MANAGEMENT
ETHICS

Sage Series in Business Ethics

Series Editor: Robert A. Giacalone
The E. Claiborne Robins School of Business
University of Richmond

Editorial Board

MANAGEMENT ETHICS
Integrity at Work

Joseph A. Petrick
John F. Quinn

Sage Series on Business Ethics

SAGE Publications
International Educational and Professional Publisher
Thousand Oaks   London   New Delhi

For information:

SAGE Publications, Inc.
2455 Teller Road
Newbury Park, California 91320
E-mail: order@sagepub.com

SAGE Publications Ltd.
6 Bonhill Street
London EC2A 4PU
United Kingdom

SAGE Publications India Pvt. Ltd.
M-32 Market
Greater Kailash I
New Delhi 110 048 India

Printed in the United States of America

Library of Congress Cataloging-in-Publication Data

Petrick, Joseph A., 1946-
    Management ethics: integrity at work / authors, Joseph A. Petrick
and John F. Quinn.
        p. cm. — (Sage series in business ethics)
    Includes bibliographical references and index.
    ISBN 0-8039-5796-3 — ISBN 0-8039-5797-1 (pbk.)
    1. Business ethics. 2. Management—Moral and ethical aspects.
3. Business ethics—Case studies. 4. Management—Moral and ethical
aspects—Case studies. I. Quinn, J. F. (John F.) II. Title.
III. Series.
HF5387.P44 1997
174'.4—dc21   96-51271

    98 99 00 01 02 03 10 9 8 7 6 5 4 3 2

Acquiring Editor:	Marquita Flemming
Editorial Assistant:	Frances Borghi
Production Editor:	Michele Lingre
Production Assistant:	Denise Santoyo
Typesetter/Designer:	Janelle LeMaster
Cover Designer:	Lesa Valdez

With appreciation for prior generations of teacher-scholars
on whose shoulders we stand; with gratitude for the
loving encouragement of faithful spouses, supportive families,
and true friends; and with hope for improving managerial work
and the quality of work life for future generations.

Contents

Table 1 Minicases, Management Functions, and Allied Management
Application Clusters

Application Clusters	Planning	Organizing	Leading	Controlling
1. *Accounting/ Auditing*	4A: Beverly Hills Savings & Loan (p. 150)	5A: E. F. Hutton (p. 195)	6A: MiniScribe (p. 249)	7A: BCCI (p. 302)
2. *Finance/ Investment*	4B: Campeau Corporation (p. 152)	5B: Kidder Peabody (p. 196)	6B: Drexel Burnham Lambert and Michael Milken (p. 251)	7B: Barings Bank (p. 303)
3. *Marketing/ Advertising*	4C: Kellogg Company (p. 153)	5C: Investors Center Inc. (ICI) and Telemarketing Boiler Rooms (p. 198)	6C: Nestlé Infant Formula (p. 254)	7C: Dow Corning and Implants (p. 306)
4. *Business Management/ Human Resources/ Business Law*	4D: Forklift Systems (p. 155)	5D: J. C. Penney (p. 199)	6D: Price Waterhouse (p. 259)	7D: The Xieng Case and Accent Discrimination (p. 310)
5. *Technology/ Quality Operations/ Organizational Behavior*	4E: Microsoft Corporation (p. 158)	5E: Sears Auto Centers (p. 202)	6E: Johns-Manville (p. 261)	7E: A. H. Robins (p. 314)
6. *Public/Nonprofit/ Health Care Administration*	4F: Sikorsky and Government Purchasing (p. 160)	5F: United Way (p. 204)	6F: Mercy Hospital and the U.S. Health Care System (p. 265)	7F: The HUD Scandal (p. 318)
7. *International/ Environmental/ Public Policy*	4G: International Hazardous Waste Trade (p. 161)	5G: Indonesian Deforestation (p. 205)	6G: Industrial Ecosystem of Denmark (p. 273)	7G: Komineft and the CIS Oil Spill (p. 321)
Application Clusters	*First Function*	*Second Function*	*Third Function*	*Fourth Function*

Preface

The primary objective of this book is to *enhance and link ethics and management competence* in planning, organizing, leading, and controlling for management integrity in private and public sectors, domestically and globally. The major philosophical assumption underlying our approach is that just as the unexamined personal life is not worth living, the unexamined work life is not worth working. When managers regularly use the theories and tools in this book to handle moral complexity and build integrity responsibly, the quality of work and work life will improve markedly.

We have witnessed these improvements in managerial performance and quality of work life as organizational ethics consultants in the United States and abroad. With a combined total of more than 50 years of academic research and training experience and corporate consulting experience, we have field-tested the theories and tools in this book for ease of understanding, managerial effectiveness, and organizational advancement. They work! Our multidisciplinary, certified backgrounds in business management, organizational development, human resource management, cultural anthropology, law, engineering, statistical quality control, philosophy, and religion, along with years of first-hand managerial experience, provide a wealth of reflective practitioner guidance in improving ethical decision making for today's pressured manager.

Distinctive features of this book include: (a) sound treatment of major types of key ethics theories, with practical application to and examples in the four microphases of each managerial function (planning, organizing, leading, and controlling); (b) interdisciplinary and coordinated treatment of management, communication, legal, and ethics theories to balance individual ethical judgment; (c) quantifiable assessment tools for practitioners to measure and improve management ethics and the three dimensions (judgment, process, and developmental dimensions) of management integrity; (d) a comprehensive qualitative ethical decision-making tool to structure moral analysis and resolution systematically; (e) explicit recognition that quality performance and management integrity require dealing with both people and processes ethically; (f) 28 ethics minicases related to each management function in seven allied management application clusters (see Table 1, on page x, containing cases with page numbers for easy reference); (g) inclusion of specific management integrity issues faced in the private and public sectors; (h) inclusion of international ethics and law concepts, cases, and challenges; (i) treatment of the impact of communication styles and theories on managerial integrity; (j) explicit treatment of the major types of key legal theories and their impact on managerial integrity; (k) detailed treatment of how to plan, organize, lead, and control with greater integrity as a manager; (l) inclusion of sustainable development conduct within the mainstream of managerial performance responsibilities; (m) raising of important conceptual and operational differences between and among managerial expediency, consistency, congruence, and integrity; (n) disclosure of implicit ethics theory commitments embedded in styles of managerial decision making; (o) disclosure of parallel processes of ethical awareness, judgment, intention, and conduct in all managerial functions; and (p) discussion questions and experiential exercise opportunities at the end of each chapter.

This book redefines what it means for a manager to function with integrity. It builds upon the theoretical work of others in both descriptive and normative ethics, weaves new conceptual frameworks, applies these new frameworks to a wide range of managerial minicases, and offers practical tools to assess and improve management ethics and integrity on an ongoing basis. It challenges management educators and practitioners to take integrity, not only rights, seriously and add it to the performance expectations of all current and future managerial leaders. It convincingly shows how management integrity makes an indispensable difference in individual, professional, and collective performance. Furthermore, because of our broad sense of management and inclusive set of minicases/examples, this book relates to domestic and global private-sector managers (accounting, marketing, advertising, finance, investment, information systems, human resource, quality operations, environmental, corporate, and small business managers), public-sector administrators (elected, appointed, and recruited government employees charged with managerial responsibility at the global, national, regional, state, and local levels), and nonprofit institutional directors (heads of educational, religious, health care, and charitable service organizations worldwide).

This book consists of seven chapters divided into two parts: "Management Ethics and Integrity: Theory and Tools," and "Management Ethics and Integrity: Practice and Minicases in the Functions of Management." Part I presents the need for improved ethical decision making by private and public managers, the theoretical nature of management and ethics, and the three major theoretical dimensions of management integrity. In addition to these theories, specific tools contained in the appendices are supplied to enhance proficiency in handling management ethics issues. Part II applies the theories and tools to microphases of each management function (planning, organizing, leading, and controlling) to build integrity. Twenty-eight ethics minicases related to each management function in seven allied management application clusters are provided for analysis and discussion by using the theories and tools in Part I.

Targeted markets for this book include its use: (a) as a primary text for undergraduate and graduate management ethics, business ethics, business professionalism, public administration ethics, professional ethics, and/or government ethics courses in academic settings; (b) as a supplementary text in undergraduate and graduate principles of management, business and society, business law, principles of public administration, public policy, managerial communications, leadership, health care/nursing administration, and/or nonprofit management courses in academic settings; (c) as a reference text and practical tool repository for corporate, governmental, and nonprofit ethics trainers and consultants worldwide; (d) by private, public, and nonprofit sector practicing managerial leaders at all levels in search of ways to ennoble work and empower employees with the tools to enhance integrity at work; (e) by professional, trade, and industry associations interested in addressing managerial performance and professional integrity issues for their respective memberships; (f) by the millions of "Dilberts" who daily endure abusive managers, cynical work groups, and hostile work environments who urgently need to find their voice and the power of the dream for a better work future that this book provides; and (g) by the interested citizen and general reader concerned about the prevalent costs of the erosion of managerial ethics and integrity, eager to use the constructive tools in this book to improve the situation.

Many persons and groups deserve our thanks for their helpful comments and support. We wish to thank the series editor, Robert Giacalone, for his enthusiastic encouragement; the acquisitions editor, Marquita Flemming, for her sound editorial judgment; and the many technical professionals at Sage Publications for their production/marketing expertise. The University of Dayton and Wright State University, and their respective Liberal Arts and Business Colleges, as well as their respective Philosophy and Management Departments, provided the enabling university contexts for this book. The Wright State University Institutional Integrity Task Force, chaired by President Harley E. Flack and actively supported by Janet Achterman, John Fleischauer, Teresa Timm, Jack Dustin, and Robert Scherer, continues to support implementation of organization integrity training. Other Wright State University colleagues and students who provided research or editorial feedback include Charles Hartmann, William Slonaker, Paul Wren, Claire Timmer, and Jeffrey Meyer. Three Wright State University students deserve special thanks for their technical support: Jackson Moses, Ramesh Gangadharan, and Ty Manley. In addition, the entire support staff at Organizational Ethics Associates in Cincinnati is to be commended.

Finally, we wish to offer a special tribute to our wives, Kimberly Petrick and Grace Quinn, whose patient understanding, faithful love, smiling encouragement, and personal sacrifice sustained our energy while writing this book. Our parents, extended families, and supportive friends also provided a socially nurturing context.

The extent to which *Management Ethics: Integrity at Work* adds value to your personal and professional lives and contributes to the development of management integrity will be the final measure of our success. Please let us hear from you by giving us both your positive and negative feedback.

Joseph A. Petrick
Wright State University
FAX: 937-775-3545
PH: 937-775-2428
e-mail: jpetrick@
discover.wright.edu

Organizational Ethics Associates
PH: 513-984-2820

John F. Quinn
University of Dayton
FAX: 937-229-4200
PH: 937-229-3013
e-mail: quinn@
chekhov.udayton.edu

Organizational Ethics Associates
PH: 513-984-2820

PART I

Management Ethics and Integrity:
Theory and Tools

Introduction and Overview

The focus of Chapter 1 is on four areas: (a) the nature and value of manage-ment, (b) management challenges in the private and public sectors, (c) the need for improved ethical decision making by managers, and (d) the over-view of the book. After disclosing the nature and value of private and public sector management, the authors demonstrate the need for improved ethical decision making by managers.

▨ NATURE AND VALUE OF MANAGEMENT

Management can be defined as *the process of reaching organizational goals by working with and through human and nonhuman resources to continuously improve value added to the world.* Reaching organizational goals is an indication of *effectiveness;* not wasting resources along the way is an indication of *efficiency;* continuously improving output and process is an indication of *innovation;* and adding value to the world is an indication of focused *stakeholder responsibility.* This book is devoted to enhancing managerial performance by integrating managerial and ethical competence.

World-class management reaches goals without wasting resources and generates competitive innovation while sustaining responsible commitments in the private, public, and/or nonprofit sectors domestically and globally. When the managerial process is well executed, it is a "visible hand" that plans, organizes, leads, and controls the use of resources to supplement, integrate, and enhance the positive effects of the "invisible hand" (Chandler, 1977, 1980; Werhane, 1991a). Well-managed organizations have a competitive advantage over poorly managed ones for a number of reasons:

- They influence their competitive external environments through more productive and focused activities, thereby providing a more stable horizon for planning and progress.
- They monitor and coordinate internal resource usage through an organized process that leverages the full, rather than partial, impact of their assets.
- They manage system changes more successfully by negotiating favorable contracts and creatively adapting to external forces.
- They have a more flexible, committed workforce because their managers routinely exhibit the sound human relations practices that build a strong work community.

When management is poorly executed, however, organizational ineffectiveness, inefficiency, inertia, and/or irresponsibility are overt and covert (Carillo & Kopelman, 1991; Porter, 1985, 1990; Premeaux & Mondy, 1993). Overt ineffectiveness leads to loss of market share in the private sector and to loss of citizen confidence in the public sector. Overt inefficiency leads to increased operational costs in the private sector and to wasted tax dollars in the public sector. Overt inertia leads to obsolete products and services in the private sector and to bureaucratic mediocrity in the public sector. Overt irresponsibility leads to corporate sabotage in the private sector and to defensive uncooperativeness in the public sector. In many instances, the invisible hand in the private sector and government intervention in the public sector eliminate and/or control severe overt mismanagement.

Nevertheless, covert organizational ineffectiveness, inefficiency, inertia, and/or irresponsibility can be as subversively debilitating as overt inadequacies (Boatright, 1997; Bounds, 1996; Collins, 1989; Stahl & Bounds, 1990; Stahl, 1995). For example, an organizational ethics consultant relates an incident involving a lumber company client in which the firm had invested in new technologies, including a new lumber shredder, nicknamed "the hog," but was not experiencing the expected profits from effective sales volume increases and efficient processing cycle times (Navran, 1995a). In other words, overt measures of performance could not account for the lower than expected results, nor could other mainstream management consultants. In conducting an ethical work culture assessment, the consultant heard the phrase "feeding the hog" and asked the employee respondent to explain the phrase. The employee informed the consultant that whenever managers abused employees, covert retaliation would take place in the following manner: Subsequent to the abuse, an elaborate informal network became activated, and expensive grades of lumber (e.g., mahogany, cherry) would be rerouted to the lumber shredder and turned into fragments for the least expensive lumber product (e.g., particle board). In effect, "feeding the hog" was a covert expression of retaliation for unjust treatment—lack of managerial responsible treatment.

In many organizations today, employees "feed the hog" in a variety of ingenious ways—for example, actively engaging in subtle sabotage, withholding the committed performance necessary for world-class competitive success. Managerial mistakes of commission and/or omission contribute to retaliatory sabotage activities by employees (Hartley, 1994; Milo, 1984). When companies experience external competition from better-managed companies, the knee-jerk response has been to engage in layoffs, downsizing, and restructuring to eliminate overt bottom-line symptoms of profit loss, rather than change management practices to address the enduring, covert causes (Navran, 1995b).

Because in the United States many states have employment-at-will laws that, in effect, legally protect incompetent managers from being held accountable for managerial "malfeasance" (substandard performance of managerial roles), management mistakes have been perpetuated and a tradition of adversarial managerial/labor relations has become commonplace in many industries (Murray, 1984; Steiner & Steiner, 1991). With the advent of global competition, however, domestic managerial irresponsibility cannot be concealed with impunity.

Furthermore, as awareness of professional standards and sanctions for managerial malfeasance increase, managerial incompetence is being criticized because of the widespread growth of professionalism across borders, industries, and occupations (Bayles, 1989; Koehn, 1995). Public expectations to professionalize managerial performance have escalated (Larson, 1977). The following dimensions of professionalism are pertinent to managerial practice (Armstrong, 1993; Bayles, 1989; Schein, 1972):

- Specialized knowledge and skills
- Service orientation based on objective client/customer needs
- Decision making based on broad principles and theories

- Autonomy of judgment in performance
- Self-regulatory associations for establishing and enforcing performance standards

Managers today who act unprofessionally—that is, ignore objective client/customer needs or are unable to base decision making on broad principles and theories—are vulnerable to public censure, loss of business, and ultimate dismissal. To enhance professional management practice, therefore, knowledge of management, ethics, legal, and communication theories is mandatory.

The competing values framework, depicted in Figure 1.1, is a useful construct for understanding the meaning of management used in this book (Quinn, Faerman, Thompson, & McGrath, 1996). It contains four theories on management, each of which has historical roots in the Western world and each of which is necessary for the dynamic, well-rounded balance exhibited by excellent managers.

The relationships among the four theories can be seen in terms of two axes. In Figure 1.1, the vertical axis ranges from flexibility at the top to control at the bottom, and the horizontal axis ranges from an internal organizational focus at the left to an external organizational focus at the right. Each theory fits into one of the four quadrants.

The *rational goal theory*, which Frederick Taylor introduced at the beginning of the 20th century, stresses the director and producer role responsibilities of setting goals, taking initiative, increasing productivity, and maximizing output by emphasizing goal clarification, rational analysis, and action taking (Taylor, 1911). The *internal process theory*, which Max Weber and Henri Fayol developed in the first quarter of the 20th century, stresses the monitor and coordinator role responsibilities of information management, documentation control, efficient processing, and consolidated continuity by emphasizing process measurement, smooth functioning of organizational operations, and structural order (Weber, 1921). The *human relations theory*, which was made famous by Elton Mayo and the Hawthorne studies in the second quarter of the 20th century, stresses the facilitator and mentor role responsibilities of fostering openness, participation, team morale building, and commitment by emphasizing involvement, humane conflict resolution, and consensus building (Mayo, 1933). Finally, the *open systems theory*, which was advocated by Paul Lawrence and Jay Lorsch in the third quarter of the 20th century, stresses the innovator and broker role responsibilities of cultivating organizational learning capabilities and developing the competitive power of continual creativity,

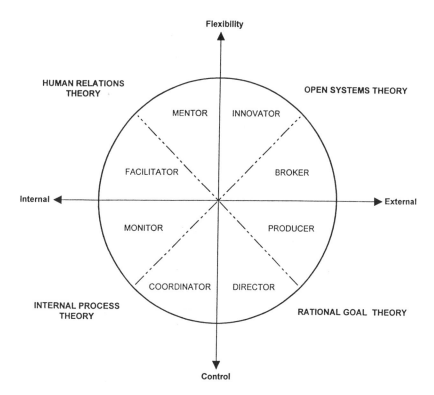

Figure 1.1. Competing Values Framework of Management Theories and Roles
SOURCE: *Becoming a Master Manager,* by R. E. Quinn, S. R. Faerman, M. P. Thompson, & M. R. McGrath. Copyright © 1996 by John Wiley & Sons, Inc. Reprinted by permission of John Wiley & Sons, Inc.

political adaptation, and negotiated external resource acquisition by emphasizing external trend scanning, creative system change and development, and negotiated contractual agreements and networking (Lawrence & Lorsch, 1967).

Each theory within the competing values framework construct consists of two roles to be mastered and is related insofar as the theories both contrast and complement each other. Thus, if one regards management as being defined by a single theory, management activity can be regarded as simple, repetitious, and unilinear; for example, if some coordinated monitoring of employees for internal control is perceived as good management, more of the same is even better and total employee control is best. Whereas if management is defined by the dynamic tension of multiple theories, management activity can be regarded as complex, creative, and holistic; for example, if some coordinated monitoring of employees for internal control is perceived as good management, total employee control may be regarded as undesirable because there is no counterbalancing, dynamic tension allowing for employee innovative flexibility. To sustain the synergistic balance of outstanding management, all four theories need to be understood and mastered. Taken alone, no one theory or set of role competencies has the range of perspectives, the increased choice, and the potential effectiveness provided by considering them all as part of a larger integrated framework (Senge, 1990).

Each theory has a perceptual opposite. The human relations theory, defined by flexibility and internal focus, stands in stark contrast to the rational goal theory, which is defined by control and external focus. In the first, for example, people are inherently valued; in the second, people are of value only if they contribute greatly to goal attainment. The open systems theory, defined by flexibility and external focus, runs counter to the internal process model, which is defined by control and internal focus. Whereas the open systems theory is concerned with adapting to the continuous change in the environment, the internal process theory is concerned with maintaining stability and continuity inside the system.

Parallels among the theories are also important. The human relations and open systems theories share an emphasis on flexibility. The open systems and rational goal theories share an emphasis on external focus. The rational goal and internal process theories emphasize control; the internal process and human relations theories share an emphasis on internal focus.

Management excellence is achieved by mastering all eight managerial roles and balancing the competing roles in an appropriate manner. In fact, the capacity to draw on and use competencies from all four management theories builds the behavioral complexity of managers and enhances their performance. *Behavioral complexity* includes cognitive complexity and is the ability to act out a cognitively complex strategy by playing multiple, even competing, roles in a highly integrated and complementary way (Hooijberg & Quinn, 1992; Quinn, Spreitzer, & Hart, 1992). Several studies suggest a link between behavioral complexity and effective managerial performance. In a study of 916 CEOs, Hart and Quinn (1993) found that the ability to play the multiple and competing roles produced better firm performance. The CEOs with high behavioral complexity saw themselves as focusing on broad visions for the future (open systems theory) while also providing critical evaluation of present plans (internal process theory). They also saw themselves tending to relational issues (human relations theory) while simultaneously emphasizing the accomplishment of tasks (rational goal theory). The firms with CEOs having higher behavioral complexity produced the best firm performance, particularly with respect to business performance (growth and innovation) and organizational effectiveness. The relationships held regardless of firm size or variations in the nature of the organizational environment.

In a study of middle managers in a Fortune 100 company, Denison, Hoojiberg, and Quinn (1995) found behavioral complexity, as assessed by the superior of the middle manager, to be related to overall managerial effectiveness of the manager, as assessed by the subordinates. In a similar study, behavioral complexity was related to managerial performance, charisma, and the likelihood of making process improvements in the organization (Quinn et al., 1992).

Without balanced behavioral complexity, a manager's strengths can become the source of his or her failure (Quinn, Sendelbach, & Spreitzer, 1991; Quinn et al., 1992; Sendelbach, 1993). Extremely low or high behavioral complexity on the part of a manager can lead to undesirable managerial role performance, as indicated by Figure 1.2.

In Figure 1.2, three circles are divided into four quadrants, parallel to those in Figure 1.1. In the middle circle is the positive zone of moderately balanced role competencies characteristic of the master manager. The inner and outer circles are negative zones of managerial under- and overdevelopment. The extreme underdevelopment of the inner circle represents the lack of ability and motivation to perform any roles. The extreme overdevelopment of the outer circle represents the set of positive values pushed until they become negative performance factors. In the lower right quadrant, for example, extreme overemphasis on the director and producer roles—in line with rational goal theory—will offend individuals and destroy cohesion. In the lower left quadrant, extreme overreliance on the coordinator and monitor roles—in line with internal process theory—stifles progress and neglects possibilities. In the upper left quadrant, extreme dependence on facilitator and mentor roles—in line with human relations theory—slows production and abdicates authority. Finally, in the upper right quadrant, extreme overreliance on broker and innovator roles—in line with open systems theory—disrupts continuity and wastes energy.

In Appendix A, the Management Style Assessment (MSA) provides a useful self-assessment tool of current, personal managerial styles. On completion of this instrument, individuals will be aware of the management theory

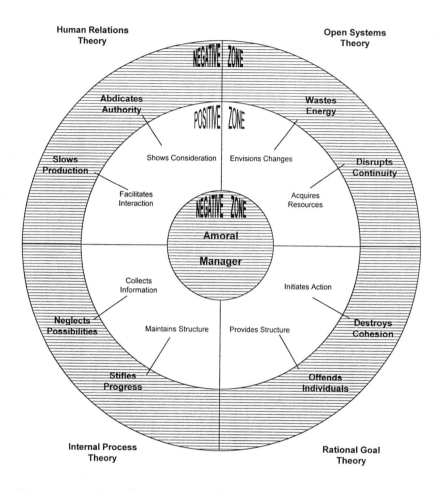

Figure 1.2. Positive and Negative Zones of Managerial Role Performance

SOURCE: *Becoming a Master Manager*, by R. E. Quinn, S. R. Faerman, M. P. Thompson, & M. R. McGrath. Copyright © 1996 by John Wiley & Sons, Inc. Reprinted by permission of John Wiley & Sons, Inc.

and role competencies that their normal work conduct exemplifies. The authors recommend that the reader complete Appendix A at this time.

Although the four management theories are universal, their relative appropriacy may vary in different transnational and national cultures. Ultimately, the world can be divided into three global transnational classifications: tribalism, collectivism, and pluralism (Leaptrott, 1996). *Tribalism* is the transnational conceptual framework that maintains that the individual derives his or her identity from the nuclear and/or extended hereditary family, that conformity to the power hierarchy is to be demanded of all members, and that socioeconomic advancement is based on seniority, not on individual merit; for example, in Latin America, absolute loyalty to the family business interests may customarily override government regulatory standards, thereby promoting patronage, human relations management theories, and a strong sense of in-group morality and out-group indifference (Mead, 1994). *Collectivism* is the transnational conceptual framework that maintains that the individual derives his or her identity from affiliation with a large, nonhereditary group's functional hierarchy (town, nation, or company hierarchies); that conformity of all members is assumed, rather than demanded; and that socioeconomic advancement is based on maintaining the homogeneity and contributing to the welfare of the whole group, rather than to individual achievement; for example, in the Pacific Rim region, group improvability through conflict avoidance, consensus decision making, individual humility, and emphasis on human relations and open systems management theories to promote harmonious flexibility may customarily override individual freedom and the importance of a separate self. *Pluralism* is the transnational conceptual framework that maintains that the individual is free to construct his or her own personal identity independent of or in loose affiliation with a combination of various groups (e.g., peer groups, political organizations) formed by mutual consent; that conformity is neither demanded nor assumed, but is accepted within a group as a means for maintaining the group's identity; and that socioeconomic advancement is based on responsible individual performance because no group will ultimately care for individuals; for example, in the United States, parts of western Canada, and parts of northern Europe, individual independence and emphasis on rational goal and internal process management theories may customarily override family pressures and group norms because social conformity is interpreted as a sign of dependent weakness.

The three transnational global classifications and their combinations are depicted in Figure 1.3 in the World Culture Map. Although these transnational global cultures may alter the appropriacy boundaries of management theories—for example, Pacific Rim managers may appropriately expect more emphasis on harmonious work relations than those in northern Europe—they cannot afford to neglect the other management theories in practice without sacrificing competent management performance (Petrick & Russell-Robles, 1992).

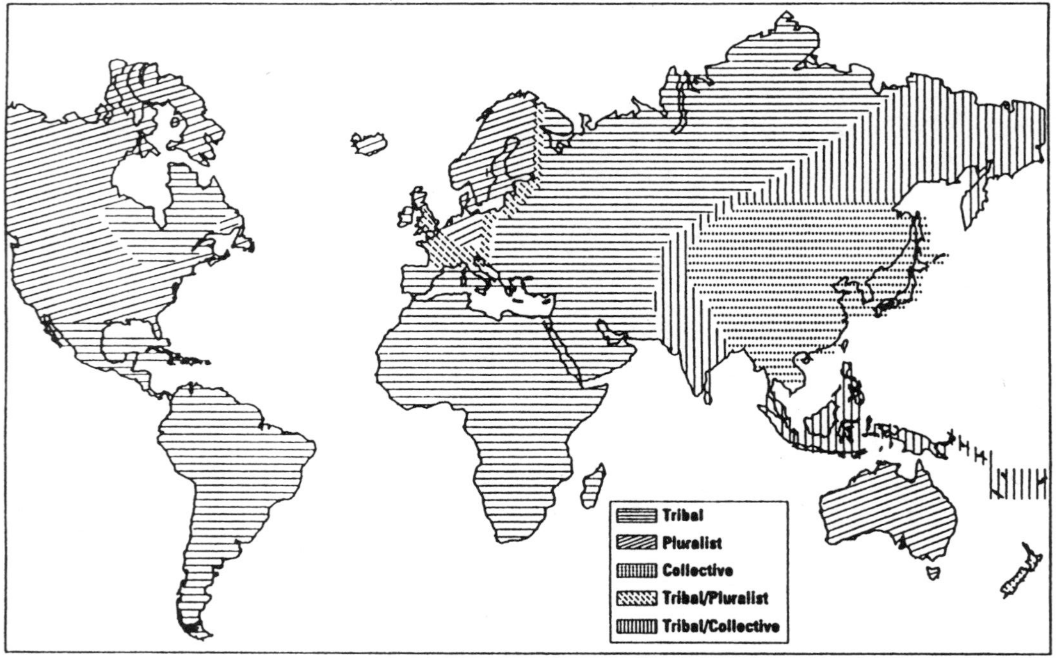

Figure 1.3. World Culture Map

SOURCE: From *Rules of the Game: Global Business Protocol* by Nan Leaptrott. Copyright © 1996 by South-Western College Publishing, a division of International Thomson Publishing Inc., Cincinnati, Ohio 45227.

National cultural influences on management practice also affect the relative appropriacy of management theory emphases. The five major national cultural variables that influence managerial performance are: (a) power distance, (b) uncertainty avoidance, (c) individualism/collectivism, (d) masculinity/femininity, and (e) long-term/short-term orientation (Hofstede, 1980, 1991, 1993; Hofstede & Bond, 1988). *Power distance* is the national cultural value accorded inequality between individuals at different socioeconomic levels in a hierarchy; for example, low power distance values in Norway, as opposed to high power distance values in Malaysia, would alter the management theory appropriacy boundaries for practitioners in their respective countries. *Uncertainty avoidance* is the national cultural value that indicates the relative need to be certain about the future; for example, high uncertainty avoidance values in France, as opposed to low uncertainty values in Canada, would alter the management theory appropriacy boundaries for practitioners in their respective countries. *Individualism/collectivism* is the national cultural value that determines the relative priority of individuals or groups in relationships; for example, high individualism values in Australia, as opposed to low individualism values in Korea, would alter the management theory appropriacy boundaries for practitioners in their respective countries. *Masculinity/femininity* is the national cultural value that determines the gender-linked division of role responsibilities in society; for example, high feminine values in Sweden, as opposed to low feminine values in South Africa, would alter the management theory appropriacy boundaries for practitioners in their respective countries. Finally, *long-term/short-term orientation* is the national cultural value that determines the relative importance accorded expectations for quick results, immediate consumption behavior, and a lack of willingness to subordinate oneself for deep-rooted collective innovation; for example, high Confucian long-term orientation values in China that emphasize human relations theory, as opposed to low long-term orientation values in Pakistan, would alter the management theory appropriacy boundaries for innovations by practitioners in their respective countries.

Nevertheless, although transnational and national cultural values alter the appropriacy boundaries of the four key management theories, they do not preclude the necessity for applying all four major management theories to arrive at competent managerial performance and staying within an acceptable range of variation in the positive zone. In some global contexts, the upper control limit of managerial practice variation in the positive zone would be "normal," whereas in others, approaching the lower control limit would be more culturally appropriate; for example, Chinese managers as collectivists might emphasize human relations cooperation more than U.S. managers as pluralists, but excellent managers worldwide accord over- and underemphasis on one approach by staying within the acceptable range of variation in the positive zone of managerial practice in Figure 1.2. *Managerial conduct within the acceptable variation range of good management practice remains a cross-cultural standard.* These extraorganizational factors, however, are important contingencies in the fruitful balancing of the four key management theories and their location in the range of acceptable, positive variation in diverse international contexts (Lindsay & Petrick, 1997; Quinn, 1995).

The value of competent management in today's turbulent, global environment lies in the balanced performance of concurrent roles over time that elicits the collective resources of an organization to meet complex challenges effectively (Vaill, 1991). Just as the ability to handle behavioral complexity enhances performance, so also does the capacity to handle *moral complexity,* whether in the private or public managerial realms.

▨ MANAGEMENT CHALLENGES IN THE PRIVATE AND PUBLIC SECTORS

The challenges in handling behavioral and moral complexity occur in the private and public sectors domestically and globally (Lewis, 1991; Osborne & Gaebler, 1992). At least six substantive differences, however, are found in the goals and processes used by private- and public-sector managers, as indicated in Figure 1.4.

The first substantive difference between private- and public-sector managers is the former's goal of optimizing market value. Optimizing market value is the *raison d'être* of the private-sector manager and may include increasing investor wealth, expanding market share, generating profits, and/or providing high-quality, low-cost goods and services for those with investment and purchasing power. The public-sector manager's goal is to optimize public value by enacting mandated standards (what is required by the letter of the law and elected officials) and by exploring innovative ways to define and serve the long-range public interest (what is permitted by the spirit of the law and

Private-Sector Managers	Public-Sector Managers
1. Goal: Optimize market value	1. Goal: Optimize public value
2. Priority of individual ownership interest and consumer sovereignty	2. Priority of collective public interest and citizen sovereignty
3. Reductionist economic value system	3. Nonreductionist diverse value system
4. Source of power: Meets economic demands of the buying public	4. Source of power: Meets political demands of the enfranchised public
5. Operational priority of efficiency with urgent market pressures to rapidly improve quantity and quality and reduce cost and cycle time of service delivery	5. Operational priority of fairness without market pressures to rapidly improve quantity and quality and cost and cycle time of service delivery
6. Business as major institution	6. Government as major institution

Figure 1.4. Substantive Differences Between Private- and Public-Sector Managers

appointed officials) (Heymann, 1987; Moore, 1995; Moore & Sparrow, 1990; Thompson, 1987). Public-sector managers who increase public value by operationalizing only what is legally required or what democratically elected authorities mandate tend to be more *bureaucratic* (Wilson, 1989). Their managerial orientation is *downward* toward the reliable control of organizational operations, rather than either *outward* toward the achievement of innovative public-service results or *upward* toward renegotiated policy mandates that may be too restrictive (Moore, 1995). Public-sector managers who increase public value by envisioning new general (as opposed to special) interests and renegotiating existing policies to improve them tend to be more *entrepreneurial* (Cohen & Bran, 1993; Doig & Hargrove, 1990; Lax & Sebenius, 1986; Osborne & Gaebler, 1992). Both private- and public-sector managers can suboptimize market and public value, respectively, by being either excessively risk averse or risk loving.

The second substantive difference between private- and public-sector managers is the former's priority of individual ownership interests and consumer sovereignty over collective public interests and citizen sovereignty. Protecting and expanding the exclusive bundle of *divisible* rights associated with individual proprietary ownership (e.g., the right to use and enjoy one's home) is more important to private-sector managers than addressing the *indivisible* rights/needs of society at large; for example, no one owns clean air or national defense, but they are collectively owned and experienced in a way that private property rights do not adequately protect, by providing inclusive assistance to owners and non-owners alike. Private-sector managers/owners are "individual economic masters" by virtue of legal property rights that protect what they have earned, been given, or inherited, whereas public-sector managers are "collective political servants" entrusted by their public masters, through democratic processes, with the authority to administer to their long-range common needs. Public managers are to serve natural individuals (persons) and artificial individuals (businesses) in such a way that common needs are met now and in the future. Public managers appeal to the priority of the collectively chosen public ends and democratic processes when they use the coercive power of taxation to deprive individual owners of their accumulated wealth and individual consumers of their purchasing power (Moore, 1995).

In addition, the private-sector managers ultimately accede to consumer sovereignty because products/services will be removed from the market when consumers decide not to buy them in sufficient quantities. On the one hand, profit is the reward that accrues to private-sector managers who satisfy customer demands repeatedly by efficiently beating competitors. Conversely, public-sector managers ultimately accede to citizen sovereignty because they can be voted out of office or not reappointed if they are perceived as detracting from public value. On the other hand, political power is the reward that accrues to public-sector managers who accurately perceive and respond to constituency interests, who are skillful at compromise and negotiation, and who can persuade people that they can be entrusted with power to use for the public interest.

The third substantive difference between private- and public-sector managers is the former's reductionist economic value system. In the private sector, managers assume that the worth of a person's labor, the worth of a particular product/service, and/or the worth of a share of stock can all be reduced to tangible economic exchange values (e.g., everything and everyone has a price). Furthermore, they expect that human and nonhuman resources will go where the price, wage and salary, or return on investment are highest until supply equals demand so that resources are efficiently allocated by the impersonal, invisible hand of the market to produce the greatest wealth for society. The public-sector manager assumes that the worth of individual labor, the worth of a particular product/service, and/or the worth of an investment is determined by diverse values and cannot be reduced without significant loss in value diversity to economic exchange values. The visible, personal, democratic process, rather than market exchanges, is expected to provide the way to aggregate the irreducible diversity of people's values to make trade-off decisions; for example, voting is required to decide whether to reduce smokestack emissions or pave new highways when a limited public budget precludes both being accomplished and when no common value system is acceptable, realistic, and appropriate in a multicultural political arena.

The fourth substantive difference between private- and public-sector managers is the former's source of power in meeting the current economic wants and anticipated needs of the buying public. Most private-sector managers assume that, by producing whatever the buying public demands, they are providing what all members of society want, when in fact the wants of large segments of the enfranchised, nonbuying public (the poor and the disadvantaged) are not necessarily met because they cannot participate in the marketplace. The source of power for the public-sector manager, however, is in meeting the current political demands and anticipated needs of the enfranchised public (those eligible to vote, with or without purchasing power), where citizen sovereignty is accorded a higher moral priority than consumer sovereignty.

When groups have neither purchasing power nor voting power, non-profit-sector managers expand their domain of influence by serving them, often relying on voluntary labor and tax-deductible charitable donations. The Association for Research on Nonprofit Organizations and Voluntary Action (ARNOVA) and Yale University's Program on Nonprofit Organizations (PONPO) provide in-depth research and education in this area and timely updates through the periodical *Nonprofit and Voluntary Sector Quarterly.*

The fifth substantive difference between private- and public-sector managers is that the former experience urgent market pressures to accord operational priority to efficiency or "go out of business." Private-sector managers must rapidly improve the quantity and quality of goods/services to secure market share/profitability and simultaneously reduce costs and cycle time to avoid bankruptcy. The public-sector manager does not experience these intense market pressures for operational improvement because government organizations/agencies rarely go out of business. Rather, the public-sector manager accords more operational priority to fairness in processes and outcomes so that all the enfranchised can democratically participate. In fact, rapid operational efficiency in formulating and implementing public policy may give the appearance of procedural unfairness, so most seasoned public managers move at a slower, less efficient but more inclusive pace to avoid the appearance of impropriety by "rushing to judgment."

The sixth substantive difference between private- and public-sector managers is that, for the latter, government, whether federal, state, or local, is the principal institution for shaping collective conduct. For public-sector managers, government lends legitimacy to policies by making them regulatory or legal obligations that command the loyalty and compliance of all citizens, not only the buying public. Only government can legitimately imprison violators of its policies. For private-sector managers, business is the major productive institution in the world. While taking consumer preferences into account, businesses actively determine the allocation of society's resources and rewards for the production of private goods and services.

In addition to the six substantive differences, public-sector managers are expected to champion the public interest by uniquely emphasizing four standards that sustain public trust: (a) avoidance of conflicts of interest, (b) maintenance of impartiality, (c) avoidance of the appearance of impropriety, and (d) submission to extensive public disclosure to ensure fitness for public office (Cooper, 1986; Dobel, 1990; Gortner, 1991; Lewis, 1991; Mosher, 1982; Wamsley et al., 1990).

Avoidance of Conflicts of Interest

Public managers have a special obligation to put the public interest ahead of personal/special interests. A public manager has a *conflict of interest* when any financial, social, or political relationship or transaction may compromise or give the appearance of compromising his or her objectivity, independence, or honesty with respect to duties. No public manager owns his or her office; the manager is a trustee, not a proprietor, in the use of authority for the common good. So, the use of the public office (as if one owns that office) by a public manager for personal gain for oneself or favored others—whether by bribery, extortion, nepotism, gifts, or other forms of favoritism—is unethical domestically and usually illegal (Common Cause, 1989; General Accounting Office [GAO], 1987). For example, although nepotism is contrary to U.S. public-service conflict of interest standards, a parent hiring a child to work in a family-owned business is accepted, even expected, in the private sector.

Federal, state, and local political scandals continue to incite the public clamor for compliance with higher standards that prevent conflicts of interest in public managers. Conflict of interest prohibitions are central to new federal standards of conduct (Fiorelli, 1992). Ranging from affirmative ideals to unequivocal restrictions and on to the criminal code, these standards include (a) the more positive, prescriptive Code of Ethics for Government Service (P.L. 96-303) enacted in 1980; (b) detailed prescriptions administratively adopted by executive orders; (c) regulations from the U.S. Office of Government Ethics (OGE) and individual agencies; and (d) criminal conflict-of-interest statutes in 18 U.S.C. 201-209. The legal compliance emphasis at the federal level is evident from two facts: (a) In 1989, 76% of all designated agency ethics officers (DAEOs), whose primary duties include training and counseling public-agency employees in conflict-of-interest matters, were in legal offices; and (b) the official title of the widely distributed 1986 OGE training publication was *How to Keep Out of Trouble*. Many states likewise have conflict-of-interest codes that extend to state and county public managers (e.g., California, Massachusetts, Alaska), as do municipalities (e.g., Los Angeles, Minneapolis, San Antonio), but their content and enforcement lack uniformity. Among the commonly restrained conflict-of-interest activities from the 1990 report of the Council on Government Ethics Laws and the New York State Commission on Government Integrity are: (a) using public position for personal benefit, (b) providing benefits to influence official actions, (c) using confidential government information, (d) accepting gifts from internal or external officials, (e) representing private clients before public bodies, (f) competitive bidding, (g) accepting fees or honoraria, outside employment, or business activities, and (g) revolving-door postemployment influence restrictions (Lewis, 1991).

Maintenance of Impartiality

Public managers must avoid bias, prejudice, or favoritism in decision making. Because competing claims make impartiality problematic, ethical public managers retain objectivity and eliminate prejudice in action by steering away from any avoidable influence that may cloud vision, bias decision, or appear as if it may. In a survey of members of the National Association of State Budget Officers, impartiality was the most frequently cited ethical concern of public managers (Mensen, 1990). This is where formal and informal standards of professional associations are key in imparting to domestic and international public managers, from top federal administrators to state purchasing managers or elected officials or police chiefs, the importance of objectively serving the public interest. Among the relevant public professional associations whose codes advocate impartiality from their respective memberships are the following: the American Society for Public Administration (ASPA), Government Finance Officers Association (GFOA), National Association of Counties Code of Ethics for County Officials (NAC), National Association of Purchasing

Management (NAPM), International City Management Association (ICMA), International Personnel Management Association (IPMA), International Association of Chiefs of Police (IACP), and International Association of Purchasing Management (IAPM).

Of particular importance to public managers is the pressure to abandon the impartiality standard because of political party affiliation. Terms such as *party boss* and *machine politics* conjure up negative images of public managers without integrity who choose to toe the party line and donate time, money, and even votes to partisan campaigns that may or may not be in the public's long-term interest. The intensity of political party affiliation pressure is usually not experienced by the private-sector manager. The move to make some managerial positions part of the civil service system, and thereby interpose merit over partisanship, mitigates party pressures on some public managers.

Avoidance of the Appearance of Impropriety

Public managers are expected to attend to the public perception of how their activities and decisions reflect on their office and to preclude adverse publicity. It is not enough for managers just to uphold the law and be ethical. Public service must look right, smell right, feel right; in short, it must avoid the appearance of impropriety (Lewis, 1991). Avoidance of negative publicity is particularly meaningful in public service, where obligations are linked to public confidence and trust. Some public managers interpret this standard to imply that looking good is as important as doing good (Greenberg, 1996). Avoiding the appearance of impropriety for public managers usually means anticipating not only what a reasonable person would reasonably regard as impropriety but also what the most suspicious person would construe as impropriety in the community setting.

For this reason, public-sector managers are often more circumspect than private-sector managers about initiatives for generating revenue for public coffers. Whereas a private-sector manager would prioritize and be rewarded for revenue-generating projects that enlarge the economic pie for everyone, a public-sector manager would prioritize and be rewarded for the public perception of the equitable distribution of a limited economic pie because the enlargement of the economic pie by his or her office might invite the appearance of impropriety (e.g., economic self-advancement). The goal, of course, is economic growth with equity, but the negative publicity resulting from the perception of inequitable distribution of benefits and burdens is much more likely to adversely affect public-sector than private-sector managers (Baily, Burtless, & Litan, 1993). This standard is not intended to be a substitute for ethical action, however. Instead and ideally, it points to the public manager's obligation to reinforce public perception of legitimate authority exercised on behalf of the public interest that is above suspicion.

Despite criticisms and cautions, this standard drives public service. In no small measure, it even defines it (Cohen & Eimicke, 1995; Lewis, 1991). This standard is geared to maintaining public confidence in public service and, therefore, voluntary compliance. In many instances, in the absence of negative publicity or scandals, public managers are reelected or reappointed at such a high rate that incumbency in the public sector carries far more weight than in the private sector (Gortner, 1991; Sandel, 1996).

Submission to Extensive Public Disclosure

Public managers usually must be able to withstand more intense public scrutiny into their private lives than private managers. The rationale behind this level of private disclosure is that the right of the electorate to know that a person is fit for public service is a more compelling interest than respecting the right of privacy for the average person. When the right of the people to be informed about public leadership does not intrude upon constitutionally protected, intimate, personal matters, which are unrelated to fitness for public office, the public manager or candidate is expected not to complain that his or her privacy is paramount to the interests of the people.

In addition to detailed financial disclosure requirements, many public managers must expose themselves to continual probing of their past official actions and any current public activities, as well as any private conduct that might raise issues of questionable character for an official entrusted with public resources. The visibility of public managers triggers their vulnerability to extensive scrutiny and the threat of unfavorable disclosure; public scrutiny intensifies the higher one climbs in government service. Part of this public scrutiny is media attention from investigative journalists. Although these journalists have their self-censorship standards of fair play (see Figure 1.5, from the Fair Play section of the 1987 revised code of ethics of the Society of Professional Journalists), they experience the urgent market pressures for breaking a story, exposing a personal scandal, or at least not being "scooped" by other media.

1987 CODE OF ETHICS OF THE SOCIETY OF PROFESSIONAL JOURNALISTS

SECTION ON FAIR PLAY

Journalists at all times will show respect for the dignity, privacy, rights, and well-being of people encountered in the course of gathering and presenting the news.

1. The news media should not communicate unofficial charges affecting reputation or moral character without giving the accused a chance to reply.
2. The news media must guard against invading a person's right to privacy.
3. The media should not pander to morbid curiosity about details of vice and crime.
4. It is the duty of news media to make prompt and complete correction of their errors.
5. Journalists should be accountable to the public for their reports and the public should be encouraged to voice its grievances against the media. Open dialogue with our readers, viewers, and listeners should be fostered.

Figure 1.5. Media Standards of Fair Play

Today, so much is in the public record that it is difficult to distinguish privacy from anonymity. Computer systems, public information, and freedom-of-information statutes join together as the speed, capacity, and standards of public disclosure change. The quality of deliberation in a democracy is debased, however, when sensationalist exposés of private activities displace reasonable discussions of issues of public concern. Furthermore, when ethics is used as a negative political weapon and cynically abused for partisan purposes, public managers and employees, their morale, and the image of public service are wounded in the crossfire. For this reason, until a material boundary of privacy for public managers is determined (e.g., a statute of limitations or amnesty on prior wrongdoing), they must be hardy enough to endure the additional public scrutiny to which they will be subjected. So, although private- and public-sector managers have different demands, they still must be able to handle behavioral and moral complexity.

Too often, however, private- and public-sector managers are overdeveloped, underdeveloped, or involved in adversarial relations when mutually beneficial development and partnership would further both their domestic and global objectives. The nature and extent of business/government relations is always controversial and varies globally. Whether government plays a big or small role as a percentage of national gross domestic product (GDP) depends on the country in question, as indicated by recent figures from the Paris-based Organization for Economic Cooperation and Development (OECD) shown in Figure 1.6.

Country	Outlays (%)
U.S.	33.5
Japan	37.6
U.K.	42.2
Germany	49.5
EU average	51.0
Italy	52.5
France	53.7
Sweden	66.7

Figure 1.6. Government Outlays as a Percentage of GDP (Organization for Economic Cooperation and Development Government Outlay Group, 1996).

Relative to those of many other industrialized countries, the U.S. government plays less of a role in economic activity. Between 1974 and 1992, roughly 30 million private-sector jobs were created in North America. The number of European Union (EU) private-sector jobs was less than 5 million for the same span. New low-cost competition from Asia and Eastern Europe has highlighted competitiveness gaps in Europe, where businesses have been losing market share and have often reacted by transferring production elsewhere. Restructured U.S. industries and the competitive dollar add new challenges for the EU.

A consensus of long-term forecasts for key European economies reveals expectations that average growth rates in the EU economies will be subpar, at little more than 2% through the year 2006, according to Consensus Economics, Inc., a London forecasting firm. European nations face dwindling tax returns as their economies stagnate under the strain of high taxes and an average unemployment rate of nearly 11% of the workforce. The result is that, bogged down by big budget deficits, high unemployment, and anemic growth, European governments are attempting to fast-forward their overhaul of the social-welfare state—a political model that, though sustaining low-risk prosperity for European citizens, has become unfundable.

The worldwide trend toward privatization after the Cold War in both developed and developing countries continues to highlight the importance of private-sector managers in the economic development of the world (Dinavo, 1995; Zahariadis, 1995). Global privatization is one attempt to institutionalize the operational efficiencies of private-sector management when public-sector management proves to be inadequate. In turn, when private-sector management ignores social responsibilities to achieve profitability efficiently, public-sector management intervenes and redresses the imbalance.

Recent politico-economic experience in the former Soviet Union and the Eastern Bloc countries demonstrates the need to simultaneously develop efficient private-sector managers who are responsive to market pressures and effective public-sector managers who are responsive to democratic pressures in order to add value to the political and economic spheres. The absence of strong private- and public-sector managers accountable to market and democracy pressures has contributed, for example, to the gross neglect of ecological responsibilities prevalent in the region. In Eastern Europe, official government bureaucrats did not develop the public-management skills to anticipate and respond to vocal democratic pressure to preserve natural resources for future generations because they were protected by the Soviet military and Communist Party allegiance. Western European private- and public-sector managers were more ecologically responsible because they were never free from market and democratic pressures. Today, Western private-sector managers are flooding into the Commonwealth of Independent States (CIS) and Eastern Europe to enhance market efficiencies, but the relative underdevelopment of comparable sophisticated public managers in the region has led to a disastrous lack of adequate public infrastructure—for example, substandard law enforcement that jeopardizes basic public safety; inadequate roads, transportation, housing, health care, food distribution, and telecommunications that erode economic opportunity and quality of life. The dual need, therefore, for competent private- and public-sector managers warrants mutual understanding and partnership to undertake and sustain value-added enterprises in any society. Although substantive differences are found between private- and public-sector managers, in important ways the domestic and global interests are best served by the balance and dynamic tension between the two as they resolve behavioral and moral complexity problems.

▧ NEED FOR IMPROVED ETHICAL DECISION MAKING BY MANAGERS

Although there is a general need for improved managerial performance in the private and public sectors, there is a special need for improved ethical decision making by managers. For five reasons, managers need to improve ethical decision making: (a) the costs of unethical workplace conduct; (b) the lack of awareness of ethically questionable, managerial, role-related acts; (c) the widespread erosion of integrity and exposure to ethical risk; (d) the global corruption pressures that threaten managerial and organizational reputation; and (e) the benefits of increased profitability and intrinsically desirable organizational order.

Costs of Unethical Workplace Conduct

Tangible and intangible costs of unethical workplace conduct are found at the individual, group, and organizational levels (Nash, 1990; Navran, 1991; Zemke, 1986). The 1994, Klynveld, Peat, Marwick, and Goerdeler (KPMG) Fraud Survey of 3,000 top large and medium-sized U.S. companies documented the awesome cost of one form of unethical and illegal conduct—fraud (KPMG, 1994). The annual amount of U.S. work fraud reported in the survey was $224 million, with the median cost of work fraud being $117,000. In 1994, 18% of companies reported frauds aggregating $1 million or more per company, and 56% of respondents indicated aggregate annual losses of more than $100,000 (KPMG, 1994). The two most expensive types of fraud were medical/insurance claims fraud and fraud from the preparation of false financial statements, averaging more than $622,000 and $765,000, respectively, per company involved (KPMG, 1994). Managers who neglect to control such losses or who contribute by their conduct to such losses must be held accountable.

In addition, the intangible personal, group, and organizational costs mount in a variety of forms: customer dissatisfaction increases, productivity and profitability decrease, low morale and organizational cynicism permeate the work setting, inattention to methods and procedures becomes the norm, lack of cooperation because of workplace fear and distrust mounts, projects run over time/budget limits, high personal stress levels and employee turnover predominate, frequent disrespectful treatment of employees occurs, employee substance abuse and absenteeism skyrocket, social activities on the job routinely preempt work performance responsibilities, loss of work pride and meaning pervade the organization, personal and organizational reputations erode in the eyes of key stakeholders, callous disregard for integrity leads to shameless loss of work commitment, and, increasingly, violence from disenfranchised employees erupts (Giacolone & Greenberg, 1997; Hosmer, 1994b, 1995; Navran, 1995a, 1995b; O'Leary-Kelly, Griffin, & Glew, 1996).

The aggregate loss of unethical work conduct is the opportunity cost of lost cooperation (Axelrod, 1984; Axelrod & Dion, 1988). The opportunity cost of lost cooperation is best conveyed through the Prisoner's Dilemma posed by contemporary game theory (Axelrod, 1984; Poundstone, 1992; Velasquez, 1996).

The Prisoner's Dilemma gets its name from a story that is supposed to illustrate the kind of situation it represents. The story goes like this:

> Two thieves arrested for a crime vow not to betray each other. But the police put them into separate rooms and tell each thief the same thing: "If your partner confesses and you keep silent, he goes free and you get 5 years in prison; if you confess and he keeps silent, you go free and he gets 5 years in prison. If you both confess, then you both get 3 years in prison. If you both keep silent, then we'll give you each 1 year in prison on a lesser charge."

The Prisoner's Dilemma is graphically illustrated in Figure 1.7. The situation summed up in the 2 × 2 matrix indicates the ethical options of prisoners A and B, along with the individual risks of years lost in prison.

Although the optimal ethical resolution and integrity challenge of the Prisoner's Dilemma would involve honestly admitting the crime, doing the appropriate amount of jail time, reforming one's character, and giving up a life of crime, even honorable criminals adhere to a minimal code of cooperative silence. This code is regarded as superior to untrustworthy, self-interested betrayal. A preferable outcome (e.g., the minimal aggregate number of years lost in prison) in a Prisoner's Dilemma, therefore, is for both parties to cooperate and remain silent. Mutual cooperation will leave them better off than if both defect (confess against oneself or betray the other). As early inquiries in the game theory showed, however, if the parties are rational and only self-interested, they will both choose to defect. Each party will reason as follows:

> The other party will either cooperate or defect. If the other party cooperates, I will gain more by defecting than by cooperating; and, if the other party defects, I will also gain more by defecting than cooperating. In either case, I will be better off by defecting.

Thus, both prisoners end up losing out by defecting (they serve 3 years in prison, rather than 1 year). Prisoner's Dilemmas, in short, are situations in which *only* self-interested behavior of two parties leaves both worse off than cooperative behavior.

	Prisoner B Defecting	Prisoner B Cooperating
Prisoner A Defecting	−3, −3	−5, 0
Prisoner A Cooperating	0, −5	−1, −1

Figure 1.7. The Prisoner's Dilemma and the Opportunity Costs of Lost Cooperation

Although Prisoner's Dilemmas technically involve only two parties in the criminal justice system, their lessons can be generalized to managerial and social dilemmas, situations in which several parties each face a Prisoner's Dilemma situation with respect to the other parties (Glance & Huberman, 1994). Ethical norms can be interpreted as norms that put managers in a Prisoner's Dilemma situation. For example, when two managers talk with each other, they have a choice of cooperating in the norm of telling the truth or trying to take advantage of each other by lying to each other. When two employees make an agreement, they have a choice of cooperating in the norm of keeping their word or trying to take advantage of each other by breaking the agreement. When investors who each own a piece of property interact, they have a choice of cooperating in the norm against theft or trying to take advantage of each other by stealing each other's property. Being ethical, on the one hand, can be thought of as a kind of cooperation between individuals; it is cooperating in the moral norms that sustain fundamental institutions such as the institutions of language, contract, property, and more generally, the social and organizational conditions that make an orderly and flourishing human life possible (Velasquez, 1996). Being unethical, on the other hand, can be conceptualized as an attempt to take advantage of others by breaking the moral norms that others follow, usually leaving all worse off than if cooperation had taken place.

Although taking advantage of another may pay off in a one-time meeting, this unrealistic condition rarely exists in a managerial environment, where stakeholder interactions are repetitive and ongoing (Bhide & Stevenson, 1990). Consequently, if a business attempts, through unethical behavior, to take advantage of stakeholders in today's context, they can usually find some way to retaliate against the manager in tomorrow's interaction. The retaliation can consist of as simple an act as refusing to buy from, work for, or do business with the unethical manager; or it may be a more complex form of retaliation such as sabotage, absenteeism, pilferage, organizing boycotts or other forms of getting others to refuse to do business with the manager, or getting even by inflicting other kinds of covert or overt injuries. Furthermore, the opportunity cost of lost cooperation deprives a manager of important reputational benefits that gain him or her access to mutually advantageous exchanges (Frank, 1988).

Because people have the ability to eventually identify ethical and unethical predispositions in others and tend to seek out those who are ethical and avoid those who are unethical, the unethical manager's negative reputation will more often force him or her to risk exchanges in mutually destructive, rather than beneficial, relationships (Frank, 1988). The opportunity cost of lost coopera-tion, therefore, belies the cynical claim that ethical behavior is only for suckers. Habitually ethical people may well end up with larger gains, through mutually cooperative relationships, than habitually unethical people (Velasquez, 1996).

Lack of Awareness of Ethically Questionable, Managerial Role-Related Acts

Managers are people whose identities are composed of a network of *roles*, which are clusters of rights and duties with a socioeconomic function (Downie, 1971; Emmet, 1966). Part of being a good manager is being aware of the moral dimensions of one's various roles (Bowie, 1982). Managers can unwittingly engage in a wide range of types of role-related acts that are regarded as ethically questionable and demonstrate the need for improved ethical decision making processes, as indicated in Figure 1.8.

In the nonmanagerial role acts, the actor is performing outside his or her role as manager. *Nonmanagerial role acts* are any acts that involve direct gain for the actor at the expense of the firm; they are managerial only in the sense that they take place in organizations and frequently involve people who hap-pen, by title, to be called managers (Waters, 1988). Ethically questionable acts of this type, such as expense account cheating, embezzlement, and stealing supplies, are committed against the firm in the self-interest of the individual. Formal auditing, internal control accounting systems, and codes of ethics in

Type	Direct Effect	Examples
1. Nonmanagerial role	Against the firm	—Expense account cheating —Embezzlement —Stealing supplies
2. Managerial role failure	Against the firm	—Superficial performance appraisal —Not confronting expense account cheating —Palming off a poor performer
3. Managerial role distortion	For the firm	—Bribery —Price fixing —Manipulation of suppliers
4. Managerial role overexertion	For the firm	—Unauthorized high-risk investments —Perpetuating currently legal but harmful environmental practices —Failure to cooperate completely with regulatory agencies

Figure 1.8. Types of Ethically Questionable Managerial Role-Related Acts
SOURCE: Waters (1988). Reprinted with permission.

most organizations are largely concerned with this category (Vanasco & Quinn, 1995).

In *managerial role failure,* acts are directly related to managerial roles and amount to a failure to competently perform those roles that one could have and should have performed. Role failure acts can be acts of either commission or omission, such as superficial performance appraisals, not confronting expense account cheating, and palming off a poor performer to another work unit. In any case, role failure acts involve direct personal advantage (often not financial gain) at the expense of the firm (or other stakeholders).

In *managerial role distortion,* managerial acts of low scope and visibility involve conduct that gives direct advantage to the firm in the short run, indirectly provides gains to the individual actor in the short run, but displaces direct costs onto selected stakeholders outside and inside the organization. Managerial role distortion acts, such as bribery, price fixing, and manipulation of suppliers, are rationalized by managers who claim they were acting on behalf of the firm's interests in carrying out their duties. The distorted preoccupation with bottom-line results and performance goals reveals the disrespect accorded other stakeholders.

In *managerial role overexertion,* managerial acts of large scope and visibility involve conduct that excessively exerts influence to adhere to the letter of the current law. These acts violate the spirit of the law, however, in a way that gains short-term advantage for the firm and the actor while displacing long-term costs onto selected stakeholders outside and inside the organization. Managerial role overexertion usually uses position power to promote aggressively the short-term advantage of the firm and to trivialize the interests of some stakeholders at the expense of other stakeholders. Managerial role overexertion acts, such as unauthorized high-risk investments, perpetuation of currently legal but harmful environmental practices, and failure to cooperate completely with regulatory agencies, are rationalized by managers who have closely identified with the firm and routinely speak for and act on behalf of the firm. Media attention is often focused on managerial role overexertion when its public image conveys a callous disregard for public concerns (e.g., the ethically questionable acts engaged in by Ivan Boesky, John DeLorean, or Charles Keating) (Binstein & Bowden, 1993).

Although the first and fourth types of questionable managerial ethical acts are usually spotlighted and addressed, the second and third types receive the least attention in the form of proactive management control. Ironically, however, when most managers are asked to describe ethical questions that occur in their professional lives, they overwhelmingly fall within the second and third types of concerns (Toffler, 1991; Waters, 1988).

Managerial role failures and role distortions comprise the vast majority of everyday ethical challenges faced on the job and, though not publically obvious, are costly to those affected, corrosive of moral standards, and undermine the substance of corporate character. Senior management that ignores, condones, or neglects to address questionable ethical acts in the second and third categories indirectly creates widespread moral stress and intractable, ethical dilemmas within organizations, which impair the ability of competent managers to act with total integrity (Jackall, 1988). Learning to act with total integrity requires managers to be aware of and critically review questionable ethical acts related to all role and nonrole conduct and to engage only in acts that have withstood critical scrutiny.

Widespread Erosion of Integrity and Exposure to Ethical Risk

Managers who want to improve their ethical performance need to attend to the erosion of integrity and, indirectly, to conscientiously managing ethical

	Intentional	Unintentional
Commission	Deliberate harm to integrity	Morally negligent harm to integrity
Omission	Deliberate exposure to harmful risks	Morally negligent exposure to harmful risks

Figure 1.9. Intentional and Unintentional Managerial Offenses That Increase Ethical Risk

risk as it pertains to individuals, groups, and organizations. *Ethical risk* is the exposure to the possibility of the loss of integrity or the presence of harmful dangers. Although individuals may take private ethical risks, as managers they take public risks that may impose burdens on others: *costs of harm* (e.g., medical bills, pain); *costs of avoiding harm* (e.g., pollution control mechanisms); and *transaction costs incurred in allocating harm* (e.g., litigation, negotiation, regulation) (Shrader-Frechette, 1991). Integrity can be eroded and unreasonable ethical risk assumed through intentional and unintentional commissions of unethical acts and omissions of ethical acts, as depicted in Figure 1.9.

Intentional commission of unethical acts by an organizational manager is the classic case of destroying personal and organization integrity (e.g., the intentional fraud by Charles Keating in the Lincoln Savings and Loan debacle). In addition, intentional commission of unethical acts recklessly disregards the ethical risks to stakeholders created before the act and callously discounts the increased distribution of ethical risks imposed on other stakeholders after the fact (e.g., the cigarettes produced by the U.S. tobacco industry, which have been shown to be addictive carcinogens, increase health risks/costs among exposed users and non-users, domestically and globally). The further deliberate cover-up of misconduct to evade accountability compounds the offense and whets media frenzy (e.g., Watergate in the public and private arenas, industry cover-ups of the production of nicotine-induced levels of addiction in cigarettes).

Another form of intentional commission of unethical acts is manipulating career image impressions and engaging corporate public relations efforts to cover up the lack of genuine integrity (Giacolone & Rosenfeld, 1991). One popular sense of integrity entails "walking the talk" in a variety of contexts, which overcomes the moral problem of divided ethical selves—that is, individuals who are "two faced" by compartmentalizing relationships and switching personalities and values at home, work, or play. The process of maintaining integrity, in popular parlance, requires substantive, moral alignment in word and deed. *Ultimately, managing organizations is a relational enterprise whose foundation is not money, technology, or power, but trust.* Gambling with personal, interpersonal, and public trust has major adverse consequences for managers and organizations (Kramer & Tyler, 1995). Charles Keating, the man found guilty of promulgating the largest bank failure in U.S. history because of financial mismanagement at Lincoln Savings and Loan, was notorious for compartmentalizing relationships and manipulating his image in a variety of contexts to gain the confidence and trust of defrauded investors; his lack of personal integrity could not ultimately fool everyone for long (Binstein & Bowden, 1993). In the popular culture, ethical integrity is the basis of genuine self-respect and realistic self-esteem; self-promotional efforts that exaggerate self-esteem or misrepresent public image to conceal the absence of personal integrity are counterfeit substitutes for authentic, responsible management.

Intentional omission of ethical acts by an organizational manager also destroys personal and organization integrity (e.g., the A. H. Robins managers who neglected to test adequately for product safety and rapidly remove the Dalkon Shield from the global market). Furthermore, intentional omission of ethical acts has the same adverse impact on ethical risks to other stakeholders (e.g., by omitting the $11 safety improvement to the design of Pinto gas tanks, Ford managers increased the ethical risks to life and limb of a wide range of stakeholders).

Unintentional commission of unethical acts by organizational managers who are *culpably ignorant* (could have or should have known of a better course of action), harms personal and organizational safety; for example, the managers of Union Carbide, in designing and maintaining the Bhopal plant in India, did not intend to kill more than 2,000 people, but their culpable moral negligence destroyed corporate integrity (Crawford & Quinn, 1991). In addition, increasing ethical risks through unintentional commission of unethical acts can impose suffering on human and nonhuman stakeholders; for example, the Exxon managers who overworked skeleton crews in their oil shipping division and who inadequately responded to substance abuse among employees created substantial risks in the *Exxon Valdez* disaster for natural ecosystems, other industries, and indigenous populations.

Unintentional omission of ethical acts by organizational managers who are culpably ignorant harms personal and organization integrity (e.g., the managers of the Washington office of the former accounting firm Price Waterhouse who denied promotion to a qualified female candidate because they unintentionally discriminated against her on the basis of stereotypical judgments). Again, unintentional omission of ethical acts by managers can injure not only immediately affected individuals but also entire categories of stakeholders; for example, managers at Texaco who engaged in employment patterns that precluded the promotion and integration of qualified women and blacks disparately affected and damaged those protected classes of people.

This perceived erosion of integrity extends to the highest levels of public management as well. More members of the U.S. Congress, for example, have been investigated and subjected to sanctions for ethical misconduct in the past decade and a half than in the entire previous history of the institution (Thompson, 1995)! There is no irrefutable evidence, however, that the character of members in recent Congresses is worse than that of their predecessors (Davidson & Oleszek, 1994).

At least two factors account for this increased number of ethics cases: (a) violations of ethics rules are now more likely to be discovered and institutionally investigated, and (b) there are more offenders because there are more offenses. With regard to the first factor, in addition to increased media attention on congressional ethics, the Federal Office of Government Ethics has expanded. In its first year, that office had fewer than 20 employees and contact with only a small network of part-time agency officials, but by 1993, the Office had tripled in size and was coordinating some 8,000 officials who devote at least part-time to ethics work in federal agencies (Thompson, 1995). With regard to the second factor, the Ethics in Government Act in 1978 not only tightened existing rules on regulated practices but also prohibited practices that had previously been unregulated (Congressional Ethics Committee Staff, 1992). Given these factors, one should expect to see more ethics cases of all kinds even if actual individual corruption were decreasing. In fact, a comparative study of 25 countries with the most developed ethics rules for national legislators found that regulations in the United States are clearly more restrictive (Congressional Research Service, 1994).

Nevertheless, the growth of interest in managerial ethics is a legitimate response to the escalating demand for public accountability in an increasingly complex moral and political environment. More complex forms of corruption are becoming more common, and the traditional codes of conduct have become inadequate. The task of ethics reform has expanded to include both individual and institutional corruption (individual managerial ethics and organization integrity).

Global Corruption Pressures

Because global competition imposes pressure on managers to condone and/or go along with unethical practices, strengthened managerial ethical decision-making skills are important in international transactions, especially in the absence of just, background institutions (e.g., regulatory agencies and enforced legal systems) (De George, 1993; Quinn & Petrick, 1994). In 1996, for example, a Global Comparative Ranking of Perceived Corruption was compiled from 10 international surveys, coordinated by Transparency International and Gottingen University, ranking countries from 1 to 10, 10 being least corrupt and 1 being most corrupt (Crosette, 1995; Transparency International, 1996). In 1995, the International Corruption Perception Index was compiled by *The New York Times* from seven global surveys of businesspeople and journalists, closely paralleling the later corruption findings from Transparency International and Gottingen University (Crosette, 1995). Nations from the major regional global triads (Europe, America, and East Asia) were compared with regard to their aggregate perceived levels of corruption. Selected results of the 1996 International Corruption Perception Index, including at least three nations from each of the major triads, is depicted in bar graphs in Figure 1.10.

In Figure 1.10, managerial compliance with East Asian standards may vary considerably from China (2.43) to Japan (7.05) to Singapore (8.80), from more perceived corruption to less perceived corruption. A similar range from more to less corrupt environments can also be illustrated in both the European triad from Italy (3.42) to France (6.96) to Sweden (9.08) and in the American triad from Venezuela (2.50) to the United States (7.66) to Canada (8.96). In other words, the more corrupt the extraorganizational environment, the more important strong managerial character and responsible organizational conduct are to achieve ethical integrity in the global marketplace. Managers with weak characters and poor ethical analysis skills, who inadequately monitor organizational conduct, are much more likely to put their firms in a compromising position than managers who demonstrate personal integrity and build organization integrity (Lozano, 1996; Premeaux & Mondy, 1993). The net result is that, without improved managerial ethical decision making, in the context of corrupt national environments, managers risk ruining their careers, their firms' reputations, and the opportunity to compete in a free market on a level playing field.

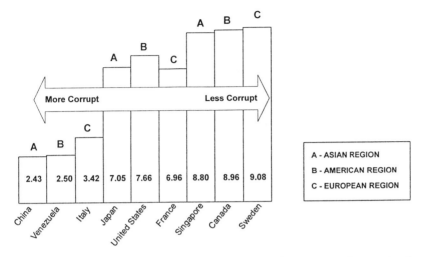

Figure 1.10. International Corruption Perception Index (Transparency International, TI, and Goettinger University, 1996). Used by permission.

Benefits of Improved Management Ethics

Improved managerial ethical decision making and moral performance can lead to both increased profitability and intrinsically desirable organizational order. They can accomplish the former objective in five ways. First, progressively managed workplaces boost shareholder returns by 45% (Kurschner, 1996). A recent Rutgers University study documented that companies that use proactive grievance procedures, incentive programs, information sharing, and job designs have much better financial performance than companies without such progressive workplace processes. Investors in progressively managed firms that did more for their employees realized an annual shareholder rate of return about 45% higher than firms that did the least for their employees (Kurschner, 1996).

Second, managing organizations with a sense of social responsibility attracts customers. A 1995 study done by Cone Communications in Boston and Roper Starch Worldwide in New York found that 31% of respondents viewed a company's sense of social responsibility as a key factor in their purchasing decisions (Kurschner, 1996). In addition, 54% of adults said they would pay more for a product that supported a cause they care about; and 66% of adults said they would switch brands and 62% said they would switch retailers to support a cause they care about. Nearly 90% of consumers surveyed by The Walker Group in New York in 1995 said that when quality, service, and price are equal among competitors, they are more likely to buy from the company that has the best reputation for social responsibility (Kurschner, 1996).

Third, responsible environmental management pays; low organizational polluters outperform high ones 80% of the time (Kurschner, 1996). Recent studies conducted by Stuart Hart at the University of Michigan-Ann Arbor on the impact of financial performance related to pollution cutbacks made at 127 firms listed on the Standard & Poor's 500 Index demonstrated that pollution reduction pays. Similar findings were reported in an analysis published in 1995 by the Investor Responsibility Research Center in Washington, D.C. Among other things, it found that firms with a relatively large number of environmental lawsuits, as compared with their industry peers, earn a lower level of return on assets and return on equity (Kurschner, 1996).

Fourth, managers who develop sound community relations have companies that achieve better financial performance, higher employee morale, and more customer loyalty than companies in the industry with poor community relations. David Lewin, a UCLA Business School professor, conducted two studies involving 188 companies in 1989 and 1992 and confirmed the positive correlations between sincere corporate-community ties and tangible financial gains, higher employee morale and more sustained customer loyalty (Kurschner, 1996).

Fifth, in firms that practice responsible participative management, productivity grew 52% after employee stock option plans (ESOPs) were created and implemented, according to a recent U.S. General Accounting Office study (Kurschner, 1996). Studies from the National Center for Employee Ownership show that a company will grow 6 to 11 times faster than its competitors if it combines employee ownership with a participatory management style (Kurschner, 1996).

The evidence that improved managerial ethics will lead to an intrinsically desirable organizational order comes from psychosocial empirical research on organizational justice (Alexander & Ruderman, 1987; Greenberg, 1996; Kahneman, Knetsch, & Thaler, 1986; Minton, 1988). Basically, if managers ensure outcome and procedural justice at work, they will create an intrinsically desirable organizational order (Lind, Kanfer, & Earley, 1990; Lind & Tyler, 1988; Velasquez, 1996). This intrinsically desirable organizational order communicates value, respect, and dignity; elicits trust, commitment, and loyalty; and leads stakeholders to attribute legitimacy to organizational leaders and their decisions (Greenberg, 1996). In turn, managers and employees who perceive their organization as just are more likely to accept and rapidly implement organizational decisions (Alexander & Ruderman, 1987; Greenberg, 1996).

With regard to *managing outcome justice at work,* research studies document that employees regard managerial adherence to the appropriate principle of distributive justice (distribution proportionate to contribution, equal distribution, or distribution based on need) as intrinsically desirable entirely apart from the personal advantage (or disadvantage) of that form of distributive justice (although personal advantage always remains a competing motivator) (Folger & Konovsky, 1989; Minton, 1988; Tyler & Dawes, 1993).

With regard to *managing procedural justice at work,* research studies document that employees regard managerial processes that allow affected parties direct input and democratic voice as more likely to be intrinsically respected, accepted, and followed; more likely to be intrinsically seen as legitimate by the parties involved; and more likely to evoke managerial trust (Folger & Konovsky, 1989; Lane, 1988; Lind & Tyler, 1988; Tyler, 1994).

Simply put, organizations that are justly managed in terms of fair outcomes and processes are intrinsically better organizations in that they function better than those that are not. This is demonstrated in terms of assessment of organizational effectiveness (Velasquez, 1996). *Organizational effectiveness* has been variously defined as: (a) an organization's ability to attain its goals, (b) an organization's ability to secure needed resources from its external environment, (c) the quality of an organization's internal processes and information, and (d) an organization's ability to at least minimally satisfy all its strategic constituencies, including suppliers, consumers, and employees (Cameron, 1980; Stone & Eddy, 1996). The empirical research on organizational effectiveness demonstrates that the management of organizational justice has a positive impact on each of these elements (Cameron & Freeman, 1991; Lindsay & Petrick, 1997).

In short, there are at least five compelling reasons for improving managerial ethical decision making today. Four of the prior five reasons help managers avoid the costs of unethical workplace conduct, the lack of awareness of ethically questionable role-related acts, the widespread erosion of integrity and exposure to ethical risk, and the temptation to succumb to global corruption pressures. Finally, improved managerial ethical decision making and conduct can lead to both increased profitability and intrinsically desirable organizational order during turbulent, competitive times.

▨ OVERVIEW OF THE BOOK

This book takes management ethics and integrity seriously. It is divided into two parts: "Management Ethics and Integrity: Theory and Tools" and "Management Ethics and Integrity: Practice and Minicases in the Functions of Management." Part I provides the normative, theoretical, and descriptive empirical integration necessary for cultivating, building, and sustaining management integrity over time and the management ethics tools to professionalize managerial moral decision making. Part II demonstrates the performance difference that management ethics and integrity make in practically handling the managerial functions of planning, organizing, leading, and controlling.

By detailed analysis of the microphases of each management function (planning, organizing, leading, and controlling), guidance is offered to improve managerial performance in ethical awareness, judgment, intention, and conduct. Finally, 28 ethics minicases related to each management function in seven allied management application clusters—Accounting/Auditing, Finance/Investment, Marketing/Advertising, Business Management/Human Resources/Business Law, Technology/Quality Operations/Organizational Behavior, Public/Nonprofit/Health Care Administration, and International/Environmental/Public Policy—provide ways to practice ethical planning, organizing, leading, and controlling in different fields. The table *Minicases, Management Functions, and Allied Management Application Clusters* (p. x) provides a graphic spreadsheet of all 28 minicases by management function and application cluster for the reader's convenience.

Part I begins with Chapter 1, "Introduction and Overview." In it, the nature and value of management, and management challenges in the private and public sectors, are treated. In Appendix A, the Management Style Assessment (MSA) tool is provided for practical self-assessment of preferred managerial orientations, which are later linked with personal ethics orientations. Next, the need for improved ethical decision making by managers is established, and finally the book overview is provided.

In Chapter 2, "Management Ethics and Management Integrity," after treating the nature and value of management ethics and rendering explicit the implicit logical connections between management theories and ethics theories, managerial ethical integrity is defined and distinguished from expediency, consistency, and congruence in moral decision making.

In Chapter 3, "Dimensions of Management Integrity," the three major dimensions of integrity are treated: judgment integrity, process integrity, and developmental integrity. In Appendix B, "Caux Roundtable Principle for Business"; Appendix C, "A Business Charter for Sustainable Development"; Appendix D, "Qualitative Ethical Decision-Making Tool (QL-TOOL)"; and Appendix E, "Organization Ethics Development System (OEDS) Components and Their Collective Work Culture Environments" are provided as ways to integrate the dimension of integrity in resolving moral issues. Finally, as the number of stakeholders who regularly demonstrate judgment, process, and developmental integrity increases, moral progress results.

Part II begins with Chapter 4, "Management Ethics: Planning With Integrity." After a review of the dimensions of planning, a detailed treatment of the four microphases in the ethical planning process, which parallel the four ethics processes that build integrity, is undertaken and exemplified. Finally, management ethics and planning with integrity minicases in various disciplines are provided for practice application.

In Chapter 5, "Management Ethics: Organizing With Integrity," after a review of the dimensions of organizing, a detailed treatment of the four microphases in the ethical organizing process, which parallel the four ethics processes that build integrity, is undertaken and exemplified. Finally, management ethics and organizing with integrity minicases in various disciplines are provided for practice application.

In Chapter 6, "Management Ethics: Leading With Integrity," after a review of the dimensions of leading, a detailed treatment of the four microphases in the ethical leading process, which parallel the four ethics processes that build integrity, is undertaken and exemplified. In Appendix F, the Leadership Empowerment Readiness Assessment (LERA) tool is recommended as one way to ascertain the self-directed leadership readiness of followers and leaders. Finally, management ethics and leading with integrity minicases in various disciplines are provided for practice application.

In Chapter 7, "Management Ethics: Controlling With Integrity," after a review of the dimensions of controlling, a detailed treatment of the four microphases in the ethical controlling process, which parallel the four ethics processes that build integrity, is undertaken and exemplified. Finally, management ethics and controlling with integrity minicases in various disciplines are provided for practice application.

SUMMARY

In summary, this chapter delineates the nature and value of management and the management challenges presented by private- and public-sector managers. It established the need to improve ethical decision making by managers and provided a conceptual overview of the entire book so that readers can appreciate its logical organization and anticipate future topic coverage.

Because the need to proceed with an investigation into management ethics is urgent, the next chapter focuses on the topic of management ethics and management integrity.

DISCUSSION/EXPERIENTIAL EXERCISES

Discussion Questions

1. Discuss the four management theories and the need for balanced managerial competencies in handling behavioral complexity at work.
2. Why do you agree or disagree with the following claim: Although the four management theories are universal, their relative appropriateness may vary in different transnational and national cultures.
3. Discuss the major differences between private- and public-sector managers and the four standards that sustain public trust.
4. Discuss five reasons why managers need to improve their ethical decision-making skills to enhance their performance at work.

Experiential Exercises

5. After completing your MSA in Appendix A, identify and prioritize areas for personal management style improvement and devise a 1-year and a 3-year plan for management development that specifically develops your strengths and addresses your areas for improvement.
6. From your own work/life/school experiences, give examples of occasions that demonstrate the need for improved managerial ethical decision making and/or share current events/news articles that do the same.
7. Using the concepts from this chapter, examine with the entire class the ethical decision-making process of private- and public-sector managers in the NASA *Challenger* disaster. (See "Ethical Controlling Scanning" in Chapter 7 on p. 287 for a brief treatment of the NASA case.)
8. Using the concepts from this chapter, examine in small groups the following minicases: 4F Sikorsky and Government Purchasing and 5D J. C. Penney Company, Inc.

2

Management Ethics and
Management Integrity

*The focus of Chapter 2 is on two areas: (a) the nature and value of manage-
ment ethics and (b) management integrity in ethical decision making. After
treating the major types of key ethics theories that are implicitly adopted by
managers who exhibit certain management styles, the authors distinguish
management integrity from expediency, consistency, and congruence.*

◪ NATURE AND VALUE OF
MANAGEMENT ETHICS

Ethics can be defined as the systematic attempt to make sense of individual,
group, organizational, professional, social, market, and global moral experience in such a way as to determine the desirable, prioritized ends that are worth
pursuing, the right rules and obligations that ought to govern human conduct,
the virtuous intentions and character traits that deserve development in life,
and to act accordingly. Put more simply, *ethics is the study of individual and
collective moral awareness, judgment, character, and conduct.*

Sometimes the term *morality* is used interchangeably with *ethics* in everyday conversation, but at other times it can be conceptually distinguished from
ethics (Wellman, 1975). The morality of a society is related to its *mores*—the

customs accepted by a society or group as being right and wrong—as well as to those laws of a society that add legal prohibitions and sanctions to many activities considered to be immoral (Shaw & Barry, 1995). *Morality,* therefore, can be defined as the customary, sociolegal practices and activities that are considered importantly right and wrong; the rules that govern those activities; and the values that are embedded, fostered, or pursued by those conventional, sociolegal activities and practices.

In some instances, management morality and management ethics are diametrically opposed to each other. For example, in the South before the Civil War, the fugitive slave, if recaptured, was often maimed by his or her managers/owners, frequently by chopping off one foot. Although this act of maiming was condoned by customary morality and sociolegal practices at the time, some ethically sensitive, progressive managers objected to it. They argued that this cruel and vindictive act may have been morally acceptable but was ethically repulsive. Whereas management morality may allow one to succeed temporarily by conforming to current social norms or organizational mazes, management ethics calls for a sensitive, reflective, and systematic endorsement of those norms only after they have withstood critical challenge (Ferrell & Fraedrich, 1997; Jackall, 1988). A classic business example of a transition from stakeholder morality to stakeholder ethics is represented in the *Ford v. Dodge* lawsuit from the turn of the century. Henry Ford wanted to share profits from his automobile company with his employees to improve the quality of their lives, but the Supreme Court sided with the position of Dodge that the fiduciary moral relationship with investors precluded the ethical sharing of profits with employees. Subsequent to that case, however, profit sharing and gain sharing with designated stakeholders has been ethically justified in terms of prioritized ends and obligations that overcame the conventional morality of earlier forms of capitalism. Many times, moral managers and ethical managers engage in the same behavior patterns, but the latter must critically challenge accepted norms before endorsing them (Green, 1994; Walton, 1988).

The study of ethics can occur on at least three levels of analysis: macro/global, molar/organizational, and micro/individual. *Macro/global ethics* focuses on world economic contexts—conflicts between market and command economies. *Molar/organizational ethics* addresses ethical issues encountered within and between institutions—company codes of business conduct or ethical issues in mergers and acquisitions. Finally, *micro/individual ethics* focuses on personal group conduct—lying, cheating, or stealing at work by employees. The primary emphasis in this book is on the latter two levels.

In addition, moral values are part of a person's philosophy of life. A *philosophy of life* consists of ongoing, critical reflection about logically fundamental beliefs regarding what is real, true, and of value and acting in accord with those reasoned commitments, as graphically illustrated in Figure 2.1. Moral values, along with economic, aesthetic, political, and other values, indicate what people regard as important in life and worth acting on. Reflection on beliefs about what is real, called *metaphysics,* and reflection on beliefs about what is true, called *epistemology,* can result in either religious or secular conclusions, and both can provide conceptual foundations for moral values. For example, a person who believes that a real God created the world and humanity, that these truths are known by faith in divine revelation disclosed through sacred writings, and that his or her highest ethical value is spiritual salvation after death has adopted a *religious foundation for ethics.* Another person who believes that nature is the only reality that always existed, that humans created gods out of fear, that these truths are known through science and reason, and that the highest moral value is ethical integrity in this life has adopted a *secular foundation for ethics.* Both persons can act ethically, but from different metaphysical and epistemological foundations (Petrick, Von der Embse, & Wagley, 1991).

In addition to reducing tangible and intangible costs, management ethics adds value to individual, group, and organizational performance. *Management ethics can be defined as the descriptive and normative study of moral awareness, judgment, character, and conduct as they relate to all levels of managerial practice.* Individual business judgment and performance can be enhanced through management ethics in the following ways:

- Stimulation of the moral imagination
- Moral identification and ordering
- Moral evaluation
- Tolerating moral disagreement and ambiguity
- Integrating managerial competence and moral competence
- Eliciting a sense of moral responsibility (Callahan & Bok, 1980; Powers & Vogel, 1980)

Although it is tempting for managers to suppose that economic and legal factors determine rational business decisions, empathy for the web of moral relationships and obligations imaginatively enlarges the awareness of the busi-

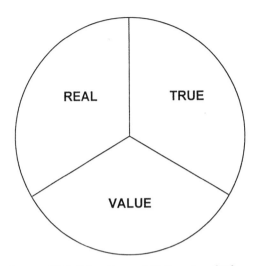

Figure 2.1. Fundamental Beliefs in a Personal Philosophy of Life

ness impact of integrity (DeGeorge, 1997; Ferrell, Gresham, & Fraedrich, 1989; Zey-Ferrell & Ferrell, 1982).

For a manager, exhibiting ethical integrity involves achieving good consequences or ends (outcome-oriented theories emphasized in *teleological ethics*), by adhering to standards of right conduct (duty-oriented theories emphasized in *deontological ethics*), while habitually being motivated by proper intentions and developing virtuous character traits (character-oriented theories emphasized in *virtue ethics*), in an ethically supportive, holistic context (system-oriented theories emphasized in *system development ethics*). Although all four theories of ethics (teleological, deontological, virtues, and system development) can be isolated, the main point is that all four theories are necessary to understand moral phenomena fully, to make balanced ethical judgments, and to act with managerial integrity. Just as handling behavioral complexity is required of master managers, handling moral complexity is required of ethical managers.

More important, as indicated in Figure 2.2, management theory and practice implicitly endorse some ethical values over others. For example, *rational goal*, "bottom line" managers who use results as the exclusive performance standard logically endorse and tacitly choose to accord outcome-oriented ethical values preeminence over other ethical values. Rational goal managers,

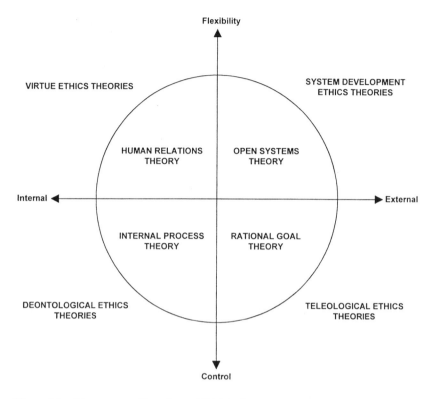

Figure 2.2. Management Theories and Ethics Theories

who have strong role competencies in directing and producing, implicitly subscribe to outcome-oriented ethical values in their daily practice. *Internal process* managers, who exhibit strong role competencies in monitoring and coordinating, implicitly subscribe to duty-oriented ethical values in their daily practice. These "by the book" managers who use compliance with internal policies as the exclusive performance standard are tacitly endorsing and logically choosing to accord duty-oriented ethical values priority over other ethical values. *Human relations* managers, who have strong role competencies in facilitating and mentoring, implicitly subscribe to a virtues-oriented ethical value in daily practice. These "true grit" managers who focus on "the right stuff in persons" and use virtuous character as the exclusive performance standard are tacitly endorsing and logically choosing to accord character-oriented ethical values preeminence over other ethical values. Finally, *open systems* managers, who excel in innovating and brokering for resources, implicitly subscribe to systems-oriented ethical values in daily practice. These "change agent" managers who use continuous system improvement as the exclusive performance standard, are tacitly endorsing and logically choosing to accord systems-oriented ethical values priority over other ethical values.

Teleological Ethics Theories

Teleological ethics theories maintain that good ends and/or results determine the ethical value of actions. If, on balance, more benefits than costs are obtained by the relevant stakeholder(s) than by any other alternative, teleological ethics endorses the goodness of that choice. Three major types of teleological ethics are egoism, utilitarianism, and eudaimonism. They and other major types of the key ethics theories are depicted in Figure 2.3.

Ethical Egoism

In the lower right quadrant of Figure 2.3 *Ethical egoism,* is a teleological theory that holds that an action is good if it produces or tends to produce results that maximize a particular person's self-interest as defined by the individual, even at the expense of others. Ethical egoism denies that a person should help others when the person will get nothing out of it. *Psychological egoism* is different from ethical egoism in that the former theory clams that people always and only want something out of it for themselves when they act, thereby denying the reality of genuine altruism. While genuine *altruism*, as the intentional sacrificing of one's self-interest or welfare for the sake of others, has been used to refute psychological egoism, it has provided a rationale for enlightened egoism. *Enlightened egoism* emphasizes long-range self-interest while allowing for altruistic concern for the well-being of others (Gauthier, 1986; Holmes, 1993; Olson, 1965). An enlightened egoist, for example, may well avoid cheating and support community projects, not so much because these actions benefit others, but because they help achieve some ultimate goal for the egoist, such as social image enhancement that could lead to career advancement within an organization.

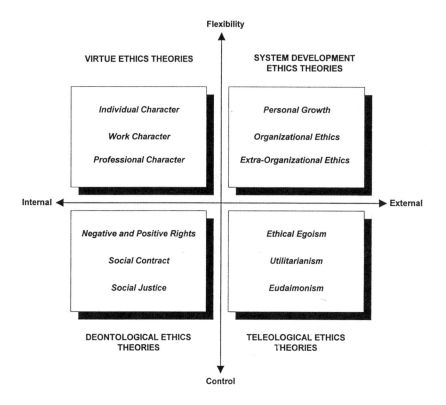

Figure 2.3. Major Types of Key Ethics Theories

Utilitarianism

Utilitarianism is a teleological theory that holds that an action is good if it produces or tends to produce the greatest amount of satisfaction for the greatest number of stakeholders affected by the action; for example, if I as a manager create an annual employee vacation schedule only after soliciting vacation time preferences from all employees and honoring those preferences, then I would be acting in a way that would maximize the pleasure of all employees (Bentham, 1789/1948; DeGeorge, 1997).

Most business students routinely adopt either an egoist or a utilitarian perspective (whether act or rule-based) because of their conceptual roots in classic economic theory and emphasis on maximizing investor wealth (self-interest and utility). Growing businesses to increase profits, market share, and sales has led to high-consumption societies and widespread material satisfaction in the economically developed world.

Eudaimonism

Eudaimonism is a teleological theory that holds that an action is good if it promotes or tends to promote the fulfillment of goals constitutive of human nature and its happiness; for example, if I as a manager enforce employee health and safety standards at work, I am ensuring fundamental, natural components of human happiness (Aquinas, 1250/1959; Aristotle, 350 B.C./1985; Finnis, 1980; Pegis, 1945). Aristotle maintained that *happiness* was the quality of a whole human lifetime characterized by the degree to which the following "goods" were achieved and sustained: health, wealth, friendship, knowledge, good luck, and virtue. He argued that there was a difference between having a good time (maximizing pleasurable utility) and leading a good life (maximizing happiness) and that the latter outcome was to be preferred to the former. Impulsive and unrestrained acquisitiveness and consumption, though pleasurable, are vices of immoderation for Aristotle that ultimately lead to unhappiness.

The rational goal theory of management, therefore, stresses productivity and profits as the criteria of effectiveness, and managers who excel in or endorse this approach demonstrate conscious or subliminal support for teleological ethics. In concrete terms for managers, this approach emphasizes the bottom line and the timely achievement of organizational objectives. Managers who adopt this perspective implicitly accept the dictum "All's well that ends well," regardless of the means used to produce the results.

Deontological Ethics Theories

Deontological ethics theories maintain that responsibly fulfilling obligations, following proper procedure, "doing the right thing," and adhering to moral standards determine the ethical value of actions. Deontological ethics maintains that actions are morally right independent of their consequences; for example, for the secularist, it is right to keep promises and for the religious, it is right to obey the Ten Commandments regardless of personal costs or benefits. Among the major types of deontological ethics are negative and positive rights theories, social contract theories, and social justice theories.

Negative and Positive Rights Theories

In the lower left quadrant of Figure 2.3 *Negative rights theories,* hold that an action is right if it protects an individual from unwarranted interference from government and/or other people in the exercise of that right; for example, if I have a right to privately use, sell, or dispose of my personal property as I choose, this means that every other person has the correlative *duty not to prevent* me from privately using, selling, or disposing of my property as I freely choose (Locke, 1690; Nozick, 1974). *Positive rights theories* hold that an action is right if it provides any individual with whatever he or she needs to exist; for example, if I have a right to adequate health care to survive, this means that other agents (perhaps the government) have the correlative *duty to provide* me with my entitled adequate health care, not merely to avoid interfering with its competitive acquisition (Dworkin, 1978; Kant, 1785/1938). Much of domestic and global public-policy conflict over moral rights can be interpreted as differences over the kind and degree of dignity that is to be accorded to persons and whether negative or positive rights should be accorded priority. Political conservatives, for example, argue that government activities should be restricted to protecting people's negative rights (e.g., right not to be killed, injured, or deprived of property), rather than also providing for people's positive rights (e.g., right to health care, welfare benefits, housing, and jobs), as political liberals maintain (Bowie, 1991; Etzioni, 1988; Shue, 1980).

Social Contract Theories

Social contract theories hold that an action is right if it conforms to the terms agreed upon, conditions, or rules for social well-being negotiated by competent parties; for example, the U.S. Uniform Commercial Code and the United Nations Code of Conduct of Transnational Corporations both specify normative guidelines arrived at by consensus (Donaldson, 1994; Donaldson & Dunfee, 1994; Mayer, 1994; Rousseau, 1762/1959-1969).

Social Justice Theories

Social justice theories hold that an action is right if it promotes the duty of fairness in the distributive, retributive, and compensatory dimensions of social benefits and burdens; for example, if secondhand smoke injures nonsmokers at work, the fair distribution of that health risk burden, the imposition of reasonable punishments on responsible parties, and the compensation due injured parties would all be factors in social justice determinations (Plato, 367 B.C./1968; Rawls, 1971; Velasquez, 1994).

The internal process model of management, therefore, stresses dutiful compliance with stable standards as the criterion of efficiency, and managers who excel in or endorse this approach often exhibit conscious or subliminal support for deontological ethics. In concrete terms for managers, this approach stresses monitoring adherence to standard operating procedures and rewarding persons for adhering to contractual agreements in a coordinated manner. Managers who adopt this perspective tend to "run a tight ship" and to make decisions "by the book," regardless of the consequences.

Virtue Ethics Theories

Virtue ethics theories maintain that habitual development of sound character traits determines the ethical value of persons. For the virtue ethicist, building character is what life is all about. *Character* is the pattern of intentions, inclinations, and virtues that dispose a person or organization to be ready to act ethically. Persons with strong character have soundly cultivated intellectual, moral, emotional, and social virtues to achieve the self-discipline to do the right thing or want what is truly good for them (Himmelfarb, 1994). Persons with weak character find themselves doing the wrong thing or wanting what is truly harmful to them and making excuses for their irresponsible life choices. Character is to be distinguished from *personality* in that the former provides the substantive moral foundation for one's actions, whereas the latter projects the psychosocial image that creates surface impressions; for example, a manager may be fair but not look fair and vice versa (Giacalone & Rosenfeld, 1991; Greenberg, 1990; Paine, 1991). The alignment of strong character and hardy personality is one indication of individual integrity (Josephson, 1992; Slote, 1992; Srivastva & Associates, 1988).

Virtue ethics maintains that the sound, balanced character, motivation, and intention of an individual is more important than the person's actual conduct and its consequences (Pincoffs, 1985; Slote, 1992). The difference between merely desirable and truly admirable lives is captured in virtue ethics; the wholesome readiness to act out of good intentions constitutes the character of the good person for a virtue ethicist. Three major types of virtue ethics theories focus on individual, work, and professional character.

Individual Character Ethics

In the upper left quadrant of Figure 2.3 *Individual character ethics,* maintains that the identification and responsible development of the human traits of nobility—such as courage, moderation, justice, prudence, gratitude, sense of humor, self-discipline, reliability, benevolence, authenticity, caring, sincerity, understanding, and wisdom—determine both the instrumental and intrinsic value of all human ethical interactions; for example, if as I age I lose my health, my wealth, and my loved ones through no fault of my own, I retain my dignity and prospects for happiness by living a virtuous life (Aristotle, 350 B.C./1985; Gilligan, Ward, & Taylor, 1989; McAllister, 1995; Nussbaum, 1986; Sheaffer, 1988; Solomon, 1990b; Taylor, 1987; Wilson, 1993).

Work Character Ethics

Work character ethics maintains that the identification and responsible development of noble, reflective, practitioner traits at work—such as competence, creativity, honesty, fairness, trustworthiness, coworker appreciation, task completion, honor, loyalty, shared work pride, diligence, resourcefulness, levelheadedness, tolerance, dependability, civility, empathy, conscientiousness, discretion, patient urgency, cooperativeness, and supportiveness—determine both the instrumental and intrinsic ethical quality of work life; for example, as a manager facing global competition, heightened productivity expectations, and the need for effective teamwork, it is essential that the character of my work performance serve as a role model for task accomplishment and considerate relations at work (Cavanagh, 1984; Hosmer, 1994a, 1996; Kruschwitz & Roberts, 1987; Schon, 1983; Solomon, 1992). As more and more occupations, including management, undergo the process of "professionalization," standards for work character ethics increase (Bayles, 1989; Fukuyama, 1995; Larson, 1977; Trevino & Youngblood, 1990). As managers and information specialists, for example, are required to have extensive training with a significant intellectual component in order to provide services vital to the organized functioning of society, they are acquiring more technical autonomy, developing more organizational networks for members, and expecting to be treated in a more "professional" manner. In turn, as more employees become empowered in their work units, they expect a high degree of cognitive moral development, appropriate positive affect, and behavior consistent with "professional" moral norms at work from their managers (Conry & Nelson, 1989; Fox, 1994; Gilligan, 1982; Kohlberg, 1973; Petrick & Furr, 1995).

Professional Character Ethics

Professional character ethics maintains that credentialed expertise, licensed monopoly, self-regulation, collegiality, altruism, trust, truthfulness, autonomy, impartiality, loyalty, independence of judgment, and public service determine both the instrumental and intrinsic ethical quality of individuals in associational communities; for example, as a business manager for a firm of surgeons who detects a pattern of double billing Medicare insurance claims, my professional character ethics would require me to bring this matter to the immediate attention of the surgeons-in-charge, to exhaust internal remedies to correct the situation in-house, and to be prepared to engage in responsible, external whistle blowing if all else fails, because of loyalty to a professional code of ethics (Armstrong, 1993; Bayles, 1989; Flores, 1988; Gahl, 1984; Koehn, 1995; Kupfer & Klett, 1993; Maniero, 1992; Sullivan, 1995; Walzer, 1983). Furthermore, research has demonstrated that managers who reason at more principled levels make a positive difference in group moral performance; individual ethical decision making thereafter benefits from the earlier group moral experience (Dukerich, Nichols, Elm, & Vollrath, 1990). Managerial moral development, therefore, shapes work unit moral development (Moberg, 1994).

The human relations theory of management, therefore, stresses interpersonal development and team-building skills as the criteria of flexible work communities, and managers who excel in or endorse this approach demonstrate conscious or subliminal support for virtue ethics. In concrete terms for managers, this approach emphasizes supporting character development, building cohesion and morale, facilitating participative decision making, fostering win-win dispute resolutions, and recognizing employee contributions on a regular basis. Managers who adopt this perspective endorse the dictum "Character counts" and avoid pressuring people to use means or achieve ends that violate their conscience.

System Development Ethics Theories

System development ethics theories maintain that the nature and extent of the supportive framework for continuous improvement of ethical conduct determines the ethical value of actions. Managers who are sensitive to the need to assess and develop work cultures supportive of ethical conduct implement ethics development systems that will sustain integrity-building environments. Managers who rely exclusively on the character of employees to sustain sound business practices, while neglecting to implement morally supportive intraorganizational systems and stable (variation reducing) processes, are unintentionally exposing their organizations to future ethical risk. Managers who do not implement recognition processes for exemplary moral conduct by employees or refrain from implementing processes for swift, fair enforcement of sanctions on wrongdoers at work are guilty of both moral and managerial malfeasance. Three major types of system development ethics theories are personal improvement, organizational, and extraorganizational ethics.

Personal Improvement Ethics

In the upper right quadrant of Figure 2.3 *Personal improvement ethics,* holds that an action is good if it promotes or tends to promote personal responsibility for continuous learning, system holistic development improvement, and moral excellence; for example, a manager who generates new ideas out of a commitment to personal improvement directed toward company goals uses her company's educational benefits package to improve herself and her organization (Covey, 1989, 1994; Martin, 1986; Norton, 1976; Schminke, 1997; Schutz, 1994). Both in the western and non-western traditions, family and friends who support personal improvement and moral progress provide the resources to energize ongoing personal development.

Organizational Ethics

Organizational ethics holds that an action is good if it promotes or tends to promote the formal and informal organizational processes that enhance procedural, outcome, and systemic justice, respectful caring, and innovation in ethical work cultures; for example, if the organization in which I as a manager work has neither a fair reward system nor an employee voice system for feedback, part of my responsibility is to improve those systems so that there are contextual forces that support individual and organizational moral development and override inertia or intense resistance to moral development (Cohen, 1993; Jones, 1991; Lindsay & Petrick, 1997; Payne & Giacalone, 1990;

Petrick & Manning, 1993; Sheppard, Lewicki, & Minton, 1992; Trevino & Nelson, 1995).

Extraorganizational Ethics

Extraorganizational ethics holds that an action is good if it promotes or tends to promote the improvement of collaborative partnerships and collective and global justice creativity in the human and natural environments; for example, as a manager, I have a social responsibility to consider and respect global and domestic constituencies that represent diverse economic, political, legal, social, philanthropic, and ecological concerns that affect the firm (Carroll, 1991, 1996; Frederick, 1986, 1995; Gittines, 1993; Israedel & Crutzen, 1995; Jones, 1995; Mitnick, 1993; Wood, 1994).

The open systems theory of management, therefore, stresses innovative adaptability and acquisition of external resources as the criteria of effectiveness, and managers who excel in or support this approach exhibit conscious or subliminal endorsement of system development ethics. In concrete terms for managers, this approach emphasizes creative change management, entrepreneurial resourcefulness, respectful and sophisticated global negotiation, and collaborative networking with diverse global interests. Managers who adopt this perspective implicitly encourage organizational flexibility to adapt to reality better and to accept the system dictum that, to make organizational moral progress, it is necessary to concurrently manage both people and processes ethically (Schminke, 1997).

Moral Complexity and Management Integrity

Just as the master manager requires a behavioral complexity repertoire to ensure the dynamic balance of all four managerial theories, the master ethical manager also requires a moral complexity repertoire to ensure the dynamic balance and use of all four ethics theories. Managers who rely exclusively on their natural affinity for one ethical perspective, whether based on religious or secular foundations, develop unilinear "ethical blind spots" in dealing with moral complexity. They fanatically rush to judgment with an inadequate appreciation of the multidimensionality of moral decisions. For example, a manager devoted to the internal process theory may dismiss an employee for not following proper bureaucratic procedures (a deontological ethical concern), whereas another manager devoted to the open systems approach would reward the same employee for demonstrating creativity in overcoming the antiquated procedures of the existing system (a system development ethical concern). The insertion of ethics within a multidimensional managerial action framework indicates the authors' assumption that management ethics is most usefully employed as an integrity development guide. Approaching conscience as a remindful coach challenging one to more responsible, balanced action, is more useful than regarding it as a reproachful critic; and constantly geared up to engender scrupulous defensiveness or engage in workplace "witch hunts." Managers are persons who must decide and act; the study of management ethics helps managers do so with integrity by expanding their moral repertoire. Today's managers do not have the luxury to contemplate every move critically; management ethics helps managers become more responsible and effective practitioners.

In addition, just as extreme overdevelopment and underdevelopment of management role competencies can lead to negative managerial performance, extreme overdevelopment and underdevelopment of ethics competencies can subvert managerial integrity. On the one hand, extreme underdevelopment of ethical competencies represents the lack of ability and motivation to act morally, typical of *amoral managers,* who make all business decisions without any awareness of the ethical dimensions of those decisions. On the other hand, extreme overemphasis on achieving moral results, in line with teleological ethics theory, risks treating people with disrespect to get results and jeopardizes cooperative, noncompetitive relationships. Extreme dependence on fulfilling duties, in line with deontological ethics theory, may lead to rapid, righteous condemnation of moral progress because it involves change and prolonged resistance to moral creativity. Extreme emphasis on building character, in line with virtue ethics theory, leads to the paralysis of self-absorbed perfectionism and neglect of the improvement of organizational systems that would preclude the necessity for managers to feel like "moral lone rangers" when they have to "go out on a limb" to do the right thing. Extreme emphasis on developing systems, in line with system development ethics, unduly disrupts the continuity of traditional relationships and risks wasted creativity.

Just as the transnational and national cultural factors altered the appropriacy emphasis of management theories in different international contexts, the same is true of ethics theory emphases; for example, the customary Chinese Confucian emphasis on intellectual and social virtues and the opposing German emphasis on duties and obligations alter the ethics theory appropriacy boundaries for agents in their respective global cultures (Cooper, 1996; Fernandez, 1991; Solomon & Higgins, 1996). In some global contexts, the upper control limit of ethical practice variation in the positive zone (near the outer rim of the positive zone circle) would be "normal," whereas in others, approaching the lower control limits (near the inner rim of the positive zone circle) would be more culturally appropriate. Yet ethical conduct beyond or below the acceptable variation range of good conduct (outside the positive zone circle) remains a crosscultural standard. Although the boundaries of the globally acceptable range of moral conduct variation are currently being determined, those boundaries do set limits and counter the skeptics' claim that good managers and good corporations are defunct in today's hypercompetitive, relativistic global arena (Daufman, 1994; D'Aveni, 1994; Houck & Williams, 1996).

Traditional Phases of General Ethics

To place the four prior ethics theories in proper perspective, it is helpful to realize that general ethics has three traditional phases: descriptive ethics, normative ethics, and metaethics (Holmes, 1993). *Descriptive ethics* consists of the application of empirical methodologies to obtain facts, explain behavior, and predict the causal/correlational factors that contribute to moral phenomena—for example, the social anthropologist's account of actual moral dilemmas encountered in organizational decision making. *Normative ethics* consists of the application of critical analysis and constructive synthesis to interpret, evaluate, proscribe, and prescribe virtues, actions, ends, and contexts supportive of moral practice; for example, the philosophical criticism of excessive U.S. CEO compensation on the basis of justice and the recommendation for greater equity. Normative ethics may rely on descriptive ethics, but its aim is not merely to accurately describe, but to prescribe what is right or wrong.

One recent nationwide descriptive ethics survey of U.S. managerial values, consisting of responses from more than 1,000 members of the American Management Association (AMA) representing diverse industries, organizations, functions, and levels, compared the changes and constants in the way U.S. managers viewed themselves and their work between 1981 and 1991 (Lee, 1988; Posner & Schmidt, 1984, 1992; Schmidt & Posner, 1982). This decade comparison of U.S. managerial values highlights the national normative value shifts among managers and is displayed in Figure 2.4.

Changes in U.S. Managerial Values

1. Quality and customer service have become clear and deliberate corporate and managerial values; neither were [sic] really even on the nation's agenda ten years ago.
2. More managers feel that improvements in the quality of life require a society with a cooperative value system.
3. Home and personal considerations are taking greater precedence over the demands of employers.
4. Greater attention is being focused on others in the organization, rather than being directed toward personal needs.
5. Increased appreciation for the importance of government, and the partnerships required between the public and private sectors, now exists.
6. Greater challenges face managers in aligning personal and organizational values.

Constants in U.S. Managerial Values

1. Managers value honesty and competence above every other quality in the people whom they would be willing to take direction from and follow.
2. They are still optimistic about the future (or at least the future they can most directly influence).
3. The relative importance of various organizational priorities (goals) remains stable.
4. Customers still hold center stage as a firm's key stakeholders and stockholders are best served when the organization meets its corporate objectives.
5. Ethics codes and workshops remain a peripheral part of the corporate environment.
6. The behavior of those in charge continues to be the principal determinant in setting the firm's ethical tone.

Figure 2.4. Changes and Constants in U.S. Managerial Values

SOURCE: Copyright © 1992, by The Regents of the University of California. Reprinted from the *California Management Review*, Vol. 32, No. 3. By permission of The Regents.

Among these national value shifts is a strong preference for total quality over traditional management practice because global competition enhances the importance of democratic participation over hierarchic paternalism. Public standards of U.S. managerial conduct, in turn, have been distinctively raised in the light of these new expectations (Vogel, 1992). Both descriptive and normative ethics are dealt with in the four ethics theories depicted in Figure 2.3. Every responsible manager today needs to correctly describe moral facts; analyze and evaluate character, actions, results, and systems; and resolve ethical issues by appeal to a set of normative priorities (Victor & Stephens, 1994; Weaver & Trevino, 1994). These value changes also account for the shift of managerial focus from individual rights to system integrity at work.

Metaethics, in contrast, consists of the study of the meaning of moral terms and with the logic of moral reasoning; for example, a language analyst may clarify the meaning and extent of role responsibility for a manager. Among the major metaethical assumptions the authors make is that humans are capable of autonomous activity both at work and away from work. This means they can be held accountable for their moral intentions, reasons, actions, and results (Feinberg, 1970). Furthermore, humans are morally responsible for their adoption and performance of management roles in a way that reflectively integrates managerial and ethical competence (Bird & Waters, 1989). Finally, humans are regarded by the authors as capable of managerial and ethical improvement and of being held accountable for their development of competence in both areas or the lack thereof (Crawford & Quinn, 1991; Ewing, 1977).

Several additional metaethical distinctions are helpful with regard to the following terms: ethical relativism, ethical universalism, and ethical pluralism. *Ethical relativism* is a theoretical claim that when two or more cultures or two or more persons hold opposing moral views of an action, all views can be right, without the appeal to justified normative frameworks. Its opposite, *ethical .universalism,* is a theoretical claim that the general principles and norms of morality are either currently everywhere and always the same or, ideally, will be through collective effort in the future. The former version of ethical universalism claims that a uni-theoretical, simple, unchallenging, external set of moral principles and norms exists somewhere—perhaps in the mind of God. The latter version of ethical universalism claims that a multi-theoretical, complex pattern of moral principles and norms emerges over time by having survived the collective, critical scrutiny of multiple stakeholders, who engage in continuous collaboration to extend the domain of moral cooperation in the world. Finally, *ethical pluralism* is a theoretical claim that general principles and norms of morality, which are justified by normative frameworks, are either currently everywhere and always different or, ideally, will be different through divergent effort in the future. The former version of ethical pluralism claims that the adversarial tension of irreconcilable diversity among opposing moralities precludes any meaningful, cooperative, global society. The latter version of ethical pluralism claims that the creative tension of diversity among moralities weaves a loosely knit, tolerant, enriching, patchwork quilt of human and nonhuman global variety.

In addition to general ethics, special ethics applies general ethics in at least two ways: (a) solving specific problems (e.g., *casuistry,* as the art of solving moral problems through careful application of moral principles obtained from general ethics, can address ways to comply minimally with the letter of the law); and (b) investigating the morality of specialized areas of human endeavor (e.g., managerial and organizational ethics). This book covers both general and special ethics to enhance management education by enlarging the vision and appreciation of the moral dimension of everyday managerial decision making in six ways.

1. It is tempting to suppose that financial, economic, legal, technological, and political factors totally determine rational managerial decisions. Sustained exposure to management ethics, however, reveals the web of moral relationships that embed managerial practice and how properly anticipated moral intentions, actions, and consequences can add to or detract from managerial performance.

2. Just as a manager learns to sort out, prioritize, and weigh the financial factors that bear upon a responsible organizational decision, sustained exposure to management ethics helps the manager sort out, prioritize, and weigh the moral factors that bear upon a responsible organizational decision.

3. Managers can learn to apply an objective ethical analysis framework routinely to diagnose a moral situation and arrive at a well-reasoned, justifiable, principled resolution of an issue, after considering alternative solutions, so that any individual can be held professionally accountable.

4. At a time of increasing workforce diversity, management ethics helps individuals develop a tolerant perspective that encourages people to voice rational and emotional challenges to workplace morality without being overwhelmed with the fragmenting intensity of pluralism but insisting on respectful regard for others in the process of moral dialogue.

5. Just as levels of managerial competence in process control, human relations, directing productivity, and system change move from novice to expert levels of mastery, the same levels of moral competence exist in character, action, result, and contextual analyses as individuals morally mature and organizations morally develop. Managers learn that moral and managerial competence are interdependent and need to be concurrently developed.

6. Sustained exposure to management ethics usually evokes an enlarged sense of the moral community and stimulates committed and principled conduct.

◤ MANAGEMENT INTEGRITY IN ETHICAL DECISION MAKING

Reframing the relationship between management and ethics theories discloses subtle connections that point toward the crucial role of management integrity in ethical decision making. Three connections have been identified: (a) Managers who emphasize a particular management theory in their pattern of daily decision making are now aware that they are *implicitly* subscribing to a parallel ethical theory; (b) managers are now aware that extreme overdevelopment and underdevelopment of managerial and ethical competencies adversely affect their performance and integrity; and (c) managers are now aware that to make sound ethical decisions with integrity precludes their denial of moral complexity or settling for a simple, narrow-minded resolution based on less than the four key ethics theories.

Integrity can be defined as *the individual and collective process of repeated alignment of moral awareness, judgment, character, and conduct that demonstrates balanced judgment and promotes sustained moral development:* Three dimensions of integrity, therefore, are part of its definition: judgment, process, and developmental dimensions. Individuals with integrity demonstrate balanced moral judgment in resolving issues; routinely align their psychological process of awareness, judgment, character, and conduct (they practice what they preach) in behaving responsibly, and sustain their development of moral reasoning from narrow self-interest to universal principled regard for others. *Management integrity is* the individual process of repeated alignment of moral awareness, judgment, character, and conduct that demonstrates balanced judgment and promotes sustained moral development at all levels of managerial practice. Likewise, three dimensions of managerial ethical integrity contribute its theoretical core: judgment, process, and developmental management integrity. Although these three dimensions are explored in more detail in the next chapter, one aspect of management judgment integrity is treated at this time.

This aspect of management judgment integrity in ethical decision making entails developing the capability of managers to handle moral complexity by using all four quadrants of ethics theories. Figure 2.5 distinguishes managerial integrity from managerial expediency, consistency, and congruence in terms of the scope of judgment exercised (the number of ethics theory quadrants exercised) in decision making. The avoidance of the latter three approaches to ethical decision making establishes the opportunity to build management judgment integrity.

Managerial expediency is an amoral type of decision-making style that ignores, represses, or denies the ethical point of view. Too often, managers are forced by deadlines and other pressures to look at a problem and simply ask, "How can I resolve this in the quickest way?" Questions about long-term

Ethical Decision-Making Style	Ethics Quadrants Exercised in Decision Making

A. Expediency
  1. Opportunist
  2. Chameleon
  3. Hypocrite
	0

B. Consistency	1
C. Congruence	2-3
D. Integrity	4

Figure 2.5. The Comparative Scope of Management Judgment Integrity in Ethical Decision Making

consequences, about the direct and indirect effects of the decision on others, and about whether the decision "squares" with their own sense of fairness and propriety are too often set aside. Impulsive decision making, without regard for any moral parameters, may appear decisive, but when managers assume the ethical point of view, they broaden their perspective beyond the immediacy of expedient resolution to principled resolution (Driscoll, Hoffman, & Petry, 1995).

Three examples of moral expediency in Figure 2.5 are the opportunist, the chameleon, and the hypocrite. The *opportunist* is motivated by the manipulative disregard of others and exploitation of situations for self-advancement at the expense of others. The blind ambitions of "fast trackers" in the private and public arenas are particularly susceptible to this amoral orientation (Dean, 1976). The *chameleon* is without strong personal convictions and is motivated by the excessive need for approval/popularity and/or the avoidance of disapproval/unpopularity to abdicate moral autonomy and conveniently adapt to any context. Management integrity, however, demands the development of a self-governing conscience, built around core moral principles (not merely the changing reflection of different social expectations), whose boundaries are circumscribed by stalwart loyalty and fidelity to the ethical point of view (M. W. Martin, 1995). Finally, the *hypocrite* feigns the moral point of view to gain the facade of a good reputation without the substance of a virtuous character. The self-fragmentation and self-deception that is consonant with the hypocrite's proclivity to say one thing and do another is antithetical to the straightforward sincerity and "follow through" of managerial integrity (Parks, 1992).

Managerial ethical consistency, in contrast, is the adoption of a narrow moral point of view in ethical decision making that provides a one-dimensional, single-quadrant resolution to all management problems. This perspective is captured succinctly in the Emersonian dictum that consistency is the hobgoblin of small minds. For example, knee-jerk cost-benefit analysis and resolutions of complex moral issues, without regard for the legitimacy of other moral perspectives, expose the lack of skill in handling moral complexity required of managerial integrity and often lead to perceptions of rigidity and biased judgment that provoke backlash. Managerial integrity resists the temptation to reach for and stubbornly insist on "quick fixes" and simpleminded answers to complex moral quandaries (Kilmann, 1984).

Managerial ethical congruence is the adoption of an intermediate moral point of view in ethical decision making that provides a multidimensional (two or three quadrants) but inadequate resolution to all management problems. For example, many traditional, moral managers hold employees accountable for personal ethics in terms of obtaining results, fulfilling duties, and developing character. However, by neglecting to institutionalize organizational ethics systems in the workplace to empower employees, they abdicate their responsibility to provide a supportive context for employee integrity. Where the ethical course of action is clear, employees must be certain that they will be organizationally supported if they choose to do what they know to be right. Where the ethical course of action is unclear, there must be clarification/training processes within the organization to help the individual employee arrive at an appropriate ethical decision. In all cases, when the employee takes the ethical point of view, he or she expects and should have the support of an organizational ethics system. Its absence is an indication of a lack of management integrity (Hoffman, 1995; McFall, 1987; Petrick, Scherer, & Claunch, 1991).

Finally, *management judgment integrity* requires the balanced use of all four ethics theories in the analysis and resolution of moral issues. There are no short-cuts to management judgment integrity. This means that managers who make one-sided, snap decisions may be perceived as decisive but lack judgment integrity. Inevitably, the inadequacy of expedient, consistent, and/or congruent decision making to deal effectively with moral complexity will redound to the original manager's lack of good judgment. In fact, patterns of expedient, consistent, and/or congruent decision making will erode management judgment integrity (Robinson, Kraatz, & Rousseau, 1994). Yet, why do these integrity-eroding patterns persist among managers?

One explanation for the erosion of management integrity has been the prevalence of popular rationalizations of five key, interrelated ideological movements in the 20th century: relativism, pragmatism, positivism, behaviorism, and psychologism (Driscoll et al., 1995). *Relativism* is the denial of ethical absolutes and the abandonment of rational justification of beliefs because all opinions are regarded as equally valid. *Pragmatism* is the belief that something is right if it works, and its popular converse (what works is right) has led to the modern fascination with technology, bereft of a sense of responsibility for its adverse impacts. *Positivism* is the belief that only scientific knowledge, which is observable, public, and repeatable, can be regarded as embodying truth. Because the experience of personal ethical integrity and the imagined needs of future generations are not strictly scientific, they are accorded no legitimate, cognitive status. *Behaviorism* is the explanation of human behavior as totally determined and predictable, thereby denying the freedom and rationality necessary to hold people accountable for unethical conduct. Finally, *psychologism,* in its popular sense, is a belief that accords subjective, introspective experience the highest cognitive status, whether it be Freudian individual unconscious sexual urges or Jungian collective unconscious archetypes. This movement denies the guiding roles of reason, responsibility, freedom, and dignity in human endeavors, regarding morality as arbitrarily, externally imposed, rather than arising from the common moral sense of individual and collective responsibility (Wilson, 1993).

The thread unifying these five ideologies is the denial of the power of reason, the trivialization of freedom and character, the curtailment of a sense of responsibility, and the neglect of conduct that would sustain future generations. It is easy to see why management integrity has been relegated to the realm of ephemeral rationalization—certainly second-class status.

Consider how the five ideological movements have shaped popular discourse. How often do we hear discussions about ethical issues—whether on talk shows or around kitchen tables—degenerate suddenly into the modern-day mantra "Oh, well, it's all just a matter of opinion anyway" (relativism)? We're told "What is important is not what is right or wrong, because no one can rationally justify anything; what is important is what we personally feel" (relativism, positivism, and psychologism).

As the verbal exchange continues, it is often assumed that behavior, especially misbehavior, "is not our fault, but rather the product of our environment and our genes" (behaviorism). Inevitably, the session's conclusion is a round of practical advice about what will work to fix the problem, with scant attention paid to whether the solution is right, but only to whether it will work. The idea is to "just do it" (pragmatism).

In addition to devaluing key components of management integrity (e.g., reason, freedom, character, responsibility, conduct, dignity, sustainability), this worldview also has the effect of making the individual the be-all and the end-all. If ethics is only opinion and if all that matters is feeling good and finding a solution that works for you, then you, your opinions, and your feelings become all-important. Feelings and ego issues become the substitute for serious ethical reflection and discussion.

Something about this sterile and self-centered picture, however, provokes resistance from mature human beings. Today, more and more people are searching for a different ideology, one that will preserve our human dignity, reconnect us as a work and human community, and provide our lives with more meaningful value. There is a growing sense of urgency and a recognition that the five ideologies that have dominated our century have left us morally adrift. Management integrity, far from being simply the latest managerial fad, is arising out of the moral crisis created by our century's inadequate philosophies (Baily et al., 1993; Sandel, 1996). Management integrity is an attempt, at least in part, to revive the importance and legitimacy of making moral claims in the world of practical affairs (Driscoll et al., 1995).

SUMMARY

In summary, this chapter delineates the nature and value of management ethics by treating the major types of key ethics theories that are implicitly adopted by different managers. Next, it defines management integrity and distinguishes it from expediency, consistency, and congruence. Managers are now aware of three insights: (a) that their management style implicitly aligns them with an ethics theory, (b) that extreme overdevelopment and underdevelopment of their managerial and ethics competencies adversely affect performance and integrity, and (c) that inadequate analysis and resolution in their ethical decision making risks the erosion of management integrity. The next chapter focuses on the dimensions of management integrity and their impact on moral progress.

▧ DISCUSSION/EXPERIENTIAL EXERCISES

Discussion Questions

1. Discuss the four key ethics theories and the need for managerial competency in handling moral complexity at work.
2. Discuss the major types of the four key ethics theories.
3. Discuss how all major types of ethics theories would explain and resolve the unequal distribution of wealth in the United States and globally.
4. Discuss the changes and constants in U.S. managerial values.
5. Discuss the nature of management ethical integrity and its differences from expediency, consistency, and congruence in performance appraisal decisions at work.

Experiential Exercises

6. Obtain *Dilbert* or *Dilbert*-like cartoons that humorously depict the lack of management ethics and integrity and discuss them in group settings.
7. From your own work/life/school experiences, provide two examples of how moral issues have been faced with and without integrity. What lessons regarding moral responsibility for personal integrity have you learned?
8. From your own work/life/school experiences, apply all the major types of ethics theories to the following topics: "freeloading," cheating, cynicism, power, courage, success, physical attractiveness, child labor, and population control.
9. Engage in a role-play exercise in which individuals adopt the roles of the expedient manager, the consistent manager, the congruent manager, and the manager with integrity by using and responding to the five ideologies that erode management integrity in making a hiring, firing, and/or promotion decision at work.
10. Using the concepts from this chapter, examine with the entire class the management integrity of U.S. tobacco industry managers. (See the "Ethical Controlling Formulation" section of Chapter 7 on p. 289 for a brief treatment of the U.S. tobacco industry case.)
11. Using the concept from this chapter, examine in small groups the following minicases: 6C Nestle Infant Formula and 7B Barings Bank.

3

Dimensions of Management Integrity

The focus of Chapter 3 is on three areas: (a) management judgment integrity, (b) management process integrity, and (c) management developmental integrity. These areas constitute the key dimensions of management integrity, that, when simultaneously cultivated, produce moral progress individually and collectively.

⬛ MANAGEMENT JUDGMENT INTEGRITY

Management judgment integrity is defined as *the balanced use of all four ethics theories and their cognate resources in the analysis and resolution of moral issues.* The last chapter emphasized the balanced use of all four ethics theories to achieve part of judgment integrity. Now, the emphasis shifts to include three cognate resources that support ethical conduct domestically and globally: management, legal, and communication theories. The extent of managerial, legal, and communication resources available provides varying levels of support for management judgment integrity.

The last chapter also depicted the correlation between ethics theories and management theories in Figure 2.2. Managers who regularly adhere to certain management theories and styles implicitly endorse particular ethics theories. Conversely, managers who adhere to certain ethics theories find that correlative management theories and styles reinforce (serve as resources for) their moral analyses and resolutions. For example, managers who regard character as an important factor in personal and employee development are not likely to find supportive managerial resources in their workplace if all other managers are adamantly and exclusively rational goal oriented. In addition, managers who demonstrate judgment integrity do so by exhibiting a versatile repertoire of management resources (competencies) from all four quadrants to support judgment integrity initiatives.

Now it is time to treat the two other cognate resources of judgment integrity: legal theories and communication theories.

Legal Theories and Ethics Theories

Increasingly, global and domestic social and economic problems are being resolved by laws, regulations, and public policy (Bork, 1990; Metzger et al., 1995). The United States has become a litigious society and has been referred to as a "nation under lawyers" (Glendon, 1994). Managers need to stay abreast of legal and regulatory changes that affect their organizations, but they can also adopt more proactive responses to influence public policy and the legal environment of business (Arpoes & Braithwaite, 1992; Buchholz, Evans, & Wagley, 1994; McAdams, Freeman, & Pincus, 1995). Laws aid business managers by enforcing contracts, protecting property rights, preventing fraud and conflicts of interest, and establishing boundaries for acceptable business practice, e.g., the federal sentencing guidelines which either aggravate or mitigate base financial penalties for offenses against federal law (Fiorelli & Rooney, 1996). In this century in the United States, however, business has come to be viewed as an important socioeconomic institution whose activities must sometimes be regulated in the public interest by various levels of government (Blackburn, Klayman, & Malin, 1994; Wood, 1994). As a result, today's managers need to combine their market system proficiency (emphasizing self-interest, economic roles, consumer sovereignty, and profits as reward) with public-policy proficiency (emphasizing public interest, political roles, citizen sovereignty, and power as reward) (Buchholz, 1994). This dynamic interrelationship of law and ethics is such that what is legally permissible today but ethically questionable may well become legally proscribed tomorrow (Paine, 1994a). Responsible managerial performance, therefore, requires that managers be aware of their legal theories and be able to use them as resources.

Different legal or jurisprudential theories emphasize different moral traditions, which, in turn, as the authors have shown in Chapter 2, are implicitly linked with different managerial responsibilities. Business law case discussions reflect different jurisprudential emphases, which, in turn, implicitly endorse different ethics theories. The way managers incorporate legal theories into their decision-making patterns either enhances or detracts from management judgment integrity (Paine, 1994b). The capacity of managers to balance legal traditions, rather than to espouse one tradition narrowly, is crucial in fostering ethics dialogue about sensitive issues, lest value conflicts deteriorate into adversarial and litigious debates. Hostile verbal crossfire may produce provocative media entertainment or courtroom theatrics, but it does not strengthen work communities, nor does it promote a shared search for the optimal resolution of moral issues.

Figure 3.1 depicts the relationship between legal theories and ethics theories. Just as the manager with ethical integrity must be able to balance and use all four ethics theories, the legally competent manager must be able to balance and use all four legal theories. Managers who rely exclusively on their natural affinity for one legal perspective develop "legal blind spots" and rush to judgment with an inadequate appreciation of law as a supportive resource for maintaining management integrity in the face of moral complexity.

Positive Law

The four major types of legal theories related to management ethics are positive law, natural law, civic responsibility, and social reform legal theories (Berman & Greiner, 1980). In the lower right quadrant of Figure 3.1 *Positive law legal theories* hold that law is the received body of authoritative commands motivated by and resulting in external control that courts are to enforce, not create; for example, according to U.S. constitutional law, Congress has the power to impose taxes on the estates of deceased individuals, even if it excessively deprives his or her offspring of the natural inheritance of real property, in order that wealth may be transferred in an orderly manner (Austin, 1885/1954; Hart, 1961; Kelsen, 1957; Shiner, 1992). The objective of positive law is to maintain external order through preserving legal precedents, *stare decisis,* and social continuity.

Two variants of positive law legal theories are the interpretations of law referred to as *utilitarian jurisprudence* and *law and economics jurisprudence.* They and other major types of key legal theories are depicted in Figure 3.2.

In the lower right quadrant of Figure 3.2 *Utilitarian jurisprudence* is a cost-benefit approach to legal interests that holds that the number of persons

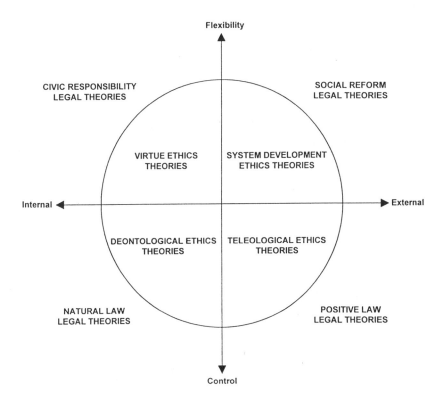

Figure 3.1. Legal Theories and Ethics Theories

who are likely to benefit from a law must be far greater than the number who must bear the cost of being harmed by it; for example, the Executive Order for Administrative Agencies No. 12296 requires that all agency decisions undergo a cost-benefit analysis before regulatory enactment (Hand, 1958; Mitnick, 1980; Posner, 1986; Schnitzer, 1983). The external control preferred by positive law legal theories has been used by managers who appeal to principles in order to oppose arbitrary and capricious regulatory impositions and to resist excess discretionary flexibility inside and outside the organization. *Law and economics jurisprudence* is a classic market economics approach to legal interests that holds that court decisions and the legal doctrines they depend on are best understood as instruments by which efficient economic outcomes are achieved; for example, excessive environmental regulations to preserve wetlands are a form of unfair "takings" of justly acquired property and should be opposed in favor of free-market incentives (Posner, 1986). It contends that good law reflects good economics as its goal. For example, the implementation of the Gramm-Rudman Act to handle U.S. deficit reduction is regarded by this approach to be both good law and good economics because it promotes fiscal accountability.

The positive law focus on external order through either utilitarian results or economic outcomes implicitly endorses teleological ethics. If managers overemphasize this legal theory, they will be regarded as callously ignoring the rights and needs of particular human communities, fair distributions of benefits and burdens, and the intrinsic value of employees. Authoritative decisions that regulate and maintain current external order are taken very seriously in this tradition.

Natural Law

In the lower left quadrant of Figure 3.2, *natural law legal theories* hold that rational dictates of conscience regarding universal common goods exist, are based on what is immutably constitutive of human nature, and provide an absolute internal basis for acceptance or rejection of any current social order; for example, any government enactments that deprive an individual or a group of natural rights, such as survival, reproduction, and property, are void— regardless of legal precedent (Aquinas, 1250/1959; Epstein, 1985; Finnis, 1980; Fuller, 1964; Shiner, 1992; Simon, 1965). The internal control preferred by natural law legal theories has been used by managers to rationally discover the likely outcome of legal enactments and to resist immoral, activist, judicial legislation that relies on the merits or outcomes of selected legal policies; for example, positive law tort reform of the civil justice system supports congressional legislation that imposes upper limits on damage tort awards, in contrast with natural law theorists, who leave damage decisions up to the conscience of the jury (Dworkin, 1978, 1985, 1986; Hart, 1961).

One key variant of natural law legal theories is the interpretation of law referred to as contemporary natural law jurisprudence. *Contemporary natural law jurisprudence* is the approach that emphasizes the standard of universal, free, practical reasonableness developed by the mature choice of ordinary persons in a single generation, rather than legal specialists or absolute standards for future generations, as the determinant of the legitimacy of laws; for example, in the Johnson Control case of 1991, the absolute right of mature women

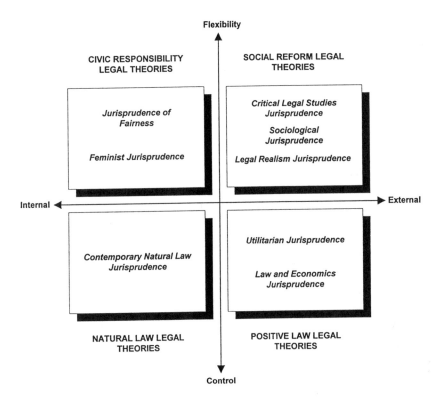

Figure 3.2. Major Types of Key Legal Theories

to freely choose to accept workplace risks for their generation was accorded more priority than the traditional natural law legal theory of absolute protection of life and health of unborn children and future generations (Beck-Dudley & Conry, 1995; Finnis, 1986). Rational discovery of the dictates of human conscience that constitute universal rights, responsibilities, and freedoms in the legal arena are taken very seriously in this tradition.

Civic Responsibility

In the upper left quadrant of Figure 3.2, the *civic responsibility legal theories* hold that law is a guide to more virtuous social relations and character formation, based on active, responsible citizenship. The increase in violent crime rates, the decrease of prison sentences, the reduction in voting rates, and the increase of children relying on Aid to Families with Dependent Children (AFDC) demonstrate the need for restoration of civic responsibility to its independent normative role in legal/public policy theories to supplement current natural law and positive law theories. The immediate U.S. post-World War II orthodoxy regarded citizenship as essentially a matter of ensuring that everyone was treated as a full and equal member of society by claiming and according people civil rights, political rights, and social rights, not out of charity, but because of legal entitlement (Brest, 1981; Dworkin, 1978, 1985, 1986; Ely, 1980; Grey, 1975, 1978, 1984; Marshall, 1965; Michelman, 1979). In the classic Supreme Court case *Goldberg v. Kelly* (1970), Justice William Brennan, writing for the majority, argued that welfare was not a gratuity or form of charity, but more like a property right to which individuals are entitled (Pierson, 1991; Reich, 1964; Rose, 1995).

This approach to citizenship has been criticized because of its emphasis on passive entitlements and its absence of any obligation to participate in public life (Andrews, 1991; Glendon, 1991, 1994; Howard, 1995; Macedo, 1990; Vogel & Moran, 1991). Conservative and liberal critics both have recommended either replacing or supplementing nonparticipatory entitlements with the active exercise of civic responsibility and virtue, including economic self-reliance, responsible political participation, and ordinary civility (Martin, 1985; Olasky, 1992; Walzer, 1992). With regard to the exercise of economic civic responsibility, conservative New Right theorists argue that citizenship inclusion requires the fulfillment of the common obligation of financial self-sufficiency (Heater, 1990; King, 1987; Shklar, 1984, 1991). Because the welfare state discourages people from becoming economically self-reliant, conservatives argue that the safety net should be cut back and that any remaining welfare benefits should have obligations tied to them—for example, "workfare" programs (Olasky, 1992). Responsible political participation and civility in the liberal tradition requires the following citizenship virtues: (a) general virtues: courage, law-abidingness, loyalty; (b) social virtues: independence and open-mindedness; (c) economic virtues: work ethic, capacity to delay self-gratification, adaptability to economic and technological change; and (d) political virtues: capacity to discern and respect the rights of others, willingness to demand only what can be paid for, ability to evaluate the performance of those in office, and willingness to engage in public discourse (Galston, 1991).

The ability to question authority and the willingness to engage in public discourse are, however, two liberal virtues, that, when carried to extreme, offend the conservative sensibilities of respect for legitimate institutions, common decency, and polite civility in public exchanges (Heater, 1990; Peck, 1993). What is needed is education for "public reasonableness," which requires that all citizens give reasons for their political claims, not just state preferences, invoke traditions, shout demands, hurl insults, or make threats. Workplace violence has increased dramatically and can be exacerbated by the lack of managerial skills in providing publicly reasonable justifications for policies and procedures and the lack of employee skills in articulating publicly reasonable criticisms of workplace practices (Kingwell, 1994; Macedo, 1990). In fact, the prevalent employee outsourcing strategy that relies heavily on temporary/part-time/virtual employees to reduce costs challenges the legal cultivation of civic responsibility and community building in the workplace because it treats temporaries as mobile, economic immigrants never entitled to the respect of full-time citizens. The civic responsibility approach holds that it is legally necessary to put civility back into civil society, as well as into the workplace, as a civil community (Peck, 1993).

Two variants of civic responsibility legal theories are the interpretations of law referred to as the jurisprudence of fairness and feminist jurisprudence. The *jurisprudence of fairness* is a commonsense approach to legal interests that holds that a worthy rule of law should not be insisting on individual rights, but rather should be promoting civic responsibility, virtuous character formation, and decent behavior; for example, the narcissistic individual who claims that he can verbally abuse others out of anger because it is his legal right of free speech to do so and that he is entitled to the mental health benefits resulting from emotional outbursts at the expense of others is a classic case of an individual who has not learned that free speech is a way of talking civilly with another, rather than a form of verbal dominance. This tradition does not take individual rights talk too seriously, but instead emphasizes the virtuous character formation that results from fulfilling personal and civic responsibilities, restraining self-indulgence, and engaging in civil discourse that builds communities.

Feminist jurisprudence is an approach to legal interests that assumes the primacy of gender and equality in law, wherein the virtue of caring, though it has priority over perceived male virtues (justice, fairness) and/or rights (free speech), may itself be a source of victimization; for example, the First Amendment's protection of pornography as a form of free speech is a protection of noncaring violence against women (Bartlett, 1993; Freeman, 1993; Larrabee, 1993; Liedtka, 1996; Tronto, 1993). Feminist jurisprudence advocates a call for a reevaluation of the traditional U.S. legal rule that a person has no duty to rescue a stranger, even though he or she has the ability to do so, because it evidences a lack of caring virtue expected in human relations and erodes commitment to the human community (Blackburn et al., 1994; Littleton, 1987).

Social Reform

In the upper right quadrant of Figure 3.2, *social reform legal theories* hold that law is both a reflection of the current sociopolitical system, which warrants criticism, and a way to systematically promote general social responsiveness and flexible judicial decision making. These theories promote external change either through negative criticism of the legal status quo or through positive extension of the system and its actors to meet the new demands of current concerns.

Three variants of social reform legal theories are the interpretations of law referred to as critical legal studies jurisprudence, sociological jurisprudence, and legal realism jurisprudence. *Critical legal studies jurisprudence* is an oppression-focused approach that criticizes judges who render decisions that preserve the existing political and economic elitist system and advocates radical, democratic egalitarianism; for example, the current U.S. legal distribution of hazardous waste sites and incinerators has been criticized as a form of legal, environmental racism because it unduly imposes risks on inner-city minorities (Kubasek, Brennan, & Browne, 1996; Noonan, 1980).

The second variant, *sociological jurisprudence*, is a sociological approach to legal interests that holds that the "living law" should be flexible enough to reflect a people's current needs, conduct, and aspirations; for example, during the 1930s, Depression mortgage moratorium laws were enacted to bar banks that held mortgages from foreclosing, because the overwhelming economic needs of the time were accorded higher priority than positive contractual obligations (Ehrlich, 1913/1936). As new domestic and global stakeholder interests have become identified and articulated, the judicial inflexibility typical of positive law reliance on precedence and convention, has become unable to address the demands of legal progress adequately. To operationalize the living law approach, legislators and judges are to implement inventories of contemporary interests to familiarize themselves with those new standards and to legislate or render decisions in conformity with those changing expectations.

The third variant, *legal realism jurisprudence*, is a change process approach to legal interests that holds that law is the product of various sociopolitical influences on the official discretion of actors in the legal/judicial system; for example, if a speed limit sign on a highway states that the speed limit is 55 mph but the police officers on patrol do not pull a driver over unless he or she drives over 65 mph, a legal realist would say the law was, in fact, 65 mph because the law is what the official legal actors say it is (Llewellyn, 1950).

World Legal Systems: Resources
for Global Management Integrity

Law is an important resource for sustaining management integrity because it provides a concrete, public way to achieve feasible moral ideals and prevents collective moral regression—for example, political and economic corruption (Senge, 1993; Sigler & Murphy, 1988). It is often referred to as the external forum; for example, the court of law can follow or precede the internal forum (the court of conscience) (Crawford & Quinn, 1991). Managers who adhere to public regulation and legal compliance as standards of conduct are comparatively more morally developed than those who are fear-ridden or advantage-driven or those who have one set of rules for inside members and another set for outside strangers (AFL-CIO Committee on the Evolution of Work, 1994; Sigler & Murphy, 1988). Managers are particularly interested in classifying legal and regulatory expectations to reduce arbitrariness and uncertainty in strategic planning. Domestic and international law, therefore, provide practical guidance on the acceptable rules of managerial activity so that a level playing field can support, rather than undermine, free-market transactions. For this reason, if for no other, prudent managers work to develop just background institutions in all global sociopolitical environments (DeGeorge, 1993). The range of legal institutions and paralegal nongovernmental organizations (NGOs) that are "drawing the line" on acceptable global business practices include the following: United Nations (UN), International Court of Justice (ICJ), International Monetary Fund (IMF), International Bank for Reconstruction and Development (IBRD), International Development Association (IDA), Court of International Trade (CIT), International Trade Commission (ITC), and Organization for Economic Cooperation and Development (OECD).

Just as transnational and national cultural factors influence the appropriacy boundaries of ethics and management theories, the same is true with respect to the emphases accorded legal theories in diverse global environments. Although many cultures distinguish between *ius* (law that is both declared and enforced) and *lex* (law that is declared but is not necessarily enforced), the world's major legal systems can be classified into six types: civil law, common law, Islamic law, socialist law, sub-Saharan African law, and Far East law (Richards, 1994). In Figure 3.3, the six major legal systems of the world are depicted.

The *civil law system,* derived in ancient Rome and currently predominant in Germany, France, Japan, and Latin America, stresses the formulation of comprehensive codes, systematic rules, and abstract principles that regulate behavior in advance. Judges who deductively apply the legal codes establish stable and predictable external order and are more likely to emphasize the positive law tradition.

The *common law system,* derived from England and currently predominant in the United States, Canada, Australia, and Nigeria, stresses the process of inductively formulating law on a case-by-case analysis in a way that relies on case precedents rather than abstract rules, holds procedural issues on a par with substantive issues, and allows for incremental change in response to external events. Judges, lawyers, and juries who resolve cases differently on the basis of the unique merits of each case are, in fact, establishing the range of external legal flexibility with regard to common practices and are more likely to emphasize the social reform legal theories.

Islamic law, derived from the Koran and currently predominant in Iran, Saudi Arabia, Libya, and the Muslim countries, stresses absolute compliance with unchanging moral law as divinely imparted to the prophet Mohammed and interpreted by Islamic scholars. Because Islamic law is an outgrowth of neither rationally derived principles nor inductively emergent practical needs, but rather emanates from fundamental religious belief and obligations, its adherents are most likely to emphasize natural law legal theories.

Socialist law, derived from Marxist ideology and currently predominant in Vietnam, North Korea, and Cuba, stresses adherence to communist collectivist standards that are based on state ownership and control of the means of production and justified in terms of a need-based distribution system that will lead to a classless society. Political bureaucrats who apply socialist law regard themselves as agents of a future classless society that will naturally evolve and who are merely enacting a form of egalitarian distribution, historically advocated through Marxist socioeconomic analysis, and are more likely to emphasize the natural law legal tradition.

Sub-Saharan African law, derived from traditional tribal norms and currently predominant in Uganda, Zaire, Ethiopia, and other sub-Saharan countries, stresses law as a means to conserve family loyalties and tribal groupings,

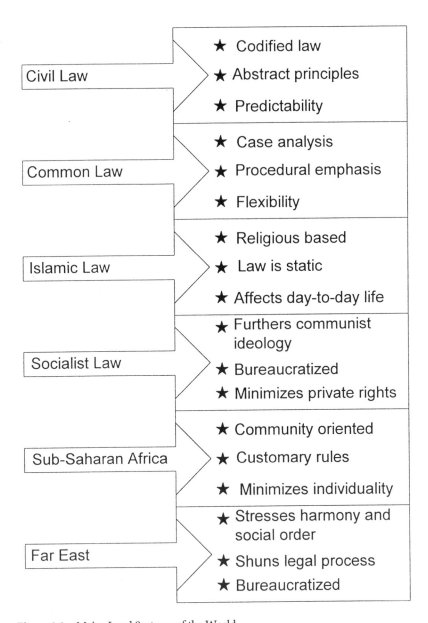

Figure 3.3. Major Legal Systems of the World

SOURCE: Richards, E. *Law for Global Business,* Irwin, 1994, p. 40. Reprinted with permission of the publisher.

as well as a means to maintain public order. Most legal disputes in the system are resolved by judges/arbitrators who use unwritten customary rules to achieve external order in tribal communities and are more likely to emphasize the unwritten positive law tradition.

Finally, *Far East law,* derived from ancient Confucian China and currently predominant in China, Singapore, South Korea, and selected Pacific Rim countries, stresses the priority of collective harmony over individual rights, social character development over economic self-interest, and the avoidance of legal processes that might erode the sense of community harmony. Far Eastern legal bureaucrats regard themselves as responsible for preserving the social fabric of the national character and are more likely to emphasize the civil responsibility legal tradition.

Although these six world legal systems emphasize different jurisprudential theories, they still must address all four legal quadrants to some extent in order to sustain management integrity.

The richness of different legal systems that can support just background institutions provides a framework within which managers can sustain integrity and prevent corruption. In those contexts where balanced legal enforcement is weak, the strain on management integrity may be overwhelming; in those contexts where balanced legal enforcement is strong, public expectation of moral conduct on the part of managers is fortified and realistic. In other words, legal theories, both domestic and global, are crucial resources for reinforcing the legal support of management integrity.

Another cognate resource for professional management integrity is awareness of communication theories and how they affect managerial practice and ethics.

Communication Theories and Ethics Theories

If managers are to discharge their role responsibilities in a manner that sustains management judgment integrity, they also need to be aware of their communication theories and the communication styles that flow from them (Ivy & Backhind, 1994). Different communication theories emphasize different managerial role responsibilities, which, in turn, as the authors showed in Chapter 2, are implicitly linked with different ethics theories. *The way managers communicate either enhances or detracts from management judgment integrity.* In other words, managers who are aware of their communication theories and styles can use them to build individual and collective integrity.

Communication styles vary by gender, age, class, ethnicity, and locale and can make or break constructive relations with others at work (Glass, 1992; Hecht, Collier, & Ribeau, 1993; Tannen, 1993). Sometimes a lack of understanding of these different communication styles leads managers to impute motives to others and indict them for being unethical—that is, attributing communication difficulties to employee abilities ("they" can't follow instructions); to flawed employee character ("they" are rude, disrespectful, and inconsiderate); to employee attitudes ("they" always ignore formal policies and procedures); and/or to employee intentions ("they" are being intentionally uncooperative to aggravate me). The work environment is a special communication world because as individuals communicate to get jobs done, they are also being evaluated. How managers get employees to do what is necessary and how managers/employees accept or avoid responsibility for mistakes, display or challenge authority, reveal or conceal what they don't know—all affect how managers are regarded and rewarded at work (Pepper, 1995; Rahim, 1986; Tannen, 1994c). Although no one style of communication is uniformly superior in all work contexts, managers need to be aware of and learn from other communication styles. They need to broaden their communications repertoire to adapt flexibly to workplace diversity in order to minimize unnecessary conflicts and managerial stress and to maximize cooperative productivity at work (Donahue & Kolt, 1992; Johannsen, 1990; Yarbrough & Wilmot, 1994).

In today's workplace, managers also must be able to recognize and flexibly adapt to different communication styles in order to successfully inform, persuade, entertain, and stimulate employees with diverse communication styles (Lakoff, 1990; Shockley-Zalabak, 1994; Tannen, 1994b). Destructive conflicts in the workplace are evidenced by the escalation of hate speech, the spiraling avoidance behavior away from cooperative conflict resolution, excessive rigidity in and retaliation against patterns of dominance and subordination that suppress differences, and demeaning/degrading verbal and nonverbal communication that intensifies hostilities that need to be understood and transformed into constructive conflict and community-building dialogue by managers (Hocker & Wilmot, 1995; Samovar & Porter, 1994).

To improve management judgment integrity, awareness of the major management communication theories, corresponding communication styles, their relative degrees of assertiveness and responsiveness, and their communication goals need to be increased (Bolton & Bolton, 1984; Merrill & Reid, 1981; Quinn, Hildebrandt, Rogers, & Thompson, 1991). Figure 3.4 depicts the conceptual relations among the key factors in communication theories.

Theories	Styles	Assertiveness	Responsiveness	Goals
Instructional Communication	Driver	High	Low	Direct Action
Informational Communication	Analytic	Low	Low	Provide Facts
Relational Communication	Amiable	Low	High	Build Trust
Transformational Communication	Expressive	High	High	Stimulate Change

Figure 3.4. Communication Theories, Styles, Assertiveness, Responsiveness, and Goals

Instructional Communication

Instructional communication is a management communication theory that explains communication patterns that direct action by means of a driver communication style high in assertiveness and low in responsiveness. Managers who effectively direct action implicitly endorse this theory by communication patterns that can be described in the following manner: decisive, practical, realistic, conclusive, engaging, absorbing, and action-oriented. This theory is paralleled by a driver communication style high in assertiveness and low in responsiveness. *Assertiveness* is the degree to which individuals know and act on perceived personal needs and their external verbal and nonverbal behavior patterns that influence others by telling or asking. *Responsiveness* is the degree to which individuals know and respond to perceived needs of others and their verbal and nonverbal behavior patterns that react toward others by controlling (according priority to achievement) or displaying emotion (according priority to acceptance). Drivers, therefore, use instructional communication theory and prefer to assertively direct action in a manner that may not be as responsive as other managers to the needs of others.

For example, a paternalistic CEO who is results-oriented and ambitious may predictably resort to a driver communication style to direct action when confronted with multiple deadlines in order to achieve timely results. Managers who routinely implement instructional communication in all contexts justify their exclusive reliance on this approach by appeals to teleological ethics (it gets results). They expect and morally value *effective communication;* anything less can be interpreted not only as inept communication but also as a moral failure to achieve goals. Carried to an extreme, however, the driver communication style may lead to a domineering and unfeeling workplace that offends individuals and provokes resistance; for example, Dabney Coleman's role in the movie *Nine to Five* is that of a hardworking male chauvinist who exploits and verbally abuses female employees for personal gain and who provokes a retaliatory workplace mutiny by the female employees that results in his ouster.

Informational Communication

Informational communication is a management communication theory that explains communication patterns that provide facts by means of an analytic communication style low in assertiveness and responsiveness. Managers who precisely provide facts implicitly endorse this theory by communication patterns that can be described in the following manner: rigorous, clear, logical, organized, controlled, technically correct, and efficient. This theory is paralleled by an analytic communication style low in both assertiveness and responsiveness. Analytics, therefore, use informational communication theory and prefer to convey accurately facts in a low-key manner that neither asserts their needs nor responds to the needs of others.

For example, a computer programmer who is designing a new program may predictably resort to an analytic communication style to convey precise information to the computer and expect others to be similarly exacting in their communication to arrive at factual knowledge. Managers who routinely implement informational communication in all contexts justify their exclusive reliance on this approach by appeals to deontological ethics—that is, telling the truth and doing the right thing at all times. They expect and morally value *precise communication;* anything less can be interpreted not only as inept communication but also as a moral failure to convey the truth. Carried to an extreme, however, the analytic communication style may lead to a regidity that neglects promising opportunities and stifles nonroutine progress; for example, Lily Tomlin's role in the movie *Nine to Five* is that of an industrious, no-nonsense office manager whose operational and technical expertise ensure that routine procedures continue in an uninterrupted, impersonal manner when Dabney Coleman, the titular head of the department, is not in the office.

Relational Communication

Relational communication is a management communication theory that explains communication patterns that build trust by means of an amiable communication style low in assertiveness and high in responsiveness. Managers who considerately build trust implicitly endorse this theory by communication patterns that can be described in the following manner: perceptive, sensitive, friendly, discerning, compassionate, conventional, and receptive. This theory is paralleled by an amiable communication style low in assertiveness and high in responsiveness. Amiables, therefore, use relational communication theory and prefer to build trust considerately and responsively in a manner that may not be as assertive as that of other managers in meeting their own needs.

For example, a sensitive, compassionate, nursing manager who permits wide scheduling latitude in response to employee preferences may predictably resort to an amiable communication style to build trust and expect others to be similarly considerate in their communication to sustain trust (Kingwell, 1994). Managers who routinely implement relational communication in all contexts justify their exclusive reliance on this approach by appeals to virtue ethics; that is, the cultivation of trust and other virtues builds character and workplace community. They expect and morally value *considerate communication;* anything less can be interpreted not only as inept communication but also as a moral failure to build trust. Carried to an extreme, however, the amiable communication style may lead to the avoidance of constructive conflict, the abdication of authority, the reduction of productivity, and the absorption of work stress without asserting realistic limits that inevitably leads to workplace disillusionment, resentment, and burnout; for example, Jane Fonda's role in the movie *Nine to Five* is that of a new employee who begins crying after Dabney Coleman, the hard-driving manager, publicly criticizes her operational incompetence regarding duplicating office documents, and she later forms a coalition of fellow abused workers to sabotage the manager's authority.

Transformational Communication

Transformational communication is a management communication theory that explains communication patterns that stimulate change by means of an expressive communication style that is highly assertive and highly responsive. Managers who fervidly stimulate change implicitly endorse this theory by communication patterns that can be described in the following manner: emphatic, powerful, insightful, innovative, fresh, visionary, and expansive. This theory is paralleled by an expressive communication style that is highly assertive and highly responsive. Expressives, therefore, use transformational communication theory and prefer to stimulate change fervidly in a highly assertive and responsive manner.

For example, an energetic, outgoing sales manager who has a flair for stimulating change may predictably resort to an expressive style to motivate her sales representatives to exceed their monthly quotas and expect others to communicate likewise. Managers who routinely use transformational communication in all contexts justify their exclusive reliance on this approach by appeals to system development ethics—that is, the improvement of system innovation and creative adaptability in human and natural environments. They expect and morally value *stimulating communication;* anything less can be interpreted not only as inept communication but also as a moral failure to promote change. Carried to an extreme, however, the expressive communication style may lead to undisciplined impulsiveness, wasted emotional energy, disrupted operational continuity, and overbearing affect in the advocacy of external flexibility. For example, Dolly Parton's role in the movie *Nine to Five* is that of an outgoing, competent, and promotable administrative assistant whose workplace development talents are ignored by Dabney Coleman, the sexually harassing manager, and she sabotages him by imaginatively redesigning a new, supportive work environment.

World Communication Styles:
Resources for Global Management Integrity

Just as transnational and national cultural factors influence the appropriacy boundaries of management, ethics, and legal theories, the same is true with respect to the emphases accorded communication theories in diverse global environments. Communication is influenced by high-, intermediate-, and low-context national and transnational cultures (Deresky, 1997; Leaptrott, 1996; Mead, 1994). In *high-context cultures,* the external environment, covert social cues, subtle influences, and nonverbal symbolic behavior are crucial in creating and interpreting communications; for example, in the Japanese language, much is left unspoken, but to a high-context Japanese, all is understood. In *low-context cultures,* the external environment needs to be supplemented with overt social cues, clear directions, explicit clarifications (preferably written), and unambiguous behavior to accurately convey and properly interpret communications. For example, in northern Germany, there are more than seven times as many lawyers as in Japan in order to resolve communication disputes by means of a precisely structured legal system with explicit distinctions and categories.

With respect to transnational communication, collectivist cultures are essentially high context, with highly symbolic language, tacit implied meanings, instructions that are best shown as well as verbalized, and inferences drawn from "reading the situation." For example, much of the Pacific Rim region has adopted communication practices that indicate that the self, referred to in the personal pronoun *I*, is merely an aggregate reflection of group relationships, not a distinct, separate reality (Leaptrott, 1996). Tribal cultures are essentially intermediate context, with verbal language used in a nonspecific sense, accompanied with body language, reliance on direct personal experience or informal networks for interpretation, and oral inflection added for emotional content. For example, for most of the Arab world, words are powerful expressions of intention (unlike the tacit collectivist cultures), but not necessarily precise indicators of action (as in pluralist cultures) because emotional threats are often sufficient to preclude overt action. Finally, pluralist cultures are essentially low context, with precise verbal language demanded, detailed questions and specific instructions encouraged, and unambiguous linkage between oral intention and actual behavior expected. For example, for most of the Scandinavian region, communication is direct, straightforward, and egalitarian, but because of the region's perspective, its members are often inept at recognizing paralanguage when used by members of collectivist or tribal cultures.

Nevertheless, although national and transnational cultural values alter the appropriacy boundaries of the four key communication theories, they do not preclude the necessity for applying all four major communication theories to arrive at competent work communication. These extraorganizational factors, however, are important contingencies in the fruitful balancing of the four key communication theories in diverse international contexts. In fact, an important domain of current ethics dialogue, discussion, and debate involves determining the acceptable global boundaries of ethical communication patterns (Harkness, Edwards, & Super, 1981; Stewart & Donleavy, 1995). The relationship between communication theories and ethics theories is graphically depicted in Figure 3.5.

In the lower right quadrant of Figure 3.5, managerial drivers assume the presence of the instructional communication theory at work and implicitly endorse teleological ethics. If they overuse this style, however, they will be regarded as overbearing, domineering, and disrespectful communicators. In

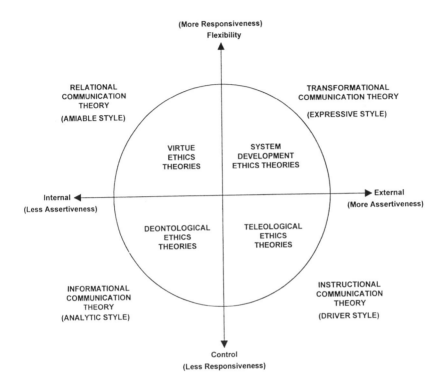

Figure 3.5.   Communication Theories and Ethics Theories

the lower left quadrant, managerial analytics assume the priority of the informational communication theory at work and implicitly endorse deontological ethics. If they overuse this style, however, they will be viewed as nitpicking, unrealistic, rigid, and exacting communicators. In the upper left quadrant, managerial amiables assume the preeminence of the relational communication theory at work and implicitly endorse virtue ethics. If they overuse this style, however, they will be regarded as hypersensitive, overreactive, cowering, and overly solicitous communicators. In the upper right quadrant, managerial expressives assume the priority of the transformational communication theory at work and implicitly endorse system development ethics. If they overuse this style, however, they will be viewed as loud, boisterous, overwhelming, and intrusive communicators.

The way managers self-consciously develop and expand their communication styles is correlated with their ethical values. It is not enough for managers to know *why* and *what* to do but also *how* to communicate effectively and respectfully about workplace goals, processes, human relations, and system innovations in a way that builds high performance commitment. Communication style may be a supportive resource or counterproductive barrier to management judgment integrity. How a manager communicates is as ethically important as what and why a manager communicates. For example, managers who want teamwork but are extremely task-oriented, subconsciously use a highly assertive, less responsive, directive communication style to get things done. The way they communicate, however, provokes employee resistance because of perceived disrespect, which precludes the very teamwork the managers originally wanted.

Just as the manager with judgment integrity must be able to identify and use all, management, and legal ethics theories in an appropriate, balanced manner, s/he must be able to identify and use all communication theories as well. Managers who rely exclusively on their preferred unilinear style of communicating develop "communication blind spots," exacerbate conflicts, minimize cooperation in the workplace, and ultimately undermine management judgment integrity.

In short, management judgment integrity is put at risk by unbalanced use of ethics theories, unbalanced use of cognate theories, and/or inadequate cognate resources to support ethical judgments. Management judgment integrity entails the balanced use of all ethics theories and the balanced use of the three cognate theoretical resources (management, legal, and communication theories) to adequately support responsible analysis and resolution of moral issues.

▨ MANAGEMENT PROCESS INTEGRITY

The second dimension of management integrity is process integrity. *Management process integrity is the repeated individual alignment of ethical awareness, judgment, intention, and conduct at all levels of managerial practice.* These four psychological processes (awareness, judgment, intention, and conduct) each consist of subcomponent steps that can be identified and improved.

Collectively, their stage alignment can be strengthened so that building personal management integrity is a continuous improvement process. In other words, building moral integrity requires managing processes and people ethically so that the steps of each stage are adequately addressed (Paine, 1996; Schminke, 1997).

Ethical Awareness

Ethical awareness is the capacity to perceive and be sensitive to relevant moral issues that deserve consideration in making choices that will have significant impact on others. The stage of ethical awareness, therefore, is composed of two steps: *ethics perception* and *ethics sensitivity*. The awareness of an ethical situation is, in part, determined by its definition as formed by the perceptions and sensitivities possessed by people. An *ethical situation* is a situation in which ethical dimensions (moral norms, standards, and/or principles) are relevant and deserve consideration in making some choices that will have significant impact on others—for example, an employer's routine neglect of worker safety standards that results in employee deaths and government sanctions/fines. Individuals differ in their degree of ethical awareness; some have "ethical blind spots" that lead them to act callously and ignore the moral point of view because they have been socialized to do so, whereas others are so paralyzed by the fear of offending others that their morally scrupulous perspective precludes normal human interaction.

Ethics perception is the capacity to "see," recognize, or discover the ethical dimensions or features of a situation. Perception involves three elements: (a) attention, (b) cognitive organization, and (c) interpretation in the information-processing cycle. The first element, *attention,* is the actively focused selection of what will be noticed and processed and what will be ignored. Ethics attention is influenced by external environmental factors (moral issue intensity, moral contrasts, encounter frequency, situational novelty) and individual internal factors (moral expectations, cognitive moral development, moral needs and interests, and psychological locus of control). Just as individuals attend only to certain ethics issues, organizations pay attention only to those moral issues that they "see" through the eyes of selected stakeholders (Ball, Trevino, & Sims, 1994; Earley, 1993; Lord, 1985). Managers who experience "moral attention deficit disorder" exhibit the following characteristics: inattention to ethical situations (e.g., they do not observe, listen to, or concentrate on ethical conflicts and are easily distracted by the flow of business activity); impulsive urge to be decisive (e.g., they act without prior reflection and are prone to rationalize after acting, rather than reason to a conclusion before acting); and hyperactive need to perform (e.g., rather than dwell in the stillness of ethical awareness or listen to their moral feelings, they rush about with restless energy and feel pressure to keep busy at work). Sustained exposure to and systematic analysis of a broad range of moral issues, combined with intensive personal feedback, develops individual and organizational capacities to recognize and pay attention to the moral dimensions of most situations.

Cognitive organization is the second element in the information-processing cycle in which many discrete bits of perceptual information are arranged into unifying configurations or schema. Schema that simplify moral understanding for individual or organizational decision-making efficiency may or may not adequately and accurately represent moral complexity—for example, Dennis Gioia's experience during the Ford Pinto crisis as a Field Vehicle Recall Coordinator who refused to recall defective Pintos because he had already internalized a cognitive and affective pattern or script for acting automatically on the company's behalf, without reviewing every case of vehicular safety in detail (Gioia, 1992). Managers who organize information by handling ethical situations as if they were only following scripts or resorting to stereotypical characterizations are likely to exclude important moral dimensions from consideration because complex ethics dilemmas do not lend themselves to "automatic pilot" decisions.

Interpretation is the third element of the information-processing cycle in which meaning is attached to the relation among abstract concepts and in which the perceiver goes beyond the descriptive identification to uncover the reasons behind conduct (Wagner & Hollenbeck, 1995). Too often, managers make irresponsible, snap decisions about an identified moral issue and misinterpret the ethical situation because of a lack of training in interpreting moral facts. To interpret information correctly and arrive at an adequate representation of a moral case, it is necessary to address certain topics and avoid certain biases. Because moral facts are not perceived as isolated bits of information, but occur in relations, moral interpretations are ways in which moral facts are constructed so that consensus, consistency, completeness, relevance, and sound common sense are preserved. Employees expect managers to routinely interpret ethical situations responsibly (Brown, 1990). To do this, managers make interpretive assumptions that may or may not be correct about the following topics: cause-and-effect relations (e.g., "Because the computer malfunctioned after you ended your shift, it happened because of your neglect");

part and whole relations (e.g., "Because your racial/ethnic group as a whole has a reputation for poor work habits, you must have poor work habits as well"); generalization and specific relations (e.g., "Because I 'went out on a limb' to support a younger colleague, only to have him take away my job, I will never mentor anyone else in the future"); abstract and concrete relations (e.g., "Because several employees in my office have complained to me about headaches at work, I will continue to interpret these as unrelated, concrete instances requiring concrete remedies, such as taking two aspirins, rather than as indications of a more generic, abstract condition, such as an occupational health problem related to sick-building syndrome"); and comparison and contrast relations (e.g., "Because training today's high tech employees is just like training dogs with positive and negative conditioning, only behavioral approaches to training will be used").

Not only must the above topics be addressed, but the following interpretation biases must also be avoided: factual overconfidence bias (e.g., being overconfident can make managers fail to search for additional corroborating evidence or for documented support of alleged facts already interpreted); confirmation trap bias (e.g., managers who regard their own performance as above reproach seek and accept only feedback that confirms their self-assessment); and story pull bias (e.g., by either abbreviating or extending factual interpretations, managers can arbitrarily impose a convenient narrative slant to an ethical situation that suits their own needs but distorts the actual situation).

Training and practice in ethical interpretation can develop ethical awareness by equipping managers with the skills to interpret ethical situations correctly, adequately, and actively, rather than passively accept the misinterpretations of others or avoid moral conflict completely out of a "felt" sense of incompetence.

After addressing ethics perception as the first step in ethical awareness, it is now time to focus on the second step in ethical awareness—ethics sensitivity. *Ethics sensitivity* is the capacity to value the relative importance of the ethical dimensions or features of a situation. Some managers may be morally perceptive but morally insensitive; that is, they "see" the ethics issue but assign little importance to it. Typically, management education is technically focused and managers are professionally socialized to prevent value conflicts from "getting in the way of business," rather than to spend time sensitively resolving ethics issues as they arise.

To be morally sensitive is to appreciate the moral situation with insight. Being morally sensitive does not necessarily mean that we agree with or even like a moral concern or position; for example, managers may not agree with or even like affirmative action policies, but it is necessary for them to be sensitive to the ethical concerns that gave rise to these policies. Being morally sensitive, however, does entail the capacity to appropriately demonstrate four key elements of sensitivity: the natural moral feelings of empathy, sympathy, moderation, and indignation. *Empathy* is the habitual ability and willingness to sense a situation from someone else's point of view. It is a cultivated sense of reciprocity and tolerance in which one switches roles hypothetically with others and feels imaginatively as they feel. Managers who are self-centered have difficulty empathizing with people who have diverse moral concerns (Cederblom & Dougherty, 1990; Hoffman, 1975, 1976).

Sympathy is the human ability and willingness to be affected by or share the feelings of others. It goes beyond the hypothetical imagination of empathy to the compassionate concern for innocent victims. It restrains people from acting cruelly. Sympathetic managers are more disposed to help people in genuine need and to take their feelings into account than hard-hearted ones. Managers who lack sympathy may engage in ruthless tactics to ensure personal career advancement or organizational success; their example legitimates organizational moral apathy and disregard for dissenters. On the one hand, individuals who oppose the actions of unsympathetic managers are often demonized, ostracized, and become the objects of vindictive retaliation because unsympathetic managers cannot or will not grant that their moral opponents may be aroused by different aspects of a moral situation. On the other hand, moral "con artists" play on the sympathies of some managers to take advantage of perceived weaknesses. To counter this ploy, managers need to avoid becoming "moral doormats" and retain their natural sense of setting moderate limits on self-sacrifice (Colby & Damon, 1994; Werhane, 1991b; Wilson, 1993).

Moderation is the ability and willingness to set limits, control self-indulgence, and delay immediate gratification. Many of the problems of contemporary western society, including domestic abuse, violent crime, drug addiction, verbal aggression, and predatory sexuality, overflow into the workplace. When managers are confronted with poor work habits, greedy acquisitiveness, disrespect for authority, unrestrained hate speech, physical violence, unbounded revenge, antisocial hostilities, employee sabotage, substance abuse, addictive dependencies, and sexual harassment, all these can be viewed as results of a lack of self-control (Bennett, 1993; Giacolone & Greenberg, 1997; Wilson, 1993). These forms of incontinence are problems of immoderate dispositions. Provided that self-disciplined managers are not carried to the extreme of self-righteous asceticism, moderate managers are more likely to persevere in order to keep promises, resist temptations, and reciprocate affections than are intemperate ones. Managers who lack moderation refuse to curb self-indulgence, and when ethical issues are front and center, they do not have the disposition to restrain themselves from preferring their own immediate advantage over the rightful but more distant interests of others.

Finally, *indignation* is a moral sentiment of appropriate anger aroused by something unjust, mean, intolerable, or unworthy. When contracts are broken, promises rescinded, trust betrayed, confidences divulged, friendships cast aside, loyalty ridiculed, one's work belittled, one's love derided, one's values dismissed, and workers ruthlessly exploited, sensitive managers naturally feel moral indignation. This righteous indignation, appropriately expressed, demonstrates that moral sensitivity entails a courageous sense of outrage that may be necessary to redress an intolerable ethical situation. Indignation often provides the emotional energy to proceed in earnest to the second process stage, ethical judgment. Indignation unexpressed can lead to workplace cynicism and resentment; indignation overexpressed can lead to inappropriate adult temper tantrums at work. Managers who lack indignation are not respected; they are often regarded as cowards because they do not challenge the status quo, avoid necessary confrontation, will take all manner of abuse, and do not stand up for themselves or for any principles (Rion, 1990; Solomon, 1977; Tavris, 1982).

In short, ethical awareness is the key introductory process based on the steps of ethics perception and ethics sensitivity. As managers enhance their personal ethical awareness, their example as morally perceptive role models stimulates similar perceptiveness in the workplace. In turn, the workplace can become a place where people become more morally sensitive, rather than callously desensitized and dehumanized.

Ethical Judgment

The result of the ethical awareness process is a properly framed ethical issue/dilemma on which a judgment can be made. *Judgment* is the stage of the information-processing cycle in which recalled information is weighted and aggregated to come up with a single overall resolution. Managers and organizations that demonstrate sound judgment use accurate information, appropriately weighted and aggregated, to resolve conflicts. Therefore, *ethical judgment* is the capacity to engage in the analytic process of critical appraisal of recognized moral options to arrive at a reasonable decision/resolution/policy that provides a standard for future determinations.

Ethical judgment, therefore, is composed of two steps: *ethics analysis* and *ethics resolution*. Ethics analysis without resolution leads to the paralysis of analysis; ethics resolution without critical appraisal leads to unfounded decisions. Today's managers can ill-afford either deficiency in ethical judgment.

Ethics analysis is the rational step of moral argumentation and dialogue designed to identify, interpret, prioritize, and weigh the key resources for managing and/or resolving ethics conflicts. Ethics analysis entails appropriate moral reasoning based upon the four major ethics theories cited in Chapter 2: teleological, deontological, virtue, and system development theories. The process of moral argumentation and dialogue has been logically modeled in a narrative format and graphically illustrated by using a baseball diamond in Figure 3.6 (Brown, 1990; Toulman, 1984).

The model of moral argumentation and dialogue is rendered in the following generic, narrative format that proceeds as follows (Brown, 1990):

1. *"We should do V."* (Initial Proposal)
2. "Why?"
3. *"Because of observations W."* (Observations)
4. "So what? How do you connect the observations and the proposal, and why is that important to you?"
5. *"Because we place a high value on X for the following normative reasons from the four major ethics theories."* (Value Prioritization)
6. "Why should you place such a high value on X?"
7. *"Because we assume Y in our philosophies of life."* (Assumptions)
8. "What about opposing views Z?"
9. *"After considering the voiced concerns of Z in dialogue, we should do V with qualifications."* (Opposing Views)
10. "What next?"
11. *"We should enact proposal V as appropriately qualified."* (Enacted Proposal)

In the ethics baseball diamond in Figure 3.6, individuals and groups can score "integrity runs" by sequentially following the six-step dialogue process from initial proposal to enacted proposal.

The benefits of using this ethics dialogue format for managers include: (a) it expects rational justification, rather than political muscle, in policy formation;

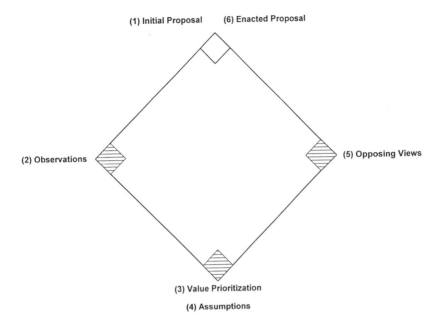

Figure 3.6. Model of Argumentative Ethics Dialogue That Promotes Process Integrity
SOURCE: Brown (1990). Reprinted with permission.

(b) it requires proposal proponents to be open to qualifying their policy recommendations in light of the strengths of opposing views; and (c) it allows for the respectful inclusion of multiple stakeholders into the moral ball game. Managerial decision making that neglects these six critical managerial components is likely to result in poor policy. Furthermore, ethical judgment is affected by managerial capacities for moral reasoning and analysis.

To assess moral reasoning and analysis skills at the managerial level, the following assessment instruments are available: Moral Judgment Interview (MJI), Defining Issues Test (DIT), and Multidimensional Ethics Scale (MES) instrument. With regard to individuals, because the capacity for integrity in action is a function of their moral reasoning development, it is important for managers to determine the levels of moral reasoning in themselves and in their employees (Blasi, 1980). The MJI and the DIT are two instruments designed to assess individual moral reasoning development (Colby & Kohlberg, 1987; Kohlberg, 1984; Rest, 1979). These instruments are reliable and valid, and although both are based on Kolhberg's moral development stage theory, referred to later in this chapter, their methodological differences warrant interpretive attention. The MJI's administrative process is an oral or written interview with open-ended responses, whereas the DIT's administrative process is a written survey with Likert scale responses. In effect, the MJI demands that an individual be able to formulate or produce a verbal justification for a decision, whereas the DIT only requires an individual to recognize, rate, and rank statements in terms of their importance in considering how to resolve an ethical dilemma (Elm & Weber, 1994). Because the outcome of the MJI is a moral stage score for an individual, whereas the outcome of the DIT is a p score, which measures the individual's moral reasoning capacity, no direct equivalence between outcomes exists; each outcome is method-specific (Elm & Weber, 1994). Properly administered and interpreted, however, both the MJI and DIT instruments can be used to measure individual moral reasoning development. (For more information on the DIT and the MJI, contact the Center for the Study of Ethical Development, University of Minnesota, Minneapolis, MN 55455. FAX: 612-624-8241.)

The MES is an individual ethical awareness and judgment instrument designed to predict behavioral intent (Reidenbach & Robin, 1990; Robin & Reidenbach, 1991). The instrument consists of context-specific scenarios of ethically questionable situations. The perceptual interpretation grid that is offered to respondents consists of eight scaled items categorized into three dimensions: moral equity, relativism, and contractualism (Robin, Gordon, Jordan, & Reidenbach, 1996). Respondents are asked to evaluate a specific ethical/unethical action by one of the actors in each scenario by using the perceptual interpretive grid. Next, a behavioral intent measure follows in the form of a question about the probability that the respondent would behave in the same manner as the actor in the scenario.

The MES has been used successfully to correlate ethical awareness in context-specific situations with behavioral intent (Cohen, Pant, & Sharp, 1993). (For more information on the MES, contact Dr. Donald Robin at the University of Southern Mississippi, Hattiesburg MS 39406. FAX: 601-266-4630.)

In addition to the MJI, DIT, and MES assessments, systematic, ongoing ethics training develops moral reasoning skills. A variety of qualified providers of ethics training are available in the United States, including: the Center for Business Ethics at Bentley College (Waltham, MA); the Center for Law and Ethics at Wharton in Philadelphia; the Ethics Resource Center in Washington,

D.C.; the Business Ethics Education Certification from the American Legal Studies in Business Association in Denver; Navran Associates in Atlanta; the Center for the Advancement of Applied Ethics at Carnegie-Mellon University (Pittsburgh, PA); the Business Enterprise Trust at Stanford University; the Center for Ethics in Economics (Columbus, OH); and Organizational Ethics Associates (Cincinnati, OH).

Once the first step of ethical analysis has taken place, the next step of ethics resolution begins. *Ethics resolution* is the rational step of making a firm, justified decision and bringing ethics analysis to a final conclusion. Decisive managers demonstrate sound ethical judgment by knowing how and when to bring closure to prolonged ethics analyses that risk becoming procrastination rituals rather than constructive preludes to ethics conflict resolution. Indecisive managers are unable to bring about moral closure. Ethics resolution often flows naturally from a thorough ethics analysis. In the absence of adequate ethics analysis, managers may find themselves imposing their resolutions or forming political alliances to coerce compliance with their decisions. Inevitably, people resist these manipulative efforts to achieve rapid resolution and resort to defensive routines that may inhibit more responsible ethics resolution—for example, withholding information, circumventing ethics processes, sabotaging group ethical decisions, or outright defiance.

The judgment outcome should be one that is sound, inclusive, and defensible. Sound judgments are arrived at by arguments that have factually true premises and factually true conclusions and are valid. Training in accurate observation and logical reasoning is crucial to arriving at sound moral judgments. Moral sentiments may disclose emotional truths, but these are only part of the moral argument; emotional intensity alone does not necessarily lead to sound moral judgment—for example, where there is emotional "heat," there is not necessarily rational "light." Group emotional intensity is also no substitute for thinking through a moral issue by means of a comprehensive analysis and justified resolution. The justified resolution is not infallible, but if it follows the ethics dialogue format for inclusive argumentation and incorporates all the elements of management judgment integrity, it is a justifiable resolution. Everyone may not agree with it, but the justified moral resolution is conscientiously reached and rationally defensible.

Part of resolution justification is the reasoned prioritization of ethics theory-based principles. A justified moral resolution requires that the moral issue at hand be resolved by prioritizing teleological ethics theory-based principles (utility and happiness), deontological theory-based principles (dignity, freedom, and social justice), virtue theory-based principles (justice and caring), and system development theory-based principles (growth and creativity). The relative weight and extent of resources to be allocated to these principles will depend on the quality of moral reasoning used to support them. Quick-fix resolutions or agreements based on coerced assent or political manipulation erode process integrity; only moral dialogue based on rational arguments grounded in prioritized moral principles contributes to process integrity. In the rational prioritization process, explicit arguments will carry more weight than implicit arguments, sound arguments more weight than unsound arguments, more inclusive arguments more weight than partial arguments (congruent arguments will be accorded more weight than merely consistent ones), and more multitheoretical and balanced arguments more weight than unitheoretical and unbalanced arguments.

This treatment of resolution justification accords legitimacy to the balanced consideration of all four major ethics traditions. It does not automatically grant the deontological tradition "moral trump priority status" over teleological approaches, nor individual rights over collective system responsibilities. But it does argue against ethical relativism in favor of an enriched but bounded tradition of moral pluralism. Essentially, for managers in organizations to take integrity seriously, overemphasizing individual rights to the detriment of system responsibility may not solve organizational problems of moral complexity. In other words, justifiable resolutions that increase process integrity must address both the barrel (the system) and the apple (the individual), or the complex interdependent nature of management integrity will be neglected.

In addition, two tools often used to sharpen managers' moral resolution capacities are the Ranking Responsibilities Test (RRT) and the Moral Threshold Test (MTT) (Rion, 1990; Stewart, 1994). The RRT is a useful approach to setting moral priorities when avoiding harm is of paramount concern. It draws on the type of moral claim made and emphasizes the relative stringency of moral demands. Ranked in terms of the moral stringency of claims are the following prioritized guidelines for managers in deciding how to handle moral dilemmas with limited resources:

- Avoid harm to person or property—the most stringent negative obligation for managers.
- Provide remedy or relief for problems that managers provoke.

- Provide affirmative aid for problems that others cause, starting within managerial jurisdiction areas and extending outward.
- Do good works through voluntary, charitable activity, starting "at home" and extending outward.

Good managers prioritize the allocation of their limited budgets and avoid depleting financial reserves for high visibility, charitable projects while neglecting to protect constituents from direct harm or deferring relief for management-induced hardships.

The MTT is a useful approach to use when a moral problem arises that a manager did not cause. The more that each of the following four factors applies, the more moral intensity should exist behind the managerial obligation to act: (a) vulnerability: a need or problem clearly exists and presents potential harm; (b) proximity: the manager knows or should know that a need or problem exists in his or her area; (c) capability: the means exist to help without excessive risk (danger, liability); and (d) dependency: the manager is the last resort—no one else is apt to help current and future generational victims. The more vulnerable, proximate, capable, and dependent the moral situation, the more the threshold for moral managerial action should be breached; that is, managers should act first on the most intense aggregate need. This is particularly important for public managers who may tend to react only after clear legal, ethical, and effectiveness guidelines are provided, whereas certain moral situations require a heightened sense of moral urgency and a more rapid, proactive response.

The net result of sound ethical judgment is the avoidance of narrow, single-quadrant judgment consistency and incomplete two- or three-quadrant judgment congruence. The lack of sound ethical judgment eventually comes back to haunt managers and organizations who have neglected the legitimate interests of ignored stakeholders in their rush to judgment. Ethical resolutions based on management process integrity attest to the power of balance, rather than the balance of power (Torbert, 1991). The power of balance includes the force of multiple theories that constitute judgment integrity, as well as the process integrity fit between the ethics issue analysis and the proposed moral resolution. In short, ethical judgment is the second process stage based on the steps of ethics analysis and ethics resolution. As managers improve the soundness of their ethical judgments, their example as morally analytical and resolute decision makers stimulates similar thoughtfulness at work.

Ethical Intention

The result of the completed ethical judgment process is the conceptual resolution of a moral issue, for which different kinds and degrees of motivation to enact exist. In traditional parlance: "What is first in intention, is last in execution"; that is, our intentions or motivations logically precede our conduct, but at times what we intend to do and what we actually do are not the same. Nevertheless, the clarity and strength of our moral intentions shape our characters and usually determine what we do (e.g., "Where there's a will, there's a way"). As the former president of RCA, David Sarnoff, was fond of saying: "The will to persevere is often the difference between failure and success." The desire to act ethically and to expend the requisite effort to do so makes the character difference in individual and collective moral performance.

The word *character* can be used broadly to refer to whatever pattern of attitudes, dispositions, and qualities a person exhibits. It can also be used narrowly to refer to a certain core group of positive qualities or virtues. In the latter sense, *character* as used in this book is fluid; that is, it expands or shrinks with the exercise of virtue. In addition, character admits of degrees of developmental integrity; that is, strong characters identify with commitments that provide continuity and unity through the course of life, through conduct that reflects espoused principles, and through regular self-assessment and self-control. Well-developed, expansive characters routinely exercise their virtues (intellectual, emotional, social, and moral) to add depth to their moral resolve. Strong characters have strong intentions to act ethically; they are ready to act morally (Paine, 1991).

Ethical intention is the degree of cognitive and volitional readiness to act, whose sustained development leads to character formation for which one can be held responsible. Ethical intention, therefore, is the third stage of management process integrity, composed of two steps: cognitive readiness to act and volitional readiness to act. *Cognitive readiness to act ethically,* the first step, is the capacity to conceive current role responsibilities accurately, imagine a preferred future, and wisely prepare a plan of action to achieve that future, which constitute the "intellectual" life of a good person. Individuals differ in their current role conception accuracy, their moral ambitions for a preferred future, their capacity to imagine vividly and create a path wisely to that preferred future, and/or their ability to prudently prepare a detailed, feasible plan of action to achieve that future state (Kupperman, 1989; Paine, 1991; Wilkins, 1989).

Role conceptions and moral ambitions are shaped by individual moral development, ethical work cultures, and other external environmental influences. As individuals develop their cognitive moral understanding of the possibilities, conditions, and benefits of moving from selfish to cooperative role behavior, they come to appreciate their stake in endorsing social arrangements (Rest, 1986). Ethical work cultures that fully implement ethics development programs model and reinforce the expectation for and feasibility of postconventional work roles and moral ambitions. Finally, some individuals are fortunate enough to intuit role responsibilities correctly and absorb sound moral ambitions from families, peers, schools, media, professional associations, or other agents of moral socialization. They easily crystallize and voice their vision of a future professional life in terms of prioritized moral ideals. Usually, the clearer one's cognitive moral vision, the more motive power that vision will generate (Rest, 1984). For example, the following cases of Maria, Takaku, and Erik provide concrete examples of differences in moral ambition. Maria, a Chicana graduate business student, has moral imagination, personal appreciation for cooperative professional conduct, and a view of balanced work/family life, but she has always worked in a manipulative work culture and has never been exposed to mainstream professional socialization experiences. Takaku, a Japanese American graduate business student, has always worked in small Japanese-owned firms that value collaboration and principled cooperation, and he has been exposed to mainstream professional socialization experiences, but he has merely conformed to work expectations without independently envisaging a balanced view of work/family life. Finally, Erik, a Swedish American graduate business student, has independently envisaged a principled approach to his professional life and a balanced view of his work/family obligations, is employed in an integrity-driven work culture, and has routinely been exposed to mainstream professional socialization experiences. The cognitive readiness to act, all other things being equal, will be far superior for Erik than for Takaku or Maria because Erik's moral ambitions have been clarified and honed through personal development and education, and his plans to achieve them are more likely to be realistic and prudent in light of his concrete experience with wholesome work/family environments and successful, principled professionals.

The key element of the cognitive readiness to act ethically is the cultivation of intellectual virtue. *Intellectual virtue* consists of knowing and appreciating what is ethically desirable. The responsibility of managers to develop their intellectual virtues (e.g., understanding, knowledge, prudence, creativity, resourcefulness, tolerance, level-headedness, appreciativeness, and wisdom) is warranted in order to sustain the cognitive readiness to act ethically at work. On the one hand, managers with impoverished moral imaginations who resist intellectual virtue development and role clarification, who settle for manipulative work environments, and who avoid professional socialization eventually shrink their moral characters and erode organizational character by depriving both of cognitive stimulation. The range of their envisaged ethical options becomes narrow, their ignorance of feasible alternatives restricts their freedom to act differently, and their practical wisdom degenerates. On the other hand, managers who take responsibility for their intellectual virtue cultivation and serve as role models for their work organizations, expand their moral characters and improve organizational character by strengthening cognitive readiness to act ethically (Kupperman, 1989).

The second step of ethical intention, *volitional readiness to act ethically*, is the capacity for regularly experiencing emotional, social, and moral virtues that constitute the "passionate" life of a good person and the capacity for resolute commitment to a chosen virtuous pattern of sustained character development. Volitional readiness to act is, therefore, composed of three elements: emotional, social, and moral virtues.

Emotional virtue consists of feeling and expressing joy only when acting ethically or regularly experiencing "moral" passions. The evolutionary phases of this element move from apathetic intentions or passionlessness, through "immoral" passions, and onto "regularly experienced moral passions." In the first phase, apathetic individuals lack volitional readiness to act; they imagine a preferred future, but they are unable or unwilling summon up the will to act and, consequently, do not experience the moral passion of moderate acquisitiveness (Viscott, 1996). For example, some business students may passively watch and be absorbed in a movie or videotape on financial success but lack the passionate drive that motivates personal successful behavior. They may feel entitled to success without any exertion of their will or expenditure of effort. Apathy, in this case, is a volitional defect even if accompanied by the cognitive readiness to act ethically.

In the second phase of emotional virtue development, traditional examples of *"immoral" passions* to be resisted include the following: arrogance, greed, envy, gluttony, lust, jealousy, slothfulness, hatred, and resentment (Midgley, 1984; Shklar, 1984; Wallace, 1978). These passions are immoral because they erode the natural volitional readiness to act ethically (Solomon, 1977, 1990a).

- *Arrogant people,* for instance, have an excessively high opinion of themselves and feed their feelings of conceit by denying others appropriate dignity and refusing to share pride in collective accomplishments; for example, always having to "look better" at another's expense erodes respectful regard for others, as well as oneself (Dean, 1976).

- *Greedy people* have an excessive and unbounded acquisitiveness, and rather than being satisfied with a desire for moderate wealth, they are driven by the unbridled "hunger for more"; for example, always having to "have more" erodes the moral capacity to enjoy moderate acquisitiveness (Shames, 1989).

- *Envious people* feel covetous of another's qualities and/or possessions and desire to obtain them by whatever means are necessary. Instead of the moral passions of admiration and emulation, which naturally inspire one to do one's personal best to achieve one's goals, this "immoral" passion begrudges the accomplishments of others, diminishes the willingness to acknowledge the rightful claim of others, and rationalizes rapacious conduct toward others—for example, Manager A, who envies the professional reputation and attractive spouse of Manager B and is motivated to destroy the reputation and marriage of Manager B in order to "get what that person has," rather than build his or her own reputation and marriage.

- *Gluttonous people* feel dominated by a need for inordinate and obsessive consumption of food or other substances. Instead of enjoying moderate consumption, gluttonous people prefer unrestrained self-indulgence; for example, an employee who routinely engages in binge drinking, which leads to work absenteeism, tardiness, and substandard performance, allows her inordinate consumption to interfere with her work life and preclude the joy of moderate consumption.

- *Lustful people* feel sustained by inordinate sexual cravings to the detriment of a respectful, productive work environment; for example, individuals who only pay attention to the sexually attractive and ignore others transform the workplace into a predatory, erotic arena (Maniero, 1992; Powell, 1993).

- *Jealous people* feel apprehensive about the possible loss of position, affection, or trust and become excessively vigilant and possessively watchful of their claimed rights and interests in light of perceived rivals or imagined betrayals; for example, managers who, to protect their personal "perks," jealously hoard resources that were originally intended for departmental use are less virtuous than managers who share resources to enhance the aggregate achievement of the unit.

- *Slothful people* feel an aversion to work and are disposed to becoming "free riders" on the efforts of others. Slothful persons may feel entitled to the benefits of the workplace but are too lazy to earn them; for example, rather than being diligently active, slothful managers waste their talents, depreciate industriousness, and corrode their healthy desire for meaningful work.

- *Hateful people* feel animosity toward others and may indulge in vicious cruelties, hostile speech, violent acts, or terrorist activities; for example, a fired employee who perceives his dismissal as wrongful may feel hateful toward his employer and resort to verbal abuse and/or physical violence.

- *Resentful people* feel bitter animosity, because of their inferiority, toward people who succeed, and through devious, surly, and vengeful strategies, take advantage of the vulnerabilities of others in order to delight in their misfortune; for example, resentful Manager A feigns concern for Manager B's stressful work situation, only to delight in taking advantage of their intimacy to destroy Manager B's reputation and career (Himmelfarb, 1994; Sheaffer, 1988).

Finally, in the third phase, traditional examples of *"moral" passions* to be fostered include the following *emotional virtues:* self-respect, moderate acquisitiveness, emulation (doing one's personal best), joy in moderate consumption, hardy resilience, appropriate erotic intimacy, trust, appropriate industriousness, loving respect for others, genuine admiration, sense of justice, warranted shame and guilt, appropriate and timely expression of hurt, eventemperedness, sincerity, sense of responsibility, sense of dignity, fidelity to commitments, natural tranquility, and self-acceptance (Bunker & Rubin, 1995; Himmelfarb, 1994; Solomon, 1977; Taylor, 1987). Cultivating and cherishing "moral" passions stimulate the emotional propensity to act ethically.

In addition to experiencing and cultivating emotional virtues, the volitional readiness to act is enhanced by its second element, social virtue. *Social virtue* consists of the spontaneous fondness for the company of good people, demonstrated by congenially relating to and valuing others. Unlike ethical judgment, which requires abstract analysis of rules and principles, the expression of social virtue does not require analytic deliberation; in fact, deliberation is evidence that one does not have certain social virtues (Solomon, 1992). Among the key social virtues, which demonstrate that getting along with others is as important a character trait for managers as efficient coordination of resources to compete against an external threat, are the following: sense of humor, wittiness, charm, amiability, cheerfulness, robust good-natured toughness, gentleness, humane interaction, openness, politeness, pleasantness, decency, liveliness, caring, cooperativeness, generosity, civility, playfulness, and citizenship. Social virtues prevent managers from becoming overly controlled, rule-bound, grim, boring, and dreary and introduce unpretentious congeniality into the workplace. For example, a manager faced with personal shortcomings gains a sense of perspective on him- or herself and builds congenial coworker relations by being able to laugh at him- or herself while addressing the character flaw that needs attention. Even in cost-cutting times, employees are likely to respond favorably to a manager who has high standards but regularly displays a sense of humor, playfulness, and caring decency.

Emotional and social virtues are the key elements that energize the volitional readiness to act ethically, but the third element, *moral virtue,* which consists of resolutely heeding the call of conscience with a discerning sense of right and wrong, determines the extent to which ethical conduct ultimately occurs. Emotional and social virtues must be reinforced by the third element, moral virtues, to sustain character development. Managers who demonstrate "weakness of will," either occasionally or habitually, reveal their moral virtue deficiency regardless of the intensity of their emotional and social virtues (Hill, 1991). Among the key moral virtues necessary to sustain character development are courage, self-discipline, justice, truthfulness, patience, dependability, moderation, loyalty, trustworthiness, perseverance, patient urgency, benevolence, caring, honesty, and gratitude (Kruschwitz & Roberts, 1987; MacIntyre, 1984, 1988; Pincoffs, 1986). Strong-willed managers exercise moral virtue repeatedly; for example, strong-willed managers who experience workplace frustration resist abusive temper tantrums and emotional outbursts at coworkers by practicing self-discipline, perseverance, and truthfulness in order to provide a moral role model for others. Courageous managers do not cower before superiors, do not curry favor with employees by belittling upper management, do not shrink from confronting employees with constructive criticism in a benevolent manner, and do not cave in to pressures when the going gets tough (Walton, 1986).

In contrast, weak-willed managers demonstrate a loss of self-control that undermines moral virtue in themselves and others (Mele, 1987; Mortimer, 1971). Weakness of will is a failure to live up to self-imposed, moral standards; it entails a willful and intentional lapse of commitment and/or a change in desired priorities with opportunities for alternative intentions. For example, a weak-willed manager may begin the fiscal year with a resolve to treat people fairly, but within a few weeks, she or he backslides, forgetting to be impartial in performance appraisal decisions. The initially firm resolution to treat people fairly becomes diluted into a wavering and vague commitment that lacks clear implications for implementing procedural fairness. As time passes, only half-hearted efforts are made, and the struggle to avoid favoritism is abandoned, succumbing eventually to discrimination that distorts managerial judgment about employee actual performance. The inner conflict experienced by a weak-willed manager between his or her ethical judgments and his or her will to act eventually erodes employee confidence in the sincerity of the weak-willed manager's commitments to fairness. Employees who are victimized by weak-willed managers, in turn lose respect for the manager; assume that weak-willed, inconsistent conduct is acceptable; and act accordingly. The end result is that weak-willed managers and their work units morally degenerate and resort to excuse making and scapegoating to protect themselves from legitimate criticism (Snyder, Higgins, & Stucky, 1983; Walton, 1986).

In summary, the internalization of intellectual, emotional, social, and moral virtues develops strong ethical intentions, i.e., cognitive and volitional readiness to act ethically. Some theorists even claim that settled virtuous character traits that have become "second nature" eliminate the need for extensive ethical deliberation and conscious decision making (Kupperman, 1968). However, the combination of sound ethical judgment incorporating careful moral analysis, combined with firm ethical intention, embodying virtuous character development, makes for a more robust readiness than either factor alone could provide on the part of managers to act ethically, especially in complex moral situations. Although managers are responsible for their own character development, it is through the collaborative partnership among all key organizational stakeholders that the *organizational character*, as the collective set of posiive qualities and virtues, provides a supportive foundation for strong individual ethical intentions.

Ethical Conduct

The result of the prior decision-making process is a manager and an organization clear about what should be done and ready to act. *Ethical conduct* is the process of engaging in and carrying out justifiable actions. Justifiable actions have met the rigorous standards of ethical judgment and are ready to be enacted.

Ethical conduct, therefore, is conceptually different from moral behavior. *Behavior* is the response of an organism to the whole range of factors constituting its environment for which only descriptive, causal explanations are appropriate. For example, when managers and their companies are said to have behaved well, this means that they have responded appropriately by conforming to the rules and/or pressures in the business environment. In contrast, *ethical conduct* is the action of an agent for which both descriptive, causal explanations and prescriptive, normative justifications are appropriate. Whereas a descriptive explanation will disclose what caused conduct, an ethical justification will argue for the legitimacy of the principles, methods, virtues, or values the actor used in making his or her choice (Brown, 1990). Because managers can use value-laden language to control behavior by pressuring others to submit to moral rules or can use ethical language to empower others by engaging them in the process of ethics discourse, the authors have selected the term *ethical conduct* to emphasize the importance of responsibility, both individually and collectively, for whatever is done in a moral situation. Managers and organizations are not behavioral robots; they can and should be held responsible for their ethical conduct and reputation (Fombrun, 1996).

The stage of ethical conduct can be divided into two key steps: responsible responsiveness and sustainable development. *Responsible responsiveness* is the voluntary ownership of intentional conduct for which one can be held morally accountable. The significance of the first step, responsible responsiveness, emerges out of the extensive literature dealing with the conceptual relationship between social responsibility and social responsiveness (Ackerman & Bauer, 1976; Carroll, 1996; Frederick, 1986; Miles, 1987; Sethi, 1975). The basic difference between the two concepts is that whereas *social responsibility* implies a static state or condition of having assumed (internalized) an obligation, *social responsiveness* implies a dynamic, action-oriented external process indicating the extent to which internal and external stakeholder needs are being met. Responsiveness to stakeholders can result from governmental and nongovernmental (special-interest groups) imposition or from voluntary assumption. The former case of imposed obligation is referred to as *irresponsible responsiveness;* the latter case of assumed obligation is referred to as *responsible responsiveness.* These conceptual relations are depicted in the Responsible Responsiveness Grid in Figure 3.7.

In the lower right quadrant of Figure 3.7, *irresponsible responsiveness* entails pressured compliance with externally imposed standards and stakeholder expectations, without acknowledging or internalizing any sense of social obligation for management and organization integrity—for example, AK Steel's 1996 begrudging compliance with OSHA safety standards in Middletown, Ohio, only after severe fines and penalties were assessed. In the lower left quadrant, *irresponsible unresponsiveness* to stakeholders entails a lack of compliance with external standards and stakeholder expectations, without acknowledging or internalizing any sense of social obligation for managerial and organization integrity—for example, the Dayton Walther Company in Dayton, Ohio, which routinely violated and ignored EPA air pollution standards and community noise pollution standards and finally relocated elsewhere in 1993

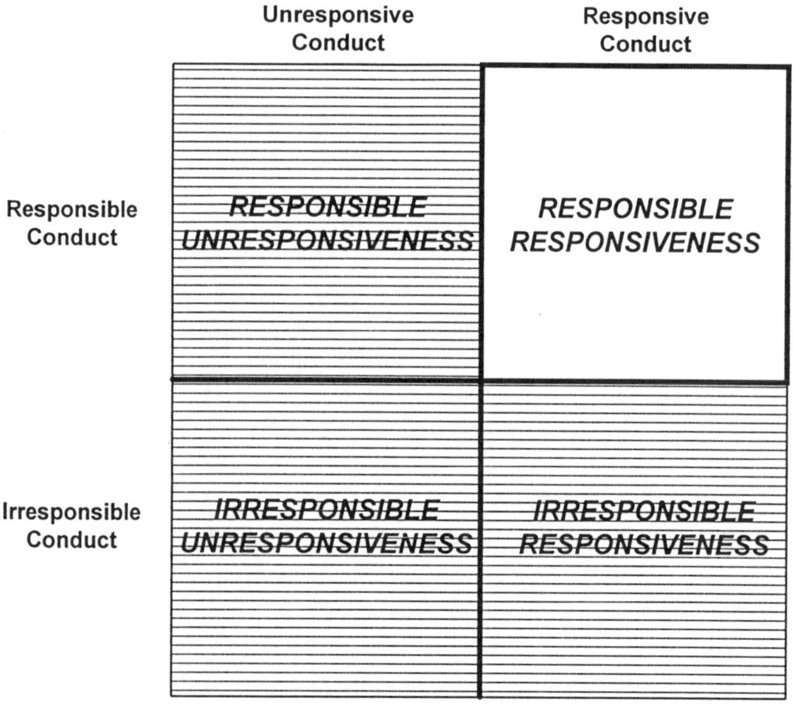

	Unresponsive Conduct	Responsive Conduct
Responsible Conduct	*RESPONSIBLE UNRESPONSIVENESS*	*RESPONSIBLE RESPONSIVENESS*
Irresponsible Conduct	*IRRESPONSIBLE UNRESPONSIVENESS*	*IRRESPONSIBLE RESPONSIVENESS*

Figure 3.7. Ethical Conduct and the Responsible Responsiveness Grid

without prior notice. In the upper left quadrant, *responsible unresponsiveness* entails a lack of compliance with external standards and stakeholder expectations but acknowledging or internalizing a sense of social obligation for management and organization integrity—for example, the Body Shop's lack of compliance with cosmetic industry conventional marketing standards and refusal to meet traditional customer expectations for glamorous product packaging in the name of maintaining organization integrity. In other words, the company refused to claim dishonestly that its products would make people look younger or manipulatively create beauty needs that did not exist, but rather would only provide products that would make one look one's best. Finally, in the upper right quadrant, *responsible responsiveness* entails assumed compliance with external standards and stakeholder expectations, with an acknowledged and internalized sense of social obligation for management and organization integrity; for example, St. Paul Companies, major insurance providers based in St. Paul, Minnesota, has been rated the best company for social responsibility in the United States by *Business Ethics* magazine (Kurschner, 1996). They have voluntarily assumed responsibility for management and organization integrity through a comprehensive OEDS and have voluntarily complied with external standards and multiple stakeholder expectations through multi-million-dollar philanthropic community donations, installation of organization ethics officer(s), and regular ethics training programs. Again, responsible responsiveness in the area of public policy has been demonstrated by Johnson & Johnson, which more than complied with external standards and stakeholder expectations by voluntarily removing Tylenol from distributors' shelves in 1982 and 1986 to avoid risks (from poison tampering) in accordance with their own prioritized corporate values designed to ensure management and organization integrity.

The growth of U.S. legal and regulatory standards, originating from executive, legislative, judicial, and administrative agency sources, has challenged the capacity for responsiveness among managers (Ayres & Braithwaite, 1992; Breyer, 1982; Carroll, 1996; Peery, 1995; Weidenbaum & Warren, 1995). In the private sector, market failures disclosed by inadequate consumer information, product defects, monopolistic practices, prevalence of negative externalities, and the necessity to provide for public goods all invite government regulation (Carroll, 1996; Peery, 1995). Although the balance of regulatory expansion and contraction varies with political changes over the years, managers and organizations that exercise responsible responsiveness can institute self-regulatory standards and practices to preempt or preclude government intervention.

In some organizations, some managers try to evade responsible responsiveness by disowning their accountability for substandard performance (e.g., "My boss made me do it"). Others try to avoid responsible responsiveness by claiming that an expected outcome is not within the scope of their role responsibility (e.g., "That's not my job"). Ethical managers take responsibility for actions and are willing to be held accountable; they do not make excuses, scapegoat others, or plead ignorance. Ethical conduct is essentially the result of ethical judgment intentionally enacted. Because process, developmental, and judgment integrity are interdependent, the organization integrity that is built by their interaction provides a normative standard for ethical conduct. In common parlance, "Actions speak louder than words"; there is no substitute for ethical conduct, whether it be supported or resisted. Ethical conduct is principled and justifiable but not quixotic; it appropriately addresses the practical circumstances that constrain conduct (Feinberg, 1995).

Managers and organizations are also held accountable for their conduct in competing with integrity both domestically and internationally. In the U.S. domestic arena, a range of background institutions (e.g., legal, social, economic, technological, cultural, and ecological) constrain selfish abuses of managerial and organizational power. U.S. managers as individuals and organizations as legal persons can engage in responsible conduct by means of external and/or internal regulation. For instance, the U.S. legal background institutions regulate responsible corporate conduct by means of judge-made common law, legislated statutory law, global treaties, and executive-made orders. U.S. *common law* is composed of *criminal law* (lawsuits over public wrongs committed by the accused against the state), *civil law* (lawsuits over private wrongs, usually classified as torts [personal injuries] or breaches of contract, committed among or between individual parties called plaintiffs and defendants), and *agency law* (lawsuits over private and business wrongs stemming from voluntary relationships among and between agents, principals, and third parties, usually within the context of business partnerships, corporate relationships, and employment relationships). U.S. *statutory law* is composed of any law made by a government body designated to enact legal regulations formally—for example, Congress enacting the federal bankruptcy code, the Uniform Commercial Code, and Administrative Agencies enforcing statutes, administrative rules, and regulations (e.g., securities regulations by the SEC) affecting corporations. *Global treaties* are bilateral or unilateral compacts negotiated to determine rights and responsibilities; for example, the Warsaw Convention determines the rights and remedies available to those who are injured or whose property is damaged while traveling on commercial aircraft (August, 1993, 1995). Finally, U.S. *executive-made orders* by the president or other duly-elected, political executives may further constrain corporate conduct—for example, Executive Order 11264 authorizing affirmative action programs.

These legal background institutions provide external regulation of business conduct to ensure compliance with socially accepted standards of moral responsibility. Involvement in the public policy and legal enactment processes that affect organizational conduct become an important responsibility for domestic managers. Proactive involvement early in the public-policy process helps ethical managers identify and shape latent and emerging issues, rather than become merely reactively defensive after the fact (Buchholz et al., 1994).

In addition, in the absence of adequate background institutions that externally regulate and reinforce good conduct, managers and organizations of integrity need to develop self-regulatory guidelines to supplement and/or complement external regulations. For instance, a central difference between conducting business on a national level and conducting it on a global level is the relative absence in the latter setting of restrictive background institutions relating to business conduct; for example, the absence of clear legal safety standards and evacuation plans by the Indian government allowed unsafe practices to exist at Union Carbide, which resulted in the chemical-leak catastrophe at Bhopal, India.

Some companies that are irresponsibly responsive feel no moral obligation beyond obeying the legitimate laws in each country in which they operate, and then only to the extent that the laws are effectively enforced (Allinson, 1993; DeGeorge, 1993; Donaldson, 1989). Other companies that are responsibly responsive, however, compete with integrity and adopt a universal set of principles that exercise responsible self-regulation, either specifically by industry (e.g., the Responsible Care Program of the Chemical Manufacturers' Association) or generically for all global organizations (Quinn & Petrick, 1994).

Despite the pulls of pluralist, collectivist, and tribalist transnational cultures, an acceptable range of normative guidelines is emerging for responsible responsiveness among international organizations. DeGeorge (1993), for example, recommends the specific normative guidelines for responsible international organizational conduct listed in Table 3.1.

In addition, the Caux Round Table Principles for Business, in Appendix B, combine both domestic and global normative principles for international business conduct. They include general principles of conduct promoting innovation, justice, world community, human dignity and trust, *kyosei* (mutual cooperation and prosperity), and respect for nature, along with stakeholder principles relating to customers, employees, owners/investors, suppliers, competitors, and communities (Skelly, 1995).

The second step in ethical conduct goes beyond an isolated instance of responsible responsiveness to a sustained pattern of reputable practices, which ultimately leads to sustainable development. *Sustainable development* is the intentional adoption of a set of morally justifiable practices and long-range policies that address equity between present and future generations and equity in North/South relations by appropriately blending socioeconomic, biological, and ecological development. Sustainable development can occur at the individual, group, organizational, industry, governmental, and global institutional

Table 3.1 Normative Guidelines for Responsible International Organizational
Conduct

---

1. Multinationals should do no intentional harm.
2. Multinationals should produce more good than harm for the host country.
3. Multinationals should contribute by their activity to the host country's development.
4. Multinationals should respect the human rights of their employees.
5. To the extent that local culture does not violate ethical norms, multinationals should respect the local culture and work with and not against it.
6. Multinationals should pay their fair share of taxes.
7. Multinationals should cooperate with the local government in developing and enforcing just background institutions.
8. Multinationals are responsible for making due compensation for any harm they do, directly or indirectly, intentionally or unintentionally.
9. Majority control of a firm carries with it ethical responsibility for the actions and failures of the firm.
10. If a multinational builds a hazardous plant, it has the obligation to make sure that it is safe and that it is run safely.
11. In transferring hazardous technology to LDCs, multinationals are responsible for appropriately redesigning such technology so that it can be safely administered in the host country.

SOURCE: DeGeorge, Richard T. (1993). *Competing With Integrity in International Business.* New York: Oxford University Press, 46-54, 90-93. Reprinted with permission.

levels (Gladwin & Krause, 1997; Shrivastava, 1996; Starik & Rands, 1995; Stead & Stead, 1996). Management process integrity requires that managers assess and develop ecologically sustainable organizations that meet internal and external standards of sustainable development (Gladwin, Kennelly, & Krause, 1995; Shrivastava, 1995b).

In traditional treatments of nature in strategic management, organizational theory, and social responsibility literatures (Buchholz, Marcus, & Post, 1992; Porter, 1980), the environment is usually "denaturalized" and regarded as an infinitely exploitable resource of marginal organizational concern. The independence and fundamental status of nature, however, imposes certain responsibilities on managers who want to engage in ethical conduct and sustain long-term relationships with nature, the ultimate stakeholder. The first responsibility requires an acknowledgment that management of organizations involves input-throughput-output systems of production and destruction; dismissing all destruction of nature as a mere inevitable "externality" of production is an attempt to evade moral accountability. Managers need to develop and use accounting procedures that measure, not ignore, the true costs of natural environment degradation (Naess, 1987; Shrivastava, 1995b). A second responsibility is to adhere to principles of environmentally responsible conduct contained in the domestic CERES principles and the global Business Charter for Sustainable Development; the latter is contained in Appendix C.

Finally, a third responsibility is to manage organizational relations with nature in such a way as to blend socioeconomic, biological, and ecological development. Socioeconomic systems have goals such as increasing production of goods and services, satisfying basic human needs or reducing poverty, improving equitable exchanges, increasing or maintaining cultural diversity, achieving social justice and gender equality, promoting education, democratic participation, protection of indigenous populations, and population control. Biological systems have goals such as increasing or maintaining genetic diversity, building individual species resilience and biological productivity for human and nonhuman use. Ecological systems have goals such as conserving weather patterns, building multisystem resilience, and preserving subtle, fragile networks of relationships among humans and nonhumans (Buchholz, 1994; Holmberg, 1992; Shrivastava, 1995b). Given the convergence and relative strength of these three systems, the trade-offs necessary for sustainable development will not magically occur without ongoing ethical conduct at many levels (Miller & Quinn, 1993; Petrick & Quinn, 1994a; Starik & Rands, 1995).

The ways that sustainable development can be converted into sustainable organization management include the following methods: (a) total quality environmental management (TQEM), (b) ecological sustainable competitive strategies, (c) technology transfer equity, and (d) population impact control (Shrivastava, 1995a). First, TQEM involves organizations and industries in systematically minimizing life cycle costs for all resources and continuous improvement of quality output, spearheaded by such organizations as the Global Environmental Management Initiative (GEMI) (FitzGerald, 1996; Lindsay & Petrick, 1997; Sayre, 1996; Wever, 1996; Willig, 1994). Second, ecologically competitive sustainable strategies include incorporating sustainability variables (e.g., operational improvements, supplier relationships, employee/customer education) into least cost, differentiation, and niche strategies to gain first-mover advantages in environmentally sensitive markets; for example, authorized eco-labels on products made in Europe give them competitive advantages over comparable products made in America without authorized eco-labels (Quinn, 1995). Third, organizations can engage in technology transfer equity by developing ecologically friendly technologies—

for example, DuPont's development of chlorofluorocarbon (CFC) substitute technology for refrigerants and air conditioning, following the Montreal Protocol agreements. Next, managers can consider technology-for-nature swaps with developing countries rich in natural resources and in urgent need of new sustainable technologies for their teeming populations, so that North/South equity disparities can be remedied within a marketlike, exchange framework (Kimball, 1992; Kothari, 1990; Sachs & Huizinga, 1987). Finally, because extreme poverty and unavailability of birth control information and devices significantly contribute to excessive population growth, organization managers can choose to locate production facilities in global rural sites to generate employment, use advertising resources to educate the public about family planning options, and, in cooperation with local institutions, distribute birth control devices to rural households (Hollist & Tullis, 1987; Merchant, 1992; Shrivastava, 1995a, 1995b). In addition, promoting responsible consumption in developed countries by moderating the wasteful habits of throw-away consumer societies also has an impact on population behavior patterns (Hirschman & Holbrook, 1992). The fundamental assumptions of responsible conduct in this area are treated in the Sustainable Development Grid in Figure 3.8.

In the lower right quadrant of Figure 3.8, the assumptions of *non-sustainable development* are contained in *anthropocentric development and conservation*—private- and public-sector managers who economically exploit natural resources for rapid profit and modernization but degrade ecosystems, biological populations, and human communities while conserving whatever remains for future human economic use. For example, lumber industry managers who engage in forest clear-cutting rationalize their non-sustainable practice as legitimated by the use of private property in a competitive free market. Replanting is done only to conserve future economic prospects. In fact, some "free market environmentalists" argue that market incentives alone should be the only method to safeguard nature, so that the "trading and banking" of pollution rights, for instance, regardless of the net deterioration of global ecosystems, ought to be the preferred method of internalizing the costs of pollution externalities while fostering growth in production (Baxter, 1974; Elkins, 1992). As this response gains sociopolitical support, some managers work to roll back environmental regulations, resist any government "takings" policy, and emphasize tax relief for free-enterprise development that creates jobs.

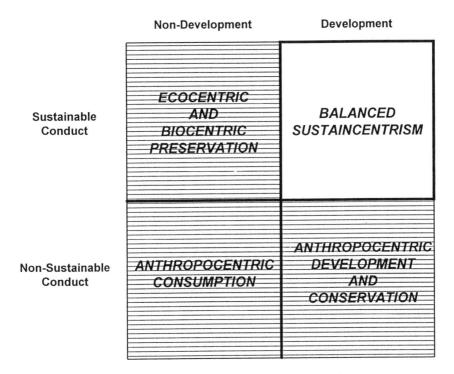

Figure 3.8. Ethical Conduct and the Sustainable Development Grid

In the lower left quadrant, the assumptions of *non-sustainable non-development* are contained in *anthropocentric consumption*—the mindless consumption and "trashing" of perceived unlimited resources that degrade ecosystems, biological populations, and human communities without any form of economic development. For example, bureaucratic, entrenched, multinational executives, smugly accustomed to economic superiority and to routine neglect of any adverse impact on nature, would rather do nothing than risk "rocking the boat" economically, socially, ecologically, or biologically. In the developing world, swidden farming that involves slash-and-burn techniques to build slipshod migrant dwellings aggravates this problem. As this approach gains sociopolitical support, nature becomes the global sink and people squander opportunities for productive investment in economic development, ecological preservation, and/or biological conservation (Bazerman, Messick, Tenbrunsel, & Wade-Benzoni, 1997; Petrick & Quinn, 1994a, 1994b).

In the upper left quadrant, the assumptions of *sustainable non-development* are contained in *ecocentric and biocentric preservation*—preserving and protecting wilderness, holistic natural ecosystems, and individual endangered species/habitats while resisting economic development through government regulation and special-interest resistance movements (Armstrong & Botzler, 1993; Naess, 1987; Nash, 1989). For example, managers of public lands in a developed country may refuse to award drilling rights domestically to companies that would promote economic development and instead purchase wetlands in developing countries by means of debt-for-nature swaps in order to preserve global undeveloped wilderness. As this response gains more sociopolitical support, membership in special-interest environmentalist groups increases: the Sierra Club, Friends of the Earth, National Wildlife Federation, National Resources Defense Council, Environmental Defense Fund, and Nature Conservancy to name a few.

Finally, in the upper right quadrant, the assumptions of *sustainable development* are contained in *balanced sustaincentrism* (Gladwin et al., 1995)—the complex, interdependent, and balanced anthropocentric (human socioeconomic realm), ecocentric, and biocentric development that supports both growth and nature (Holmberg, 1992; Petrick & Quinn, 1994a, 1994b; Quinn, 1995; Schmidheiny, 1992; Shrivastava, 1996). For example, managers at Allied-Signal, one of the world's oldest integrated chemicals corporations and a corporate member of GEMI, implemented a worldwide pollution-prevention and waste-reduction program, upholding the new chemical industry norms contained in the Responsible Care Initiative for sustainable development, explicitly balancing socioeconomic, ecosystem, and biocentric concerns. Furthermore, industrial ecology networks allow groups of companies to provide socioeconomic benefits to communities while minimizing their total impact on biological and ecological systems (Shrivastava, 1996). "Integrated greening" inside and outside the organization requires complex managerial skills in handling diverse environmental and socioeconomic issues; anything less, however, ultimately leads to unethical conduct. As this response gains sociopolitical support, individuals will reduce irresponsible consumption, revise and recycle products, renew natural resources, and expect others to do likewise.

In short, ethical conduct entails both responsibly responsive and sustainably developed over time. Managers and organizations can develop standards of ethical conduct at work that incorporate the following processes: (a) The routine, cumulative steps in improving ethical awareness, judgment, intention, and conduct set formal norms and provide informal momentum for future ethical conduct; (b) the regular referral to the tradition of business ethics cases and legal precedents provides ongoing, concrete guidance in analogous domestic and global situations; and (c) the regular practice of ethics dialogue, open forums, and moral argumentation in training sessions enhances management process integrity in everyday work discourse and action. In turn, ongoing ethical conduct builds strong reputations that constitute the foundation of sustained management process integrity (Fombrun, 1996).

◪ MANAGEMENT DEVELOPMENTAL INTEGRITY

The third dimension of management integrity is developmental integrity. *Management developmental integrity is the improvement of individual cognitive moral reasoning capacity from preconventional, self-interested regard through a stage of conforming to external conventional standards and finally to a stage of post-conventional commitment to universal ethical principles as guides to working and living.* Until postconventional reasoning and commitment to universal ethical principles is internalized, management developmental integrity is more of a hope than a reality. Whereas judgment integrity deepens and sustains management integrity, and process integrity broadens and builds that integrity, developmental integrity cultivates and grounds management integrity.

Managers choose to take the "high road" or the "low roads" to developmental integrity. Among the lower of the low roads to developmental integrity are direct political force and indirect economic force—both of which assume that humans are only self-interested beings instrumentally useful for political or economic advantage. When managers treat themselves and others in abusive and manipulative ways for political and economic success, however, they arrest their own and others' moral development. They create an atmosphere of hypercompetitive, untrustworthy *connivance* and workplace fear—for example, strict adherence to classic microeconomic theory of impersonal market forces that determine human nature and human worth.

To overcome the preconventional moral jungle of the lower of the low roads, some managers choose the higher of the low roads, interpersonal conformity and *compliance* with external authority. Managers may overcome self-interested impulsiveness by deciding to adhere to conventional legal and regulatory standards that gain them greater social approval and require some moral concern for others. Managers look up and around for ethical guidance on this conventional road but ultimately opt for the least legal constraint on their activity—for example, the global rush by transnational managers for the least regulated environments in which to maximize profits legally (Korten, 1996).

To overcome the stagnation of arbitrary external authorities and the abuses of legalized global economic warfare, some managers finally take the high road to integrity. Then they challenge authority, promote democratic participation at work, and appeal to universal moral principles in key business decisions. External compliance for managers on the high road is necessary but not sufficient when internalized, *commitment* to universal, postconventional principles is fostered and expected.

The metaphor of roads is empirically supported by studies of individual cognitive moral development that proceeds through six stages of sequential growth (Gilligan, 1982; Gilligan et al., 1989; Hansen, 1992; Kohlberg, 1973, 1984; Larrabee, 1993; Rest, 1986; Robin & Reidenbach, 1991). Although Kohlberg's final stage emphasis is on justice and Gilligan's final stage emphasis is on caring, both agree that the study of ethics should stimulate moral development toward principled conduct and caring communities, rather than toward selfish manipulation or cliquish compliance (Noddings, 1984; Rest & Narvaez, 1994; Robin & Reidenbach, 1991). Figure 3.9 depicts stages and examples of oral reasoning that lead to management developmental integrity at the postconventional morality level.

Stages One and Two: Preconventional Morality. The first stage, obedience and punishment orientation, is a preconventional egoistic approach to morality characterized by obedience out of fear of pain and punishment—for example, employees obeying managerial orders *only* out of fear of dismissal. The second stage, instrumental purpose and exchange orientation, is a preconventional egoistic approach to morality characterized by calculated pleasure seeking involving "deal making" and/or reciprocal manipulation in order to succeed—for example, forming power alliances to obtain preferential treatment and the benefits of favoritism at work.

Stages Three and Four: Conventional Morality. The third stage, interpersonal accord, conformity, and mutual expectations orientation, is a conventional approach advocating acting in a way that meets the expectations, or at least avoids the disapproval, of those close to you—for example, refraining from challenging your boss or fellow workers when you know they are wrong

Individual Cognitive Moral Development Stages	*Examples of Cognitive Moral Reasoning at Work*
Stage 1: Obedience and Punishment Orientation	
At this stage, physical consequences determine moral behavior. Avoidance of punishment and deference to power are typical of this stage because they promote self-interest.	"I won't disobey the boss because he/she may fire me."
Stage 2: Instrumental Purpose and Exchange Orientation	
At this stage, individual pleasure needs determine moral behavior. Using people for personal benefit is routine.	"I will help him/her only because he/she may help me advance my career."
Stage 3: Interpersonal Accord, Conformity, and Mutual Expectations Orientation	
At this stage, the approval of significant others determines behavior. The good person is one who satisfies family, friends, and work unit associates.	"I will go along with my work group, not because I agree with them, but because I want to be accepted by them."
Stage 4: Social Accord and Authority Maintenance Orientation	
At this stage, compliance with internal and external authority, upholding of the social order, and "doing one's duty at work" are primary ethical concerns.	"I will comply with company policy even though it involves personal sacrifice and incurs the disapproval of my work group because it is right to respect legitimate, hierarchic authority at work."
Stage 5: Majority Agreement and Due Process Orientation	
At this stage, active participation, tolerance for rational dissent, due process in grievance procedures, reasoned challenges to authority, and acceptance of majority rule become primary ethical concerns.	"I vote and participate in processes that voice the will of the majority at work, and I support the majority decision even when it challenges legitimate authority, incurs the disapproval of my work group, and/or causes personal hardship, while tolerating minority viewpoints."
Stage 6: Ethical Principle-Based Orientation	
At this stage, what is right and good is a matter of individual conscience and responsibly chosen commitments to principles of justice, dignity, caring, freedom, equality, and rights. Morality is based on principled personal conviction.	"I use ethical principles to clarify, justify, and/or criticize my company's policies whether these policies are supported by the majority at work, enforced by legitimate authority, accepted by my work group, and/or cause personal hardship."

Figure 3.9. Stages of Individual Moral Development With Examples of Moral Reasoning at Work

in order to be accepted as a "team player" in a work unit. The fourth stage, social accord and authority maintenance orientation, is a conventional approach advocating the fulfillment of one's role responsibilities in a hierarchic and/or legal authority setting—for example, as a manager, complying with new company policies regarding the accurate reporting of lateness and absences although unpopular with your work unit. It is projected on the basis of research studies that most adult Americans and managers are at the conventional level of cognitive moral development; they look up and around for ethical guidance (Bazerman, 1994).

Stages Five and Six: Postconventional Morality. The fifth stage, majority agreement and due process orientation, is a postconventional approach advocating the challenging of traditional and/or social authority that does not represent the will of the majority, by means of due process that supports future changes that will enhance the well-being of most of the parties affected—for example, supporting improvement suggestions put forth by a majority of surveyed workers that would change standard operating procedures but inconvenience me personally. The sixth stage, ethical principle-based orientation, is a postconventional approach advocating actions that are in accord with the principles of justice, caring, dignity, rights, and freedom—for example, providing designated whistle-blower protection against work retaliation because it is the right thing to do in principle.

Empirical research indicates that principled managers make a positive difference in group work moral development but that many employees and groups will remain at the conventional level of morality unless supportively challenged to morally mature (Dukerich et al., 1990). Managers need to structure work environments to nurture principle-based conduct because most employees are influenced by looking up and around to their supervisors and peers for moral guidance (Trevino & Nelson, 1995). Failure to structure supportive and maturing ethical work environments is a case of managerial malfeasance.

To guide managers in fostering collective developmental integrity through systems, the following two approaches are endorsed: (a) group and organizational moral development stages that parallel those of individual managers and (b) 16 components of an Organization Ethics Development System (OEDS) that lead to three different ethical work cultures.

With regard to the first approach, individual managers can morally develop from preconventional, self-interest through conventional conformity and on to postconventional principled conduct. Similarly, groups and organi-

zations can morally develop from a preconventional stage of collective connivance, through a conventional stage of collective compliance, and on to a
postconventional stage of collective commitment.

Collective connivance is a molar stage of moral development characterized
by the use of direct force and/or indirect manipulation to determine moral
standards. Managers who sustain this stage of collective development are either
issuing threats of force (e.g., "Get it done now or else") or developing exclusively exploitive relationships based on mutual manipulation (e.g., "What's in
it for me and forget the others?") (French & Granrose, 1995). *Collective
compliance* is a molar stage of moral development characterized by the use of
popular conformity to work processes and/or adherence to externally imposed
standards. Managers who sustain this stage of collective moral development
are either admonishing employees to secure peer approval by "getting with the
program" or commanding them to comply with organizational hierarchy
and/or externally imposed regulations. *Collective integrity* is a molar stage of
moral development characterized by the use of democratic participation
and/or principled regard for others to determine moral standards. Managers
who sustain this stage of collective moral development are either surveying
majority trends or responding to the question, "What principled system is
worth multiple stakeholder ongoing commitment?" In effect, the cumulative
outcome of individual management development integrity over time forms the
group and organizational ethical work culture, which can either support or
inhibit collective commitment. Ethical work culture environments, in turn,
both reflect and influence the level of management developmental integrity
achieved. Collective work cultures support individual and group developmental integrity.

Collective commitment work cultures, however, emerge by design, not by
accident (Petrick, Scherer, & Claunch, 1991). System development skills of
managers are pivotal in creating a committed rather than a conniving or
conforming work culture. The infrastructure components needed for collective
commitment can be found in the Organization Ethics Development System
(OEDS) that is identified in Appendix E and consists of the following 16
components:

1. Moral leadership and ethical influence patterns
2. Ethical work culture and ethics needs assessments
3. Ethics in organizational strategy and structure
4. Ethics steering committee

 5. Formal statement of prioritized values and written codes of conduct (Manley, 1991)
 6. Ethics policy and procedure manuals
 7. Ethics in the human resource selection, socialization, and performance subsystems
 8. Ethics in human resource appraisal, reward/recognition/incentive, and development subsystems
 9. Ethics in formal and informal communication processes and work attitudes
 10. Ethics training and education programs
 11. Ethics in decision-making processes
 12. Ethics officer and/or delegated organizational ethics operational role responsibility
 13. Ethics reporting and conflict resolution processes
 14. Enforcement processes of ethical standards
 15. Ethics audit and evaluation subsystems
 16. Ethics system and work process control and improvement

The caliber of managerial system development skills determines the extent to which are the OEDS components implemented to build collective commitment. In turn, managers influence ongoing system improvement in such a way that collective moral progress or regression is in the hands of every manager.

In essence, managers will not achieve developmental integrity by merely controlling connivance or enforcing compliance of oneself or others (Petrick & Manning, 1990). The moral commitment required for developmental integrity entails a mind shift from manipulative self-interest patterns of conduct to a principled concern for others. Not only must managers become role models of healthy, moral altruism, but they must also develop similar helping patterns in work unit groups and the organization as a whole. To further clarify the extent of managerial responsibility for moral development at work, Figure 3.10 depicts the progression of *forms of managerial egoistic and altruistic conduct.* Figure 3.10 provides a guide based on helping or harming concerns that produce benefits or costs to oneself or others.

In the lower right quadrant of Figure 3.10, *vindictive/self-destructive egoism* is a prescriptive theory that is immoral because it intentionally harms both oneself and others; for example, homicide, which is now the leading cause of workplace death for women, is often due to spiteful, aggressive retaliation by workers toward perceived managerial violence (O'Leary-Kelly et al., 1996). The Biblical story of the Good Samaritan can illustrate the remaining distinc-

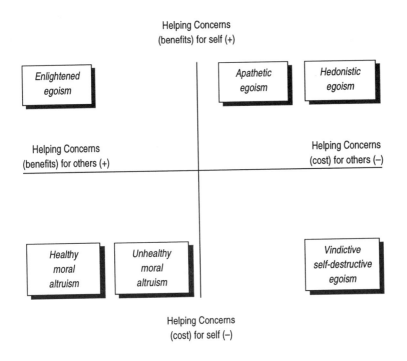

Figure 3.10. Forms of Managerial Egoistic and Altruistic Conduct

SOURCE: Kanungo and Mendonca (1996). Reprinted with permission.

tions between types of managerial egoism and altruism. In the upper right quadrant, *hedonistic egoism,* a prescriptive theory that maintains that maximizing personal pleasure or self-interest at the intentional expense of others is the highest good, is typified by the thieves who robbed the traveler for their own benefit and left the victim harmed on the roadside. This prescriptive theory endorses immorality by condoning pleasure seeking while intentionally inflicting harm on others. Managers who delight in abusing their power by firing employees with impunity in employment-at-will states are good examples. Also in the upper right quadrant, *apathetic egoism,* as the prescriptive theory that maintains that maximizing personal pleasure while being disinterested in the needs of others (not actively providing help or causing harm is the highest good) is typified by the conduct of the priest and the Levite who pass the victim by, absorbed in their own agendas. Apathetic egoism is a step beyond hedonistic egoism (though not highly commendable) and provides the moral minimum for ethical egoism. Managers who demonstrate legal, benign neglect of work problems are good examples. In the upper left quadrant, *enlightened egoism* is a prescriptive theory that maintains that helping others in a way that serves long-term, if not short-term, self-interest is the highest good. This type of egoism is illustrated in the conduct of the Biblical innkeeper story who helps the injured traveler only after being assured of compensation by the Good Samaritan. Managers who publicly contribute to community improvement projects in order to gain visibility for corporate citizenship behavior, which can be parlayed into future career advancement, are good examples. Next, *unhealthy moral altruism* is the prescriptive theory that maintains that helping others to the point of extreme self-sacrifice is the highest good—for example, women who sacrifice personal health to meet family wants or men who sacrifice personal health to workaholism. Managers who burn out at 50 because of overwork are good examples. Finally, *healthy moral altruism* is the prescriptive theory that maintains that helping others when it moderately harms oneself or involves moderate personal sacrifice is the highest good; it is typified by the conduct of the Good Samaritan himself. The shift from egoistic self-interest to principled concern for others signals the moral developmental maturity required of responsible managers with integrity.

In fact, *the best managers are corporate Good Samaritans who nurture Good Samaritan work habits in groups and nurture healthy, moral, altruistic patterns throughout the workplace.* These are two major moral development challenges for today's managers: demonstrating personal developmental integrity and building collective healthy, moral altruism work habits in a committed work culture.

The aggregate impact of simultaneously improving management judgment integrity (depth), management process integrity (breadth), and management developmental integrity (height) is to produce multidimensional moral progress. *Moral progress* is the increase in stakeholders who regularly demonstrate judgment, process, and developmental integrity domestically and globally. Although every person has some general obligation to promote moral progress, managers have special role responsibilities, unique opportunities, and effective tools to do so.

In addition to the management ethics tools already mentioned and contained in the appendices, the Qualitative Ethical Decision-Making Tool (QL-TOOL) in Appendix D is a comprehensive, systematically structured framework and checklist to operationalize management integrity. It incorporates all the dimensions of management integrity and all the steps in the ethics dialogue process, so its repeated use will promote both management integrity and moral progress.

SUMMARY

In summary, this chapter examine the three major dimensions of management integrity: judgment integrity, process integrity, and developmental integrity. By applying the management ethics tools and simultaneously cultivating all three dimensions, managers can promote personal integrity and collective moral progress. The remaining chapters of the book focus on the application of the theories and tools in the prior chapters to the functions of managerial practice: planning, orga-nizing, leading, and controlling with integrity.

▧ DISCUSSION/EXPERIENTIAL EXERCISES

Discussion Questions

1. Discuss the legal theory resource components of management judgment integrity.
2. Discuss the communication theory resource components of management judgment integrity.
3. Discuss the first three key steps and their subcomponents in management process integrity.
4. Discuss the last key factor (ethical conduct) and its subcomponents in management process integrity.
5. Discuss the stages of individual and collective moral development entailed in management developmental integrity.
6. Discuss Good Samaritan healthy moral altruism and implementation of the OEDS as important managerial integrity responsibilities.

Experiential Exercises

7. From your own life/work/school experiences, initiate an ethics proposal and, by using the ethics dialogue format in a group setting, employ rational arguments to arrive at an enacted ethics proposal.
8. Review your own current or past workplaces to determine the extent to which all 16 components of an OEDS were operational. Devise a plan and timetable for their implementation, being careful to anticipate and overcome resistance to their enactment.
9. Using the concepts from this chapter, examine with the entire class the dimensions of management integrity in the A. H. Robins minicase 7E.
10. Using the concepts from this chapter, examine in small groups the following minicases: 7D the Xieng case and Accent Discrimination and 4A Beverly Hills Savings & Loan.

PART II

Management Ethics and Integrity:
Practice and Minicases in the
Functions of Management

4

Management Ethics:
Planning With Integrity

Now that the theoretical first part of the book has been completed, the application of the theories and tools to planning, organizing, leading, and controlling takes place in Chapters 4 through 7 (Quinn, 1988). The focus of Chapter 4 is on three areas: (a) the dimensions of planning, (b) ethical planning processes that build integrity, and (c) management ethics and planning with integrity minicases. By addressing the ethical issues involved in the managerial function of planning and by applying those lessons to the analysis and resolution of planning minicases, skills in ethical planning can enhance management ethics and integrity.

▨ DIMENSIONS OF PLANNING

Planning is the intended, coordinated, emergent, and realized pattern of integrated, multidimensional decision processes and actions that provide organizational direction and prioritize objectives. It is the fundamental function on which all subsequent management functions (organizing, leading, and controlling) rely; that is, inadequate planning adversely affects all other management functions. Meritorious planning energizes stakeholders by enacting plans that

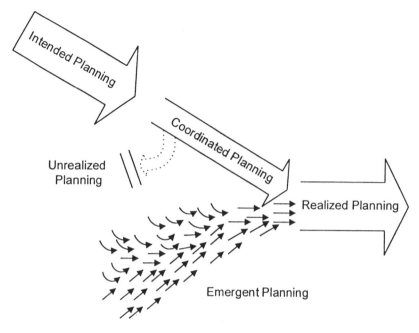

Figure 4.1. Dimensions of Planning

are expressly intended, efficiently coordinated, creatively responsive to emergent contingencies, and fully realized, as indicated in Figure 4.1.

Managers who generate and articulate a compelling vision of a desired organizational future that motivates stakeholders are involved in *intended planning*. Managers who realistically predict and arrange for proper allocation of resources to implement intended plans are engaged in *coordinated planning*. Managers who are open and responsive to unexpected events and critical planning feedback are involved in *emergent planning*. The outcome of the interaction among intended, coordinated, and emergent planning is realized and unrealized plans. *Realized plans* are fully implemented plans that incorporate the evolved patterns of the past, the expectations of the desired future, and the realistic constraints of the present. Managers who incorporate intended, coordinated, and emergent planning and analyze the historical precedents of "what worked" and "what didn't work" for organizations are engaged in *realized planning. Unrealized plans* are intended plans that never materialized because of a lack of coordinated resources or a lack of ability to respond to contingent emergencies or a lack of adequate follow-through. Among the realized plans, some are successful in that they ensure that the organization and its stakeholders survive and thrive; others are unsuccessful and become realized plans that adversely affect organizational and stakeholder performance.

Furthermore, *culpably negligent planning* includes any and all of the following: absence of explicitly intentional planning, inefficiently coordinated planning, planning that is rigidly unresponsive to emergent contingencies, inadequately realized planning, unintegrated patterns of planning processes and actions, and plans that provide unclear and unprioritized direction. The degree of moral culpability for negligent planning is dependent on the extent to which a manager could have and should have known or anticipated all the factors involved in the planning function (Petrick & Wagley, 1992).

There are two basic types of planning: tactical and strategic. *Tactical planning* is short-range (usually 1 year or less) planning that emphasizes current operations of various parts of the organization (e.g, annual production or marketing plans). Tactical plans in traditional firms are developed mainly by middle-level and lower-level managers or line associates and contain substantial amounts of factual detail based on information that is relatively easy to gather. *Strategic planning* is long-range (more than 1 year) planning that focuses on the existence and prospects of the organization as a whole (e.g., 5- or 10-year plans for the organizational future). Strategic plans in traditional firms are developed mainly by upper-level managers, contain relatively little factual detail, and are based on information that is relatively difficult to gather.

The embodiment and end result of strategic planning is *strategy*, which directs the long-range emphasis of managerial activity toward handling organizational strengths and weaknesses in order to address opportunities and threats in the external and internal environments. Strategy occurs at four levels: enterprise, corporate, business, and functional levels. *Enterprise-level strategy*, the broadest level of strategy, identifies the organization's role in the world and specifies the purposes and values upon which the firm stands—that is, addresses the question of why this organization needs to exist at all (Freeman, 1984; Freeman & Gilbert, 1988). *Corporate-level strategy* focuses on the scope, mix, and emphasis among existing businesses in order to determine growth, stability, or retrenchment options and prioritized allocation of resources to existing or new business—that is, addresses the question of what business the stakeholders are in. *Business-level strategy* deals with how the organization intends to compete in a specific business, what the role of each key functional area will be in supporting that business, and resource allocation within the business unit—that is, addresses the question of how the stakeholders will compete in a selected business. *Functional-level strategy* explicitly focuses on how each major subactivity and operation in each functional area (production, operations, R&D, information systems, finance, accounting, marketing, human resources, public relations) contributes to accomplishing the business strategy—that is, addresses the question of what the stakeholders will do in each functional unit to contribute to business strategy success. These different levels of strategy need to be mutually reinforcing to be effective guides for external adaptation and sufficiently delineated to be efficient guides for internal integration.

The dynamics of strategy development may vary among the following approaches: the top-down, bottom-up, and interactive approaches. The *top-down approach,* in which upper-level managers generate vision and initiate strategy formulation, expecting subordinates to implement corporate-level strategies, is typical of traditional, bureaucratic organizations (e.g., Maytag). The *bottom-up approach,* in which strategy formulation is initiated by the voices of business or functional unit profit centers and transmitted up to top managers for comment, is typical of decentralized organizations (e.g., the Bechtel Group). Finally, the *interactive approach,* in which strategy formulation is the result of shared vision and voices from all levels encouraging egalitarian, respectful exchanges from all stakeholders, is typical of Baldrige Award winning total quality (TQ) organizations (e.g., Motorola).

In effect, planning in traditional and TQ organizations differs not only in terms of the source of strategy generation but also in the following areas:

- Traditional firms accord financial performance top priority as a planning objective, whereas TQ firms accord increased market share top priority and view financial goals as outcomes of sustained customer satisfaction.
- Traditional firms expect compliance with top-level directives and regard factual, critical, lower-level planning feedback as indications of insubordination requiring sanctions, whereas TQ firms respect and reward the challenging voices of factually based, critical feedback in order to continuously improve acceptable variation within the planning process.
- Traditional firms grant access to planning information only on a "need to know" basis and thereby guard the information power base of top managers, whereas

Intended Plan Realized

		Yes	No
Realized Plan Successful	Yes	Coordinated Planning Success (*Efficient and Effective*) [A]	Emergent Planning Success (*Inefficient but Effective*) [C]
	No	Realized Plan Failure (*Efficient but Not Effective*) [B]	Complete Planning Failure (*Inefficient and Ineffective*) [D]

Figure 4.2. Planning Success Evaluation Matrix

> TQ firms share planning information widely to empower and leverage the collective planning feedback of all stakeholders (Lindsay & Petrick, 1997; Petrick & Furr, 1995).

In effect, determining the roles of people and processes is crucial in arriving at sound managerial planning.

To evaluate the efficiency and effectiveness of the dimensions of planning, Figure 4.2 provides a matrix based on two questions: "Was the intended plan successfully realized?" and "Did the realized plan successfully promote organizational performance?"

In Figure 4.2, the Planning Success Evaluation Matrix contains four combinations. A yes-yes designation (in Quadrant A) means that the intended, coordinated planning was successful and fully meritorious: Managers set out to do something, they did it efficiently, and the plan effectively worked. A yes-no designation (in Quadrant B) points toward a realized plan failure in which managers efficiently implemented an intended plan, which itself was only partially meritorious because that plan proved to be ineffective. A no-yes designation (in Quadrant C) points toward inefficient implementation of the intended plan but an effective emergent plan; for example, an unintended and unanticipated plan emerges that happens to be effective and is thereby partially meritorious. A no-no designation (in Quadrant D) indicates a complete failure in planning because of inefficient implementation of the intended plan and ineffective outcomes.

Now that the dimensions and success standards of planning have been treated, it is important to address the relationship of ethical planning processes to building integrity.

▧ ETHICAL PLANNING PROCESSES THAT BUILD INTEGRITY

All the dimensions of integrity—judgment, process, and developmental—are important in managerial planning with integrity. Whereas the developmental and judgment dimensions anchor and sustain planning with integrity, the process dimension builds planning with integrity.

To plan in a fully meritorious manner, therefore, some form of systematic planning process must be used (Mintzberg, 1994). The following four-step sequence of responsible planning provides a generic model of the planning subprocess and their associated developmental tasks:

1. *Planning Scanning:* planning awareness through environmental scanning of current external and internal factors by using future forecasting, surveying, and benchmarking tools to develop stakeholder voice

2. *Planning Formulation and Choice:* planning formulation, analysis, and choice through development of the vision of a desired future; gap analysis between current rhetoric and reality; mission statement with prioritized, quantified objectives and prioritized, qualitative goals; analysis of planning action options; and resolution of planning choice by using various matching tools to judge alternatives and endorsement of a justified course of action that will develop organizational processes for resource alignment

3. *Planning Implementation:* selected plan implementation to coordinate organizational readiness to act through intentional enactment of policies, processes, procedures, rules, programs, projects, and personal/unit performance standards by using scheduling, budgeting, team building, project management, and organizational character/health assessment tools

4. *Planning Evaluation, Control, and Improvement:* evaluation, control, and improvement of the results and impact of the selected plan by using a variety of measures, standards, audits, causal analyses, acceptable process variation assessments, improvement techniques, and feedback information tools to ensure organizational performance according to plan and sustained reputation development (Ansoff, 1988; Bounds, Dobbins, & Fowler, 1995; Certo, 1994; Pearce & Robinson, 1994; Quinn & Mintzberg, 1996; Wheelen & Hunger, 1992)

Each step in the generic planning process must be adequately completed to produce a successful plan that is both effective and efficient.

The four process integrity steps parallel and permeate the four steps in the generic subprocesses of planning (planning scanning, planning formulation

Processes	Step 1	Step 2	Step 3	Step 4
Ethics processes	Ethical Awareness	Ethical Judgment	Ethical Intention	Ethical Conduct
Planning subprocesses	Planning Scanning	Planning Formulation and Choice	Planning Implementation	Planning Evaluation, Control, and Improvement

Figure 4.3. Parallel Ethics and Planning Subprocesses That Build Management Integrity

and choice, planning implementation, and planning evaluation, control, and improvement). In other words, *planning with ethical integrity means addressing the elements of the four ethics processes in the context of their parallel planning subprocesses to ensure that no step in the planning function neglects its moral dimension.* Managers may lack integrity in planning by neglecting to adequately perform the substasks entailed in ethics and planning processes, thereby exposing themselves and their organizations to ethical risk (see Chapter 1). Planning with ethical integrity is facilitated by using the appropriate systematic queries from the QL-TOOL in Appendix D for each corresponding step of the generic planning process. Figure 4.3 depicts the inclusive and sequential alignment of all ethics processes and planning subprocesses that build management integrity.

Ethical Planning Scanning

With regard to the alignment of ethics and planning processes in Step 1, the scope of ethical planning scanning includes strategic stakeholder benchmarking of best practices in the global and domestic, external and internal organizational environment, specified in detail in queries 1, 2, and 3 from the QL-TOOL (external ecological, technological, economic, legal, sociocultural, and political factors and internal organizational ethics development system [OEDS] factors). Ethical planning scanning is achieved when the two elements of the ethical awareness process (perception and sensitivity) are adequately addressed by responses to queries 1, 2, and 3 of the QL-TOOL. Misperception of and insensitivity to external and internal stakeholders results in culpably negligent unethical planning scanning.

Exxon Corporation Managers and
Unethical Planning Scanning

For example, Exxon's perception of and insensitivity to the natural environment and the human stakeholders in its oil transport business has been morally and legally sanctioned. In 1989, the oil spill from the grounded *Exxon Valdez* tanker killed thousands of plants and animals, severely damaged the Alaskan fishing and tourist industries, polluted Native American lands, and altered the ecosystem of Prince William Sound for years to come. Although Exxon was indicted on violations of U.S. maritime safety and antipollution laws, the ultimate naval responsibility resides in unethical corporate boardroom policy decisions that trivialized safety and ecological concerns(Gini, 1996; Pierce, 1991; Schwartz, 1990; Sejersted, 1996; Wilson, 1996). Again, in 1990, another Exxon oil spill of 567,000 gallons of heating oil occurred off the coast of New York City from a burst pipeline. Government officials cited shoddy equipment and poor maintenance as contributing factors to the oil spill. Albert Appleton, New York City commissioner on the environment, said: "Exxon has a corporate philosophy that the environment is some kind of nuisance problem and a distraction from the real business of moving oil around." If Exxon corporate planners fail to benchmark, to perceive and be sensitive to nature and human stakeholder concerns, they incur legal, financial, and moral culpability.

The type of moral attention deficit disorder exposed by these Exxon incidents can be overcome by accurate perception of and appropriate sensitivity to natural and human stakeholders. To achieve that level of perception and sensitivity, regular, careful responses to queries 1 and 2 from the QL-TOOL are required prior to disasters. This means that training focused on developing moral attention, cognitive organization, and interpretation of ethical situations can improve ethical perception by eliminating "moral blind spots" from the planning scanning step. Similarly, developing the natural moral feelings of empathy, sympathy, moderation, and indignation can overcome planning callousness and/or affected ignorance and, thereby, improve ethical sensitivity to current or anticipated concerns—prior to disasters that require crisis management. The accumulated moral experience and legal precedents regarding ethical planning provide new organizational performance standards and information search guidelines when forecasting, benchmarking, and feedback survey tools are designed to solicit stakeholder input.

The contrast in planning perceptions and sensitivities between the Exxon code of ethics and the Johnson & Johnson code of ethics reveals opportunities

Summary Code of Ethics of Exxon Company, USA

Business Ethics
Our Company policy is one of strict observance of all laws applicable to its business.
A reputation for scrupulous dealing is itself a priceless Company asset.
We do care how we get results.
We expect candor at all levels and compliance with accounting rules and controls.

Antitrust
It is the established policy of the Company to conduct its business in compliance with all state and federal antitrust laws.
Individual employees are responsible for seeing that they comply with the law.
Employees must avoid even the appearance of violation.

Conflict of Interest
Competing or conducting business with the Company is not permitted, except with the knowledge and consent of management.
Accepting and providing gifts, entertainment, and services must comply with specific requirements.
An employee may not use Company personnel, information, or other assets for personal benefit.
Participating in certain outside activities requires the prior approval of management.

Figure 4.4. Exxon Summary Code of Ethics. Used with permission.

for improving ethical planning in the way Exxon conducts its business. In Figure 4.4, the Exxon code of ethics recommends that employees obey the law, be financially honest, and avoid conflicts of interest. The code makes no mention of worker safety, environmental protection, customer service, community concern, distributor loyalty, or prioritized responsibilities to guide decision making in crisis situations. This code represents a compliance approach to managerial responsibility, as indicated in Chapter 3.

The contrast with the Johnson & Johnson credo in Figure 4.5 is particularly revealing because the latter's credo lists, in order of priority, responsibilities to external customers, employees, communities, the natural environment, and investors. When the Tylenol tampering occurred in 1982, Johnson & Johnson managers placed the welfare of their customers, employees, and society above profits for their investors. Former CEO James Burke credited the credo for enhancing moral awareness and providing value prioritization guidance for uniform, principled, global sensitivities in corporate decision making. In effect, the presence of an organizational moral filter that scanned perceptions and sensitivities provided managers with the necessary frame of reference to exer-

Johnson & Johnson Credo

We believe our first responsibility is to the doctors, nurses, and patients,
to mothers and fathers and all others who use our products and services.
In meeting their needs, everything we do must be of high quality.
We must constantly strive to reduce our costs
in order to maintain reasonable prices.
Customers' orders must be serviced promptly and accurately.
Our suppliers and distributors must have an opportunity
to make a fair profit.

We are responsible to our employees,
the men and women who work with us throughout the world.
Everyone must be considered as an individual.
We must respect their dignity and recognize their merit.
They must have a sense of security in their jobs.
Compensation must be fair and adequate,
and working conditions clean, orderly, and safe.
We must be mindful of ways to help our employees fulfill
their family responsibilities.
Employees must feel free to make suggestions and complaints.
There must be equal opportunity for employment, development,
and advancement for those qualified.
We must provide competent management,
and their actions must be just and ethical.

We are responsible to the communities in which we live and work
and to the world community as well.
We must be good citizens—support good works and charities
and bear our fair share of taxes.
We must encourage civic improvements and better health and education.
We must maintain in good order
the property we are privileged to use,
protecting the environment and natural resources.

Our final responsibility is to our stockholders.
Business must make a sound profit.
We must experiment with new ideas.
Research must be carried on, innovative programs developed,
and mistakes paid for.
New equipment must be purchased, new facilities provided,
and new products launched.
Reserves must be created to provide for adverse times.
When we operate according to these principles,
the stockholders should realize a fair return.

Figure 4.5. Johnson & Johnson Credo. Used with permission.

cise responsible judgment. Strikingly absent from Exxon's corporate summary code of ethics are the broad stakeholder perceptions and prioritized sensitivities necessary for an integrity approach to managerial responsibility, as indicated in Chapter 2. Not surprisingly, the public outrage against Exxon management in the Exxon Valdez disaster was in stark contrast to the public adulation for Johnson & Johnson management in the Tylenol poisonings.

Ethical Planning Formulation and Choice

With regard to the alignment of ethics processes and planning subprocesses in Step 2 (in Figure 4.3), the scope of ethical planning formulation and choice includes factors in the global and domestic, external and internal organizational context and judgment, specified in query in the QL-TOOL (supportive external and internal contexts for optimal ethical analysis and resolution in demonstrating judgment integrity). Ethical planning formulation and choice is achieved when the two elements of the ethical judgment process (analysis and resolution) are adequately addressed by responses to query of the QL-TOOL. Lack of thorough, multidisciplinary ethical analysis precludes structured moral dialogue to arrive at balanced, justified resolution of ethically framed issues and results in unethical planning formulation and choice.

Ford Motor Company Managers and
Unethical Planning Formulation and Choice

For example, Ford's analysis and resolution of product safety in the Pinto case has been morally and legally sanctioned. In 1968, Ford formulated a planning strategy to design a fuel-efficient, inexpensive subcompact automobile to respond to global competition and rapidly produced the Pinto within 2 years. Multiple product safety design problems with the Pinto surfaced during the testing, inspection, and production (faulty fuel tank design, "uncrashworthy" rear bumper, and lack of reinforced longitudinal and horizontal rear cross-members all contributed to a less crash-resistant vehicle than other competitors provided) but were discounted by top management, represented by Lee Iacocca, who promoted the production, sale, and distribution of the Pinto in the 1970s. Management used two primary justifications: (a) Safety doesn't sell (U.S. consumers are more concerned with style and trunk space than with vehicle susceptibility to explosion in rear-end collisions); and (b) using a cost-benefit analysis (assuming 1971 fatality costs of $200,725 per person), the costs of recalling and repairing Pinto safety problems would total around $137 million, whereas the computed benefits of safety improvements that would have prevented 180 deaths, 180 injuries, and 2,100 burned vehicles only totaled around $49 million. Because the financial costs of recall outweighed the financial benefits of preventing future harm by almost three times, financial utility dictated the strategic choice to continue selling Pintos.

The type of error in moral judgment displayed in handling the Ford Pinto fire cases can be overcome by thorough ethical analysis and adequately justified ethical resolution of issues undertaken in a well-developed, principled ethical work culture. To achieve these analysis and resolution outcomes, ethical dialogue among diverse stakeholders must first take place in response to query from the QL-TOOL. Next, a justified resolution of an issue must evidence a weighted consideration of all four ethics theories, as well as their cognate resources (management, communication, and legal theories). Finally, the ethical work culture within which dialogue and resolution occur must have infrastructure components (ethics reporting and conflict resolution processes, enforcement processes of ethical standards) that will anchor judgment integrity. The absence of any or all of these ingredients precludes sound ethical judgment over time.

In the Pinto case, one of the Ford recall coordinators, Dennis Gioia, admitted to moral judgment failure because of acceding to personal script processing, organizational cultural role pressures, and exclusive overreliance on cost-benefit justifications (Gioia, 1992). *Script processing* is a cognitive shortcut for simplifying information overload to facilitate efficient understanding and action. The script processing adopted by Gioia reduced the capacity for personal, group, and organizational ethics dialogue because unscripted information was never accorded priority in Ford's recall decision; that is, safety factors were never the highest priority in recall decisions, or in other words, they never got off second base in the ethics dialogue. In large part, Ford's work culture context, as a collection of scripts, shaped Gioia's role perceptions and judgments to conform to the corporate cost-benefit rationale that justified not recalling Pintos and was not open to qualification from opposing views.

To correct these managerial judgment deficiencies, several steps need to be taken:

1. Select, empower, and reward managers who evidence personal integrity and sound moral judgment (integrity testing and moral commendation ceremonies), the capacity for ethics dialogue, and the ability to arrive at sound

judgments only after systematically considering all relevant ethics and cognate theories.

2. Train and develop persons to move beyond script processing, automatic role behavior, and narrow theoretical consistency toward judgment integrity that encompasses and weights all the ethics and cognate theories to resolve work issues responsibly.

3. Enact components of the OEDS to arrive at a principled work culture as soon as possible, in which the process and outcome of principled ethical decision making is supported by the organizational infrastructure and collective performance norms.

Ethical Planning Implementation

With regard to the alignment of ethics processes and planning subprocesses in Step 3 (in Figure 4.3), the extent of ethical planning implementation can be determined by fully addressing queries 5, 6, and 9 from the QL-TOOL (Galbraith & Kazanjian, 1986; Hambrick & Cannella, 1989). Ethical planning implementation is achieved when the two elements of the ethical intention process (cognitive and volitional readiness to act) are demonstrated by responses to queries 5, 6, and 9 of the QL-TOOL. Obviously, poor implementation of a rationally formulated plan can result in planning and moral failure (Wheelen & Hunger, 1992). Less obviously, refusal to consider feedback to modify originally formulated plans in light of operational experience or to replace the intended plan with a more feasible, emergent one is also a planning and moral failure. Managers may tend to underestimate potential risks because of an optimistic illusion of control, may tend to believe that they are less susceptible to risks than others because of an arrogant illusion of invulnerability, and/or may tend to ignore/devalue negative planning implementation feedback because of an irrational escalation of commitment to the originally formulated plan (Bazerman, 1994; Messick & Bazerman, 1994).

Deceptive Downsizing by Managers and
Unethical Planning Implementation

For example, the recent American Management Association (AMA) and Wyatt and Company research studies on downsizing at more than 1,500 firms have reported that two thirds of the companies that laid off also reported hiring new employees in other areas and that most laid-off positions were refilled within 2 years (Downs, 1995; Tomasko, 1990). This planning implementation process is a type of immoderate, binge-and-purge addiction that was begun in earnest in the United States in the 1980s and widely used up to the present (Knowdell, Branstead, & Moravec, 1994; Olmstead & Smith, 1994). As selected managers, employees, and communities experience the accumulated adverse impact of binge-and-purge downsizings that reveal unwise planning implementation, their readiness to act virtuously and out of organizational loyalty is eroded. Even the survivors of downsizings go through a grieving process (Knowdell et al., 1994; Noer, 1993). An anti-risk-taking environment can permeate the work setting after downsizing, further debilitating an organization from successfully and collaboratively adapting to new, critical market changes. Managers may not vividly imagine a preferred future or engage in level-headed, prudent human resource planning, but rely on arrogance, greed, resentment, distrust, inhumane toughness, incivility, dishonesty, ingratitude, and injustice in implementing plans, which inevitably reduce the cognitive and volitional readiness of the organization to act with integrity. In effect, organizational character is undermined because *organizational self-respect*, the collective pride in the way the business is managed and its people treated, is diminished. The outcome is organizations unable to respond constructively to external challenges or internal initiatives; that is, sluggish response demonstrates the weakness of will of a discouraged workforce. This erosion of organizational character is exacerbated by deceptive downsizing practices (as indicated in Table 4.1) and expanded reliance on temporary, leased, and outsourced employees (Ettorre, 1994; Feldman, Dolipinghaus, & Turnley, 1994).

The loss of the readiness to act with integrity exposed by deceptive and/or quick-profit-at-any-cost downsizing practices can be overcome by sustained management and organization character development. To achieve that level of cognitive and volitional readiness to act, regular, careful responses to queries 5, 6, and 9 from the QL-TOOL are required. Specifically, the cultivation of cognitive virtues (practical wisdom to envision controlled growth that avoids binge-and-purge extremes) and volitional virtues (the emotional virtues of joy in moderate pride and acquisitiveness; the social virtues of humane toughness, openness, and civility; and the moral virtues of courage, justice, trustworthiness, honesty, and gratitude) are paramount in times of downsizing to sustain organizational character.

To correct these organizational character deficiencies in the context of downsizing, several steps need to be taken to enact wiser controlled growth of human resources:

Table 4.1 Deceptive Downsizing Management Techniques That Erode
Organizational Character

Bait and Switch

1. Promise the employee a newly created, more desirable position.
2. Replace the employee in his or her current job.
3. Fail to get funding for the new position, change the position to something much less than promised, or eliminate the new position before it ever really gets started.

Raise the Bar

1. Raise the performance standards of the job to a level that may exceed the skills of the employee.
2. Promise the employee support and resources to meet the new standards.
3. Have the employee agree to the new standards in writing.
4. Fail to deliver the promised help.
5. Severely decrease the employee's performance rating/pay.
6. Encourage the employee to quit before getting fired/fire the employee for inadequate performance.

Reorganize

1. Redistribute the workload among employees in a manner that eliminates a job by dividing up its duties among other positions.
2. Lay off the "extra" employee.
3. After a brief period, hire another employee to take on tasks that were displaced when other employees took on the tasks of the employee previously laid off; or after a year or so, return to the old organization and rehire for the position previously eliminated.

Do Nothing, Please

1. Create a new position that has seemingly reasonable expectations but cannot be met because of hidden factors (factors that are preferably in control of the manager); or make the employee dependent on the work of two other employees who can never agree or get along.
2. Severely reduce the performance rating/merit pay of the employee.
3. Encourage the employee to quit before getting fired/fire the employee for inadequate performance.

Cut Benefits

1. Reduce or eliminate the employee's benefit package. This is particularly effective with single parents who rely heavily on company-sponsored health care benefits.
2. Wait for the employee to quit.

Rescope the Job

1. Have the human resources dependent analyze the job (based heavily on your input).
2. When the decision is made to lower the pay scale for the job, have the employee "red-lined" so that he or she won't be eligible for pay raises for the foreseeable future.

(continued)

Table 4.1 Continued

Boss From Hell

1. Move the employee to a position under a boss who is known to be impossible.
2. Privately feed the new boss your concerns about the employee's performance and ability to do the job.
3. Wait for the blowup.

Slow Death

1. Consistently reinterpret everything the employee does as mediocre or inferior.
2. Reward other employees in the department for equivalent performance.
3. Wait for the employee to quit.

Early Retirement

1. Strongly urge that the employee take early retirement.
2. Blame the situation on another executive who "has it out" for the employee.
3. Tell the employee, "Get out while you can still get something."

Behind Closed Doors (Threats)

1. Privately threaten the employee with an impending firing if he or she doesn't quit.
2. Tell the employee you are providing an opportunity to avoid a bad mark on his or her record. If the person doesn't quit, it will only be a matter of time before he or she is fired.
3. Wait for the employee to quit.

Total Withdrawal

1. Completely withdraw from the employee. Refuse all meetings.
2. Withhold critical information that the employee needs for success.
3. Wait for the employee to quit.

Dead-End Contract

1. Convince the employee of the benefits of becoming an external contractor (e.g., work at home, set your own hours, make more money, work for many companies).
2. Promise to hire the person for all the work he or she does now.
3. Once the employee resigns permanent employment status, fail to return phone calls, never sign a contract, never hire him or her for work.

SOURCE: Excerpted by permission of the publisher, from COrporate EXecutions © 1995 Alan Downs. Published by AMACOM, a division of American Management Association. All rights reserved.

1. Question the planning assumptions of reduction at any cost because lean and mean is not always effective, is often character eroding, and if carried to extreme, can preclude organizational renewal because of corporate anorexia.
2. Flatten the organizational pyramid by enacting TQ processes and projects for eliciting necessary, corrective, factual feedback and for protecting emergent

planning recommendations about alternative employment changes from adversely impacted employees (Petrick & Furr, 1995).

3. Clarify and expect virtuous norms for individual, group, and organizational character development so that programs, procedures, and/or budgets that reduce work pride and organizational self-respect are eschewed.

Management plans that disrespect associates by deceptive downsizing methods erode managerial and organizational character and thereby the collective readiness to act successfully and with integrity in the future.

Ethical Planning Evaluation, Control, and Improvement

With regard to the alignment of ethics processes and planning subprocesses in Step 4 (in Figure 4.3), the scope of ethical planning evaluation, control, and improvement includes stakeholder conduct and reputation in the global and domestic, external and internal organizational environments, specified in detail in queries 7, 8, and 10 from the QL-TOOL (extent to which responsible ecological, economic, ethical, legal, and philanthropic conduct anchors and builds reputations for integrity). Ethical planning evaluation, control, and improvement are achieved when the two elements of the ethical conduct process (responsible responsiveness and sustainable development) are adequately addressed by responses to queries 7, 8, and 10 of the QL-TOOL. Responsible responsiveness and sustainable development contribute to ethical planning evaluation, control, and improvement at the domestic and global levels.

E. I. DuPont de Nemours's Managers and
Ethical Evaluation, Control, and Improvement

For example, DuPont's handling of chlorofluorocarbons (CFCs) and global ozone depletion demonstrated a shift in corporate conduct from nonsustainable development by resisting CFC regulation to collaborative, sustainable development as industry market leader by developing reliable substitute products that avoid or minimize harmful ozone depletion (Reinhardt & Vietor, 1996). DuPont was the world's largest manufacturer of CFCs used worldwide in aerosols, air-conditioning, solvents, insulation, and refrigerants when the CFC-ozone depletion connection was raised in the 1970s. The ozone layer in the earth's stratosphere absorbs most of the harmful ultraviolet (UV) radiation from the sun, and its depletion allows excess UV radiation to damage or kill plant and animal cells, cause skin cancer and eye cataracts in humans, reduce crop yields, and reduce biodiversity. At first, DuPont opposed CFC regulation because of scientific uncertainty, but the issuance of the NASA Executive Summary Report in the late 1980s, which presented hard evidence linking CFCs to ozone depletion, caused the company to reassess its position. In 1987, the International Montreal Protocol was signed by 24 nations; this agreement sought to phase out emissions of ozone-depleting substances, such as CFCs, by 1999. In 1991, however, DuPont, as market leader, unilaterally announced plans to phase out all CFC production by 1996 (long before governmental or intergovernmental requirements) and, in the mid-1990s, to open world-scale plants that create and manufacture a reliable substitute compound called hydrofluorcarbons (HFCs), which have no potential to delete the ozone layer (Boyhan, 1992). By evaluating negative feedback about its CFC products and setting tough product change targets ahead of regulatory requirements, DuPont's industry and public reputation have been enhanced significantly in both the domestic and global communities.

The cost of complying with and/or accelerating the pace at which the Montreal Protocol is implemented is exacerbated for DuPont by the conflicting evaluations of and modifications to the CFC issue provided by more developed countries (MDCs) from the North and less developed countries (LDCs) from the South (Dove, 1994). For instance, LDCs like India and China, with enormous growing populations, prefer to use less costly, ozone-depleting, CFC-based products to promote current economic development rapidly, rather than emphasize future environmental protection. In India, the number of CFC-based refrigerants is projected to reach 80 billion units by the year 2010, up from 6 billion in 1989 (Touche Ross Management Consultants, 1990). China, meanwhile, with its gigantic economic boom and 1.2 billion people, is producing nearly 10 billion CFC-based refrigerants a year, and a 1990 survey showed that half of all government officials in China did know what ozone or CFCs were (Tobias, 1994). Because of the asynchronous development of the North (MDCs) and the South (LDCs), with the former having historically preceded the latter in technological development, the problem evaluation, temporal control emphasis, and improvement solution to the CFC issue varies, as indicated in Figure 4.6.

The CFC problem evaluation is based on the asynchronous development of the North (MDCs) and the South (LDCs). The North, on the one hand, evaluates the CFC issue as primarily one of environmental preservation, technological challenge, and protection from Southern greed because of ever-

CFC Issue	North (MDCs)	South (LDCs)
Problem Evaluation	-Environmental preservation -Protection from Southern envy -Technological mastery	-Economic development -Protection from Northern hegemony -Environmental colonialism
Temporal Control Emphasis	-Control future threat -Control any addition to problem -Control by avoiding past environmental mistakes	-Control past damage -Control cumulative problem -Control by repeating past economic success of the North
Improvement Solution	-Eliminate CFC production for future generations -Grand use of costly substitutes as reality permits -Global environmental accords	-Expand cheap CFC purification for current generations -Avoid costly substitutes as overpopulation requires -Structural change in global economy

Figure 4.6. Differences Between North and South CFC Planning Evaluation, Control, and Improvement

increasing overpopulation. The South, on the other hand, evaluates the CFC issue as primarily one of environmental colonialism, wherein LDCs need protection from Northern hegemony, which is attempting to constrain the South's rapid economic progress (Agarwal & Narain, 1991; Brookfield, 1992). Again, the North's temporal control emphasis with regard to CFCs is to focus on eliminating future CFC threats, reducing any addition to the current problem and avoiding past environmental mistakes. The South, however, focuses on retribution and compensation for past damages from Northern CFC-based production, control only of the CFC problem created in the South up to this point, with the right of economic self-determination to repeat the material successes of the North. Finally, the North's improvement solution is to eliminate CFC production to protect future generations, to leverage its wealth by expanding the design and use of costly, reliable substitutes, and to extend global environmental accords to stabilize future markets. In contrast, the South's improvement solution is a radical structural change in the global economy to redistribute developmental disparities between the two hemispheres and to expand cheap production of CFC-based products for widespread consumption by current generations, thereby avoiding unaffordable, costly substitutes or further delayed gratification.

Because the North-South conflict regarding CFCs requires planned, controlled growth to meet the needs of present and future generations, DuPont and other private and public organizations need to learn from different perspectives and to work in a committed consensus to a feasible timeline for reducing developmental disparities. Essentially, this is the approach of sustainable development in which collaborative partnership among ecological, economic, biological, and sociocultural spheres provide the framework for responsible and respectful relationships between MDCs and LDCs. How well DuPont constructs its network of global agreements for sustainable development will be a barometer of its reputation for integrity with regard to the CFC issue.

Ethical conduct and managerial reputation development are strengthened through ethical planning evaluation, control, and improvement. Managers with a reputation for responsible and sustainable planning are more likely to set higher standards of moral performance domestically and globally.

▧ MANAGEMENT ETHICS AND PLANNING WITH INTEGRITY MINICASES

To apply management ethical decision making and plan with integrity, the following minicases are offered for practice analysis by students, practicing managers, consultants, business ethicists, educators, government officials, and/or average citizens. Because the broad domain of management includes private, public, and nonprofit sectors in the domestic and global arenas in a wide variety of applied areas (e.g., accounting managers, marketing managers, finance managers, corporate managers, small business managers, information system managers, human resource managers, public administrators, nonprofit managers, health care administrators, environmental managers, international managers, and quality managers), the practical development of management integrity requires minicases in many settings. These minicases raise issues in management ethics and planning with integrity in many areas of management practice and are organized around seven allied management application clusters:

1. Accounting/auditing issues
2. Finance/investment issues
3. Marketing/advertising issues
4. Business management/human resources/business law issues

5. Technology/quality operations/organizational behavior issues
6. Public/nonprofit/health care administration issues
7. International/environmental/public policy issues

These clusters are generic categories, and specific cases in any one chapter may not cover all subfields in the cluster, but at least one minicase in Chapters 4 through 7 addresses each subfield in the cluster. Of the 18 subfields contained in the seven clusters, 28 minicases are provided, ensuring that each subfield is addressed at least once and that overlapping interfield problems are included. (See Table 1: Minicases, Management Functions, and Allied Management Application Clusters [p. x] for a graphic overview of all 28 minicases by management function and application cluster.)

In addition to the minicases presented in this text, the authors have used, cited material from, and recommend a range of ethics casebooks, including the following:

Paine, L. S. (1997). *Cases in leadership, ethics, and organizational integrity.* Burr Ridge, IL: Irwin.

Jennings, M. M. (1996). *Case studies in business ethics.* St. Paul, MN: West.

Boatright, J. R. (1995). *Cases in ethics and the conduct of business.* Upper Saddle River, NJ: Prentice Hall.

Donaldson, T., & Gini, A. (1994). *Case studies in business ethics.* New York: Oxford University Press.

Driscoll, D. M., Hoffman, W. M., & Petry, E. (1995). *The ethical edge: Tales of organizations that have faced moral crises.* New York: Master Media.

Hosmer, L. T. (1994). *Moral leadership in business.* Burr Ridge, IL: Irwin.

Newton, L., & Schmidt, D. (1996). *Wake-up calls: Classic cases in business ethics.* Belmont, CA: Wadsworth.

In addition to the immediate relevance and direct application that these minicases offer, they also can indirectly supplement the normative theoretical approaches of business ethicists from the humanities (philosophers and theologians), the descriptive theoretical approaches of business ethicists from the human sciences (psychologists, political scientists, anthropologists, and sociologists), the professional standards' approaches of industry/trade/ professional associations (lawyers, engineers, accountants, industry and trade officials, the Academy of Management, and other business professional associations), and the instructional/training approaches of management, organizational behavior and public administration professors, as well as corporate trainers.

To incorporate the tools and resources of this book to analyze and resolve planning issues with integrity, the authors recommend that each minicase be approached with three objectives in mind:

1. Systematically apply the QL-TOOL, in an individual or collective setting, to arrive at a principled, feasible resolution.
2. In accomplishing the first objective, consciously engage in ethics dialogue as the guiding method of moral discourse.
3. Select the appropriate components of the OEDS (in Appendix E) and other tools in the appendices that would cultivate, build, and/or sustain dimensions of management integrity in the future.

(1) Accounting/Auditing Minicase: (Case 4A) - Beverly Hills Savings & Loan

In 1988, of the nation's 3,178 so-called thrift institutions, 503 were insolvent (Hartley, 1994). Another 629 had less capital on their books than regulators usually require. In 1987, 630 thrifts had lost an estimated $7.5 billion, half again as much as the earnings of all the rest combined. Most of the "terminal" S&Ls got into trouble making risky loans; while fraud also contributed to the failures of nearly 50. More than half of the troubled thrifts were in Texas, thrifts in other states were also crashing. Beverly Hills Savings and Loan (BHSL) in California, which had much of its $2.9 billion in assets invested in dicey real estate ventures and junk bonds, closed in 1985, leaving taxpayers to foot the bill for managerial and auditing incompetence.

By early 1989, the Federal Home Loan Bank Board (FHLBB) had suits pending against a number of auditors, including the future merger partners Deloitte Haskins & Sells and Touche Ross. In many ways, the Touche Ross case, involving the audit of BHSL, reflected in microcosm the reckless practices of the thrift industry and the alleged role of the big accounting firms in the emergence of this national scandal.

The roots of the episode date back a half century to the founding of BHSL as a federal savings and loan association. For the first 44 years of its existence, the thrift operated in the tried-and-true S&L format, taking deposits and using the proceeds to make standard mortgage loans. It was a reliable, steady-as-you-go business. All of this changed abruptly in 1980, when BHSL, which in 1979 had converted to a state-chartered association, embarked on an aggressive campaign to achieve rapid growth.

Before the FHLBB seized and closed down BHSL in 1985, it had gone through three of the future Big Six public accounting firms—Touche Ross, Ernst & Whinney, and Coopers & Lybrand—and had a negative net worth of approximately $65 million. The specific causes for the decline included (a) imprudent managerial real estate and junk bond investment decisions; (b) the untimely slump of the California real estate market; (c) the Touche Ross treatment of the Stout Apartment deal as a loan, rather than as an investment, enabling BHSL to artificially build up a nonexistent net worth; and (d) with the Stout Apartment deal treated as a loan, Coopers & Lybrand determined that the collateralized assets were overinflated, substantially exceeding the thrift's real net worth.

Clearly, the carnage in the S&L industry, and BHSL in particular, cannot be blamed solely on Touche Ross or the other Big Six firms. As the auditors claim, thrift managements must be held primarily accountable for the practices that led to the failure of their institutions. But what is so troubling about the auditors' role in the S&L debacle is that they are licensed to maintain a higher standard and ultimately to protect the public's interest. Here, Touche Ross and other Big Six firms failed repeatedly. Forget the all-too-common excuse that complex fraud committed by devious management in collusion with others is hard to detect. To people who invest in thrifts or who entrust their life savings to them, this kind of don't-blame-us-if-the-bad-guys-are-real-smart buck-passing is hardly what they have in mind when they see a Big Six signature blessing a financial statement.

No one should know this better than the auditors. Unless they work harder to eliminate, rather than to excuse, lapses in professional standards, the imprimaturs that the public relies on and that bring them billions of dollars in fees will be worthless.

Planning and auditing without integrity in order to expand revenues or to keep accounting clients ultimately results in lost revenues, loss of professional status, loss of respect for independent auditing judgment, and erosion of confidence in future certifications of accounting records and financial statements. (For more details, see Stevens, M. [1991]. *The big six: The selling out of America's top accounting firms.* New York: Simon & Schuster.)

(2) Finance/Investment Minicase: (Case 4B) - Campeau Corporation

Robert Campeau, a French Canadian real estate developer, was a major hostile raider in the latter 1980s who relied on junk bonds and leveraged buyouts (LBOs). In May 1988, Campeau scored a major victory over R. H. Macy & Co. in a bitter battle for the Federated Department Store Corporation and its prestigious division, Bloomingdale's. Less than 2 years earlier, Campeau had acquired another major department store corporation, Allied Stores, through the *street sweep technique,* a process that circumvents SEC disclosure requirements by accumulating multiple small lots of stock.

On January 15, 1990, however, the Campeau Corporation filed for Chapter 11 bankruptcy protection from its creditors. Campeau had lost wealth that took him a lifetime to accumulate—nearly $500 million; the Reichmann family of Toronto's $700 million investment in Campeau's acquisition was largely depreciated; First Boston Corporation also lost millions and had its debt rating downgraded by Moody's; thousands of retailing employees lost their jobs; and prestigious retail firms besmirched their hard-won reputations. The scale of damage because of planning without integrity in investment management by Campeau provoked an avalanche of regulatory intervention.

Like many successful people, Campeau came from humble beginnings and was driven by fierce economic ambition. He allowed his rampant drive for financial success and power to blind him to imprudent investment risks, with little concern for debt accumulation or liquidity constraints. His justifiable personal pride in his Canadian real estate development competence became overextended arrogance in his assumption of easy transferability of management planning competency from commercial real estate financing to retail operations management.

First, in his acquisition binge, Campeau paid $500 million too much for Federated. Second, after incurring mountainous debt to gain the hostile takeover victory, his sale of assets to pay off a portion of the debt in a timely fashion failed. The imagined synergy between real estate and retailing did not materialize in time to handle interest payments on the remainder of the debt. Finally, the net result of Campeau's irresponsible intended and coordinated investment management planning victimized the plans of more responsible stakeholders, inside and outside the Campeau empire.

Four reasons have been proposed to account for the failures of hostile takeovers done mainly or solely for quick-fix profit: (a) myopia, (b) wasted talent, (c) excessive debt, and (d) distrust (Reich, 1991). First, although myopic investors benefit at the outset when the market price of their stock is bid up, those prices can fall after the takeover attempt, and junk bond holders can find themselves in a collapsed market. Investors can, then, experience long-term losses in a hypervolatile market. In addition, the myopic short-term investment perspective does not enable firms to develop new technologies. Profit pressures inhibit real technological growth. Second, "asset rearranging" by "paper entrepreneurs" wastes the energy of talented managers. The short-term profit perspective does not grow business and technological talent. Third, hostile takeovers require financial borrowing and leveraging—often excessive debt. The average U.S. firm paid 16 cents of every dollar on pretax earnings in interest on its debt 25 years ago. This figure was 33 cents in the 1970s. The Brookings Institution predicted that if the level of debt that existed in the 1980s prevails, 1 in 10 American firms will go bankrupt in the coming decades. Finally, an economy based on asset rearranging foments distrust and plays one group's gain against another's loss. Without trust, people won't dedicate themselves to common organizational goals. They will turn their energies instead to defending their own careers and interests. In a corporation, this means declining productivity. (For more details, see Rothchild, J. [1991]. *Going for broke: How Robert Campeau bankrupted the retail industry, jolted the junk bond market, and brought the booming eighties to a crashing halt.* New York: Viking.)

(3) Marketing/Advertising Minicase: (Case 4C) - Kellogg Company

Founded and still located in Battle Creek, Michigan, Kellogg Company produces breakfast cereals and other food products. Kellogg has 40% of the U.S. cereal market and 52% of the foreign market and produces 9 of the world's 10 best-selling cereals. Concerned with nutrition, Kellogg pioneered nutrient labeling in the 1930s, produced the first combination grain product (1943) and first high-protein cereal (Special K, in 1955), and became the first cereal company to label sugar (1977) and salt (1979) content. While Kellogg's leadership in the cereal market remained strong, public interest groups, such as the Center for Science in the Public Interest (CSPI) and Action for Children's Television (ACT), pointed toward a lack of corporate moral awareness with regard to two issues and jointly petitioned the Federal Trade Commission (FTC) in 1977 to address these issues: (a) inadequacy of the nutritional value of children's cereals because of their high sugar content and (b) unfairness of advertising to children by the use of manipulative selling techniques.

With regard to the first claim, the public interest groups demonstrated that presweetened children's cereals were advertised as being highly nutritious. Then the groups countered that cereals, many of which were highly processed so that their intrinsic nutrient content and density were very low, particularly when combined with sugar (the prototype of empty calories), were not a complete food even if fortified with 8 or 10 vitamins and were potentially harmful. Experts testified to the number of cases of dental problems and argued that although children need calories, they have no need to get them in a form relatively devoid of other nutrients.

With regard to the second claim, the public interest groups claimed that misleading and manipulative advertising exploited young children's vulnerability to commercial suggestion. Since a Harvard Business School survey found that 5- to 7-year-olds successfully influenced parental purchases of cereals 88% of the time, shaping children's preferences for cereals ultimately led to parental purchase of those cereals (Micheli, 1979). All kinds of attractive cartoon characters—talking elves, Easter bunnies, cuddly animations—sang the praises of cereal products and made magical promises of future physical attractiveness, prowess, and peer group acceptance. The public interest groups argued that the unfairness of manipulating children, who are not capable of acting as rational, self-interested consumers, as a means of selling to their parents warrants governmental intervention because marketers had done an absolutely pitiful job of professional/industry self-regulation and had filled children's television programs with junky food and junky promotional toys.

The efforts of the public interest groups and others were successful in 1983 and 1990 in getting the Council of Better Business Bureaus, Inc., to adopt Self-Regulatory Guidelines for Children's Advertising, shown in Table 4.2.

In 1984, the public interest groups were successful in getting the Federal Communications Commission (FCC) to adopt "voluntary" guidelines that limit the number of advertisements during children's shows to 9.5 minutes each hour on Saturday and Sunday and 12 minutes each hour on other days. In 1990, the Children's Television Act was passed; it prohibited the airing of commercials about products or characters during a show about those products or characters.

In effect, the lack of marketing planning with integrity in advertising cereal products to children provoked governmental regulation. Increased company/industry moral awareness, judgment, intention, and self-regulatory conduct could have precluded this type of extraorganizational control and censorship. (For more details, see Walsh, D. [1994]. *Selling out America's children*. Minneapolis: Deaconess.)

Table 4.2 Self-Regulatory Guidelines for Children's Advertising

Product Presentations and Claims Guidelines in Advertising to Children

Children look at, listen to, and remember many different elements in advertising. Therefore, advertisers need to examine the total advertising message to be certain that the net communication will not mislead or misinform children.

1. Copy, sound, and visual presentations should not mislead children about product or performance characteristics. Such characteristics may include, but are not limited to, size, speed, method of operation, color, sound, durability, and nutritional benefits.
2. The advertising presentation should not mislead children about perceived benefits from use of the product. Such benefits may include, but are not limited to, the acquisition of strength, status, popularity, growth, proficiency, and intelligence. Social stereotyping and appeals to prejudice should be avoided.
3. Care should be taken not to exploit a child's imagination. Fantasy, including animation, is appropriate for younger as well as older children. However, it should not create unattainable performance expectations nor exploit the younger child's difficulty in distinguishing between the real and the fanciful.
4. The performance and use of a product should be demonstrated in a way that can be duplicated by the child for whom the product is intended.
5. Products should be shown being used in safe environments and situations.
6. What is included and excluded in the initial purchase should be clearly established.
7. The amount of product featured should be within reasonable levels for the situation depicted.
8. Representation of food products should be made so as to encourage sound usage of the product with a view toward healthy development of the child and development of good nutritional practices. Advertisements representing mealtime in the home should clearly and adequately depict the role of the product within the framework of a balanced diet.
9. Portrayals of violence and presentations that could unduly frighten or provoke anxiety in children should be avoided.
10. Objective claims about product or performance characteristics should be supported by appropriate and adequate substantiation.

SOURCE: *Self-Regulatory Guidelines for Children's Advertising* (3rd ed.). Children's Advertising Review Unit, National Advertising Division, Council of Better Business Bureaus, Inc., 1983, pp. 4-5.

(4) Business Management/Human Resources/ Business Law Minicase: (Case 4D) - Forklift Systems, Inc.

Teresa Harris was employed by Forklift Systems, Inc., an equipment rental company, as a manager from April 1985 until October 1987 (Solberg, 1995). Charles Hardy was the company's president. During Harris's tenure at Fork-Lift, Hardy was alleged to have done the following to her:

Often insulted her because of her gender

Often made her the target of unwanted sexual innuendos

Told her on several occasions, in front of other employees, "You're a woman, what do you know," and, "We need a man as the rental manager"

Called her a "dumb ass woman"

In front of other employees, suggested that they "go to the Holiday Inn to negotiate (Harris's) raise"

Occasionally asked her and other female employees to get coins from his front pants pocket

At times, would throw objects on the ground in front of Harris and other female employees and ask them to pick them up

Made sexual comments about her and other women's clothing

Finally, after she complained to him about his conduct and he promised to stop, he commented to her in front of other employees, "What did you do, promise the guy . . . some [sex] Saturday night?" regarding a business deal Harris was arranging. After this last incident, Harris quit. She sued the company, alleging the above conduct amounted to a hostile work environment.

Under Title VII, protection from sexual harassment was passed as part of the Civil Rights Act of 1964. The act prohibits workplace discrimination based on race, religion, color, sex, and national origin. The Supreme Court, in *Meritor Savings Bank v. Vinson,* ruled that sexual harassment was a type of sexual discrimination and is thereby prohibited by Title VII. The term *sexual harassment* is defined as follows by the Equal Employment Opportunity Commission's guidelines:

> Unwelcome sexual advances, requests for sexual favors, and other verbal or physical conduct of a sexual nature constitutes sexual harassment when (1) submission to such conduct is made either explicitly or implicitly a term or condition of an individual's employment, (2) submission to or rejection of such conduct by an individual is used as the basis for employment decisions affecting such individuals, or (3) such conduct has the purpose or effect of unreasonably interfering with an individual's work performance or creating an intimidating, hostile, or offensive work environment.

Sections 1 and 2 of the definition describe a type of sexual harassment known as *quid pro quo.* Section 3 relates to a type of sexual harassment known as a *hostile work environment.*

To be successful in a hostile work environment sexual harassment claim, a plaintiff must prove, inter alia, that the conduct was sufficiently severe or pervasive to alter the conditions of employment and create an abusive working environment. This last element consists of a subjective, psychological component and an objective, behavioral one.

At first, the district court ruled in favor of Forklift, when it concluded that even though the objective behavior would have offended a reasonable woman, it failed to affect Harris's subjective psychological well-being and was therefore nonactionable (did not meet the two requirements of subjective and objective harm). The Sixth Circuit Court of Appeals affirmed the decision of the lower trial court. The Supreme Court, however, disagreed with both the trial and appeals courts.

The Supreme Court changed the law and decided that proof of psychological harm was not a prerequisite to a successful sexual harassment claim, arguing that Title VII comes into play before the harassing conduct leads to a nervous breakdown. The *Harris* case sets out the following factors for determining whether conduct was objectively harassing:

1. Behavior more likely to be considered harassing:
   a. extreme physical contact—though not present in this case, it is probably a safe assumption that this type of conduct is harassing
   b. intimidating behavior—can include any number of specific behaviors
   c. property destruction of the victim
   d. vulgar derogatory terms
   e. graphic sexual talk
   f. graphic photos
   g. pervasive behavior—would include almost any type of sexual conduct done repeatedly
   h. victim-directed behavior—as opposed to behavior directed at other employees, but heard or observed by the victim
2. Behavior less likely to be considered harassing:
   a. sexual banter—innuendos and other sexual talk of a nongraphic nature
   b. occasional outburst—would include an epithet or a vulgar expression
   c. moderate physical contact
   d. nonrepetitive behavior—unless extreme

Because of the Supreme Court change in the sexual harassment law, relieving Harris of the unnecessary burden of proof for psychological impairment, she won her case against Forklift Systems.

In effect, the legal clarification of the behavioral boundaries of sexual harassment, which cost the company thousands of dollars, could have been prevented by implementing human resource policies and controlling harassing conduct of any kind with standards based on moral integrity, rather than only on current legal compliance. (For more details, see Rapaport, J. O., & Zevrick, B. L. [1994]. *The employee strikes back.* New York: Collier; and Slonaker, W., & Wendt, A. [1991]. Profile of employment discrimination in micro-business. *Journal of Business and Entrepreneurship, 3*[2], 33-46.)

(5) Technology/Quality Operations/Organizational Behavior Minicases: (Case 4E) - Microsoft Corporation

Microsoft Corporation, headquartered in Redmond, Washington, is by far the world's largest and richest company dedicated to PC software development, and thanks to an expanding stream of new products, it continues to grow with astounding speed domestically and globally.

Current chairman and CEO Bill Gates (born in 1955), regarded as one of the richest persons in the world, cofounded Microsoft in 1975 with Paul Allen (born in 1953). Microsoft's revenues surged from $16,000 in 1975, when the company consisted of 1 product and 3 people, to nearly $6 billion in 1995, when the company had some 200 products and approximately 17,800 employees. Microsoft controls between 80% and 85% of the most important market segment for PC software: operating systems, the programs that determine the basic functions of the computer. It produces 25% or more of all PC applications products (or "packaged software"), which run on top of the operating system.

MS-DOS (which stands for "Microsoft Disk Operating System") is probably Microsoft's best-known product. It has sold in the millions each year since 1981, when IBM adopted it as the operating system for its personal computers. Windows is probably Microsoft's second best-known product. This is a graphical or picture-based "user interface" and operating system that works with MS-DOS and makes the computer easier to use. Perhaps the third best-known set of products are the Windows applications, such as Word (a word-processing program) and Excel (a spreadsheet program) that are market standards, with more than half of their sales coming through Microsoft's low-priced Office "Suite" of applications. Microsoft has also entered or is planning to enter just about every market that relates to computers and information technology, from children's video games to corporate networking, interactive television, entertainment, on-line network services, and the information superhighway. No manager in any industry related to computers or information technology, and no current or future user of a computer, can really avoid or afford to ignore what Microsoft does.

What Microsoft does is especially suited to fast-paced markets with complex systems products, short life cycles, and competition based around rapidly evolving product features and technical standards. In particular, the work of any large team building many interdependent components that are continually changing requires a constant high level of communication and coordination while still allowing designers, engineers, and marketing people the freedom to be creative. Achieving and sustaining this balance is perhaps the central mark of management integrity at Microsoft.

In short, Microsoft engages in ethical planning through a number of key strategies: (a) extensive use of best-practices benchmarking, (b) selection of innovative people to rapidly pioneer products in evolving mass markets, (c) use of synchronization and stabilization processes to implement strategies, and (d) use of postmortem evaluations to accelerate organizational learning.

Microsoft makes extensive use of *best-practices benchmarking,* a process of comparing one's own operations with the best practices of other companies and other industries. The company's historical planning approach is to benchmark against the best in the industry and eventually create a superior product; for example, Excel was created after benchmarking with Lotus. Microsoft's rigorous selection process screens for smart people with high IQs, who have strong technical and business skills, and who are ambitiously entrepreneurial. The urge to rapidly create drives these associates to excel in constantly pioneering new products for mass markets. Microsoft's product planning and development process entails *daily "builds"* at 2 and 5 p.m. to determine product progress, *daily synchronization* of the contributions of multiple teams through direct feedback, and *daily stabilization* through debugging by parties responsible for errors ("breaking the build") to maintain project implementation momentum. Finally, by requiring *written project postmortems,* Microsoft managers become driven by honest self-criticism, peer feedback, and shared learning.

In essence, the world's most powerful software company creates technology, shapes markets, and manages people and processes by planning with integrity at all levels. Every manager at every level is held accountable for performance and is expected to improve through continuous self-critiquing, feedback, and sharing. The impact of this vigorous collective integrity is demonstrated in market success and global customer demand. (For more details, see Cusumano, M., & Selby, R. [1995]. *Microsoft secrets.* New York: Free Press.)

(6) Public/Nonprofit/Health Care Administration Minicase: (Case 4F) - Sikorsky and Government Purchasing Management

On April 27, 1983, Marine Lieutenant David A. Boyle died off the coast of Virginia Beach, Virginia, when the helicopter he was piloting crashed and sank into the ocean. Although neither Boyle nor the other crew members of the helicopter were killed in the impact of the craft, Boyle, unlike the others, was apparently unable to escape because his escape hatch did not open outward against the pressure of the water. The cause of the initial failure of the helicopter was a malfunction of the control system. An investigation after the accident revealed that a small chip of metal wire had been improperly introduced into the pilot valve of the helicopter's servo, a primary element of the control system.

Delbert Boyle, the father of the victim, sued the Sikorsky division of United Technologies Corporation, the manufacturer of the CH-53D that crashed, in the United States District Court for the Eastern District of Virginia. He alleged negligence and breach of warranty in both the design of the escape hatch and in the repair of the helicopter's servo.

The *Boyle* case involved an independent contractor performing its obligation under an authorized federal procurement contract, not an official performing a duty. Therefore, the Supreme Court found that if an authorized federal procurement contract is honored by meeting three criteria in order to fulfill a uniquely federal interest, both the federal government and the authorized contractor are legally immune from lawsuits. For an authorized federal procurement to be favored in a particular case, three criteria must be satisfied. First, the government must have established the specifications for the product. Second, the product manufactured by the defendant must meet the government's specifications in all material respects. Third, the government must have known as much or more than the defendant about the hazards associated with the product.

These criteria were established in *In Re Agent Orange Product Liability*. In this case, Vietnam veterans and members of their families brought suit against chemical companies that served third-party complaints against the United States. "Agent Orange" was a herbicide used by the United States military in Southeast Asia. The court held that if the chemical companies established that the specifications for Agent Orange were established for the government, that if all the specifications were met, and that the government knew as much or more than the company about the hazards to the people, the claims against them would be dismissed. The chemical companies argued that they were immune from liability for injuries arising out of the government's use of Agent Orange because it was manufactured under contract with the United States and in strict compliance with its specifications (Quinn, 1989).

The majority opinion of the Supreme Court stated that if the elements are properly established, the manufacturer will be shielded from all claims. Therefore, in the *Boyle* case, if the manufacturer satisfies all three criteria, the plaintiff cannot recover. In other words, if there is a uniquely federal interest, "the king and his entourage" are legally immune (Quinn, 1989).

In the minority opinion of the Supreme Court, the dissenting justices argued that the extension of legal immunity to nonmilitary products that injure both military personnel and innocent civilians by a defense contractor unfairly burdens individual citizens with no legal recourse for remedies. The adverse impact on the morale of the armed forces and the civilian population are inadequately weighted to sustain the financial, legal, and political cooperative relations with defense contractors.

The key distinctions between legal guilt/immunity and moral guilt/immunity occur at individual, institutional, and national levels in this case. Planning government procurement without integrity, therefore, can clearly result in personal injury, loss of property, and widespread public distrust of government. (For more details, see Pekkever, J. [1986]. *My father, my son.* New York: Dell.)

(7) International/Environmental/Public Policy Minicases: (Case 4G) - International Hazardous Waste Trade

The export of hazardous wastes by the MDCs to the LDCs is escalating beyond control and depicts global waste planning without integrity (Singh & Lakhan, 1989). The ethical implications and environmental consequences of this trade in hazardous wastes highlight the need for international controls and regulations in the conduct of business by corporations in the MDCs. One recent dramatic case is that of Koko, Nigeria, where more than 8,000 drums of hazardous wastes were dumped, some of which contained polychlorinated biphenyl (PCB), a highly carcinogenic compound and one of the world's most toxic wastes, causing extensive human and ecological damage. The government of Nigeria detained a number of Nigerians in connection with the incident and indicated that they may face a firing squad if found guilty of illegal dumping.

Hazardous waste is any material that may pose a substantial threat or potential hazard to human health or the environment when managed improperly. These wastes may be solid, liquid, or gaseous form and include a variety of toxic, ignitable, corrosive, or dangerously reactive substances. Hazardous wastes not only contaminate ground water, destroy habitats, cause human disease, and contaminate the soil, but also enter the food chain at all levels and eventually damage the genetic material of all living things. Since World War II, the amount of toxic by-products created by the manufacturers of pharmaceuticals, petroleum, nuclear devices, pesticides, chemicals, and other allied products has increased almost exponentially. From an annual production of less than 10 million metric tons in the 1940s, the world now produces more than 320 million metric tons of extremely hazardous wastes per year. The United States is by far the biggest producer, with more than 275 million metric tons of hazardous waste produced each year. The total is well over 1 ton per person. But the United States is not alone. European countries also produce millions of tons of hazardous wastes each year. Recent figures indicate that the 12 countries of the European Community produce about 35 million tons of hazardous wastes annually.

The U.S. Environmental Protection Agency (EPA) estimates that as much as 75% of waste exported from the United States is disposed of in Canada. In addition, the United States and certain European countries are now turning to areas in Africa, Latin America, and the Caribbean to dump their wastes.

Why do companies and countries export wastes? A major reason is that many of them are finding it difficult to build disposal facilities in their own countries because of the NIMBY (Not In My Back Yard) syndrome. Other reasons are that better technologies may be available in another country, facilities of a neighboring country may be closer to a generator of waste than a site on national territory, and economies of scale may also be a factor. To these reasons must be added the fact that corporations may be motivated to dispose of waste in another country where less stringent regulations apply. Although more stringent regulations, higher disposal costs, and heightened environmental awareness are pushing many companies in industrial countries to export hazardous wastes, it must be realized that the governments of LDCs are allowing such imports into their countries because of the need for foreign exchange. These governments are willing to damage their environment in return for hard currency and the creation of jobs.

Several key ethical implications of the international hazardous waste trade are (a) respecting the moral and legal right to a livable environment, (b) corporate social responsibility, and (c) racist and/or North-South discrimination. First, the moral right to a clean, safe environment is seen as a positive human right because the absence of such a condition would prevent one from fulfilling one's human capacities. Sustainable development extends that right to future generations. Although the need for and enforcement of international law on this issue is both needed and conspicuously absent, the international environmental group Greenpeace has routinely called for a global ban on transboundary movements of wastes. Greenpeace bases its legal appeal on Principle 21 of the 1972 Declaration of the United Nations Conference on the Human Environment, which declares that each state is responsible for ensuring that activities within its jurisdiction or control do not cause damage to the environment of other states or of areas beyond the limits of its own national jurisdiction.

Second, the international trade in hazardous wastes basically involves three parties: the generators of wastes, the exporters of wastes, and the importers of wastes. These entities, if they are to act in a socially responsible manner, should be accountable to the public for their behavior. A corporation involved in the international trade in hazardous wastes is not likely to be a responsibly responsive firm. The importer of hazardous wastes is clearly engaged in activities that will damage the environment, whereas the exporter, being aware that this is a possibility, nevertheless sends these wastes to the importer. The generator of hazardous wastes, however, is the most culpable in this matter. Production and consumption patterns need to be altered to reduce wastes.

Third, the recent trend of sending more shipments of hazardous wastes to Third World countries has led to charges of racism. *West Africa*, a weekly magazine, referred to the dumping of toxic wastes as the latest in a series of historical traumas for Africa. The other traumas cited by the magazine were slavery, colonialism, and unpayable foreign debt. Charges of racism in the disposal of wastes have been made before at the national level in the United States. A study of waste disposal sites found that race was the most significant among variables tested in association with the location of commercial hazardous waste facilities. In addition, the global toxic trash trade has been indicted as another form of Northern Hemisphere colonial domination of the Southern Hemisphere, especially when waste shipments are made "south of the U.S. border." A toxic barge from New York was turned back recently by the Mexican navy, and the incident illustrated the pattern of scorn that certain sectors of U.S. society feel toward Mexico in particular and Latin America in general.

Planning without integrity about hazardous waste management entails irresponsible and exploitative conduct that harms humans and nature, and ultimately boomerangs to form a circle of poison when the people and products of victimized countries reenter the United States. (For more details, see Valette, J. [1989]. *The international trade in wastes: A Greenpeace inventory* (4th ed.). Luxembourg: Greenpeace International.)

SUMMARY

In summary, this chapter covers the multiple dimensions of the function of planning for managers and the four ethical planning subprocesses that build management integrity. In addition, seven management ethics and planning with integrity minicases were presented. By addressing the moral issues embedded in planning ethically and applying the theories and tools from the first part of the book to the structured analysis and principled resolution of planning minicases, sharpened skills in ethical planning can enhance management integrity.

DISCUSSION/EXPERIENTIAL EXERCISES

Discussion Questions

1. Discuss the nature of managerial planning and culpably negligent planning as they relate to private- and public-sector managers.

2. Discuss the differences between traditional and TQ planning and, using the Planning Success Evaluation Matrix (Figure 4.2), provide life/work/school examples from each quadrant.

3. Discuss the parallel alignment of the four key ethics processes and planning subprocesses that build integrity, providing an example of managerial planning for each step.

4. Using the tools and resources from the first part of the book, examine the planning with integrity minicase in your major field or field of concentration.

Experiential Exercises

5. In a group setting, using the tools and resources from the first part of the book, examine two planning with integrity minicases outside your major field or field of concentration.

6. From your own life/work/school experiences, discuss times when planning occurred without integrity, identifying specific adverse effects that resulted when one or more of the ethical planning steps were omitted or inadequately completed and how you could have (in the past) or will (in the future) plan with integrity to prevent a recurrence of the problem.

5

Management Ethics:
Organizing With Integrity

The focus of Chapter 5 is on three areas: (a) the dimensions of organizing, (b) ethical organizing processes that build integrity, and (c) management ethics and organizing with integrity minicases. By addressing the ethical issues involved in the management function of organizing and applying those lessons to the analysis and resolution of organizing minicases, skills in ethical organizing can enhance management ethics and integrity.

▨ DIMENSIONS OF ORGANIZING

Organizing is the intended, coordinated, emergent, and realized pattern of integrated, multidimensional decisions and actions that assemble, arrange, and allocate human and nonhuman resources into structures, people, and technology that can activate organizational plans. Just as in architecture, the form of an organization's design follows its planned functional; that is, the organizing structure of a firm follows its strategy. Whereas planning provides directional mission, organizing provides the means to accomplish it. Meritorious organizing mobilizes stakeholders by activating organizational process systems that are expressly intended, efficiently coordinated, creatively responsive to emergent feedback, and fully realized, as indicated in Figure 5.1.

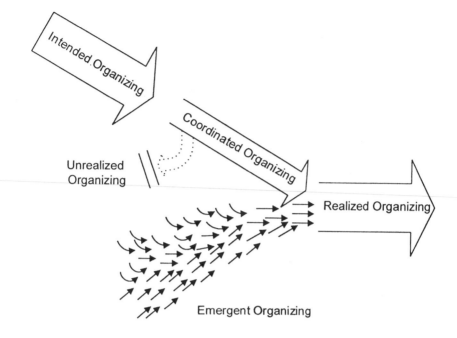

Figure 5.1. Dimensions of Organizing

Managers who generate and articulate a compelling vision of the future structure and resources of the organization that motivates stakeholders are involved in *intended organizing*. Managers who realistically design and arrange for the proper blend and allocation of human and nonhuman resources are engaged in *coordinated organizing*. Managers who are open and responsive to unexpected events and critical organizing feedback are involved in *emergent organizing*. The outcome of the interaction among intended, coordinated, and emergent organizing is realized and unrealized organizational designs. *Realized organizational designs* are fully implemented designs that incorporate the evolved patterns of the past, the expectations of the desired future, and the realistic constraints of the present. Managers who analyze the historical precedents of "what worked" and "what didn't work" for organizations are engaged in *realized organizing*. *Unrealized organizing* designs are intended designs that never materialized. Among realized organizational designs, some are successful in that they efficiently transform inputs into value-added outputs; other designs are unsuccessful, realized structures that become barriers to effective organizational and stakeholder performance.

Furthermore, *culpably negligent organizing* includes any and all of the following: absence of explicitly intended organizing, inefficiently coordinated organizing, organizing that is rigidly unresponsive to emergent contingencies, inadequately realized organizing, unintegrated patterns of organizing processes and actions, and organizing that misaligns core business processes and human resource (HR) subsystems (selection, performance, appraisal, rewards, and development). The degree of moral culpability for negligent organizing is dependent on the extent to which a manager could have and should have known or anticipated all the factors involved in the organizing function.

Management integrity in organizing can only be achieved if there is a balanced concern for both stability and change, internally and externally (Leonard-Barton, 1995). If an organization overemphasizes stability, its core organizing capacities and energies can degenerate into core organizing rigidities with the following adverse impacts: premature screening out of new external benchmarking knowledge, limited future structural and staffing experimentation, internal inability to generate diversity and innovation, and limited organizing problem-solving skills in the present. If an organization overemphasizes change, its core organizing capacities and energies can become dissipated into random, unfocused activities that cause the organization to go adrift, resulting in the following adverse impacts: uncritical openness to novelty, overreliance on future structural and staffing experimentation, squandering of organizational energy, and overreliance on solving current organizing problems by changing for change's sake.

Organizing Factors: Structure

The balance of change and stability to achieve optimal effectiveness in the organizing function is obtained by addressing the relationships among three key factors: structural factors, people factors, and technological factors. The structural, people, and technological factors require both intrafirm and interfirm organizing. The first set of key organizing factors, *structural factors,* consists of current and future work designs, processes, policies, and procedures that provide the means to achieve organizational plans. Because organizing structure usually follows planning strategy, traditional firms that emphasize the strategic priority of financial performance over market share; competitor-focused, adversarial relations over customer-focused, partnership relations;

compliance with hierarchic, centralized authority over commitment to democratic, decentralized competency networking; and "closed" financial books information over "open" financial books information sharing are likely to rely on one or more of the following organizational structures: function, division, geography, customer, product, strategic business unit, holding company, matrix, and/or hybrid.

Functional structure is a design that groups employees involved in similar or related functional activities (e.g., marketing) or who belong to the same professional or occupational group. *Divisional structure* is a design that groups all the functions necessary to semiautonomously conduct business under one category, formed on any of several bases: geography-based regional alignment (e.g., North American, European, and Asian Pacific-based headquarters), customer-based access alignment (e.g., commercial vs. residential real estate customers), and product-based development alignment (e.g., truck, van, and sedan automotive products). The structure that combines related divisions in a large corporation into homogenous groups is *strategic business unit design*, whereas the structure that combines unrelated divisions in a large corporation into heterogenous, autonomous profit centers is the *holding company structure*. *Matrix structure* leaves the functional hierarchy in place and superimposes a horizontal structure based on products or projects to achieve some coordination and integration across functional departments. *Hybrid structure* is any combination of divisional, functional, and matrix structures.

Organizing structures occur in primate societies, as well as human organizations. In societies of chimpanzees and gorillas, dominance and deference rituals rank order positions of power and influence (Goldsmith, 1991; Wilson, 1993). Dominant members provide at least five organizing services: (a) choosing the direction of group movement, (b) protecting the group from predators, (c) orienting members to their status and place, (d) controlling conflict, and (e) maintaining norms, including norms of mating and resource allocation.

In many conventional human organizations, *traditional authority* is regarded as the right to exercise dominance or to issue commands. It allows its holders, usually managers, to act in certain designated ways and to directly influence the actions of others. It also allows its holder to allocate the organization's resources to achieve the objectives of the organization. Individuals with authority are held accountable for how well they use their authority or live up to their role responsibilities.

Traditional organizations have three types of authority: line, staff, and functional authority. *Line authority,* the most fundamental traditional orga-

Advantages	_Disadvantages_
Line Authority	
1. Maintains simplicity	1. Neglects specialists in planning
2. Makes clear division of authority	2. Overworks key people
3. Encourages speedy action	3. Depends on retention of a few key people
Staff Authority	
1. Enables specialists to give expert advice	1. Confuses organization if functions are not clear
2. Frees line executives from detailed analyses	2. Reduces power of experts to put recommendations into action
3. Affords young specialists a means of training	3. Tends toward centralization of organization
Functional Authority	
1. Relieves line executives of routine specialized decisions	1. Makes relationships more complex
2. Provides framework for applying expert knowledge	2. Makes limits of authority of each specialist a difficult coordination problem
3. Tends toward centralization of organization	3. Relieves pressure of need for large numbers of well-rounded executives

Figure 5.2. Advantages and Disadvantages of Line Authority, Staff Authority, and Functional Authority

SOURCE: MODERN MANAGEMENT, 6th ed. by Certo, Samuel C., © 1994. Adapted by permission of Prentice- Hall, Inc., Upper Saddle River, NJ.

nizational authority, is the right to give orders and make decisions concerning the production, sales, or finance-related behavior of subordinates. _Staff authority_ is the right to advise or assist those who possess line authority. _Functional authority_ is the right to give orders within a limited domain of the management system in which the right is normally nonexistent. The advantages and disadvantages of these three types of traditional authority are indicated in Figure 5.2.

In contrast, _total quality authority_ is not the right to exercise dominance, but the conferred right to perform a service. This means that organizing authority in TQ firms is given and can be taken away if authority is used for self-aggrandizement, rather than for improving the work system. TQ authority is conferred as part of an exchange agreement in which power is shared to better accomplish set purposes, and failure to abide by the terms of the agreement means risking the loss of authority. Dominance relationships are based on coercion or habitual deference; TQ authority relationships are voluntary and revocable.

The extent to which different people are able to confer power, rather than defer by habit, differs markedly. Some people grow up aware that the choice to confer power lies within them. They learn to challenge conventional structures and to participate in the exchange of power for services. They come to think of authority figures with mutual regard. But many do not. Many people take their powerlessness for granted. If they have grown up disenfranchised, abused, or in a high power distance culture, they may have socialization issues to address.

The major thrust, however, of TQ authority structures is to enfranchise all employees with appropriate responsibility, power, and authority to improve the work system continually. This requires authority figures to assess and develop the empowerment readiness of organizational associates continually. TQ firms organize around horizontal network (spider web) structures, rather than vertical hierarchic (tree branch) structures.

For a TQ organization, a *process* is any set of linked activities that takes an input, adds value to it, and provide a product/service that becomes an output of the internal customers and an outcome to an external customer, as indicated in Figure 5.3.

The organizational efforts and results that have societal impact can be interpreted as sets of processes or systems. A *system* is an interrelated set of plans, policies, processes, procedures, people, and technology needed to reach the objectives of an organization. Thus, a set of processes may be seen as making up a system. A process will usually cross organizational boundaries within an operating unit and require coordination across those boundaries. A *structure* is a formal or informal organization entity that is developed to perform a certain process or set of tasks that is part of a process.

TQ systems promote internal cross-functional integration and external cross-organizational partnerships with suppliers and distributors to enact TQ marketplace strategy. Sometimes the duration of the network structure is temporary, and "virtual organizations" may use information technology to share skills, costs, and access to one another's markets. In addition, TQ organizational design streamlines processes, eliminates unnecessary middle managers, simplifies information flows, accelerates decision-making speed, and encourages employee participation through cross-functional and self-managed teams, thereby decentralizing authority and responsibility for system success.

Organizing through the use of a decentralized TQ structure, however, may permit or encourage unethical conduct at work if there are pressures from upper-level managers to overemphasize unrealistic, bottom-line quarterly

	Input (raw material)	Processes (how to do it)	Products (enroute result)	Outputs (the aggregated products of the system that are delivered or deliverable to society)	Outcomes (the effects of outputs in and for society and nature)
Examples	Existing human resources; existing needs, goals, objectives, regulations, laws, money, values, societal and community characteristics; current quality of life; natural resources	Means, methods, procedures; searching for "excellence," teaching; learning; human resource development, training, managing	Course completed; competency test passed; competency acquired; learner accomplishments; production quota met; the performance "building blocks"	Delivered automobiles, sold computer systems; program completed; job placements; certified licenses	Safety of outputs; profit; dividends declared; continued funding of agency; self-reliant, productive individual; socially competent and effective, contributing to self and to others; no addictive relationship to others or to substances; sustainable development
Scope	Internal (Organization)			External (Societal)	
Cluster	Organizational Efforts		Organizational Results		Societal Results/ Impact

Figure 5.3. Organizational Efforts and Results Model

SOURCE: Kaufman (1988). Copyright April 1988 *Training & Development*, American Society for Training and Development. Reprinted with permission. All rights reserved.

revenue objectives and if the organizational processes to guide ethical decision making are unclear (Cullen, Victor, & Stephens, 1989; Weiss, 1994). To counteract the ethical risks of a decentralized structure, it is necessary for responsible managers to address the second key factor in organizing—the people factor.

Organizing Factors: People

The *people factor* concerns the mix of knowledge, skills, abilities, and characters that affect organizational performance. The HR subsystem, including selection, performance, appraisal, rewards, and development processes, must be carefully monitored and continuously improved to ensure that optimal human resources are optimally organized (Petrick & Furr, 1995; Rousseau, 1995, 1996). Organizing people well requires attending to five key HR organizing processes: selection, performance, appraisal, rewards, and development. The first key element of organizing people is the selection process (Heneman & Heneman, 1994; Payne, 1994). Selection is the mutual process by which the individual and the organization become matched to form the employment relationship. In addition to testing for technical competence, substance abuse, and physical health, self-respecting organizations need to engage in integrity (Murphy, 1993; Ones, Visyvesvaran, & Schmidt, 1993), service orientation (Hogan, Hogan, & Busch, 1984), and organizational citizenship behavior (Van Dyne, Graham, & Dienesch, 1994) testing. In the long run, it is more cost effective to screen carefully for persons who are honest, respectful, and geared to improve the work system cooperatively prior to organizational entry, rather than to expend resources thereafter to retrain employees with major character problems.

The second key element of organizing people is the performance process. *Performance* is the contribution that individuals, groups, and systems make to the accomplishment of organizational objectives. Self-respecting organizations set performance standards in both task completion and relationship development at work. Balancing the intellectual virtues to complete technical tasks with the moral, emotional, and social virtues to build the work community is a dual performance responsibility in self-respecting organizations. The moral, emotional, and social virtues are exhibited by sincere communication styles that nurture trust and respect and by empathic interactions, such as equitable pain-sharing and gain-sharing meetings, that sustain an informal solace and incentive system when adjusting to the rapid pace of technological changes (Greene, 1993). *Pain sharing*, for example, builds community character, raises team stress thresholds, and improves organizational justice because it is important to get all employees to acknowledge visibly who is paying a price and who is not in any new work initiative. This acknowledgment of differential impact of work decisions builds the work unit social memory of who sacrificed and who benefited in the past and can later be used as an organizational equity process in "balancing the books" between and among employees in future work decisions (Greene, 1993). Persons of exceptional character who dramatically raise and meet new personal, group, and system performance standards and good, reliable contributors who incrementally improve and meet new performance standards deserve recognition for the relative range and value of their consistent contributions.

Organizing the work process with integrity entails designing performance standards within the realistic constraint of a system. The application of statistical control tools to determine upper and lower variation limits of work system capability and reasonable performance expectations is essential (Joiner, 1994; Lindsay & Petrick, 1997; Petrick & Furr, 1995). Otherwise, acceptable performances will be scapegoated for their individual performance when the system performance is at issue, e.g., rotten apples can be the result of wholesome apples in a rotten barrel (Petrick & Furr, 1995). Tampering with performance systems, without adequate knowledge of quality statistical variation, may detract from individual and collective human performance (Deming, 1982, 1988; Scherkenbach, 1991; Walton, 1989). For example, performance standards that ignore process capabilities and adequate resources to complete projects merely erode morale and reduce the cognitive and volitional readiness of employees to act with personal integrity. Ignorance of acceptable performance system variation, therefore, may result in a performance work process that erodes managerial character (Petrick & Furr, 1995).

The third key element of organizing people is the appraisal process. *Appraisal* is the feedback process for evaluating and improving individual, group, and system performance. The use of 360° feedback appraisals from peers, subordinates, internal and external customers as well as superiors provides multiple, balanced feedback for personal and group accountability (Petrick & Furr, 1995). Character flaws need to be honestly disclosed along with a concrete plan for character improvement. Omitting character appraisal feedback (e.g., both positive and negative character trait feedback) deprives individuals, groups, and organizations of moral self-understanding opportunities. In addition, factoring in organizational work system predictability and acceptable variation levels into appraisals acknowledges the organizational responsibility for maintaining a statistically stable work system that supports performance expectations. Self-respecting organizations do not expect world-class performance from their employees if they provide only inefficient, ineffective processes and inadequate resources (Harrington, 1995; Petrick & Furr, 1995). Companies that use appraisals to scapegoat managers/employees and evade responsibility for work process improvements engage in a form of self-deception and abuse of power, which ultimately erodes their self-respect (Martin, 1985; McLaughlin & Rorty, 1988).

Many traditional appraisal processes degrade the morale of employees, fail to provide useful improvement feedback, and give managers the illusion that they can identify and measure individual effort or performance in the absence of adequate statistical knowledge of the work process context (Bounds, Yorks, Adams, & Ranney, 1994; Neave, 1990; Scholtes, 1988). They fail to give direction, enable empowerment, or constructively motivate people to do a better job (Petrick & Furr, 1995). TQ appraisal alternatives to provide direction, empower employee improvement, and identify and acknowledge superior performers, while fostering the intrinsic motivation that individuals bring to the job. These need to be explored if appraisal with integrity is to occur (Lindsay & Petrick, 1997; Petrick & Furr, 1995).

Balanced, honest appraisal is the breakfast of moral champions; it provides the nourishment for organizational self-respect. It is the formal locus for moral understanding in the workplace and the springboard for ongoing individual, group, and organizational character improvement. In other words, it should be an important organizational self-respect goal to engage in character appraisal because organizational self-respect requires ongoing character development. Individuals and groups should not only survive but also become better every day in a self-respecting organization, or else collective work activity becomes barren and futile. Not only is the unexamined personal life not worth living, but the unexamined work life is not worth working.

The fourth key element of organizing people is the reward process. *Rewards* are all forms of financial and nonfinancial returns to individuals, groups, and systems for their contributions as part of the employment relationship. The challenge for self-respecting organizations is to design a reward system that takes advantage of the extrinsic and intrinsic motivational effects of rewards, satisfies norms for equity, meets external market competitiveness challenges, complies with appropriate laws and regulations, is consistently and efficiently administered, and encourages collaboration for team and system success. For example, when rewards are administered only to individuals, competition between individuals for limited rewards is intensified, rather than the collaboration crucial for team and system performance. In addition, when rewards are viewed as extrinsic returns for instrumental work activities, the intrinsic motivation to take moral pride in a job well done is jeopardized.

To avoid eroding organizational character and demotivating employees through inappropriate reward subsystems, self-respecting organizations have a mix of extrinsic and intrinsic rewards that include the full range of financial returns and nonfinancial recognition (Petrick & Furr, 1995). For instance, a company like Ben & Jerry's has profit sharing for employees, recognition ceremonies for individual and team performance, ongoing efforts to improve the meaningful content of work, interdependent collaboration in the work flow process, employee choice and control over work activities, visible vertical and horizontal remuneration equity, and, in effect, a demonstrated commitment to self-respecting business practices.

The degree of emphasis on intrinsic rewards is correlated with the adequacy of the selection process. Individuals who are likely to be strongly internally motivated would usually indicate high customer service orientations, high moral maturity from integrity testing, and a record of good citizenship behavior. These are the type of people who are ready, able, and willing to demonstrate the reciprocal altruism necessary to enjoy contributing to personal, team, and system advancement. The relationship between respect and productivity, therefore, is often one described in the extensive anthology on compensation, titled *Paying for Productivity: A Look at the Evidence:* "Changing the way workers are *treated* may boost productivity more than changing the way they are paid" (Blinder, 1990, p. 3).

Reward/discipline processes need to be designed so that they sustain a productive, fair, continually learning, and enjoyable work environment (Kohn, 1993). Too often, censure processes are set up as if employees are the only problem, not the work process itself (Petrick & Furr, 1995). When problems arise, the disciplinary search focuses on who made the error, rather than on what process allowed the error to occur in the first place (Kohn, 1993). Processes, people, and their interrelationships need to be carefully examined prior to installation and implementation of an organizational reward/discipline system (Petrick & Furr, 1995).

The fifth key element of organizing people is the development process. *Development* is the ongoing process of planned and structured activities designed to improve individual, group, and organizational performance. The identification and nurturance of potential is a never-ending, enabling responsibility of self-respecting organizations. Development occurs in three forms: career, team, and organization development. Individual and group ethics training contributes to the first two forms of development. Understanding and implementing the complete infrastructure of the ethical work culture constitutes the moral dimension of organizational development. One way, for example, that self-respecting managers demonstrate the strength of their character is by refusing to eliminate ethics training and development resources during cost-cutting times.

Organizing Factors: Technology

The third set of key organizing factors, *technological factors,* includes the employment of tools, machines, materials, and/or processes to do work, produce goods, perform services, or carry out other useful activities (Burris, 1993; Gattiger, 1990; J. Martin, 1995). Organizing technological factors requires treatment of information technologies (e.g., advanced computers, video displays, artificial intelligence, digital electronics) and non-information technologies (e.g., advanced genetic engineering and biochemistry, high-tech ceramics and polymers, advanced satellites and photovoltaic [PV] cells, along with lasers and fiber optics). Information technologies (ITs) handle information in life cycle stages, from acquiring, to processing, to storing, to disseminating, to using data. Ethical issues can arise at any of these stages. If properly organized, however, ITs can arrange large amounts of data into manageable information for responsible organizing decisions (Mason, Mason, & Culnan, 1995). Organizing information technologies (IT) can be, in large part, regarded as a form of enabling four types of companywide, electronically extended con- versations to occur rapidly to align and accelerate the decision-making processes for organizational change or stability (Austin, 1962; Fisher, 1987; Leonard-Barton, 1995; Rorty, 1989; Searle, 1969; Winograd & Flores, 1986).

The four types of IT conversations in which the computer literate engage are initiative, understanding, performance, and closure (Mason et al., 1995; Smith, 1994). First, IT *initiative* conversation rapidly calls attention to what could or should be done; for example, the university president sends an e-mail message to all administrators and faculty, proposing that the university endeavor to obtain the Baldrige Award for Quality in Education in 3 years. Second, IT conversations for generating *understanding* rapidly provide a "technological common" in which electronic dialogue eventually produces justified, measurable expectations for balancing organizational change and stability.

Employees who are "plugged into" and contribute to the electronic dialogue experience the benefits of participatory leveling, technological empowerment, and increased clarity about future measurable expectations; for example, the provost of the university may receive the president's proposal and ask, by e-mail, whether supplementary individual faculty rewards with interdepartmental faculty team rewards would be a policy change in line with Baldrige criteria. Third, IT conversations for *performance* consist of requests and promises transmitted to take action and produce specific results; for example, by e-mail, the president may formally charge the provost to be accountable for devising a feasible, cross-functional team faculty reward system in 2 weeks, and by e-mail the provost may counteroffer for a month's time period instead of 2 weeks to complete the project. Finally, when both parties agree to the month/time deadline, an IT performance promise has been enacted. Fourth, IT conversations for *closure* bring about an end to the performance agreement; for example, at month's end, the president may send a congratulatory message to the provost, with copies to the rest of the university community, publicly celebrating the successful completion of the faculty team reward project.

The extent to which IT organizational conversations occur are encouraged through nonhierarchic structures, and are facilitated by ongoing computer training for all employees will determine the quality and pace of responsible organizational decision making in a technoligically complex workplace.

In addition, organizing non-information-oriented technology to balance stability and change requires the consideration of operational efficiency, economic utility, legal/regulatory compliance, safety, health, and environmental soundness. For example, to organize an ecologically sustainable company that leads to sustainable development, managers need to coordinate at least three mechanisms among a growing number of processes (Jennings & Zandbergen, 1995): *total quality environmental management* (TQEM), *technology-for-nature swaps,* and *population impact control* (Shrivastava, 1995a, 1995b).

First, *TQEM* seeks to minimize the intra- and interorganization life cycle costs of inputs, throughputs, and outputs necessary to manufacturing products and providing services—for example, Procter & Gamble's (P&G) intraorganizational factoring in of disposal costs, legal fees, liability for product harm, and loss of environmental quality in its TQEM approach to household products. Similarly, the interorganizational extension of TQEM creates integrated industrial ecosystems, which are bioregional groups of companies that cooperate to minimize adverse ecological impact by coordinating their inputs, throughput,

Intended Organizing Realized

		Yes	No
Realized Organizing Successful	Yes	Coordinated Organizing Success (*Efficient and Effective*) [A]	Emergent Organizing Success (*Inefficient but Effective*) [C]
	No	Realized Organizing Failure (*Efficient but Not Effective*) [B]	Complete Organizing Failure (*Inefficient and Ineffective*) [D]

Figure 5.4. Organizing Success Evaluation Matrix

and outputs; for example, the network of power plants, refineries, and chemical plants in Kalundborg, Denmark, uses one another's wastes and by-products as inputs and closes the loop of output and input processes within the network (Shrivastava, 1996). Second, technology-for-nature swaps reduce North-South global and intergenerational equity conflicts—for example, DuPont's policy of swapping its chlorofluorocarbon (CFC) substitute technologies for access to sustainable cultivation and harvesting of genetic resources from Third World forests. Third, corporate population impact control in the less developed countries (LDCs) may entail encouragement of rural economic development, contributions to public education in family planning, and in cooperation with local institutions, the mass distribution of birth control devices (Shrivastava, 1995a, 1995b).

To evaluate the efficiency and effectiveness of the dimensions of organizing, Figure 5.4 provides a matrix based on two questions: (1) "Was the intended organizing successfully realized?" and (2) "Did the realized organizing successfully promote organizational performance?"

In Figure 5.4, the Organizing Success Evaluation Matrix contains four combinations. A yes-yes designation (in Quadrant A) means that the intended coordinated organizing was successful and fully meritorious: Managers set out to do something, they did it efficiently, and the organizing worked effectively. A yes-no designation (in Quadrant B) points toward a realized organizing failure in which managers efficiently implemented the intended organizing, which itself is only partially meritorious because that organizing proved to be ineffective. A no-yes designation (in Quadrant C) points toward inefficient implementation of the intended organizing but effective emergent organizing; for example, unintended and unanticipated organizing emerges that happens to be effective and is thereby partially meritorious. A no-no designation (in

Quadrant D) indicates a complete failure in organizing because of inefficient implementation of intended organizing and ineffective outcomes.

Now that the dimensions and success standards of organizing have been treated, it is important to address the relationship of ethical organizing processes to building integrity.

▧ ETHICAL ORGANIZING PROCESSES THAT BUILD INTEGRITY

All three dimensions of integrity—judgment, process, and developmental —are important in organizing with managerial integrity. Whereas the developmental and judgment dimensions anchor and sustain organizing with integrity, the process dimension builds organizing with integrity.

To organize in a fully meritorious manner, therefore, some form of systematic organizing process must be used. The following four-step sequence of responsible organizing provides a generic model of the organizing subprocess and their associated developmental tasks:

1. *Organizing Scanning:* scanning of current external and internal factors, using benchmarking, and process mapping (Camp, 1995)

2. *Organizing Formulation and Choice:* organizing formulation, analysis, and choice of relationship arrangements among structural, people, and technological factors that can most efficiently align and allocate resources to accomplish strategic plans by using inter- and intraorganizational cross-functional integration and reengineering simulation tools

3. *Organizing Implementation:* the chosen blend of structure, people, and technology is implemented and coordinated with organizational readiness to act by using scheduling, budgeting, team building, project management, and organizational character/health tools

4. *Organizing Evaluation, Control, and Improvement:* evaluation, control, and improvement of the results and impact of the chosen blend of structure, people, and technology by using a variety of performance indicators, audits, international quality standards, feedback, and process improvement tools

Each step in the generic organizing process must be adequately completed to result in a well-organized company that is both effective and efficient.

Processes	Step 1	Step 2	Step 3	Step 4
Ethics Processes	Ethical Awareness	Ethical Judgment	Ethical Intention	Ethical Conduct
Organizing Subprocesses	Organizing Scanning	Organizing Formulation	Organizing Implementation	Organizing Evaluation, Control, and Improvement

Figure 5.5. Parallel Ethics and Organizing Subprocesses That Build Management Integrity

The four process integrity steps parallel and permeate the four steps in the generic subprocess of organizing (organizing scanning, organizing formulation and choice, organizing implementation, and organizing evaluation, control, and improvement). In other words, *organizing with ethical integrity means addressing the elements of the four ethics processes in the context of their parallel organizing subprocesses to ensure that no step in the organizing function ignores its moral dimension.* Managers may lack integrity in organizing by neglecting to adequately perform the subtasks entailed in ethics and organizing processes, thereby exposing themselves and their organizations to ethical risk (see Chapter 1). Organizing with ethical integrity is facilitated by using the appropriate systematic queries from the QL-TOOL in Appendix D for each corresponding step of the generic organizing process. Figure 5.5 depicts the inclusive and sequential alignment of all ethics processes and organizing subprocesses steps that build management integrity.

Ethical Organizing Scanning

With regard to the alignment of ethics process and organizing subprocesses in Step 1 in Figure 5.5, the scope of ethical organizing scanning includes stakeholder benchmarking of best practices in the global and domestic, external and in- ternal organizational environment, specified in detail in queries 1, 2, and 3 from the QL-TOOL (external ecological, technological, economic, legal, sociocultural, and political factors and internal organizational ethics development system [OEDS] factors). Ethical organizing scanning is achieved when the two elements of the ethical awareness process (perception and sensitivity) are adequately addressed by responses to queries 1, 2, and 3 of the QL-TOOL.

Perception of and responsibility to external and internal stakeholders results in ethical organizing scanning.

Xerox Corporation Managers and Ethical Organizing Scanning

For example, Xerox's perception of and sensitivity to benchmarking for improved organizational structures and processes that enhance customer satisfaction have been economically applauded and morally acclaimed (Kearns & Nadler, 1992). In the 1980s, however, Xerox's former lion's share of the domestic copier market had dwindled to only 8%. Its functional structure compromised ethical and quality awareness in several ways: (a) it distanced people from customers and insulated them from customer expectations; (b) it promoted complex and wasteful processes and inhibited process improvement; and (c) it separated the quality and ethics responsibilities from the rest of the organization, providing people with an excuse for not worrying about quality and ethics awareness. David Kearns, former chairman and CEO of Xerox, and his top management team began organizing scanning and designed a new approach to reorganizing the relationships between people and technology. The distinctive emphasis of the new approach was the extensive use of benchmarking organizational structures, processes, technologies, and HR systems, rather than relying on internal standards and organizing traditions.

Benchmarking, the search for best practices that lead to superior performance, includes at least three major types: strategic, performance, and process benchmarking. *Strategic benchmarking* examines how companies compete and seek the winning strategies that have led to competitive advantage and market success. *Performance benchmarking* involves pricing, technical quality, features, and other quality or performance characteristics of products and services. Performance benchmarking is usually performed by direct comparisons or "reverse engineering," in which competitors' products are taken apart and analyzed. This practice is also called "competitive comparison" and involves studying products and processes of competitors in the same industry. *Process benchmarking* centers on work processes such as billing, order entry, and employee training. This type of benchmarking identifies the most effective practices in companies that perform similar functions, no matter what industry. For example, the warehousing and distribution practices of L. L. Bean were adapted by Xerox for its spare parts distribution system, and the billing processes of American Express were adapted by Xerox for its billing system. If process benchmarks are adopted from outside the industry, a company may learn ideas and processes as well as new applications that allow it to surpass the best within its own industry and to achieve distinctive superiority (Camp, 1995).

Furthermore, Xerox created a structural scanning team, known as the "Futuretecture" Team, to scan structural options for a new organizational architecture. This structural scanning team came up with a design recommendation to reconfigure Xerox in order to establish independent global business decisions that would be technologically linked. A second HR scanning team, known as the "Organizational Transformation Board," focused on the people issues of coordination and support between and among internal and external units, which were vital to the new architecture.

This combined organizational scanning approach for processes, structures, technologies, and people factors established unbiased targets based on the performance levels of world-class organizations. In the end, the process benchmarked design of an integrated supply chain of independent global business centers resulted in significant improvements in operational cycle time, reduction of inventory, and increased logistical efficiency. The net result was Xerox's dramatic competitive resurgence; its market share, revenues, and profits all have recovered substantially. In 1989, Xerox became one of the first winners of both the American and Canadian National Quality Awards. In effect, by using organization scanning, "Xerox is probably the first American company in an industry targeted by the Japanese to regain market share without the aid of tariffs or government help" (Kearns, 1990, p. 89; Kearns & Nadler, 1992).

By encouraging multiple stakeholder input into organizing scanning, Xerox managers gained access to the perceptions and sensitivities of external and internal customers. Prioritizing and satisfying these multiple stakeholders, rather than only investors, became a key part of the foundation of ethical organizing at Xerox (Boatright, 1993; Clarkson, 1991; Donaldson & Preston, 1995; Freeman, 1994; Goodpaster, 1991; Jones, 1995). In fact, organizing that ignores or neglects multiple stakeholder input capacities or that prevents voiced feedback jeopardizes managerial and organization integrity at the outset.

Ethical Organizing Formulation and Choice

With regard to the alignment of ethics and organizing processes in Step 2 in Figure 5.5, the scope of ethical organizing formulation and choice includes factors in the global and domestic, external and internal organizational context and judgment, specified in query 4 in the QL-TOOL (supportive external and internal contexts for optimal ethical analysis and resolution in demonstrating judgment integrity). Ethical organizing formulation and choice is achieved when the two elements of the ethical judgment process (analysis and resolution) are adequately addressed by responses to query 4 of the QL-TOOL. The presence of thorough, multidisciplinary ethical analysis leads to structured moral dialogue to arrive at balanced, justified resolution of ethically framed issues and results in ethical organizing formulation and choice.

Federal Express Corporation Managers and
Ethical Organizing Formulation and Choice

For example, Memphis-based Federal Express has the world's largest fleet of air cargo delivery planes and is a leader in the U.S. overnight package delivery market (Waterman, 1994). The company credo states simply: People, Service, and Profits; that is, all organizing factors (structure, human resources, and technology) and decisions are evaluated in terms of their effects on the employees (people), their customers (service), and the company's financial performance (profits)—in that order. It provides a good example of an organization that has been involved in ethical organizing formulation and choice through the four programs of its quality improvement process: the Survey Feedback Action (SFA) Program, the Guaranteed Fair Treatment (GFT) Program, the Quality Action Team (QAT) Program, and the Service Quality Indicator (SQI) Program.

First, the SFA Program is an annual employee survey of the leadership effectiveness at Federal Express, and it gives people an opportunity to express attitudes about the company, management, compensation, and service. What is different about the SFA Program is the focus of the first 10 statements that comprise the leadership index that determines annual managerial bonuses. Those 10 statements do not evaluate how closely managers supervise their people, nor do they assess how well they manage their budgets. Instead, the leadership index reveals how well managers support their people and how well they empower them, *as perceived by each manager's customers*—the people who report to him or her. A list of the SFA questions is provided in Figure 5.6.

Although individual responses are kept confidential, overall results are passed on to all managers, who must then meet with their work groups to develop an action plan for resolving any problems that surface. To ensure that this part of the SFA process really works over time, Statement 29 states: "The

1. I feel free to tell my manager what I think.
2. My manager lets me know what's expected of me.
3. Favoritism is not a problem in my work group.
4. My manager helps us to find ways to do our jobs better.
5. My manager is willing to listen to my concerns.
6. My manager asks for my ideas about things affecting our work.
7. My manager lets me do my job without interfering.
8. My manager treats me with respect and dignity.
9. My manager keeps me informed about things I need to know.
10. My manager lets me do my job without interfering.
11. My manager's boss gives us the support we need.
12. Upper management (directors and above) lets us know what the company is trying to accomplish.
13. Upper management (directors and above) pays attention to ideas and suggestions from people at my level.
14. I have confidence in the fairness of management.
15. I can be sure of a job as long as I do good work.
16. I am proud to work for Federal Express.
17. Working for Federal Express will probably lead to the kind of future I want.
18. I think Federal Express does a good job for our customers.
19. All things considered, working for Federal Express is a good deal for me.
20. I am paid fairly for the kind of work I do.
21. Our benefit programs seem to meet most of my needs.
22. Most people in my work group cooperate with each other to get the job done.
23. There is cooperation between my work group and other groups in Federal Express.
24. In my work environment, we generally use safe work practices.
25. Rules and procedures do not interfere with how well I am able to do my job.
26. I am able to get the supplies or other resources I need to do my job.
27. I have enough freedom to do my job well.
28. My work group is involved in activities to improve service to our group's customers.
29. The concerns identified in my work group during last year's SFA feedback session have been satisfactorily addressed.

Figure 5.6. Questions for Federal Express Survey Feedback Action (SFA) Program

concerns identified by my work group during last year's SFA feedback session have been satisfactorily addressed."

Second, the GFT Program is designed to ensure fair treatment at work. Anyone who arrives at an ethical judgment that he or she has been unfairly treated (for whatever reason) can have these ethical concerns addressed

Error Indicator Type Description	Weight
1. Abandoned calls	1
2. Complaints reopened	5
3. Damaged package	10
4. International	1
5. Invoice adjustments requested	1
6. Lost packages	1
7. Missed pick-ups	10
8. Missing proofs of delivery	10
9. Overgoods (lost and found)	5
10. Right day late deliveries	1
11. Traces	1
12. Wrong day late deliveries	5

Figure 5.7. Federal Express Service Quality Indicator (SQI) Factors

SOURCE: Service Quality Indicators at Federal Express—Internal Company Document. © 1984 Federal Express Corporation. All Rights Reserved.

through the management network. Every week, the chief HR officer, two ro-tating senior vice presidents, and the CEO meet to review the three-step internal process to the final stage, the appeals board. The GFT Program is one way to implement part of an ethical work culture that institutionalizes orga-nizational justice as a key component of any system development ethics.

Third, the QAT Program, which currently involves 1,000 teams all over the world, was cited by the national Baldrige Award examiners as a model for involving and training people at all corporate levels. Cross-divisional root cause teams, each led by a vice president, focus on each of the 10 major process/ project improvement indices. Divisional and work group QATs solve hundreds of organizational process problems and come up with solutions that improve service, save money, and correct strategy. Policy deployment based on QAT feedback has literally saved Federal Express millions of dollars.

Finally, the SQI Program is a 12-item error index of service quality that is weighted on a scale from 1 to 10 and provides public outcome measures for all employees, as indicated in Figure 5.7.

The total score from all 12 error indicator types provides a daily SQI measure, which is communicated to every Federal Express facility via the FedEx satellite-linked TV network, called FXTV. Surveys show that as the SQI goes down, customer satisfaction goes up. To accelerate the improvement process, an action team headed by a senior executive has been assigned to study each of the failure points to determine how they can be reduced or eliminated. In the 1st year that the SQI was instituted, Federal Express averaged 152,000 daily points. By 1991, the monthly rate was 99,959, and Federal Express continued to set new daily, weekly, and monthly records on its way to 15,000 annual SQI points. In essence, the Baldrige Award-winning ways of Federal Express are, in part, a result of its ethics and quality organizing formulation and choice with regard to its processes in addressing people, service, and profits.

In essence, managers who foster a well-developed ethical work culture infrastructure provide their employees with the moral framework and language to facilitate ethics dialogue about how best to organize structure, people, and technology that achieve planned objectives. Organizations like Federal Express, that formulate and choose processes that anchor strain ethical work cultures, are more likely than competitors to arrive at sound collective ethical judgments on a regular basis.

Ethical Organizing Implementation

With regard to the alignment of the ethics processes and organizing sub-processes in Step 3 in Figure 5.5, the extent of the ethical organizing implementation can be determined by fully addressing queries 5, 6, and 9 from the QL-TOOL. Ethical organizing implementation is achieved when the two elements of the ethical intention process (cognitive and volitional readiness to act) are demonstrated by responses to queries 5, 6, and 9 of the QL-TOOL. Obviously, poor implementation of a rationally formulated organizational design can result in organizing and moral failure. Less obviously, refusal to consider feedback to modify original organizational designs in light of operational experience or to replace the intended organization design with a more feasible, emergent one is also an organizing and moral failure. The demands of ethical organizing implementation in dealing with people, structure, and technology factors can be dramatized in the Johnson Controls case.

Johnson Controls, Inc. Managers and
Unethical Organizing Implementation

At the time of the Supreme Court decision, Johnson Controls, Inc., was a leading U.S. manufacturer of automotive lead batteries, particularly for the replacement parts market. Between its founding at the turn of the century and the late 1970s, Johnson Controls was engaged chiefly in the production of

environmental controls, automotive sealing, and miscellaneous plastic products. In 1978, the company purchased Globe Union, Inc., an independent
battery manufacturer that had been in business for more than 50 years. In 1990,
the Globe Battery Division of Johnson Controls operated 14 plants, extending
from Bennington, Vermont, to Fullerton, California, and accounted for 16%
of Johnson's sales and 20% of its income. That year, the company as a whole
posted sales of $4.5 billion and employed 43,500 workers—approximately
5,400 of them in the battery division.

Prior to the 1960s, few if any women worked in production jobs at Globe
Union, reflecting long-standing historical patterns of gender segregation in
which men worked in production jobs and women worked in office and support roles. In the 1970s, at Globe Union, as in many other businesses in those
years, women began moving in increasing numbers into traditionally male occupations. Even by the mid-1980s, however, only a small percentage of women
had production jobs. In the Bennington, Vermont, plant, for example, only 5%
of the production workforce was female. Women never penetrated the top
echelons of the company. In 1990, the company's 15 top executives and 12
directors were men. In short, the company could be described as paternalistic.

The production process used in Johnson's Global Battery Division plants
necessarily entailed exposure to lead, which is the element that enables an
automotive battery to store and deliver electricity. To make a battery, Johnson
Controls workers mixed lead oxide to form a paste, which was then compressed
to form lead plates in the core of the battery. Lead dust and vapors were
produced at multiple points in the production process. Johnson Controls, like
other battery manufacturers, had made numerous efforts to develop a non-
lead-based battery. Although several technological alternatives were currently
in the experimental stage, including a zinc-bromide battery that Johnson had
been researching for several years, none had yet been successfully developed
for commercial use.

When lead particles are inhaled or ingested, they damage the central
nervous, immune, reproductive, cardiovascular, and excretory systems of
males and females. According to the Centers for Disease Control and Prevention (CDC), lead becomes dangerous to adults at blood levels of 50 μg/dl.
Children suffer toxic effects from lead at even lower levels of 25 μg/dl. Furthermore, lead in a pregnant woman's bloodstream adversely affects a fetus at blood
levels of 10 μg/dl.

In 1977, Johnson Controls implemented a voluntary policy warning of
women in higher-paying, lead-exposed jobs about dangers to avoid lawsuits

based on sex discrimination. But by 1982, the policy of warning was changed to a fetal protection policy, a form of paternalistic exclusion to justify pregnancy discrimination through a bonafide occupational qualification (BFOQ). Johnson Controls was responding to the fact that, between 1979 and 1982, eight employees became pregnant while maintaining blood levels in excess of 30 μg/dl, the OSHA standard. Johnson Controls maintained that its policy represented a BFOQ and that it required medical certification of non-child-bearing status to avoid substantial liability for injuries.

In 1984, three Johnson Controls employees filed suit against the company on the grounds that the fetal-protection policy was a form of sex discrimination that violated Title VII of the Civil Rights Act. The three employees included Mary Craig, who had chosen to be sterilized to avoid losing her job that involved lead exposure; Elsie Nason, a 50-year-old divorcee who experienced a wage decrease when she transferred out of a job in which she was exposed to lead; and Donald Penney, a man who was denied a leave of absence so that he could lower his lead level because he intended to become a father. The trial court certified a class action and included all past, present, and future Johnson Controls employees who have been or continue to be affected by the fetal protection policy implemented by Johnson Controls in 1992.

At the trial, uncontroverted evidence was presented that exposure to lead affects the reproductive abilities of men and women and that the effects of exposure on adults are as great as those on the fetus, although the fetus appears to be more vulnerable to exposure than adults. Johnson Controls' rationale changed in court and maintained that its policy was one that resulted from business necessity.

The employees argued that fertile men, but not fertile women, are given the choice whether to risk their reproductive health for a particular job. Johnson Controls responded that its policy was not based on any intent to discriminate culturally, but rather on its concern for the health of the unborn child. Johnson Controls also pointed out that more than 40 states recognize a right for a parent to recover for a prenatal injury on the basis of negligence or wrongful death, and its policy was designed to prevent its liability for such injury or death to fetuses. Johnson Controls maintained that just because it complied with Title VII did not mean it would be exempt from state tort liability for injury to the parent or the child. The employees, however, argued that the 1982 policy of Johnson Controls, if upheld, would open the door to the exclusion of women from a very wide range of jobs entailing possible hazards to the fetus, thus effectively resegregating the workforce. According to studies by the Bureau of National Affairs, as many as 20 million jobs held by women involved exposure to possible fetotoxins; many millions more involved exposure to other risks, such as infectious agents, stress, noise, radiation, or even ordinary physical accidents such as falls or automobile accidents.

Because fertile women were just as capable of performing hazardous work as men and infertile women in traditional male-dominated and female-dominated occupations and because the parent, not the employer, has the caring responsibility to assess possible risks and protect the fetus, the Supreme Court decided that the 1982 policy was a violation of the Pregnancy Discrimination Act and, therefore, a form of illegal sex discrimination.

The moral lessons of ethical organizing implementation from the Johnson Controls case include the following:

- It is more important for managers to avoid unethical discrimination in the present than to avoid future legal tort risk.
- It is more unfair for companies to discriminate against pregnant female employees than innocent fetuses.
- It is more unethical for managers to disrespect the reproductive risk choices of adult employees than to act paternalistically in a democratic society.
- It is more important to respect female reproductive and economic autonomy than to protectively impose sexist, corporate patriarchy.
- The optimal ethical implementation response to hazardous work conditions is not to exclude fertile women, but to reduce workplace exposures through replacement technology, for all employees, male and female, insofar as it is economically feasible.

Ethical Organizing Evaluation, Control, and Improvement

With regard to the alignment of ethics processes and organizing subprocesses in Step 4 in Figure 5.5, the scope of ethical organizing evaluation, control, and improvement includes stakeholder conduct and reputation in the global and domestic, external and internal organizational environments, specified in detail in queries 7, 8, and 10 from the QL-TOOL (extent to which responsible, ecological, economic, ethical, legal, and philanthropic conduct anchors and builds reputations for integrity). Ethical organizing evaluation, control, and improvement are achieved when the two elements of the ethical conduct process (being responsibly responsive and engaging in sustainable development) are adequately addressed by responses to queries 7, 8, and 10 of the

QL-TOOL. Irresponsible and unsustainable conduct results in unethical organizing evaluation, control, and improvement.

Tokyo Electric Power Company Managers
and Ethical Evaluation, Control, and Improvement

For example, Tokyo Electric Power Company (TEPCO) is the largest private electric utility company in the world (Shrivastava, 1996). In 1992, it had revenues of 4.7 trillion yen, a generating capacity of 47,000 megawatts, employed 40,000 workers, and served about 42 million people. About 32% of power generated was nuclear. By 2001, TEPCO will generate 65,000 megawatts per year, of which 42% will be produced by nuclear energy. This high dependence on nuclear energy creates huge environmental risks and responsibility for the company. By 2050, nearly 40% of world economic production will be related to energy and environmental technologies. The demand for such power will come from developing and industrialized countries.

To meet the performance challenges in a responsible and sustainable manner, TEPCO developed an environmental management policy to minimize the impact of its operations on the surrounding environment through technological innovations and international networking. It organizes and improves its technology and interorganizational networking to balance energy production needs with environmental protection in four ways. First, TEPCO has become the world's technological leader in reduction of dioxide pollutants. All TEPCO power plants use desulfurization equipment, flue gas denitrification technology, in-furnace nitrogen dioxide reduction systems, electrostatic precipitators, tall stacks, and particulate scrubbers. The result of these measures is impressive. Per unit of electricity generated, TEPCO emits less than 0.4 g/kwh of sulfur dioxide and nitrogen dioxide, compared with an average of 6.5 g/kwh of sulfur dioxide and 3.2 g/kwh of nitrogen dioxide in the United States, Germany, the United Kingdom, and France. Second, TEPCO recently unveiled the highest-performing electric car in existence. It can drive for 340 miles at 25 mph on a single battery charge and can reach a maximum speed of 109 mph. Third, TEPCO has partnered with the Japanese government to become the world's leader in municipal solid waste management. Japan's nationwide solid-waste recycling program claims to recycle 35% of its wastes, far more than in the United States, where the figure is about 7%. This program involves stringent recycling laws, a strong recycling infrastructure, and a thriving government-supported market for recycled materials. Fourth, both TEPCO and

Japan are highly dependent on nuclear energy. They are experimenting with alterative technologies for decommissioning nuclear power plants, disposing of low-level radioactive wastes, and handling spent nuclear fuels. These technologies include robots for cutting up a nuclear reactor core, television remote control of operations, and nuclear waste-containment vessels and disposal methods. The market for decommissioning nuclear power plants is as huge as it is lucrative, potentially a trillion-dollar market in the coming decades. There are about 400 civilian nuclear power plants around the world, most built in the 1950s to 1970s, with a licensed useful life of about 30 years. They will need to be decommissioned in this and the next decade, and each decommissioning can cost more than $2 billion (Shrivastava, 1996).

In addition to responsible and sustainable organizing of environmental technologies and consumption management, TEPCO and Japan have partnered to develop interorganizational learning networks and organizational risk-sharing arrangements that form an integrated and mutually reinforcing set of standards to measure and improve organizational environmental performance. First, new international organizational partnering used by TEPCO and Japan include the creation of technology consortia to generate the expensive new technologies needed for large-scale environmental management. Groups of companies in the consortium jointly fund basic research and share research results; this cuts down the time required and reduces the financial risk for individual companies such as TEPCO. A good example of this is nuclear power plant decommissioning technologies. The technologies involved are expensive, hazardous, and financially risky. The markets for these technologies, though definite, are in the distant future. By creating a consortium of several dozen companies to develop pieces of this technology, Japan has leap-frogged ahead of the United States. Second, the tradition of government-business partnership has given TEPCO and other Japanese companies a strong competitive advantage in the global environmental industry. Government ministries work closely with TEPCO and other companies to study markets, design strategies, fund R&D projects, and open trade relationships. The Ministry of International Trade and Industry (MITI) is funding several alternative energy resources and pollution-control technologies. The Office of Development Assistance (ODA), the government's development funding agency, has earmarked funds to subsidize environmental projects in Asia. MITI proposed bundling energy aid projects in China, Malaysia, and Indonesia with ODA subsidies for Japanese environmental equipment purchases. Having these powerful governmental agencies as allies gives TEPCO and other Japanese companies direct entry into intergovernmental markets around the world. Third, TQ organizations, like TEPCO, also react to and influence their social environments by proactively building international, national, and regional societal learning networks that share information about new quality environmental practices and, in turn, place social pressure on other organizations to meet enhanced quality environmental standards.

In Japan, for example, the extended institutional infrastructure of societal learning includes six elements: (a) national promotional organizations, (b) national training in existing quality methods, (c) national knowledge dissemination of new quality methods, (d) societal learning and promotional activities, (e) national and international standard certification, and (f) sustained research and development of new TQ methods (Shiba, Graham, & Walden, 1993). Among the national promotional organizations are the Ministry of International Trade and Research (MITI), the Japanese Industrial Standards (JIS), the Union of Japanese Scientists and Engineers (JUSE), and the Japanese Standards Association (JSA). The primary roles of JUSE and JSA are national training, national knowledge dissemination, societal learning, promotional activities, and new research and development efforts. JIS, in conjunction with the International Standards Organization (ISO), certifies national and international quality standards. Although the United States has somewhat of a social network infrastructure (e.g., American Society for Quality Control, GOAL/QPC, Center for Quality Management, Department of Labor Office of the American Workplace), it is not as integrated and mutually reinforcing as the Japanese network (Reich, 1991; Shiba et al., 1993). The net result is that, in organizing the evaluation, control, and improvement of quality systems, U.S. managers and organizations are far behind Japanese managers, and their preferred methods for dealing with the issue are likely to exacerbate organizational equity issues. U.S. firms exhibit the widest range of quality implementation variation, with heavy reliance on executive incentive programs, rather than on internal system improvements to stimulate TQ initiatives. In contrast, Japanese organizations use TQ practices more intensively than do firms in other major global trading regions. In effect, U.S. firms end up overcompensating top executives, rather than improving their internal system of processes and developing interorganizational partnering networks to coordinate standards that systematically control unacceptable variation (Petrick & Furr, 1995).

Managers contribute to ethical organizing improvement, therefore, through the publicity of responsible and sustainable external relations with society and nature, which in turn sets higher moral standards of organizing for the industry, the marketplace, the nation, and the world. Managers with a reputation for responsible responsiveness and sustainable development in organizing structural, human, and technological resources are in demand because they can organize people and processes in a way that enhances management integrity.

▧ MANAGEMENT ETHICS AND ORGANIZING WITH INTEGRITY MINICASES

To apply management ethical decision making and organize with integrity, the following minicases are offered for practice analysis. They raise issues in management ethics and organizing with integrity and are categorized into seven allied management application clusters:

1. Accounting/auditing issues
2. Finance/investment issues
3. Marketing/advertising issues
4. Business management/human resources/business law issues
5. Technology/quality operations/organizational behavior issues
6. Public/nonprofit/health care administration issues
7. International/environmental/public policy issues

These clusters are generic categories, and specific cases in any one chapter may not cover all subfields in the cluster, but at least one minicase in Chapters 4 through 7 addresses each subfield in the cluster. Of the 18 subfields contained in the seven clusters, 28 minicases are provided, ensuring that each subfield is addressed at least once and that overlapping interfield problems are included.

To incorporate the tools and resources of this book to analyze and resolve organizing issues with integrity, the authors recommend that each minicase be approached with three objectives in mind:

1. Systematically apply the QL-TOOL in an individual or collective setting to arrive at a principled, feasible resolution.
2. In accomplishing the first objective, consciously engage in ethics dialogue as the guiding method of moral discourse.
3. Select the appropriate components of the OEDS (in Appendix E) and other tools contained in the Appendices that would cultivate, build, and/or sustain dimensions of management integrity in the future.

(1) Accounting/Auditing Minicase:
(Case 5A) - E. F. Hutton & Company

On May 2, 1985, E. F. Hutton & Company (Hutton) ended a 3-year probe into its cash management practices and pleaded guilty to 2,000 separate counts of criminal mail and wire fraud. Specifically, Hutton admitted to organizing and implementing *excessive overdrafts* (systematically overdrawing its bank accounts) and *chaining* (generating check-clearing delays by successively pooling deposit checks from different branches around the country). Through these and other cash management practices, Hutton was able to obtain more than $1 billion in interest-free funds from its banks during a time when short-term interest rates reached 18% to 20%. Additionally, the scale of damage due to organizing without integrity in accounting management at Hutton, which involved at least 20 branches, threatened the liquidity of unsuspecting lenders and endangered the entire U.S. banking system. The net result was that the irresponsible, intended, and coordinated cash management process of Hutton victimized the processes of many more responsible stakeholders.

In practice, Hutton's cash management system, which was endorsed by top management, targeted banks that employ the "float factor." These banks did not use computer analysis for deposits and automatically gave customer/depositors 1-day availability on all checks. By zeroing in on these banks, Hutton was able to engage in excessive overdrafts. Then, Hutton used chaining, a process in which checks that are overdrafts are funneled through the system to various banks so that the float period was an interest-earning period even when there was actually no money passing through the system. Hutton took advantage of the fact that some banks cannot differentiate between ledger and available balances. It was depositing funds that were not immediately available but was treating them as if they were. Banks were honoring those checks, and Hutton was eventually covering them, but earning interest through this check-kiting scheme.

In most states, writing checks backed by insufficient funds could be prosecuted as larceny or theft if criminal intent could be proved. Why did Hutton assume these legal risks for short-term economic gain? Thomas Rae, Hutton's general counsel, rationalized that Hutton's practices raised no legal problems, citing a 1981 U.S. Supreme Court decision that ruled 5-4 that writing bad checks was not a crime under federal law prohibiting false statements to federally insured banks (*Williams v. United States*, 458 U.S. 279, 1982). The Court reasoned that a check is not a "statement," but rather a "promise to pay," obligating the person drawing the check to pay if the check is dishonored. This extraorganizational, legal interpretation provided Hutton with the opportunity to engage in corrupt accounting practices and to use aggressive cash (check) management practices to boost company earnings, displacing risk onto other stakeholders.

In effect, the lack of organizing accounting processes with integrity resulted in excessive overdrafts and chaining, provoked government intervention, skyrocketed litigation costs, and endangered the U.S. banking system. (For more details, see Stevens, M. [1989]. *Sudden death: The rise and fall of E. F. Hutton.* New York: New American Library.)

(2) Finance/Investment Minicase: (Case 5B) - Kidder, Peabody and Company

Joseph Jett earned his master's degree in business administration from Harvard in 1987. Dismissed from his first postdegree job at CS First Boston, he then worked for Morgan Stanley but was laid off in the post-1980s Wall Street cutbacks. Despite his lack of experience in government securities, Jett was hired in 1991 by Kidder, Peabody and Company to work in the government bonds section of the fixed-income department.

The fixed-income department was headed by Edward Cerullo, a hands-off manager who emphasized profits and was credited with turning Kidder around following the late-1980s insider trading scandals. The compensation system rewarded financial results without close supervision of the processes used to achieve them; "never question success" was the informal operating norm. Some fixed-income traders so feared telling Cerullo of losses that they underreported their profits at certain times so that they would have reserves to cover any future losses.

At the time of Cerullo's tenure and Jett's employment, Kidder Peabody was owned by General Electric (GE), which had purchased it in 1986 for $602 million. The GE/Kidder strategic and operational emphases on financial success reinforced each other. To establish Kidder as a Wall Street force, GE poured $1 billion into the firm and had begun to see a return only from 1991 to 1994. In 1992, GE had tried to sell Kidder to Smith, Barney, Harris, Upham and Company, but the sale fell through when Smith Barney learned of the extent of Kidder's mortgage-backed bond inventory.

In 1991, Linda LaPrade sued Kidder, claiming she was terminated as a vice president when she brought illegal trading to the attention of Cerullo. She also claimed she was told to increase allotments from government agency security issuers by "any means necessary." Also in 1991, the National Association of Securities Dealers (NASD) fined Kidder and Cerullo $5,000 for conduct by one of Kidder's bond traders, Ira Saferstein, who profited from a customer error.

During this same period, Jett's profits bulged to 20% of the fixed-income group's total, and Jett was promoted to the head of the government bond department. Hugh Bush, a trader at Kidder raised questions, however, when he examined Jett's trades. In April 1992, Bush accused Jett of "mismarking," or misrecording, trading positions, an illegal practice. Bush's allegations were never investigated, and Bush was fired within a month. Jett's profits, in fact, did not exist. Jett had taken advantage of a financial accounting process loophole at Kidder that enabled him to earn a $9 million bonus for 1993 alone. The fictitious profits were posted through an accounting system that separated out the interest portion of the bond. Jett captured the profit on the "strip" (the interest portion of the bond) before it was reconstituted, or turned back into the original bond. Kidder's financial and compensation processes only recognized profits on the date that the reconstituted bond was entered into the system. The result was that, during $2\frac{1}{2}$ years, Jett generated $350 million in fictitious profits. When the scheme was uncovered by auditors in April 1994, GE had to take a $210 million write-off in its second quarter.

On April 17, 1994, Jett was fired, his bonus and accounts were frozen, and the SEC began an investigation that resulted in the following costly results:

1. June 22, 1994: GE fired Kidder CEO Michael Carpenter.
2. July 14,1994: Kidder's brokerage chief, Michael Kechner, quit.
3. July 22, 1994: Cerullo quit.
4. August 4, 1994: Kidder fired three additional trader managers.
5. December 1994: GE sold Kidder to Paine Webber for $670 million, requiring GE to take a $917 million loss on the value of Kidder's assets and a $500 million write-off for the fourth quarter of 1994.
6. About half of Kidder Peabody's 5,000 employees were laid off following completion of the Paine Webber deal.
7. Because GE's income dropped 48% for the final quarter of 1994, a group of GE shareholders sued GE for the loss in share value resulting from the Kidder problems, the write-off, and the subsequent sale of Kidder for a loss.

In short, the lack of organizing financial processes with integrity resulted in fraudulent profits, SEC intervention, multi-million-dollar financial losses, shareholder lawsuits, thousands of lost jobs, and shattered reputations. (For more details, see Slater, R. [1992]. *The new GE: How Jack Welch revived an American institution*. Burr Ridge, IL: Irwin.)

(3) Marketing/Advertising Minicase: (Case 5C) - Investors Center, Inc. (ICI) and Telemarketing Boiler Rooms

Investors Center, Inc. (ICI) was a penny stock brokerage firm, headquartered in Hauppauge, New York. ICI housed 900 young "brokers," each equipped with a telephone and a sales pitch. ICI used a "six-call approach," whereby brokers were expected to call a prospect six times in their efforts to persuade him or her to invest. The third and fourth calls were the most important because then the sales pitch was made and the financial relationships established. Brokers followed a script for each call, which included "excuses" or additional phrases that helped the broker make the sale or refute the client's doubts or objections.

ICI chairman Anthony Stoisich acknowledged that his brokers were primarily salespeople, with little knowledge of the securities industry; he said there was little need for brokers to have in-depth securities knowledge unless they were able to sell. ICI's strong sales tactics upset a few of its brokers, and some former employees spoke out against ICI's policies. Salespeople were expected to use high-pressure sales techniques to sell the "stock of the day." There were no organized company processes for sustained securities industry training or quality control assurances to avoid boiler room abuses.

According to the Council of Better Business Bureaus and the North American Securities Administration Association, the term *boiler rooms* originated in the 1920s to describe organizations that crammed salesmen into hot, low-rent offices to tout worthless stocks to investors. Today's boiler rooms are much the same; small, disreputable organizations peddling things as diverse as worthless stocks, precious metals, land, art, "luxury" vacations, and vitamins over the telephone to defraud unsophisticated investors. Often the phones and salespeople make up the entire business operation. Advanced telemarketing techniques, inexpensive long-distance telephone rates, and computerized dialing have eased the boiler rooms' task.

The National Association of Securities Dealers (NASD) became skeptical of ICI's practices. It claimed that ICI often inflated the prices of warrants (options to purchase stocks within a specified range) and sold them to individual customers at a tremendous markup. One former broker charged that ICI wholesaled certain warrants to other brokerages for 12 cents but sold them to customers for 50 cents. Similar incidents were reported to be commonplace at ICI. Stoisich claimed that his company was doing small entrepreneurs a favor by providing a market in which their inexpensive stock could be traded.

Nonetheless, the NASD, in response to complaints and its own investigation, imposed stricter regulations on ICI, mandating that it could no longer hold its customers' cash or securities and that it must clear all its transactions through an outside firm. When ICI brokers began selling off their clients' stocks early in 1989, the firm collapsed. The Justice Department considered filing criminal fraud and Racketeer Influenced and Corrupt Organizations (RICO) racketerring charges against the firm, using the Act.

Most telemarketing boiler room operations thrive until government investigation or angry investors' threats of lawsuits force them to close. Others choose to shut down before the law moves in. By then, the boiler room operators have typically bilked thousands of dollars out of unsuspecting investors. Many of the swindlers simply move on to another state or another country and switch to different boiler room scams.

In short, the lack of organizing sales/marketing efforts with integrity resulted in consumer fraud in the millions of dollars, federal regulatory and judicial intervention, erosion of public trust in reputable telemarketing firms, and lowered respect for securities dealers. (For more details, see Council for Better Business Bureaus & the North American Securities Administration Association. [1988]. *Investor alert: How to protect your money from schemes, scams, and frauds.* New York: Benjamin.)

(4) Business Management/Human Resources/
Business Law Minicase: (Case 5D) - J. C. Penney Company, Inc.

In April 1986, Euna Faye Blake, a 17-year employee of J. C. Penney Company, Inc., was terminated from her sales position in the shoe department. The company's contention was that she allegedly slapped another employee and that this action was in violation of the company's Personnel Procedures Manual, which had a section on "Assaulting an Associate." Blake, though not denying that she slapped another employee, contended that the employee had made several harassing remarks to her over a 2-year period and that despite her complaints to supervisors, management, and the Personnel Department, nothing was done. She contended that the repeated remarks, such as "senile old woman" and "crazy old woman," coupled with her failure to get a transfer and the stress of a family health crisis (which she made known to others in the department), prompted the slap. The 56-year-old filed an age discrimination claim, and on January 16, 1990, the United States Court of Appeals held that there was sufficient evidence to support Blake's claim of age discrimination. Furthermore, her awarded damages of $35,000 in lost wages and benefits could not be reduced by the amount she would receive from her pension/retirement plan.

Among the types of evidence offered in Blake's age discrimination case were the following:

> Her performance appraisals had been consistently high; she had often been praised as a valuable asset to the company because of her sales record and her efforts with assisting others in the department. Her last two performance appraisals prior to her dismissal reflected the highest possible rating a J. C. Penney employee could receive; she clearly had the ability to do her job well.

> One week prior to her dismissal, Blake ranked among the top 10 shoe salespersons for all J. C. Penney stores in the southeastern United States.

> Not only did Blake assist with training new employees, but she did more than her share of work when stocking the shelves. Although her responsibilities included stocking nine shelves, other, younger salespersons were responsible for stocking at most four.

> For 2 years, Mr. Hubbard, Blake's coworker, repeatedly made offensive remarks to her regarding her age. He called her a "senile old woman" and a "crazy old woman." Although Blake complained of this disrespectful treatment to her line manager on numerous occasions and also complained to the personnel manager on at least four occasions, no action was taken against Hubbard. In fact, the personnel manager advised her to put up with the treatment for 3 more years, at which time she would be eligible for early retirement.

The Court of Appeals ruled that Blake submitted evidence that J. C. Penney either tolerated or condoned Hubbard's age-directed insults. In addition to the fact that the company's personnel records did not reflect that Hubbard had ever been disciplined for his actions, the company essentially told Blake 2 weeks prior to the incident that she would have to put up with it until she retired. Additionally, the Court of Appeals found that the slap did not have to result in dismissal and that J. C. Penney had previously retained a younger worker after another incident involving physical contact with an employee. The court mentioned that employers, though free to establish standards for employee conduct, must enforce such criteria in a nondiscriminatory manner.

The Age Discrimination in Employment Act (ADEA) was passed by Congress in 1967 with three purposes: (a) to promote employment of older persons based on their ability rather than age, (b) to prohibit arbitrary age discrimination in employment, and (c) to help employers and workers find ways of meeting problems arising from the impact of age on employment. The law makes it illegal for an employer to discriminate against persons 40 years of age or older with regard to compensation, terms, conditions, or privileges of employment because of such persons' age. Thus, the ADEA requires that employers not implement policies and procedures that discriminate against an employee simply because of his or her age. The law requires that employees are evaluated on their performance, as opposed to their age.

The past few years, however, have seen an increasing number of age discrimination claims in the United States. Age discrimination claims filed with the Equal Employment Opportunity Commission jumped 34% to 19,884 in 1993 from 14,789 in 1989. Older workers and their larger salaries are prime targets for layoffs and downsizings to cut costs. Managers need to realize, however, that the penalties for engaging in age discrimination can be quite severe. A recent survey of 515 verdicts in wrongful-termination lawsuits found that the average age discrimination award was $302,914. That average is higher than those found for race, sex, and disability discrimination, in part, because juries realize that other victims of discrimination usually can move on to other jobs at comparable pay, whereas victims of age discrimination often become unemployable.

Managers need to be aware of and counter the following age stereotypes and myths: (a) "you can never teach an old dog new tricks"; (b) work capacity and ability to perform necessarily decline in all lines of work with age; (c) older workers are uniformly less adaptable to new work requirements; (d) all older people resent and will resist being managed by younger people; and (e) older people will necessarily have more absences because of illness and injury. They need to resist the "Detroit syndrome" of treating older employees in a three-stage disrespectful process by first devaluing them, then discounting them, and finally dumping them.

In short, the lack of organizing human resources and business law processes with integrity relating to older workers results in increased litigation costs, government intervention, waste of human expertise and organizational memory, incitement of intergenerational disrespect, and increased organizational cynicism. (For more details, see Crown, W. [1996]. *Handbook on employment and the elderly.* New York: Greenwood.)

(5) Technology/Quality Operations/Organizational Behavior Minicase: (Case 5E) - Sears, Roebuck and Company Auto Centers

Despite its long history of high earnings and its penetration into the U.S. market, in 1990 Sears, Roebuck and Company reported a 40% decline in earnings, with the merchandising group dropping a whopping 60%! Cost-cutting measures were designed, including the elimination of jobs, profit-centered performance standards, and new compensation systems. Sears' automotive unit, with 850 repair shops nationwide, generated 9% of the merchandise group's $19.4 billion in revenues; it was one of the fastest-growing and most profitable divisions of Sears over the previous 2 years.

In 1991, Sears implemented a productivity incentive plan to increase profits in its auto centers nationwide. Auto mechanics had traditionally been paid an hourly wage and were expected to meet production quotas. In 1991, the compensation plan was changed to include a commission component. Mechanics were paid a base salary plus a fixed dollar amount for meeting hourly production quotas. Auto service advisers (the counterpeople who take orders, consult with mechanics, and advise customers) had traditionally been paid a salary. To increase sales, however, commissions and product-specific sales quotas were introduced for them as well. For example, a service adviser might be given the goal of selling a certain number of front-end alignments or brake repairs during each shift.

In June 1992, the California Department of Consumer Affairs accused Sears of violating the state's Auto Repair Act and sought to revoke the licenses of all Sears' Auto Centers in California. The allegation resulted from an increasing number of consumer complaints and a statewide undercover investigation of brake repairs. Other states quickly followed suit. Essentially, the charges alleged that Sears Auto Centers had been systematically misleading customers and charging them for unnecessary repairs. Sears had crossed over the line from prudent preventive maintenance to culpable unnecessary repairs. This pattern was particularly ominous in an industry that was increasingly relying on computerized diagnostics for auto repairs, giving more opportunity to corporations or small independent businesses to take advantage of future consumers. Not only was the quality goal of customer satisfaction being violated, but Sears was also using its corporate image of trusted retailer to violate consumer confidence and trust. The California investigation attributed the problems to the compensation system of Sears Auto Centers.

In response to the charges, Sears CEO and Chairman Edward A. Brennan denied that any fraud had occurred, and he defended Sears' focus on preventive maintenance for older cars. He admitted to isolated errors and outlined the actions the company planned to take to resolve the issue. These included (a) elimination of the incentive compensation program for service advisers, (b) substitution of commissions based on customer satisfaction, (c) elimination of sales quotas for specific parts and repairs, (d) substitution of sales volume quotas, and (e) introduction of "shopping audits" of its auto centers in which employees would pose as customers.

On September 2, 1992, Sears agreed to pay $8 million to resolve the Consumer Affairs Agency claims on overcharging in California. The $8 million included reimbursement costs, new employee training, and coupons for discounts at the service center. Another $15 million in fines was paid in 41 other states to settle class-action suits.

In December 1992, Sears fired John T. Lundegard, the director of its automotive operations, a $3 billion per year portion of its business. Sears indicated that Lundegard's termination was not related to the controversy surrounding the auto centers.

Sears recorded a net loss of $3.9 billion despite $52.3 billion in sales in 1992 —the worst performance ever by the retailer in its 108-year history and its first loss since 1933. Auto center revenue dropped $80 million in the last quarter of 1992, and Sears paid out $27 million to settle state overcharging claims. Moody's downgraded Sears' debt rating following the loss announcement.

In 1994, Sears partially reinstated its sales incentive practices in its auto centers. Service advisers must earn at least 40% of their total pay in commissions on the sale and installation of tires, batteries, shock absorbers, and struts. Not included on commission are brakes and front-end alignments (the core of the 1992 problems). Earnings in auto centers have not yet returned to pre-1992 levels.

In short, the lack of designing organizational compensation systems with integrity that satisfy internal and external customer needs results in extensive litigation costs, government intervention, ruined careers, tarnished corporate reputations, and loss of future profitability. (For more details, see Santoro, M. [1993]. *Sears Auto Centers*. Boston: Harvard Business School.)

(6) Public/Nonprofit/Health Care Administration Minicase: (Case 5F) - The United Way

The United Way, which evolved from the local community chests of the 1920s, is a national organization that funnels funding to charities through a payroll-deduction system. In 1991, 90% of all charitable deductions were for United Way.

The United Way's system of spending came under fire through the actions of William Aramony, president of United Way from 1970 to 1992. During his tenure, United Way receipts grew from $787 million in 1970 to $3 billion in 1990. But some of Aramony's effects on the organization were less positive.

In early 1992, the *Washington Post* reported that Aramony enjoyed the following benefits: (a) was paid $463,000 per year, (b) flew first class on commercial airlines, (c) spent $20,000 in 1 year for limousines, and (d) used the Concorde for transatlantic flights. In addition, one of the taxable spin-off companies that Aramony had created to provide travel and bulk purchasing for United Way chapters had bought a $430,000 condominium in Manhattan and a $125,000 apartment in Coral Gables, Florida, for his use. Another spin-off had hired Aramony's son, Robert Aramony, as its president.

When Aramony's expenses and salary became public, he was skewered for his obscenely lavish lifestyle, and United Way was criticized for its lack of processes to ensure responsible board oversight and lack of independent outside auditor control. Aramony resigned after 15 chapters of United Way threatened to withhold their annual dues to the national office.

In August 1992, the United Way board of directors hired Elaine Chao, the Peace Corps director, to replace William Aramony at a salary of $195,000, with no perks. She reduced staff from 275 to 185 and borrowed $1.5 million to compensate for a decline in donations. By 1995, United Way donations had still not returned to their 1991 level of $3.2 billion.

In September 1994, William Aramony and two other United Way officers, including the chief financial officer, were indicted by a federal grand jury for conspiracy, mail fraud, and tax fraud. The indictment alleged that the three officers diverted more than $2.74 million of United Way funds to purchase an apartment in New York City for $383,000, interior decorating for $72,000, a condominium, vacations, and a lifetime pass on American Airlines. In addition, $80,000 of United Way funds were paid to Aramony's girlfriend, a 1986 high school graduate, for consulting, even though she did no work.

On April 3, 1995, Aramony was found guilty of 25 counts of fraud, conspiracy, and money laundering. Two other United Way executives were also

convicted. In effect, the lack of designing and implementing executive accountability processes with integrity in the nonprofit sector resulted in millions of
lost dollars in mail and tax fraud, loss of current and future charitable revenue
because of public distrust of responsible philanthropic management, lost jobs,
and shattered organizational reputations. (For more details, see Berman, M.
[1994]. *The future of workplace giving.* New York: Conference Board.)

(7) International/Environmental/Public Policy Minicase:
    (Case 5G) - Indonesian Deforestation

The deforestation of Indonesia's tropical forests is internationally recognized as a serious, multifaceted problem. The Food and Agriculture Organization of the United Nations (FAO) studies indicate that Indonesia is being
deforested at an accelerating rate from 5,500 km^2 annually in 1980 to 7,000 km^2
by the mid-1980s and now stands around 12,000 km^2 per year. This is more
deforestation than in any other country except Brazil.

World Bank studies also demonstrate that Indonesia faces difficult challenges in defining its strategies for economic growth and environmental protection in a highly competitive international economic environment. Indonesia competes with East Asian countries such as Thailand, Vietnam, Korea, and
the Philippines in natural resource processing and contends with other regional
countries, such as China, India, and Bangladesh, that have an abundance of
low-wage labor.

In addition, the Indonesian labor force grew from 40 million in 1971 to
83 million by 1984. As the fourth most populous country in the world, with a
population of 186 million and a growth rate of 1.7%, Indonesia's labor force
growth rate is currently 2.8%. These projections imply that, during the next 35
years, nearly 50 million new jobs—almost 1.5 million a year—must be created
by the private and/or public sectors to absorb those able and willing to work.

In addition to historical patterns of nonsustainable development, specific
government policies and management practices have caused Indonesian deforestation. The primary direct causes of deforestation in Indonesia are irresponsible management of agriculture, logging, large-scale development projects, transmigration and land rights policies, rising world demand for forest
products, unequal distribution of land and wealth in tropical nations, and
poverty. Tropical forests are often viewed by both public and private managers
as obstacles to expanding civilization, rather than as permanent resources. The
managers of developing countries like Indonesia are inclined to emphasize

Table 5.1   Total Economic Values of Tropical Forests

Use Values			Non-Use Values
Direct Uses	Indirect Uses	Option Values	Existence Values
Timber	Nutrient cycling	Premium/discount	Endangered species
Non-timber products	Watershed protection	on direct and	Charismatic species
Recreation	Air pollution reduction	indirect uses	Threatened species
Ecotourism	Microclimatic function		Cherished landscapes
Genetic resources	Carbon storage		Biodiverse systems
Medicine			
Education			
Human habitat			

SOURCE: Granted with permission from "The Future Shape of Forests," C. Sargent and S. Bass, in J. Holmberg (Ed.) *Making development sustainable*, © Island Press, 1992. Published by Island Press, Washington, DC & Covelo, California.

quick exploitation of timber for cash, rather than long-term sustainable development through multiple usage of forest resources.·

To appreciate the complexity of responsibly managing a forest, it is helpful to have an ecological definition of a forest and a graphic image of the many use and non-use values of tropical forests. A *forest* is a predominantly woody association of species, of variable complexity in component species and their interdependencies, that is able to reproduce and dominate a landscape both in space and over time. As living repositories of a wide range of economic values, forests require responsible, organized management.

Table 5.1 illustrates the wide range of use and non-use economic values of tropical forests. The economic use (instrumental) values of tropical forest include direct, indirect, and option values; the economic non-use (intrinsic) values are existence values. The exclusive or predominant focus on one direct use of tropical forests—obtaining timber through logging—in Indonesian tropical forests has been the major economic factor contributing to deforestation.

Because of rapid exploitation of its tropical forests for timber exports, Indonesia may eventually find itself without enough wood for domestic needs. Careless logging methods that neglect restorative forestation obligations destroy tropical forests. Negligence can also destroy the domestic economic system and the delicate balance of the ecosystem, thereby creating global environmental problems.

The Indonesian tropical forest also sustains indigenous human populations, as well as animal populations. It is home to human societies and cultures that have expert knowledge unavailable elsewhere. Deforestation, however, is displacing these societies and cultures and causing their expert knowledge to be lost before it can be captured and recorded. Government transmigration policies, for example, to shift people from the densely populated Inner Islands (Java and Bali) to the thinly populated Outer Islands (Sumatra, Kalimantan, Sulawesi, Irian Jaya, Lesser Sundas, Lombok, and Timor) have adversely affected indigenous peoples such as the Dayaks in Kalimantan and the Asmats in Irian Jaya. Because primary forests provide 80% of transmigration sites, deforestation has had a devastating impact on the forest resources of the nation.

The combined adverse impacts of current economic, environmental, and social policies have provoked widespread domestic and global criticism. Despite their contributions to the economic well-being of Indonesia, the tropical forests are decreasing in size and quality, jeopardizing long-term economic returns. This, combined with outside influences from other governments, corporations, and environmentalists, has pressured the government of Indonesia to adjust its forestry policies and be open to new policy frameworks.

The revised government forestry policies have included three elements: forest reclassification, selective cutting policy, and 20-year concessions. First, the government has classified the forested areas into different types depending on their *economic* purpose: (a) protection of forests to maintain watershed, (b) national parks, (c) limited production forests for restrictive felling, and (d) full production (commercial) forests. The intervention guidelines for each forest vary according to type of forest; for example, the teak forests of Java are managed differently from the mixed-species dipterocarp forests of the Outer Islands. Protection forests and national parks are not to be used by the timber industry, but rather are protected for environmental, aesthetic, and cultural reasons. The limited production and commercial forests are the only forests that logging companies may exploit.

Second, according to the new Indonesian selective cutting policy, a concessionaire (company that pays for rights to cut trees) may only cut trees by following certain guidelines. By law, only Indonesians can own forest concessions and the right to harvest timber on particular tracts of land. Although the intent of the law was for enterprising Indonesians to establish their own trade, what generally happens in practice is that foreign trading companies perform all actual harvesting and simply pay a fixed royalty to local concession owners. In practice, many foreign companies have cared less about the procedures used in obtaining the logs or about replanting trees than about harvesting quick profits.

Third, Indonesian loggers are granted 20-year concessions on blocks of forest land. Concession holders are allowed to log under a selective felling and planting system. Concessions are subdivided into 35 blocks. Within each block, trees above 50 cm in diameter can be cut down. At least 25 trees over 35 cm in diameter must be left standing evenly distributed throughout the block to act as seeding agents. In theory, these laws ensure that when the block is harvested again in 35 years, there will be a sufficient number of mature trees to make commercial logging sustainable. Under this system, it is hoped that the production forest will sustain itself at its original levels.

Many critics, however, claim there is no effective system for coordinating all policies and then uniformly enforcing them; there are still multiple government agencies with conflicting agendas and so many timber companies operating in Indonesia that have intensified logging activities and neglected the multiple-use opportunities of the forest.

In short, the lack of designing and implementing coordinated forestry sustainable development policies with integrity results in rapid economic depletion of a diminishing natural resource for future generations in a developing country, lost opportunities to take advantage of the multiple uses of forests, disruptive dislocations of indigenous peoples, and wanton destruction of forest ecosystems and biodiversity. (For more details, see Panayotow, T., & Ashton, P. [1993]. *Not by timber alone: Economics and ecology for sustaining tropical forests.* New York: Island.)

SUMMARY

In summary, this chapter covers the multiple dimensions of the function of organizing for managers and the four ethical organizing subprocesses that build management integrity. In addition, seven management ethics and organizing with integrity minicases were presented. By addressing the moral issues entailed in organizing ethically and applying the theories and tools from the first part of the book to the structured analysis and principled resolution of organizing minicases, sharpened skills in ethical organizing can enhance management integrity.

▧ DISCUSSION/EXPERIENTIAL EXERCISES

Discussion Questions

1. Discuss the nature of managerial organizing and culpably negligent organizing for private- and public-sector managers.
2. Discuss the three key factors in the organizing function and how they are handled in traditional and TQ work environments.
3. Discuss in detail the five key processes of organizing the HR subsystem at work and what ethics issues arise when these processes are organized in traditional and TQ ways.
4. Using the Organizing Success Evaluation Matrix (Figure 5.4), provide life/work/school examples from each quadrant.
5. Using the tools and resources from the first part of the book, examine the organizing with integrity minicase in your major field or field of concentration.
6. Discuss the parallel alignment of the four key ethics processes and organizing subprocesses that build integrity, providing an example of managerial organizing for each step.

Experiential Exercises

7. In a group setting, using the tools and resources from the first part of the book, examine two organizing with integrity minicases outside your major field or field of concentration.
8. From your own life/work/school experiences, discuss times when organizing occurred without integrity, identifying specific adverse impacts that resulted when one or more of the ethical organizing steps were omitted or inadequately completed, and how you could have (in the past) or will (in the future) plan with integrity to prevent a recurrence of the problem.

6

Management Ethics:
Leading With Integrity

The focus of Chapter 6 is on three areas: (a) the dimensions of leading, (b) ethical leading processes that build integrity, and (c) management ethics and leading with integrity minicases. By addressing the ethical issues involved in the managerial function of leading and applying those lessons to the analysis and resolution of leading minicases, skills in ethical leadership can enhance management ethics and integrity.

◪ DIMENSIONS OF LEADING

Leading is the intended, coordinated, emergent and realized pattern of decision processes and actions that induce or influence the character and conduct of organizational members in appropriate directions by using appropriate resources. Just as on a soccer team, leadership is shown by the demonstrated readiness and capacity to enact game strategy (planning) by technically executing the designed plays with the human talent on the field (organizing), in today's work environment, managerial leadership requires demonstrating organizational readiness and capacity to collectively act successfully. Meritorious leading is expressly intended, efficiently coordinated, enthusiastically responsive to emergent feedback, and fully realized, as indicated in Figure 6.1.

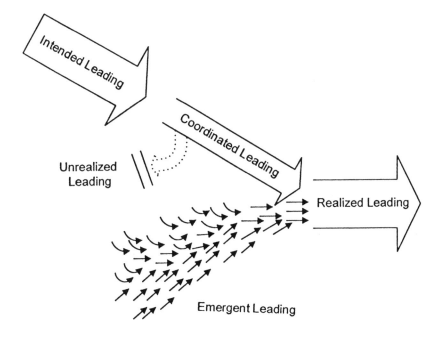

Figure 6.1. Dimensions of Leading

Managers who generate and articulate a compelling vision of future leadership dynamics for an organization that motivates stakeholders are involved in *intended leading*. Managers who realistically arrange for the proper matching of leadership and follower empowerment readiness styles are engaged in *coordinated leading*. Managers who solicit ongoing input and are enthusiastically responsive to critical feedback with regard to influencing processes are involved in *emergent leading*. The outcomes of the interaction among intended, coordinated, and emergent leading are realized and unrealized leadership opportunities. *Realized leadership opportunities* are fully implemented processes that incorporate the evolved patterns of the past, the expectations of the desired future, and the realistic constraints of the present. Managers who incorporate intended, coordinated, and emergent leading and analyze the historical precedents of "what worked" and "what didn't work" for organizations are engaged in *realized leading*. *Unrealized leading* opportunities are intended leadership projects that never materialize. Among realized organizational leadership processes, some are successful in that they effectively transform inputs into value-added outputs; other leadership processes are unsuccessful, realized projects that become barriers to effective organizational and stakeholder performance.

Furthermore, *culpably negligent leading* includes any and all of the following: absence of explicitly intended leadership vision, inefficiently coordinated leadership style matches, leading that is rigidly unresponsive to emergent contingencies, inadequately realized leadership opportunities, unintegrated patterns of leadership processes and actions, leading that misdirects core business processes, and leadership that persists in disrespecting people. The degree of moral culpability for negligent leading is dependent on the extent to which a manager could have and should have known or anticipated all the factors involved in the leadership function. The balance of change and stability to achieve optimal effectiveness in the leading function is obtained by addressing people factors (both leaders and followers/collaborators) and contextual factors.

People Factors

The first set of factors, *people factors*, consists of current leaders and followers/collaborators as individuals or groups and their interactions. Although the word *follower* is the predominant term in conventional management and leadership literature, the word *collaborator* has gained some currency in the postindustrial setting (Gini, 1996; Rost, 1993). The use of the term *follower* in the remainder of this chapter, though it adheres to the conventional standard, can be interpreted to include the denotative and connotative meanings inherent in the term *collaborator*—that is, reciprocal interaction and equality. When leaders are considered in isolation from followers and contexts, emphasis may be placed on *traits, skills, behaviors,* and *decision-making styles* (Bailey, 1988; Bass, 1990a; DuBrin, 1995; Rost, 1991; Yukl, 1994; Zaleznik, 1990). The leadership trait results can be categorized in terms of characteristics of current domestic successful leaders and characteristics of global leadership potential. In the former case, the following demonstrated leadership traits have been identified by research finding: intelligence, knowledge, emotional stability, adaptability to situations, alertness to social environment, creativity, personal integrity, resourcefulness, ambition, achievement-orientation, assertiveness, cooperativeness, decisive judgment, dependability, dominance (desire to influence others), energetic (high activity level), persistence, self-confidence, tolerance of stress, and willingness to assume responsibility (Bass, 1990a; Yukl, 1994). Among those traits that indicate leadership potential in the international arena are the following: seeks opportunities to learn, acts with integrity, adapts to cultural differences, is committed to making a difference, seeks broad knowledge base, brings out the best in people, is insightful and sees things from new angles, has the courage to take risks, seeks and uses feedback, learns from mistakes, and is open to criticism (Jeannot, 1989; McCall, 1994; Spreitzer, McCall, & Mahoney, 1995).

In addition to traits, four types of managerial leadership skill categories have been identified: (a) *technical skills* (proficiency in detailed uses of quantitative and qualitative methods, processes, tools, and equipment); (b) *interpersonal skills* (emotional expressivity, sensitivity and control, social expressivity, political sensitivity, control and manipulation, effective communication, and persuasiveness); (c) *conceptual skills* (anticipation of changing trends and opportunities, diagnostic analysis of problems, integrative prognosis of ongoing improvement and/or problem resolution, proficiency in conceptualization of complex and ambiguous relationships, creativity in idea generation and articulation, and sound logical reasoning); and (d) *administrative skills* (effective work organization, prioritized operational obligations, efficient and timely in-basket processing of information, rapid routine decision making, constant monitoring of performance, solid control of financial resources, and sharp attention to detail) (Yukl, 1994).

In addition to skills, managerial leaders demonstrate a blend of two major types of behavior: *task-centered behavior* that initiates structure and *relationship-centered behavior* that demonstrates consideration. Although each leadership practice involves some component behaviors that are concerned with both tasks and relationships, some practices are more concerned with tasks (e.g., planning, problem solving, clarifying, informing, making decisions, delegating, giving/seeking information), whereas other practices are more concerned with building relationships (e.g., motivating and inspiring, recognizing and rewarding, networking to influence people, team building, conflict management, supporting, facilitating collaboration, and mentoring) (Bass, 1990b; Kellerman, 1986; Mendl, 1989).

Finally, although leaders satisfy both task and relationship concerns, they do so by demonstrating the following four appropriate decision-making styles: (a) the *autocratic decision style* (e.g., leader solves problem, makes decisions by him- or herself using the information available at the time and tells followers); (b) the *consultative decision style* (e.g., leader shares problem with relevant followers, confers with them individually to obtain input, and then he or she makes and sells the decision, which may or may not reflect the followers' input); (c) the *participative decision style* (e.g., leader shares problem with all followers, facilitates group involvement in problem analysis and group commitment to problem resolution, with the final decision being either the result of a majority vote or consensus); and (d) the *delegative decision style* (e.g., followers identify and analyze problems among themselves and are empowered to make, carry out, and "own" their own resolutions while keeping the leader informed) (Bass, 1990a).

The quantity and quality of individual traits, skills, behaviors, and decision styles constitute the personal readiness for leadership empowerment. In addition to this personal readiness for leadership, the nature of the interaction between leaders and followers will determine leadership effectiveness.

When leaders are considered in relation to followers, emphasis is placed on five variables: (a) *follower behaviors,* (b) *power relations,* (c) *leader-member exchange,* (LMX) *theory,* (d) *transactional interactions,* and (e) *transformational/ transforming interactions* (Bass, 1990a; Burns, 1979; Yukl, 1994).

With regard to the first interactional variable, *follower behaviors,* leaders influence followers by communicating what needs to be done, providing feedback to followers in how well it is done, acting as role models for followers, and mediating between followers and their own supervisors. Followers, in turn, reciprocally influence leaders by upward influence that takes many forms as diverse as integration and establishing coalitions of influence. The followers' impact on leaders depends on the followers' competence, maturity, readiness, and compliance, as well as the leader's and followers' explanations for the followers' disposition and performance (Bass, 1990a). Follower behavior can be categorized in terms of independent critical thinking and activity level, as indicated in Figure 6.2. (Kelley, 1988).

The two-dimensional model of follower behavior in Figure 6.2 results in five types of followers. *Sheep* are followers who do not play an active role in the organization and simply comply with any order or directive given to them. *Yes people* are active followers who readily carry out orders uncritically; they support leadership egos but can be dangerous if their orders contradict societal standards or organizational policy (e.g., ollieism) and extreme obedience that violates laws (Kelman & Hamilton, 1989). *Alienated followers* are the critics of the organization who point out its negative aspects but refuse to actively improve the situation. *Effective followers* play an active role in the organization

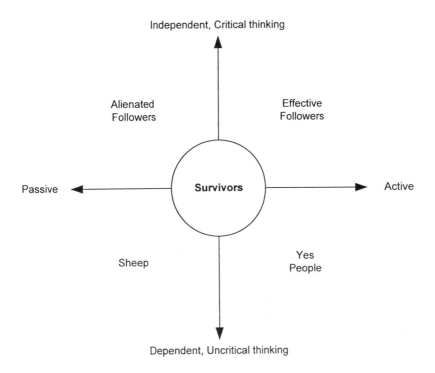

Figure 6.2. Two-Dimensional Model of Follower Behavior

Reprinted by permission of *Harvard Business Review*. From "In Praise of Followers" by R. E. Kelley, 66(6), 1988. Copyright © 1988 by the President and Fellows of Harvard College; all rights reserved.

but are not yes people; they critically assess and respectfully challenge organizational authority and propose constructive alternatives. Effective followers can play a vital role in enhancing organizational performance by improving leader-follower interactions so that the wisdom of mature followers can be brought to bear on complex decision making. Finally, *survivors* are followers who "get by" through minimal investment and risk exposure in the work environment. As reengineering, restructuring, and downsizing become domestic and global norms, organizational survivors become better at keeping their jobs than doing their jobs well (Ludwig & Longenecker, 1993; Noer, 1993). Survivors keep their jobs by carefully cultivating multiple images in order to appear to be the kind of follower the current leaders want (Noer, 1993).

	Managerial Competence	Managerment Integrity
Running the Business	Competence in running the business (e.g., understand customer needs, have a viable strategy)	Integrity in running the business (e.g., pursue the organization's interests, act honestly)
Dealing With People	Competence in dealing with people (e.g., communicate effectively, design reasonable reward systems)	Integrity in dealing with people (e.g., show genuine concern for employees, communicate sincerely)

Figure 6.3. The Domain of Organizational Cynicism
SOURCE: Dean & Brandes (1995). Reprinted with permission.

Although negative feedback of alienated followers is helpful to correct practices, their sustained whining without constructive action contributes to organizational cynicism. *Organizational cynicism* is a negative attitude toward an organization's management, and toward the organization itself, based on the belief that management will consistently fail to meet employee expectations (Dean & Brandes, 1995). The domain of organizational cynicism that is fostered by alienated followers is depicted in Figure 6.3.

The domain of organizational cynicism in Figure 6.3 incorporates employee expectations about managerial competence in running the business and dealing with people and management integrity in running the business and dealing with people (Andersson & Bateman, 1994; Brunsson, 1989; Schein, 1985). When managers fail to uncover, meet, and/or exceed employee expectations, alienated followers become organizational cynics, depicted in the sarcastic humor of the popular cartoon character, *Dilbert* (Adams, 1996). The adverse impact of organizational cynicism includes constrained use of managerial legitimate power because of discredited authority (Goldfarb, 1991; Kahn & Kram, 1994); reduced commitment to organizational change (Brooks & Vance, 1995; Wanous, Reichers, & Austin, 1994); reduced organizational citizenship behavior (Van Dyne et al., 1994); increased behavioral hostility at work (Houston & Vavak, 1991); customers turned against the organization (Dean & Brandes, 1995); and other followers converted to cynical views (Guastello, Rieke, Guastello, & Billings, 1992; Ibarra & Andrews, 1993).

In addition to follower behaviors, an interaction approach to leadership must deal with the second interactional variable—the nature, kinds, and uses of leadership power. *Power* is the ability to influence the conduct of others and to resist unwanted influence in return (Hollander & Offermann, 1990; Wagner & Hollenbeck, 1995). The five traditional interactional sources of power are legitimate power, reward power, expert power, referent power, and coercive power. *Legitimate power* is interactional power based on holding a position of formal authority. *Reward power* is interactional power based on the ability to control how desirable outcomes are distributed. *Expert power* is an interactional power based on the profession of expertise, knowledge, and talent. *Referent power* is an interactional power based on the possession of attractive personal characteristics. *Coercive power* is an interactional power based on the ability to control the distribution of undesirable outcomes. Table 6.1 provides guidelines for building and using interactional power in leader-follower relations. Although the achievement and exercise of power is necessary for improving organizational performance, it is not sufficient; and when abused, it may convert effective leaders/followers into dysfunctional leaders/followers (Heifitz, 1994; Hogan, Curphy, & Hogan, 1994).

In addition to general interaction power, the sharing of power through special reciprocal exchange relationships between leaders and "in-group" followers is addressed in the third interactional variable, the *LMX (leader-member exchange) theory* (Graen & Scandura, 1987; Graen & Uhl-Bren, 1991). This interactional approach suggests that leaders select and preferentially treat "in-group" followers, in contrast with "out-group" followers, on the basis of personal compatibility, mutual interests outside work, demographic similarity, and follower competence and dependability (Dienesh & Liden, 1986). Leaders confer on in-group followers greater status, influence, and benefits, which they secure from a favorable upward relationship with their own supervisors and, in return, expect in-group followers to work harder, to be more committed to task objectives, to be loyal to the leader, and to share some of the leader's administrative duties.

The LMX relationship has three possible stages: (a) the mutual testing phase, in which the leader and follower evaluate each other's motives, attitudes, expectations, and potential resources to be exchanged, as an out-group relationship; (b) the intermediate in-group selection phases, in which the reciprocal exchange arrangements are developed through mutual interests, benefits, and loyalty between leaders and in-group followers; and (c) the advanced exchange phase, in which exchange based on self-interest and approval seeking is changed into mutual commitment to the mission and objectives of the work unit (Graen & Uhl-Bren, 1991).

Table 6.1 Guidelines for Building and Using Power

How to Increase and Maintain Power	How to Use Power Effectively
Legitimate Power:	
• Gain more formal authority.	• Make polite, clear requests.
• Use symbols of authority.	• Explain the reasons for a request.
• Get people to acknowledge authority.	• Don't exceed your scope of authority.
• Exercise authority regularly.	• Verify authority if necessary.
• Follow proper channels in giving orders.	• Be sensitive to target concerns.
• Back up authority with reward and coercive power.	• Follow up to verify compliance.
	• Insist on compliance if appropriate.
Reward Power:	
• Discover what people need and want.	• Offer desirable rewards.
• Gain more control over rewards.	• Offer fair and ethical rewards.
• Ensure people know you control rewards.	• Explain criteria for giving rewards.
• Don't promise more than what you can deliver.	• Provide rewards as promised.
• Don't use rewards in a manipulative way.	• Use rewards symbolically to reinforce desirable behavior.
• Avoid complex, mechanical incentives.	
• Don't use rewards for personal benefit.	
Expert Power:	
• Gain more relevant knowledge.	• Explain the reasons for a request or proposal.
• Keep informed about technical matters.	• Explain why a request is important.
• Develop exclusive sources of information.	• Provide evidence that a proposal will be successful.
• Use symbols to verify expertise.	• Listen seriously to target concerns.
• Demonstrate competency by solving difficult problems.	• Show respect for target (don't be arrogant).
• Don't make rash, careless statements.	• Act confident and decisive in a crisis.
• Don't lie or misrepresent the facts.	
• Don't keep changing positions.	
Referent Power:	
• Show acceptance and positive regard.	• Use personal appeals when necessary.
• Act supportive and helpful.	• Indicate that a request is important to you.
• Don't manipulate and exploit people for personal advantage.	• Don't ask for a personal favor that is excessive given the relationship.
• Defend someone's interests and back them up when appropriate.	• Provide an example of proper behavior (role modeling).
• Keep promises.	
• Make self-sacrifices to show concern.	
• Use sincere forms of ingratiation.	
Coercive Power:	
• Identify credible penalties to deter unacceptable behavior.	• Inform target of rules and penalties.
• Gain authority to use punishments.	• Give ample prior warnings.
• Don't make rash threats.	• Understand situation before punishing.
• Don't use coercion in a manipulative way.	• Remain calm and helpful, not hostile.
• Use only punishments that are legitimate.	• Encourage improvement to avoid the need for punishment.
• Fit punishments to the infraction.	• Ask target to suggest ways to improve.
• Don't use coercion for personal benefit.	• Administer discipline in private.

SOURCE: LEADERSHIP IN ORGANIZATIONS, 3rd ed. by Yukl, Gary, © 1994. Adapted by permission of Prentice-Hall, Inc., Upper Saddle River, NJ.

Finally, the fourth and fifth interactional variables are treated in two modal leadership influence processes identified as transactional and transformational/transforming interactions (Bass, 1990b; Burns, 1979; Graham, 1995; Kanungo & Mendonca, 1996; Manz & Sims, 1989; Mayhew, 1991; Tichy & Devanna, 1986). Although full empirical verification of these conceptual distinctions awaits completion (Yukl, 1994), they provide a useful contrast in interactional influence processes, as indicated in Table 6.2.

The *transactional leader* uses the reciprocal exchange control strategy to gain compliant behavior from followers. By relying on the social exchange of valued resources, these leaders draw on their reward, coercive, and legitimate power base to perpetuate the status quo through existing exchange interactions and thereby sustain organizational continuity.

The *transformational leader* uses the empowerment development strategy to gain committed behavior for ongoing change from followers. By relying on increased self-efficacy of followers and the internalization of shared values, these leaders draw on their expert and referent power bases to institutionalize change through cooperative networks and, thereby, sustain organization development. The *transforming leader* uses the empowerment development strategy to gain committed behavior for ongoing moral improvement from followers (Burns, 1979).

Leader-follower interactions can enhance follower performance by increasing sensitivity to what motivates followers "from the outside in" (providing an externally supportive work system) to become highly motivated performers. The model of individual motivation and performance in Figure 6.4 provides a bridge from people to contextual factors in implementing leadership.

The model in Figure 6.4 is sequential and progressive and integrates both content theories of motivation (what motivates behavior) and process theories of motivation (how events and outcomes interact to motivate behavior). *Motivation* can be defined as the pattern of factors that initiate, direct, and sustain human conduct over time (Steers, Porter, & Begley, 1996; Wagner & Hollenbeck, 1995). The four outcomes (desire to perform, effort, performance, and satisfaction), shown as rectangles, normally occur sequentially, and increased work satisfaction (the last outcome) normally leads to a renewed desire to perform at ever higher standards (the first outcome). Leaders who want to enhance individual performance can, therefore, use this model to motivate performance and secure contextual resources. The model contains six components in five steps and is used to explain four outcomes.

Table 6.2 Comparison of Transactional and Transformational/
Transforming Leadership Influence Processes

Leadership Influence Process	Transactional Leadership	Transformational/ Transforming Leadership
Leadership strategy	Reciprocal exchange to control conformity	Empowerment development to improve chosen conduct
Leader goal in terms of behavioral outcomes	Emphasis on follower compliance behavior	Emphasis on follower committed, moral improvement
Underlying psychological motivator	Social exchange of valued resources	Increase self-efficacy beliefs and internalized commitment to shared values
Power base	Coercive, legitimate, and reward	Expert and referent
Relationship of leader to follower	Quid pro quo relationships	Moral challenge relationship to instill pride
Operational impacts	Tends to perpetuate primarily the short-term status quo of current leaders.	Tends to promote primarily long-term organizational change and improvement efforts
Traditions developed over time	Continuity is made appealing and vital	Change is institutionalized
Follower outcome	Followers sensitive to and compliant with externally imposed standards and sanctions	Followers sensitive to and accountable for internally chosen standards and sanctions
Leader expectation of follower	Expects compliance with rules and standards	Expects committed performance in accordance with principled integrity
Self-expectations of leaders	Use power bases to arrange fair reciprocal exchanges to perpetuate their authority	Use power bases and personal moral examples to inspire follower moral development and empowerment that continually improves organizational integrity
Organizational outcome	Organizational continuity	Organizational integrity

The six components, represented by circles in the model, are valence, instrumentality, expectancy, ability, accuracy of role perceptions, and equity of rewards. *Valence* is the preference that a person has for a particular outcome. If two outcomes are to be expected, a person may prefer a specific outcome (a positive valence), prefer *not* to attain that outcome (negative valence), or have

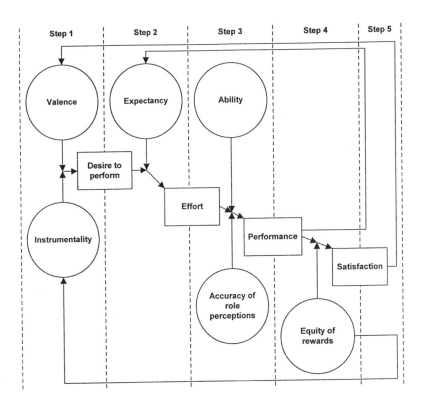

Figure 6.4. Model of Motivation and Performance
SOURCE: MANAGEMENT OF ORGANIZATIONAL BEHAVIOR 2nd ed. by Wagner/Hollenbeck, © 1992. Reprinted by permission of Prentice-Hall, Inc., Upper Saddle River, NJ.

no preference between the two possible outcomes (zero valence). A variety of need theories, including Maslow's need hierarchy, Alderfer's ERG (Existence-Relatedness-Growth) theory, Murray's theory of manifest needs, and/or McClelland's theory of achievement motivation, explain intrinsic preferences of individuals and why they differ among people (Alderfer, 1972; Maslow, 1970; McClelland, 1963; Murray, 1938). Alderfer's ERG theory, for example, proposes that people are internally motivated by the urge to fulfill three basic human needs: existence needs (physiological and safety needs), relatedness needs (belongingness and social esteem needs), and growth needs (self-esteem and self-actualization needs). Alderfer agreed with Maslow that need importance progresses up the hierarchy one step at a time and is prepotent. Alderfer maintained, however, and research has supported the claim, that failed attempts to satisfy some higher-level growth needs will often cause people to regress to satisfying only lower-level relatedness and existence needs, thereby reducing their aspiration for superior performance (Wanous & Zwang, 1977). For leaders who are aware of motivational regression, therefore, it becomes a challenge to assess and channel the strong intrinsic motivation of employee growth needs toward successful learning experiences and enhanced moral performance for the organization. Enabling personal performance "from the inside" means acknowledging and endorsing growth needs; enabling personal performance "from the outside" means removing barriers to growth need fulfillment that risk individual regression to lower performance standards.

Instrumentality is the subjective belief a person has about the relationship between performing an act and receiving an outcome. A variety of learning theories, including Watson's classical conditioning, Skinner's reinforcement, and/or Bandura's social learning theory, explain what people believe will lead to the attainment of desired outcomes (Bandura & Walters, 1963; Skinner, 1971). Bandura's social learning theory, for example, suggests that behavior to achieve desired outcomes is driven by the desire of an observer to model the behavior of persons deemed worthwhile, even to the extent of self-reinforcement of behavior in line with the learning role model (Bandura, 1976). For leaders, this provides the challenge to identify, develop, and broadcast role model behaviors that enable persons to emulate desirable role model behavior. To facilitate a total quality (TQ) system, human resource (HR) leaders must seek, find, and support their role models in both traditional and nontraditional places—not only within the pool of current managers but also among rank-and-file employees with natural leadership talent at the operational level. Internalization of TQ performance standards and self-reinforcement of those quality standards is exactly what constitutes the justification for worker self-control and self-inspection. In addition to self-reinforcement, reinforcement theory demonstrates the importance of environmentally shaping performance behavior by rewarding successive approximations of desired behavior (Wagner & Hollenbeck, 1995). For TQ system leaders, developing the ethical work culture becomes an expanded responsibility of total quality leaders to shape the moral instrumentality of all associates (Petrick & Pullins, 1992).

Expectancy is the set of beliefs regarding the link between making an effort and actually performing well (Vroom, 1964). Whereas knowledge about valence and instrumentalities indicates what an individual wants to do, knowledge of expectancies indicates what an individual will try to do. Bandura's self-efficacy theory, for example, explains how expectancies are formed and can be changed (Bandura, 1982). People high in self-efficacy believe they can master, or have mastered, some specific task and feel empowered to exert the effort to take on new responsibilities. For total quality leaders, the importance of promulgating transformational leadership styles that build confidence and empowerment skills in employees is paramount in helping employees develop the level of moral self-efficacy required to improve processes and continually innovate (Waldman, 1993).

Ability is the set of physical, psychomotor, cognitive, social, affective, and moral capabilities an individual brings to bear on a situation. People can only perform what they are capable of, although their abilities can be increased. Kanfer and Ackerman's (1989) interaction theory and Hinter's (1986) cognitive ability theory, for example, indicate that people high in cognitive ability learn quickly and are able to attend to multiple responsibilities at any one time. People high in demonstrated organizational citizenship behavior (OCB) dispositions are more capable and more likely to engage in cooperative, team performance behavior at work (Van Dyne et al., 1994). For total quality leaders, therefore, selection criteria that include high cognitive ability, moral integrity, and OCB standards are more likely to produce a capable, cooperative workforce.

Role perceptions are people's beliefs about what they are supposed to be accomplishing on the job and how (Wagner & Hollenbeck, 1995). Role perceptions are accurate when people facing a task know what needs to be done, how much needs to be done, and who will have the responsibility and authority to do it. Locke's goal-setting theory, Waldman's work performance theory, and Davenport's process innovation theory, for example, demonstrate that clear, unambiguous goals, goal commitment, hierarchy level, increased autonomy, and personal empowerment all enhance individual performance (Wagner & Hollenbeck, 1995). For total quality leaders, clarifying the new responsibilities and authority of empowered employees is a major communication challenge that affects all the traditional HR processes: selection, performance, appraisal, reward, and development (Petrick & Furr, 1995). Persuading middle managers to share power and line employees to assume more responsibility, while having all stakeholders held accountable for the quality of outputs, are major changes in role perceptions from the traditional organization. In addition, ensuring that appropriate levels of authority are delegated to handle new responsibilities becomes an important managerial task to avoid employee frustration and burnout. This is no less an employee role shift than having someone change from viewing the employer as a parent to regarding the employer as a partner.

Equity is the perceived standard whereby individuals and/or groups ought to receive outcomes (rewards) consistent with the quantity and quality of the results they produce. The key equity theories all point toward the need for equity balance to ensure work satisfaction (the relationship between my inputs and outcomes matches). The ratio relationship between a key reference person's inputs and outcomes should approximate one's own ratio relationship in order to promote satisfaction (Adams, 1963; Greenberg, 1996; Sheppard, Lewicki, & Minton, 1992; Solomon, 1990b). If these ratios are not equal, the reward structure is perceived as unfair (Greenberg, 1996). In the face of perceived inequity of rewards, employees may alter their inputs (reduce performance contributions), alter their outputs (demand a raise or threaten to strike), distort the facts (rationalize or delude themselves about the reality of the inequity), change the behavior of the reference person (socially ostracize the highest-paid performer), and/or engage in sabotage (break equipment) (Folger & Konovsky, 1989; Solomon, 1990b). In contrast, when people experience persistent justice at work through equitable rewards, several positive outcomes ensue: (a) persistent equitable pay improves performance, work satisfaction, and group morale; (b) persistent equitable pay enhances interpersonal trust, organizational loyalty, and OCB; and (c) persistent equitable pay lessens the likelihood of retaliation for occasional inadvertent injustice in the workplace (Kim & Mauborgne, 1993; Tyler, 1994). For total quality leaders, therefore, developing the ethical work culture to ensure outcome, procedural, and systemic justice in all reward decisions is crucial to achieving work satisfaction and organizational commitment (Petrick & Furr, 1995). If the total quality leader wants to build a high-performance community at work, he or she must ensure organizational justice (Lindsay & Petrick, 1997).

The five steps of the model in Figure 6.4 also show the key places where people and contextual factors combine to influence outcomes. The four outcomes, shown as rectangles, are desire to perform, effort, performance, and satisfaction. The first, *desire to perform*, is a function of valences and instrumentalities. A person's desire to perform well will be high when valences are associated with high performance. The second outcome, *effort*, is a function of desire to perform and expectancy. Effort will be forthcoming only when individuals want to perform well and when they believe they can do so. The third outcome, *performance*, is a function of effort, accurate role perceptions, and ability. Performance will be high only when individuals with the requisite abilities and knowledge of desired goals and strategies put forth their best effort. The model also shows how *satisfaction,* the fourth outcome, is a product of past performance and the perceived equity of rewards received for performing well. The dynamic nature of the motivation process is revealed in the way present levels of satisfaction, perceived equity of rewards, and performance affects future levels of valence, instrumentality, and expectancy.

A more complex variant of the transactional approach to leadership is the path-goal theory (Evans, 1986; House, 1971). This approach advocates leadership manipulation of follower motivational variables while using four different behavioral styles (directive, supportive, participative, and achievement-oriented), along with altering contextual variables such as performance appraisal and reward systems in order to manage organizational performance. In this theory, the primary purpose of the leader is to motivate followers by clarifying goals and best paths to achieve goals, but not to transform or morally develop followers. In contrast, a more complex variant of the transformational approach to leadership is the situational leadership theory (STL; Hersey, 1984; Hersey & Blanchard, 1977). This approach advocates the initial diagnosis of follower job and psychological maturity levels with regard to task demands, and on the basis of the perceived developmental maturity of the follower for the task, leaders are to use four types of task-relationship behaviors ("telling," "selling," "participating," and "delegating") that appropriately match and boost follower maturity. In this theory, therefore, effective leadership depends on transforming follower immaturity into maturity by using appropriate behavioral styles within the scope of the situational task to be accomplished.

Contextual Factors

In addition to the people factors in leadership are the additional contextual factors. Three major contextual models of leadership are *contingency leadership, servant leadership,* and *total quality leadership.* Fiedler's *contingency theory of leadership* focuses on contextual factors that enhance or detract from leadership effectiveness. The first step in Fiedler's theory is to identify leadership style by determining the degree to which a manager favorably or unfavorably describes his or her least preferred coworker (LPC scale). In short, if one can easily tolerate one's antagonists, a leader has a high-LPC or is relationship-motivated; if not, a leader has a low-LPC or is task-oriented (Fiedler & Chemers, 1982).

According to Fiedler, because leadership style (LPC scale) is a relatively permanent aspect of behavior that cannot be modified, it is important to match a leader with a suitable context; if there is a mismatch, change the leader, but do not focus on developing leader or context. Fiedler identified three context factors that determine the preferred leadership style to be used: (a) leader-member relations (how well the group and the leader get along); (b) task structure (how clearly the procedures, goals, and evaluation of the job are defined); and (c) position power (the leader's formal authority to hire, fire, discipline, and grant salary increases to group members). A summary of the findings of Fiedler's theory are provided in Figure 6.5.

The bottom portion of Figure 6.5 shows the leadership style most strongly associated with effective group performance in each context. For example, task-motivated (low-LPC) leaders perform the best in contexts of high control and low control (Cells i, ii, iii and viii), and relationship-motivated leaders are the most effective when the situation is moderately favorable (DuBrin, 1995).

The second major contextual model of leadership is servant leadership (Graham, 1991; Greenleaf, 1977; Terry, 1990, 1993). *Servant leadership* is a normative theory that espouses leaders as servants of followers and advocates of contexts favorable to the least privileged. Although the servant leadership style endorsed is not necessarily the same as Fiedler's, the style to be used is contingent on follower wants and context constraints.

The third major contextual model of leadership, *total quality leadership*, on the other hand, focuses on contextual ways to implement and measure organizational processes that transfer individual power over others into team empowerment and continuous system improvement (Camp, 1995; Conference Board, 1991; Howell & Avalco, 1992; Johnson, 1993; Olian & Rynes, 1991; Petrick & Furr, 1995; Petrick, Scherer, Wilson, & Westfall, 1994). This approach assumes that leaders and followers can be educated to shift mindsets from focusing on controlling people by blaming them for errors to developing people with the skills to improve the work process that allowed the error to occur in the first place. For example, the total quality leadership succession processes of selection, performance, appraisal, reward, and development identify people who are ready to cooperatively build teams and engage in process improvement projects.

For total quality leadership to occur, two contextual assessments must be present: organizational process assessment and team empowerment readiness assessments. The first condition, *organizational process assessment*, entails categorizing all work processes into six levels, from an unknown status to world-

CONTINGENCY FACTORS

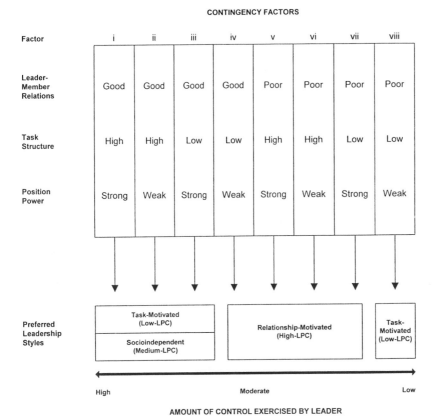

Figure 6.5. Contingency Model of Leadership

SOURCE: DuBrin, Andrew J., *Leadership: Research Findings, Practice, and Skills.* Copyright © 1995 by Houghton Mifflin Company. Reprinted with permission.

class. As organizational processes improve from Level 1 to Level 6, the ethical work culture must be simultaneously developed, as indicated in Figure 6.6, if process improvement of the system is to remain within acceptable ranges of variation and be sustained over time (Petrick & Furr, 1995).

In other words, total quality leaders need to assess and improve both the status of organizational processes in the work system and the stages of ethical work culture, which will sustain commitment to continuous improvement in each work group, work unit, and organization. The process context supports or inhibits individual and team empowerment that total quality leaders de-

Level	Process Status	Process Description/Assessment	Ethical Work Culture Status
1	Unknown	Process status has not been determined	Social Darwinism
2	Understood	Process design is understood and operates according to prescribed documentation	Machiavellianism
3	Effective	Process is systematically measured, streamlining has started, and end-customer expectations are met	Popular conformity
4	Efficient	Process is streamlined and is more efficient	Allegiance to authority
5	Error-free	Process is highly effective (error-free) and efficient	Democratic participation
6	World-class	Process is world-class and continues to improve	Principled integrity

Figure 6.6. Levels of Organizational Process and Ethical Work Culture Improvement
SOURCE: Harrington, M. (1991). *Business process improvement.* New York: McGraw-Hill. Reproduced with permission of The McGraw-Hill Companies.

velop. Cooperation makes sense in a context of world-class processes where principled integrity is the system norm upheld by total quality leaders, and is conversely resisted in a Machiavellian culture where processes are only partially understood and distrust of leadership prevails.

The second condition, *team empowerment readiness assessment,* occurs after the task, psychosocial, and moral maturity levels of leaders and followers are determined through completion of the Leadership Empowerment Readiness Assessment (LERA) in Appendix F (Petrick & Furr, 1995). Full work empowerment maturity, therefore, with regard to total quality leadership, is a condition characterized by high task competence and wide experience, high psychosocial motivation to achieve and share power, and high moral commitment to use power to enhance justice, trust, and care in the workplace. Premature empowerment of leaders and/or followers simply results in the cohesiveness of incompetent groups who make poor decisions more quickly and more often—a recipe for disaster (Giacolone & Greenberg, 1997; Janis, 1983; Jeannot, 1989). In total quality leadership, collective empowerment is expected to improve in phases from nonworking groups to high-performance teams (Fairholm, 1991; Katzenbach & Smith, 1993; Petrick & Furr, 1995).

The phases of team empowerment development, from nonworking groups to high-performance teams, can be delineated. Initially, a *group* is a collection of individuals who are in an interdependent relationship with one another. There are many types of groups. A *nonworking group* is simply a loose affiliation of individuals without a task focus. A *working group* is one for which there is no significant incremental performance need or opportunity that would require it to become a team. The members interact primarily to share information, best practices, or perspectives and to make decisions to help each individual perform within his or her area of responsibility. Beyond that, there is no realistic or truly desired "small group" common purpose, incremental performance goals, or joint work products that call for either a team approach or mutual accountability. Groups can be productive, but it is becoming increasingly evident that just bringing a group of people together to complete specific tasks is often unproductive and ineffective. Members of real teams develop strong feelings of allegiance that go beyond the mere grouping of individuals. The productive outcome is synergistic, and the accomplishments often can exceed the original goals of the group or its sponsor.

Next, there can be a collective performance improvement as groups transition into four phases: pseudo-teams, potential teams, real teams, and high-performance teams. A *pseudo-team* is a group for which there could be a significant incremental performance need or opportunity, but it has not focused on collective performance and is not trying to achieve it. It has no interest in shaping a common purpose or set of performance goals even though it may call itself a team. Pseudo-teams almost always contribute less to company performance needs than effective working groups because their interactions detract from each member's individual performance without delivering any joint benefit. In pseudo-teams, the sum of the whole is less than the potential of the individual parts.

The *potential team* is a group for which there is a significant incremental performance need and that sincerely is trying to improve its performance impact. Typically, however, it requires more clarity about its purpose, goals, or work products and more discipline in hammering out a common working approach. It has not yet established collective ability. Potential teams abound in most organizations.

A *real team* is a small number of people with complementary skills who are equally committed to a common purpose, goals, and working approach for which they hold themselves mutually accountable (Katzenbach & Smith, 1993). Its basic ingredients are diagrammed in Figure 6.7.

Real teams are the real power in TQ organizations; that is, they have the ability to guide their own conduct energetically, influence the conduct of others, and resist unwanted influence. Real teams have the skills, commitment,

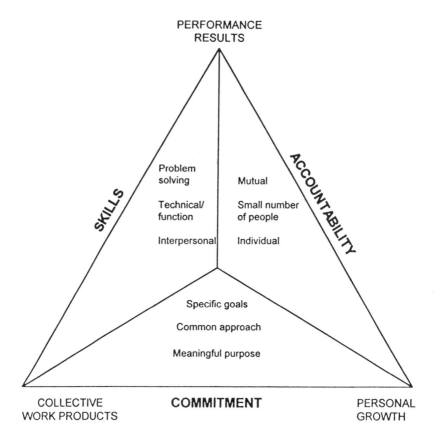

Figure 6.7. Basic Ingredients of Teams

SOURCE: Reprinted by permission of Harvard Business School Press. From *The Wisdom of Teams* by J. Katzenbach & D. Smith. Boston, MA, 1993, p. 8. Copyright © 1993 by McKinsey & Co., Inc.

and accountability for performance in TQ organizations. They require task, psychosocial, and moral maturity to exist, sustain regular interactions, and develop. Real project teams are the models to which pseudo- and potential teams aspire. Members of pseudo- and potential teams may demand empowerment as an entitlement; members of real teams deserve empowerment because they are the operational backbone of any successful total quality leadership approach. Empowerment readiness determinations for individuals, groups, and teams are necessary because diversion of scarce resources to "squeaky wheel" groups that are unable or unwilling to shoulder the commensurate responsibilities of power deprives real teams of the fuel they need to make productive contributions.

Finally, a *high-performance team* meets all the conditions of a real team, and its members are also deeply committed to one another's personal growth and success. That caring commitment usually extends beyond the team's work domain. The high-performance team significantly outperforms real teams and outperforms all reasonable expectations given its membership. It is as powerful as it is rare, but it remains a compelling aspiration for all real teams (Petrick & Furr, 1995).

To avoid premature team empowerment, therefore, the Total Quality Leadership Grid in Figure 6.8 provides a road map for matching the four appropriate contexts for managerial directing, coaching, participating, and delegating in order to promote responsible team empowerment (Johnson, 1993). The four leadership styles are placed within a two-dimensional grid of supportive and directive actions and are placed on a time line that starts at the top left and works its way through all four styles, ending at the top right quadrant. Total quality followers should progress along this time line, which is a measure of training effectiveness and ownership of the TQ process as time progresses. In fact, total quality leadership and team empowerment must be a blend of both contextual (system) adaptability and transformational leadership styles (Petrick & Furr, 1995).

The second line on the chart in Figure 6.8 places the four leadership styles along the time line. This shows the expected progression of people from their initial introduction into any work situation, from beginning employment to new process deployment under the directing style, through coaching and participating, to the ultimate payoff style afforded by delegation. In the directive style, either a high level of support is not required or there is not time. The coaching style becomes a natural progression as training and awareness of need take hold. In the participating style, high-level direction is not needed and may interfere with the team's initiative. When the delegating plateau is reached, the team is willing and able to handle the situation facing them with little support or direction; providing either would be undesirable. Because the greatest performance potential exists under the delegating style, the leader's goal must be to bring the team up to speed rapidly so that it can operate effectively in this self-directed, delegating mode.

The third line shows the activating force that powers each of these leadership styles. Positional power generally is the prime mover during the directing stages. Initial relationships with new employees do not produce personal power

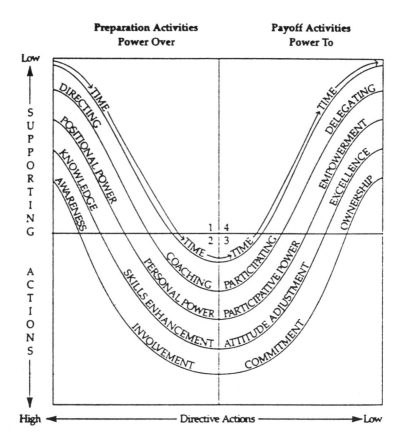

Figure 6.8.   Total Quality Leadership Style and Team Empowerment

SOURCE: Johnson, R. S. (1993). *TQM: Leadership for the Quality Transformation.* Milwaukee: ASQC Quality Press, p. 204. Reprinted with permission.

to any great degree, and the deployment of new processes requires the leader to create and sell his or her vision of work excellence. When coaching is used, the followers have been progressing long enough that the skilled coach usually has gained considerable personal power, which becomes the motivating force. The leader's influence is enough in most cases when participative leadership styles are employed and empowerment fuels the delegative style.

The fourth line illustrates the progression of training and development that supports the various leadership styles. Knowledge acquisition is the initial phase of training, which introduces the participants to the task at hand and provides them with the basics to begin their efforts. This is followed by skill enhancement, which helps people become productive. Under proper leadership, most people become more willing to perform as their ability to do the job well increases. This leads associates to collective participation, which requires psychosocial and moral attitude adjustments, OCB, and teamwork skills for maximum effectiveness. Fine-tuning the process on an ongoing basis requires the delegation style and demands collective attention to task, psychosocial, and moral excellence in every dimension of the work environment.

The fifth line of the chart in Figure 6.8 exhibits employee attitudes and contributions to the total quality management (TQM) process in part and the organization as a whole. People are initially aware of organizational needs and quality processes. As they progress in working with solid leaders, they become involved in TQM and the organization. Participation demands commitment to excellence and the organization if there is to be a payoff. The ultimate is TQM, self-directed leadership, and organizational ownership as teams are empowered through the delegating leadership style. Responsible team empowerment, therefore, is the result of work empowerment maturity in task, psychosocial, and moral dimensions between leader and followers.

The leadership flow from Quadrant 1 to Quadrant 4 is dependent on the work empowerment maturity of leaders and employees in Quadrant 1. Incompetent leaders who have positional power without commensurate work empowerment maturity (inadequate task competence and experience, low psychosocial motivation to achieve, inability or unwillingness to accept responsibility, or low moral commitment to use power to enhance justice, trust, and care in the workplace) will impede employee empowerment. Employee reactions to leaders with low work empowerment maturity are likely to include (a) lack of respect for leadership direction, position, knowledge, and awareness; (b) active or passive resistance; (c) compliance accompanied by resentment; and/or (d) exit from the organization. To avoid the prior negative sequence of outcomes, employees must be able to speak with facts (voice the truth) about leadership inadequacies with impunity.

The flow of empowerment reflected in this model is not leader-controlled as it is in a traditional organization. Employee empowerment readiness may exceed the leader's readiness to delegate and share power. Leader reactions to employees with higher work empowerment maturity may include (a) unwillingness to acknowledge obvious employee capability; (b) active or passive resistance to employee empowerment; (c) resignation and abdication of responsibility appropriate to each stage; and/or (d) exit from the organization. To avoid this negative sequence of outcomes, leaders must be able to create and adjust to new role responsibilities that relinquish traditional positional power prerogatives. Empowerment is a reallocation of responsibilities for both leaders and employees. If workforce empowerment does not result, both parties have failed, and optimal total quality leadership remains unrealized.

After the treatment of the major descriptive leadership approaches, it is important to relate them to what it normatively means to lead with integrity. *Leading with integrity means addressing the elements of the four ethics processes in the context of their parallel leading subprocesses to ensure that no step in the leading function neglects its moral dimensions and individual and collective postconventional moral development is cultivated.* It is important for managers to realize that the leadership styles they choose to use have implicit ethical values embedded in them. Expecting empowered teamwork from followers who have never been assessed with the LERA or who only experience autocratic, coercive leadership from their manager is both operationally unrealistic and morally regressive. There are many ways to lead without integrity. The victims of leadership moral immaturity include the walking wounded in most domestic and global organizations. Learning to lead with integrity entails personal, group, and organizational moral awareness and development. Leadership approaches are not value neutral; they either promote or inhibit the moral development of leaders, followers, and their work cultures (Murphy & Enderle, 1995).

Figure 6.9 delineates the relationships among the moral development stages, leadership approaches, and likely performance outcomes at the preconventional, conventional, and postconventional development levels. The pattern of leadership approaches adopted by leaders reflects and reinforces their own moral development and influences the moral development and likely performance outcomes of their followers and their work cultures.

In Figure 6.9, the preconventional cluster level of individual and organizational moral development is correlated with two leadership approaches and their likely performance outcomes. In the first row, the autocratic, coercive power leadership approach is implicitly supported by social Darwinism and is likely to generate minimal performance to keep a job out of fear (Graham, 1995). In the second row, the path-goal/transactional leadership approach is implicitly supported by Machiavellianism and is likely to generate an instrumental, "stepping-stone path" attitude toward work, wherein mutual manipu-

Moral Developmental Stages	Leadership Approaches	Likely Performance Outcomes
PRECONVENTIONAL	**PRECONVENTIONAL**	**PRECONVENTIONAL**
1. Obedience & punishment orientation/ Social Darwinism 2. Instrumental purpose/Machiavellianism	1. Autocratic, coercive power leadership 2. Path-Goal/Transactional leadership	1. Positive task accomplishment to keep job out of fear. Regular on-time attendance out of fear. 2. Following formal paths and informal paths to career success. Efficient use of resources to pursue future career options. Mutual manipulation at work for personal career advancement.
CONVENTIONAL	**CONVENTIONAL**	**CONVENTIONAL**
3. Interpersonal accord, conformity, and mutual expectations/Popular conformity 4. Social accord and authority maintenance/ Allegiance to authority	3. Leader-member exchange and interpersonal consideration leadership 4. Institutional, transactional compliance leadership, and Fiedler's contingency leadership	3. Developing group cohesiveness and competence. Sharing information, tools, and other resources. Socialization of newcomers. Assisting those with heavy workloads 4. Respecting the internal chain of command. Obedience to authority figures. Complying with external legal and regulatory standards. Maintain contingency settings that enhance the control and authority of the leader.
POSTCONVENTIONAL	**POSTCONVENTIONAL**	**POSTCONVENTIONAL**
5. Majority agreement and due process/ Democratic participation 6. Ethical principle-based orientation/ Principled integrity	5. Participative, servant leadership. 6. Total quality, transforming leadership; empowered team leadership	5. Serving constituency needs. Democratic participation to arrive at majority agreements. Enfranchising involvement with organizational success. Keeping informed about current issues of organizational importance. Attending nonrequired meetings and providing constructive input. Giving decision makers timely, accurate information. Providing reasoned arguments in ethics dialogues for proposed work changes. Tolerance of other points of view. 6. Challenging authority and majority respectfully with the facts. Providing for principled, systemic moral development and team empowerment. Consensual decision-making preferred to majority vote. Dedicated to character improvement.

Figure 6.9. Relationships Among Individual and Organizational Moral Development Stages, Patterns of Leadership Approaches, and Likely Follower/Work Culture Performance Outcomes

lation for career advancement becomes the norm. Leaders who cannot clarify organizational paths for future associate success or who lack the political savvy to manipulate others are neither respected nor promoted (Yukl, 1994).

In Figure 6.9, the conventional cluster entails a set of leadership and moral relationships designed to evoke work unit productivity by appealing to group conformity and allegiance to authority. In the third row, leader considera-tion (Bass, 1985) and cultivation of vertical dyadic exchange between leaders and a favored network of subordinates (Dansereau, Graen, & Haga, 1975) engender interpersonal loyalty and in-group cohesion to fulfill role expecta-tions above and beyond the promised payoffs for dependable task perform-ance. Furthermore, in the fourth row, a more impersonal leadership style, institutional, transactional compliance leadership or "organizational states-manship" (Selznick, 1957) may likely result in respect for the law and obedience to authority figures. Several OCB studies have found evidence connecting leader attributes, such as trustworthiness and fairness, with subor-dinate altruism/cooperation, but a different set of causal factors for obedi-ence-type OCBs (Farh, Podsakoff, & Organ, 1990; Podsakoff, MacKenzie, Moorman, & Fetter, 1990). In these latter studies, it appears that leadership style and moral reasoning help create strong interpersonal and/or social rela-tionships that broaden self-interest to include service to a dyad or group, thereby giving rise to social norms that favor cooperation as well as personal industry (Ciulla, 1995; Enderle, 1987; Graham, 1995).

Finally, the postconventional cluster in Figure 6.9 entails a set of leadership and moral relationships designed to evoke participation in organizational governance, respectful challenging of authority, and commitment to systemic and principled moral development. In the fifth row, participative servant leadership serves constituency needs, determining majority trends and enfran-chising all stakeholders in organizational governance. The servant leader elicits majority expectations about workplace governance and legitimates responding to stakeholder voiced concerns. Selfishness and naive gullibility are both lessened when democratic processes prevail and people are empowered to serve others and voice high-level moral reasoning that assesses special stakeholders' interests in terms of due process and majority values. In the sixth row, total quality, transforming empowerment leadership develops people from poten-tial to real team members dedicated to ongoing character development and consensual decision making with processes from unknown to world-class standards that support continuous system improvement (Drake & Baasten, 1990; Petrick & Furr, 1995). As followers and leaders mature, they advance beyond participative leadership into delegative leadership, wherein empowered teams assume ownership of strategy formulation and implementation, the respectful challenging of authority with facts, and the balanced application of universal moral principles in everyday ethics dialogues is the operating work norm.

In this sixth row, leading with integrity is absolutely essential. Many leaders who have been successful at lower levels of process and moral development do not aspire to lead with integrity; they and their organizations settle for safe stagnation. Other leaders who survive the battles of lower levels of process and moral development are so wounded that they are neither able nor willing to lead with integrity; they hold on to power and callously crush those who aspire to a higher level of leadership. Finally, a few leaders, by pluck and luck, have the knowledge, experience, and intact moral ambition to lead with integrity; their personal leadership inspires others to emulate their principled conduct and demand more than conventional performance from themselves and their leaders. At this level, optimal leadership effectiveness and efficiency emerge and are sustained.

To evaluate the efficiency and effectiveness of the dimensions of leading, Figure 6.10 provides a matrix based on two questions: (1) "Were the intended leading processes successfully realized?" and (2) "Did the realized leading processes successfully promote organizational performance?"

In Figure 6.10, the Leading Success Evaluation Matrix contains four combinations. A yes-yes designation (in Quadrant A) means that the intended coordinated leading was successful and fully meritorious; managers set out to lead a particular way, they did it efficiently, and the leading effectively worked. A yes-no designation (in Quadrant B) points toward a realized leadership failure in which managers efficiently implemented the intended leading, which itself is only partially meritorious because that leadership proved to be ineffective. A no-yes designation (in Quadrant C) points toward inefficient implementation of the intended leadership but efficient emergent leading; for example, unintended and unanticipated leadership emerges that happens to be effective and is thereby partially meritorious. A no-no designation (in Quadrant D) indicates a complete failure in leadership because of inefficient implementation of intended leadership and ineffective outcomes.

Now that the dimensions and success standards of leading have been treated, it is important to address the relationship of ethical leading processes to building integrity.

Intended Leading Realized

		Yes	No
Realized Leading Successful	Yes	Coordinated Leading Success (*Efficient and Effective*) [A]	Emergent Leading Success (*Inefficient but Effective*) [C]
	No	Realized Leading Failure (*Efficient but Not Effective*) [B]	Complete Leading Failure (*Inefficient and Ineffective*) [D]

Figure 6.10. Leading Success Evaluation Matrix

▧ ETHICAL LEADING PROCESSES THAT BUILD INTEGRITY

All three dimensions of integrity—judgment, process, and developmental —are important in managerial leading with integrity. Whereas the developmental and judgment dimensions anchor and sustain leading with integrity, the process dimension builds leading with integrity. To lead in a fully meritorious manner, some form of systematic leading process must be used. The following four-step sequence of responsible leading provides a generic model of the leading subprocesses and their associated developmental tasks:

1. *Leading Scanning:* scanning of current external and internal factors affecting the leadership of people and processes, such as awareness of best leadership practices inside and outside the industry, existing leadership talent at all levels within the organization, and internal system incentives and measures of leadership development progress

2. *Leading Formulation and Choice:* leading formulation, analysis, and choice of the blend of people and processes that will constitute organizational leadership by creatively combining the following three ingredients: (a) leader traits, skills, conduct, and decision making styles; (b) follower conduct, power relationships, leader-member exchanges, transactional and transformational interactions, and follower performance motivations; and (c) contingent and TQ system processes that support or inhibit leaders

3. *Leading Implementation:* strengthening the resources of people and processes through personal selection, performance expectations, appraisal, rewards, and development, as well as empowerment readiness assessment, ongoing character, and learning community development, in order to enhance the personal and organizational readiness to act responsibly

Processes	Step 1	Step 2	Step 3	Step 4
Ethics Process	Ethical Awareness	Ethical Judgment	Ethical Intention	Ethical Conduct
Leading Subprocesses	Leading Scanning	Leading Formulation and Choice	Leading Implementation	Leading Evaluation, Control, and Improvement

Figure 6.11. Parallel Ethics and Leading Subprocesses That Build Management Integrity

4. *Leading Evaluation, Control, and Improvement:* evaluation, control, and improvement of people and processes by using a variety of ethics, quality, social, and environmental audit instruments, performance indicators, acceptable process variation feedback measurements, social responsibility plus sustainable development measures, and ongoing improvement initiatives

Each step in the generic leading process must be adequately completed in order to result in a well-led company that is both effective and efficient.

The four process integrity steps parallel and permeate the four steps in the generic subprocesses of leading (leading scanning, leading formulation and choice, leading implementation, and leading evaluation, control, and improvement). In other words, *leading with ethical integrity means addressing the elements of the four integrity processes in the context of their parallel leading subprocesses to ensure that no step in the function of leading neglects its moral dimension.* Managers may lack integrity in leading by neglecting to adequately perform the subtasks entailed in ethics and leading processes, thereby exposing themselves and their organizations to ethical risk. Leading with ethical integrity is facilitated by using the appropriate systematic queries from the QL-TOOL in Appendix D for each corresponding step of the generic leading process. Figure 6.11 depicts the incusive and sequential alignment of all ethics processes and leading subprocesses that build management integrity.

Ethical Leading Scanning

With regard to the alignment of ethics and leading processes in Step 1 in Figure 6.11, the scope of the ethical leading scanning includes stakeholder benchmarking of best practices in the global and domestic, external and internal organizational environment, specified in detail in queries 1 and 2 from the QL-TOOL (external ecological, technological, economic, legal, sociocultural and political factors and internal organizational ethics development system factors). Ethical awareness leading scanning is achieved when the two elements of the ethical awareness process (perception and sensitivity) are adequately addressed by responses to queries 1, 2, and 3 of the QL-TOOL. Misperception and insensitivity to external and internal stakeholders results in culpably negligent unethical leading scanning.

Motorola, Inc. Managers and Ethical Leading Scanning

Recent research studies have indicated that most North American workers regard themselves as being poorly led by out-of-touch managers (Spitzer, 1995). To overcome this pattern of conventional leadership insensitivity, Motorola, Inc. has developed a tradition of leadership scanning of external and internal stakeholder practices to ensure global leadership (Meister, 1994; O'Toole, 1995; Petrick et al., 1994). Motorola is a U.S.-based multinational that employs nearly 130,000 workers at 53 major facilities worldwide, with headquarters in Shaumburg, Illinois (outside Chicago). It manufactures mobile and portable cellular phones (number one maker worldwide), semiconductors (number three maker worldwide), multifunction computer systems, two-way land-mobile radios (number one maker worldwide), cellular infrastructure equipment (number two worldwide), radio products, pagers, cordless phones, positioning and navigation systems, LAN systems, and data communications equipment. Founded by Paul Galvin in 1928, the family value of intergenerational dialogue has provided continuity of leadership emphasis on the part of his son, Robert, and his grandson, Christopher. Two areas in which Motorola focused its attention are external awareness of the need for system improvement through measured defect reduction and internal awareness of the need for team leadership to institutionalize organizational capacities for rapid change.

With regard to external leadership scanning, during a 1986 team benchmarking trip to Japan, Motorola executives visited various (noncompeting) electronics firms and discovered that they were operating at a defect rate that was as much as 1,000 times lower than Motorola's! The perception of a superior external process sparked an intense reassessment of existing internal processes and a sensitivity to the harm of conducting business as usual. Robert Galvin, in turn, challenged his workforce to achieve the now-famous and widely used Six Sigma defect-free process standard. In practical terms, this means only 3.4

deviations (errors) in 1 million opportunities—99.9997% perfect. The combined impact of the Six Sigma defect level standard and cycle time improvement has reduced waste, overhead, and production costs and increased responsiveness to customer orders, R&D innovative productivity, and product performance.

With regard to internal leadership scanning, Robert Galvin quickly realized that constant renewal in their high-tech facilities could not materialize without the exercise of leadership by all Motorola employees. To achieve this, operations were radically decentralized, and employees were formed into teams, each responsible for such things as quality, productivity, cost reduction, inventory control, and customer service. Because these teams were truly self-directing, and because all employees were rewarded with healthy bonuses when they met the goals they had set for themselves in consultation with management, Motorola created a system in which workers had a greater voice and stake than competing Japanese workers had in their firms. Motorola became one of the first large companies in the United States to enable its workers to be leaders themselves. Through a system of constant communication and feedback, Motorola employees came to understand their individual, team, and organizational responsibilities to scan for innovation in a way that precluded coercive leadership or complacent groupthink. Motorola invested heavily in quality staffing, training, and team rewards/recognition to develop the skills and sense of ownership necessary for world-class leadership.

The capacity of Motorola's leaders to stay in touch with external competitor practices and internal employee leadership potential had ancillary benefits in improving its supplier relations. Suppliers who wanted to maintain relationships with a Baldrige Award winner like Motorola were likewise challenged to improve their measured process and team leadership capacities. The net result was that multiple stakeholder ethical awareness was strengthened by thorough ethical leadership scanning. Leadership that ignores or neglects external and/or internal stakeholder input or prevents voiced feedback from influencing leadership styles cannot be regarded as ethical, and it undermines leadership with integrity.

Ethical Leading Formulation and Choice

With regard to the alignment of ethics processes and leading subprocesses in Step 2 of Figure 6.11, the scope of ethical leading formulation and choice includes factors in the global and domestic, external and internal organizational context and judgment, specified in query 4 in the QL-TOOL (supportive external and internal contexts for optimal ethical analysis and resolution in demonstrating judgment integrity). Ethical leading formulation and choice is achieved when the two elements of the ethical judgment process (analysis and resolution) are adequately addressed by responses to query 4 of the QL-TOOL. Sometimes, this type of ethical leadership is internally generated; at other times, qualified organizational ethics consultants help formulate and initiate moral discourse and processes that empower all company stakeholders to arrive at sounder ethical judgments (Petrick & Quinn, 1995). The presence of thorough, multidisciplinary ethical analysis leads to structured ethics dialogue and formulated processes that arrive at a balanced, justified resolution of ethically framed issues, resulting in ethical leading formulation and choice.

Texas Instruments Incorporated Managers and Ethical Leading Formulation and Choice

For example, Dallas-based, high-technology, Texas Instruments Incorporated (TI) was recently awarded the National Business Ethics Award by the Center for Business Ethics at Bentley College for formulating and choosing effective organizational measures to maintain and strengthen ethical conduct. TI's leadership has actively structured a supportive ethical sharing process that is conducive to the responsible formulation and widespread sharing of sound ethical judgments. Included in its organizational ethics infrastructure are the following practices: benchmarked peer review of its formal ethics program, whistle-blower support, ongoing ethics training, and revision of its code of ethics. In 1987, TI established an Ethics Office with three primary goals: (a) to ensure that TI's business policies and practices continue to be aligned with its ethical principles, (b) to clearly communicate TI's ethical expectations, and (c) to provide multiple channels for feedback through which people can ask questions, voice concerns, and seek resolution of ethical issues.

The Ethics Office has been accomplishing its goals and introduced an interactive way to institutionalize ethics discourse systemwide and to encourage commitment to organization integrity. TI uses protected, confidential, and interactive electronic mail (e-mail) feedback in a helpline system called "Instant Experience," which serves as a weekly clearinghouse of useful ethical experience for all TI employees worldwide. By using T-News, the company's worldwide electronic newspaper, ethical work issues can be formulated and Ethics Office answers can be broadcast; the sustained electronic ethics dialogue has sharpened moral analysis and resolution of issues regarding appropriate moral conduct at TI worldwide. This type of organizational ethics communication vehicle, however, could be replicated in any company that has a local area computer network in order to sharpen and share moral judgments.

The Instant Experience is particularly appropriate at TI because its e-mail ethics dialogues are a natural extension of that technical work environment. Furthermore, e-mail is appropriate for ethics dialogues because it allows for interaction with reflection. The Instant Experience System encourages employees to think about a moral issue at work and then to participate in relatively informal, electronic communication with others. Research on electronic communication suggests that people are less inhibited when communicating electronically and may be more willing to deal with sensitive ethical issues at the keyboard than they would be face to face. The net result of TI's leadership choice of ethics infrastructure, therefore, is the rapid inclusiveness of a wide range of moral viewpoints that provide the leadership opportunity to exercise balanced integration within and among diverse perspectives to arrive at systemwide, sound, factually based, morally justified, and supported policies.

In essence, TI's Instant Experience demonstrates the difference that ethical leading formulation and choice can make in improving an organization's collective ethical judgment and moral development by using new technological processes.

Ethical Leading Implementation

With regard to the alignment of the ethics processes and organizing subprocesses in Step 3 of Figure 6.11, the extent of the ethical leading implementation can be determined by fully addressing queries 5, 6, and 9 from the QL-TOOL. Ethical leading implementation is achieved when the two elements of the ethical intention process (cognitive and volitional readiness to act) are demonstrated by responses to queries 5, 6, and 9 of the QL-TOOL. Obviously, poor implementation of a rationally formulated and chosen leadership project can result in leadership and moral failure (Yukl, 1994). Less obviously, refusal to consider feedback to modify original leadership choices in the light of operational experience or to replace the intended leadership choice with a more feasible, emergent one is also a leadership and moral failure.

Mary Livingston of AT&T Corporation
and Ethical Leading Implementation

The benefits of ethical leading implementation in addressing people and processes can be delineated in the case of Mary Livingston, a manager who headed the Change Management Organization (CMO) of AT&T's Business Communication Services (BCS). AT&T Corporation is a New York City-based U.S. multinational that provides communications, computer, and network services and products as well as financial and leasing services worldwide; it operates more than 90 manufacturing facilities globally. AT&T has the largest long-distance network in the United States and is a world leader in telecommunication services. The BCS Group is a key component of AT&T's global success. BCS generates multi-billion-dollar revenue streams by providing businesses of all sizes with everything from long-distance calling to ultrasophisticated, global data networks. It was from BCS's highly successful salesforce that Mary Livingston broke the glass ceiling and was selected as a credible leader of the CMO within BCS (Kouzes & Posner, 1990, 1991).

The highly regarded McKinsey & Company Real Change Team identified Livingston at AT&T from among many national candidates as representative of the transformed corporate middle manager who, by tough but fair performance expectations, has become a real change leader in implementing new corporate visions. In the course of the AT&T corporate change from one of the largest corporate sales forces in the world to one of the leanest for its size, Livingston formed and guided a score of team initiatives that diagnosed current sales performance, designed and implemented sales improvement processes for different customer segments, and reengineered all of the sales force's support services—with dramatic bottom-line results. In addition to challenging performance expectations, Livingston's approach enhanced both personal and organizational cognitive and volitional readiness to act, thereby strengthening AT&T's character during the turbulent times of industry deregulation. The focused clarity of Livingston's publicized personal vision aligned her cognitive and volitional empowerment readiness for leading change initiatives, as indicated in Figure 6.12. Her cognitive virtues include a vivid imagination of a preferred organizational future to be achieved within multiple constraints. Her volitional virtues include the moral virtues of courage and justice to overcome all odds and to take risks on people and processes; the social virtues of fostering trust and cooperativeness by including people in the change

Vision Statements	Virtuous Motivations
I have a dream that one day we will be a salesforce that stands tall and commands respect from customers, business units, and competitors.	*Shared Pride*
We will be a benchmark for other sales organizations. Business cases will be written about us.	*Desire for Earned Greatness*
I have a dream that we will one day be a salesforce that consistently meets commitments and says it can do more (vs. being skilled in defending forecasts we know we can meet).	*Responsibility for Continued Improvement*
We will be a salesforce that delights customers—that is, raises the bar for customer satisfaction.	*Serving Better by Raising Standards*
We will be a salesforce that thinks more about the competition and the customer than about turf. In other words, there is an abundance mentality; we intuitively understand there is more for everybody if we do the right things versus divvying up the same pie in a different way.	*Growth With Equity*
Borrowing from Martin Luther King Jr.'s dream analogy is no accident. I respect the difficulties and obstacles, but I am not concerned about the obstacles. "For when people get caught up with that which is right, and they are willing to sacrifice for it, there is no stopping short of victory."—M.L.K.	*Courage to Overcome Obstacles*

Figure 6.12. Mary Livingston's Personal Vision

process and awarding them for their collaboration; and the emotional virtues of respect and sincerity by developing group pride in solid accomplishments and conveying honest appreciation for work well done, thereby expanding leadership capacity and character for the organizational future.

Livingston also enhanced AT&T's organizational readiness to act by combining organizational recognition self-respect with measurable organizational evaluative self-respect. She built momentum to sustain developmental results over time by avoiding changes that inflict undeserved harm on any stakeholders without their consent and requiring that AT&T employees have routine evaluations and periodic opportunities to reenlist in the character development process of working with good, dedicated people in a constant improvement process. She varied the balance of control and flexibility needed to adapt to contingent challenges but focused on organizational empowerment development, rather than on mere change activities to display power for personal career enhancement.

These leadership implementation lessons from Mary Livingston are even more important if gender is viewed as a contingent variable in effective leadership (Kanter, 1977; Morrison, 1992; Powell, 1993). Some recent gender research has indicated that women tend to adopt a more inclusive, participative leadership style that attempts to enhance follower's self-worth and rely on interpersonal skills to influence others than men, who are more likely to use a directive command-and-control leadership style that rewards follower compliance and relies on formal authority to influence others (Eagly & Johnson, 1990; Helgesen, 1990; Loden, 1985). In essence, ethical leadership implementation strengthens individual and collective character, enhancing the readiness of employees to act with integrity.

Perhaps if ethical leadership implementation styles of women in some contexts are more likely to build organizational character and to exhibit empowerment readiness by means of greater task, psychosocial, and moral maturity than men, then the traditional command-and-control leadership approaches can promote institutional integrity by learning from the Mary Livingstons of the work world (Katzenbach & the RCL Team, 1995; Vorherr, Petrick, Quinn, & Brady, 1995).

Ethical Leading Evaluation, Control, and Improvement

With regard to the alignment of ethics processes and the leading subprocess in Step 4 of Figure 6.11, the scope of ethical leadership evaluation, control, and improvement includes stakeholder conduct and reputation in the global and domestic, external and internal organizational environments, specified in detail in queries 7, 8, and 10 from the QL-TOOL (extent to which responsible, ecological, economic, legal, and philanthropic conduct anchors and builds reputations for integrity). Ethical leading evaluation, control, and improvement are achieved when the two elements of the ethical conduct process (responsible responsiveness and sustainable development) are adequately addressed by responses to queries 7, 8, and 10 of the QL-TOOL. Irresponsible and unsustainable conduct results in unethical leading evaluation, control, and improvement.

The Maxxum Group Managers and Unethical
Leading Evaluation, Control, and Improvement

The example of the Maxxum Group's leadership in its dealings with Pacific Lumber in California can illustrate the devastating impact of unethical leading evaluation, control, and improvement on people and processes. In January 1985, Pacific Lumber (PL), under President Elain, was turning a modest, steady profit for investors, generously compensating its workers and managers, conserving its giant redwood trees, and acting as a socially responsible corporate citizen in the community. In October 1985, backed by Michael Milken's junk bonds at Drexel Burnham Lambert, the New York-based Maxxum Group, led by Charles Hurwitz, made PL the target of a hostile takeover. President Elain was stunned by the attack because PL was debt-free, cash-rich (including a solid worker's pension fund overfunded by $58-$60 million), resource-rich beyond the knowledge of the board of directors (it had been 30 years since the last complete timber resource inventory), and complacent in the knowledge that its practices were ecologically sound. PL produced moderate financial prosperity and was well respected in the community. The end result, however, was that PL was acquired by Maxxum at $40 per share (rather than the $29 market price), with golden parachutes for key management personnel.

The huge debt incurred by Maxxum to seal the hostile takeover (of the $840 million spent for PL, $770 million was debt, of which $575 million was financed through junk bonds), motivated Hurwitz to terminate employee pension plans (freeing up $50 million) and to accelerate logging practices to cut redwoods faster in order to cut debt faster. Numerous lawsuits ensued, and after environmental activists tried unsuccessfully to have the California State Board of Forestry fulfill its public stewardship responsibility by denying PL's accelerated timber harvest plans, it futilely engaged in civil disobedience as a last resort to stop the new PL leadership. The net result of the hostile takeover was that Maxxum exploited people, nature, and the financial system. Hurwitz was regarded as socially irresponsible and as promoting unsustainable development to generate cash for imprudent debt obligations and for more short-term gains from takeover attempts, causing more long-term harm and unfair distribution of social and ecological burdens.

The PL case provides a number of lessons for ethical leading evaluation, control, and improvement. First, responsible corporate leaders need to know the current value of all company resources and the extent to which capital assets are being inefficiently allocated. Corporate leaders who neglect the aspect of financial responsibility do so at their peril. Second, corporate leaders need to address the system of incentives that promote counterproductive hostile take-overs by considering, for example, endorsing legislation proposed by Rep. James Flores to impose a 100% surtax on all short-term capital gains from hostile takeovers that exceed $1 million in any year (Thompson, 1995). Third, responsible corporate leaders must build integrity rationally and produce quality products/services that sustain long-term ethical conduct but must also ensure that the company's good reputation is effectively communicated to multiple stakeholders, who can appreciate and support exemplary corporate conduct, rather than opt for short-term financial benefits. Fourth, corporate leaders by word and deed need to exercise and promote moderate acquisitions and prudent debt assumption, rather than unbridled greed, as a preferred character trait. Finally, responsibly building and protecting ecologically sustainable organizations is an important social responsibility of managerial leaders and essential for maintaining a solid corporate reputation (Jennings & Zandbergen, 1995; Starik & Rands, 1995).

In essence, moral performance standards and organizational reputation development are both strengthened by ethical leading evaluation, control, and improvement. Organizations with a reputation for responsible and sustainable conduct with regard to leading people and processes with integrity are likely to develop empowered workforces, to have their good ethical conduct reinforced through deserved recognition, and to set higher standards of performance domestically and globally.

▧ MANAGEMENT ETHICS AND LEADING WITH INTEGRITY MINICASES

To apply management ethical decision making and lead with integrity, the following minicases are offered for practice analysis. They raise issues in management ethics and leading with integrity and are categorized into seven allied management application clusters:

1. Accounting/auditing issues
2. Finance/investment issues
3. Marketing/advertising issues

4. Business management/human resources/business law issues
5. Technology/quality operations/organizational behavior issues
6. Public/nonprofit/health care administration issues
7. International/environmental/public policy issues

These clusters are generic categories, and specific cases in any one chapter may not cover all subfields in the cluster, but at least one minicase in Chapters 4 through 7 addresses each subfield in the cluster. Of the 18 subfields contained in the 7 clusters, 28 minicases are provided, ensuring that each subfield is addressed at least once and that overlapping interfield problems are included.

To incorporate the tools and resources of this book to analyze and resolve leadership issues with integrity, the authors recommend that each minicase be approached with three objectives in mind:

1. Systematically apply the QL-TOOL, in an individual or collective setting, to arrive at a principled, feasible resolution.
2. In accomplishing the first objective, consciously engage in ethics dialogue as the guiding method of moral discourse.
3. Select the appropriate components of the OEDS (in Appendix E) and other tools contained in the Appendices that would cultivate, build, and/or sustain dimensions of management integrity in the future.

(1) Accounting/Auditing Minicase: (Case 6A) - MiniScribe

MiniScribe, founded in 1980 and based in Longmont, Colorado, was a disk drive manufacturer (Jennings, 1996). When MiniScribe hit a slump in the mid-1980s because it had lost its largest customer, IBM, the board of directors brought in Q.T. Wiles, a turnaround specialist in the high-technology industries. When Wiles took over at MiniScribe, he engaged the venture-capital and investment banking firm of Hambrecht & Quist to raise the capital needed for the firm's turnaround. Hambrecht & Quist raised $20 million in 1987 through the sale of debentures. Wiles was, at that time, the chairman of Hambrecht & Quist. Hambrecht & Quist purchased $7.5 million of the debentures and also purchased a 17% interest in MiniScribe.

With new capital and simultaneous cost cuts, MiniScribe's sales went from $113.9 million in 1985 to a projected $603 million in 1988. In 1987, Mini-Scribe's board asked Wiles to stay for another 3 years. That year, MiniScribe's stock climbed to $14 per share. During 1988, the computer industry underwent another slump, and by May, Wiles and other officers were selling stock. Wiles sold 150,000 shares for between $11 and $12 per share, and seven other officers sold 200,000 shares.

By the time the shares were sold, MiniScribe held the unenviable position of having high inventory and high receivables. Industry sales were down, and MiniScribe customers were not paying their bills. In early 1989, MiniScribe announced a $14.6 million loss for the final quarter of 1988. MiniScribe's ratio of inventory to sales was 33% (the industry average was 24%), and its receivables were 94 days behind (the industry average was 70 days). The amount of receivables went from $109 million to $173 million in the last quarter of 1988.

MiniScribe's release of the new financial information resulted in an in-house audit, shareholder lawsuits, and an investigation of stock trading by the Securities and Exchange Commission (SEC). Scrutiny by regulators, outside directors, and the SEC revealed that Wiles, through his unrealistic sales goals and autocratic management style, had created a high-pressure environment for managers.

The in-house audit uncovered that, by late 1986, financial results had become the sole criterion for performance evaluations and bonuses at Mini-Scribe. To be sure that they hit their quotas, MiniScribe sales personnel had used creative accounting maneuvers. For example, in one case a customer was shipped two times as many disk drives as had been ordered—at a value of $9 million. Although the extra drives were returned, the sale for all the drives had already been booked.

The investigation also revealed that, in some orders, sales were booked at the time of shipment even though title would not pass to the customer until completion of shipment. An examination of MiniScribe's financial records showed that the company had manipulated its reserves to offset its losses. MiniScribe posted only 1% as reserves, whereas the industry range was 4% to 10%. In some of the transactions the audit uncovered, shipments sent to MiniScribe warehouses were booked as sales when, in fact, customers were not even invoiced until the drives were shipped from the warehouse.

Through these creative accounting manipulations and others, MiniScribe officers kept up a rosy fiscal appearance for the firm's auditors, Coopers and Lybrand. For example, for the 1987 audited financials, company officials packaged and shipped construction bricks (pretend inventory valued at $3.66 million) so that these products would count as retail sales. When bricks were returned, the sales were reversed but inventory increased. Obsolete parts and scraps were rewrapped as products and shipped to warehouses to be counted in inventory.

It was discovered that, during the 1986 audit by Coopers and Lybrand, company officials broke into trunks containing the auditors' work papers and increased year-end inventory figures. With the disclosure of the internal audit and the discovery of these creative accounting practices and inventory deceptions, MiniScribe's stock continued to drop, selling for $1.31 per share by September 1989. By 1990, MiniScribe had filed for bankruptcy and was purchased by Maxtor Corporation.

Lawsuits against Hambrecht & Quist, Wiles, and Coopers and Lybrand were brought by Kempner Capital Management, the U.S. National Bank of Galveston, and 11 other investors in the debentures sold by Hambrecht & Quist. In February 1992, a jury awarded the investors $28.7 million in compensatory damages and $530 million in punitive damages. Coopers and Lybrand was held responsible for $200 million, Wiles for $250 million, Hambrecht & Quist for $45 million, and Mr. Hambrecht for $35 million.

In effect, the lack of accounting leadership planning with integrity resulted in multi-million-dollar compensatory and punitive damage awards, bankruptcy, loss of jobs, dramatic investor losses, and erosion of public confidence in audit certifications. (For more details, see International Federation of Accountants. [1990]. *Guidelines on ethics for professional accountants.* New York: Author.)

(2) Finance/Investment Minicase: (Case 6B) - Drexel Burnham Lambert, Inc. and Michael Milken

Drexel Burnham Lambert, Inc. (Drexel) was an investment banking firm that dominated the high-yield bond market and rose to prominence during the 1980s, only to be toppled along with the "junk bond king," Michael Milken, who served as its vice president based in Beverly Hills, California. Milken's and Drexel's rapid rise to the top came about as a result of their virtual creation and subsequent domination of the billion-dollar "junk bond" market that helped finance the 1980s takeover boom and thousands of emerging businesses usually deemed uncreditworthy. The lack of their financial leadership with integrity caused one of the biggest scandals ever to hit Wall Street.

Before Milken's ascent to the top financial circles, junk bonds were a relatively obscure financial investment shunned by most investors. *Junk bonds are debt securities that offer high rates of return at high risk.*

People familiar with the firm say Milken's office was responsible for 80% to 90% of Drexel's profits. In addition to bringing in huge profits for the company, Milken also amassed for himself a huge fortune. In the 4-year period ending in 1987, he is believed to have made over $1.1 billion. In 1987 alone, he earned $550 million in salary and bonuses—more than the firm he worked for—making him easily the highest-paid employee in history.

During the early 1980s, Milken recognized a tremendous financial opportunity in meeting the borrowing needs of relatively small companies. At that time, only about 800 companies issued bonds labeled investment grade, but there were thousands of firms with annual revenues of $25 million or more. Drexel's success was built on meeting those financing needs. Drexel's ability to raise capital through the high-yield bond market allowed many firms to borrow much-needed funds although they had not previously been considered creditworthy. In this sense, Drexel's activities supported growth, and they expanded their financial activities to fuel the bitter takeover battles of the 1980s.

In September 1988, after an investigation spanning $2\frac{1}{2}$ years, the SEC filed a 194-page civil lawsuit against Drexel. The SEC also name Michael Milken, his brother Lowell, and other Milken aides in the suit. In its most sweeping enforcement action since the securities laws were written, the SEC charged Drexel with insider trading, stock manipulation, "parking" of securities to conceal their true ownership, false disclosures in SEC filings, maintaining false books and records, aiding and abetting capital rules violations, fraud in securities-offerings materials, and various other charges. (*Parking* involved hiding ownership of securities by selling them to other parties with the understanding that they will be sold back to the original owner, usually at a prearranged time and price.) The SEC suit also raised questions about Drexel's supervision of Milken's Beverly Hills operations.

While the SEC was putting together its case, the U.S. Department of Justice was building a criminal case against Drexel and its employees. This effort was led by Rudolph Giuliani, the U.S. attorney for the Manhattan district, who later became mayor of New York City. Giuliani's office set out to prove that Drexel used Ivan Boesky, the notorious insider trader, as a front for secretly trading some stocks. By so doing, Drexel could increase the price of takeover stocks so that it could get higher fees and trigger unwanted takeovers. The profits were then funneled back into the firm by using dubious payments, with false paperwork covering the trail. In many cases, Drexel's goal appeared to be power as much as profit—the ability to control the outcome of the deals it financed. Giuliani's case against the firm centered around a $5.3 million payment Boesky made in March 1987 to Drexel for "consulting services." The prosecution alleged this amount was actually part of the profits on stock that Drexel had parked with Boesky's firm. Allegations were also made that Drexel and Boesky deliberately destroyed documents to cover up their activities. Of the six charges initially brought against Drexel, all involved transactions allegedly initiated by Michael Milken, and five of the six transactions allegedly involved Boesky. Drexel set out to discredit Boesky as Giuliani's office supported his claims against Drexel with written documentation and other informants—Charles Thurnher, James Dahl, Cary Maulteschy, and Terrence Peizer—all of whom had worked for Michael Milken.

In December 1988, after spending more than $100 million on its legal defense and denying any misconduct or wrongdoing for more than 2 years, Drexel pleaded guilty to a six-count felony indictment on charges of securities, wire, and mail fraud and agreed to pay a record $650 million in fines and restitution. Drexel also gave in to the government demand that it had most vehemently opposed—it agreed to cooperate in all continuing investigations, including investigations of some of its own clients and employees, including Michael Milken. In return, the prosecutor dropped the racketeering (RICO) charges against the company. CEO Fred Joseph said Drexel's decision was the only alternative that gave the company a chance to survive.

The settlement with the Justice Department was contingent on Drexel's settling with the SEC, which it did in the spring of 1989. Under that agreement, Drexel submitted to unprecedented federal supervision, agreed to a 3-year probation, and had to appoint board members approved by the SEC. In addition, Drexel was required to move its Beverly Hills operation back to New York and to sever ties with Milken. In the agreement, Drexel neither admitted nor denied guilt. By agreeing to plead guilty to the felony charges in which Michael Milken was also implicated and by cooperating with the prosecution in all continuing investigations, Drexel in effect withdrew all support from its most productive employee.

Drexel did manage to avoid a lengthy court trial and the accompanying expense and publicity. It avoided the severe penalties of RICO, including jail sentences for top management and the stigma of a racketeering-conviction label. In addition, Drexel was not prohibited from doing business in the junk bond market. It was, however, a convicted organizational felon and without the services of Michael Milken and other key employees. Although many clients remained loyal to the firm, others followed Milken or broke ties altogether. Drexel lost its dominance in the junk bond market. To maintain some degree of profitability, Drexel sold its retail brokerage and mutual fund businesses and trimmed about 40% of its workforce from the payroll. Despite Drexel's efforts to remain a player in financial markets, the collapse of the junk-bond market in late 1989 was the final blow to the company. Unable to maintain the liquidity needed to buy and sell huge quantities of securities, the company declared bankruptcy in February 1990.

In a plea bargain arrangement, Michael Milken pleaded guilty on April 24, 1990, to six felony charges, ranging from mail and wire fraud to conspiracy and net-capital violations. He was sentenced to 10 years in prison and 3 years of community service on his release. He must pay $200 million in fines and penalties, as well as $400 million in restitution to victims of his crimes. Additionally, he was barred forever from the securities industry. In return, prosecutors dropped all charges against Lowell Milken (although he, too, was forever barred from the securities industry) and the remaining charges filed against Michael Milken in 1989.

Michael Milken was released to a halfway house in Los Angeles on January 3, 1993. After Milken served 22 months in federal prison, his original 10-year sentence was reduced to 2 years. He spent 2 months in the halfway house work-release program arranged through his lawyer's firm, Victor and Saddler, researching civil legal cases. He also continued to work on 1,800 hours of court-ordered community service with a drug prevention program in inner-city Los Angeles. In early 1993, it was estimated that Michael Milken had paid $1.1 billion in fines and settlements connected with his work in the securities business at Drexel.

In effect, the lack of financial leadership with integrity caused the downfall of the leading junk bond institution and its top performer, resulted in billions of dollars of fines and hundreds of lost jobs, and eroded investor trust in one of the worst scandals in Wall Street history. (For more details, see Zey, M. [1993]. *Banking on fraud: Drexel, junk bonds, and buyouts.* New York: Aldine de Grayter.)

(3) Marketing/Advertising Issue Minicase:
(Case 6C) - The Nestlé Company

The Nestlé Company, formally known as Nestlé Alimentana, S.A., is headquartered in Vevey, Switzerland. It is a giant worldwide corporation with three top product groups: dairy products, instant drinks, and culinary/sundry products. Infant foods, including the controversial infant formula, and dietetic products account for less than 10% of total conglomerate sales. Nestlé developed infant formula foods in the early 1920s as an alternative to breast milk. Infant formula is a specially prepared food for infants (under 6 months); although based on cow's milk, it is scientifically formulated to approximate the most perfect of all infant foods, human breast milk. Today, a number of different artificial milk products are available for infants, and these range in nutritional value from very high (humanized infant formula) to very low (various powdered, evaporated, and sweetened condensed milks).

Sales in infant formula increased sharply after World War II and hit a peak in 1957, with 4.3 million births in developed countries. After this time, births started a decline that continued into the 1970s. The result was a steep downturn in baby formula sales and profits. Therefore, the industry began searching for new business. This was found in developing countries where the population was still increasing: the less developed countries of Africa, South America, and the Far East.

Total industry sales for infant formula alone, excluding all other commercial milk products, was about $1.5 billion. Of this, an estimated $600 million came from developing countries. Hence, this market segment represented a significant total market potential. Nestlé maintained a strong market share—40% to 50%—of the market in developing countries for baby formula. Competitors included three U.S. firms—American Home Products, Bristol Myers, and Abbott Labs—that shared 20% of the market. Foreign firms accounted for the remainder. The market was estimated to be growing at 15% to 20% per year.

The major issues for Nestlé's infant formula were the misuse of its product and its marketing practices. The incapability of a significant portion of the developing country market to use the product correctly caused thousands of infant deaths. Large numbers of consumers in developing countries live in poverty, have poor sanitation, receive inadequate health care, and are illiterate. Therefore, the misuse of infant formula was inevitable and foreseeable. Water is obtained from polluted rivers or a common well and is brought back in contaminated containers. A refrigerator is considered a luxury item, and fuel is very expensive. Consequently, powdered formula was mixed with contaminated water and put into unsterilized bottles and nipples. In addition, the mothers diluted the formula with excess water so that it would last longer.

Studies determined three reasons for the trend to less nursing and more bottle feeding in the developing countries. First, the sociocultural environment was changing, and bottle feeding was looked on as a high status practice, so the lower income groups readily followed along. Second, health care professionals in many hospitals and clinics endorsed the use of infant formula and bottle feeding. Babies were routinely separated from their mothers for 12 to 48 hours and were bottle-fed whether or not the mothers planned to breast-feed. Hospital practices were perceived as better and deserving of emulation. A third factor was the marketing and promotional practices of infant formula manufacturers.

The impact of these three forces was dramatic. In 1951, approximately 80% of all 3-month-old babies in Singapore were being breast-fed; by 1971, only 5% were. In 1966, 40% fewer mothers in Mexico nursed 6-month-old babies than had done so 6 years earlier. In Chile, in 1973, there were three times as many deaths among infants who were bottle-fed before 3 months of age than among wholly breast-fed infants.

The Nestlé infant formula fiasco then proceeded through its final stages. First, Nestlé had some serious quality control problems in its production of the formula in its far-flung plants. A quality inspection at the Nestlé Tongala plant in Australia revealed cracks in the spray drier used to turn liquid milk into powder form. The State Health Department was not informed, and Nestlé attempted to sterilize the equipment without halting production, but a unique strain of bacteria, a variant of salmonella that causes severe gastroenteritis, continued to be discovered. The drier was kept in operation for a full 8 months after the contaminants were found.

Second, Nestlé engaged in a controversial and aggressive infant formula marketing and promotion campaign directed toward consumers and health care providers. Its methods were criticized for the following reasons: (a) inadequate directions for proper use of the product; (b) inadequate warnings about the dangers of improper product usage; (c) lack of warning that bottle feeding could contribute to infant mortality in developing countries; (d) baby booklets that ignored or de-emphasized breast-feeding; (e) misleading media promotions that encouraged poor and illiterate mothers to bottle-feed rather than breast-feed their infants; (f) advertising that portrayed breast-feeding as primitive and inconvenient; (g) free gifts and samples that were direct inducements to bottle-feed infants; (h) posters and pamphlets in hospitals and "milk nurses" used as "endorsements by association" or "manipulation by assistance"; and (i) the prices of formulas at the "milk banks" that were still too expensive for most consumers, thereby tempting consumers to dilute the formula.

Nestlé employed about 200 women who were registered nurses, nutrition-ists, or midwives. These professionals were often nicknamed "milk nurses." Critics maintained that these milk nurses were actually sales personnel in dis-guise who visited mothers and gave product samples in an attempt to persuade mothers to stop breast-feeding. With their uniforms giving them great credi-bility, the nurses were criticized for being too persuasive for naive consumers. Physicians and other hospital personnel also received company-sponsored travel to medical meetings. After the publication of the two articles "The Baby Killer" and "Nestlé Kills Babies" and the subsequent lawsuit by Nestlé, which received worldwide publicity, two groups were formed: the Interfaith Center on Corporate Responsibility and the Infant Formula Action Coalition (IN-FACT). The opposition of these organizations eventually led to a boycott of Nestlé products and services.

Third, as a by-product of the growing condemnation of the industry, Nestlé and other firms began to make changes in their promotional practices, at least on paper. The changes were brought about through the auspices of the International Council of Infant Food Industries (ICIFI), which was formed in 1975 by nine infant food manufacturers, including Nestlé. The changes in-cluded the following: (a) product information would always recognize breast milk as best; (b) infant formulas would be advertised as supplementary; (c) ads would recommend that professional advice should be sought; and (d) nurse uniforms would be worn only by professional nurses.

But the self-regulation apparently did not work sufficiently to allay the criticisms. Documentation by the International Baby Food Action Network confirmed more than 1,000 violations of the "code" from 1977 to 1981. Some critics scoffed that asking for self-regulation was like asking Colonel Sanders to baby-sit your chickens. After continued reported violations, a boycott was organized in the United States in July 1977 and soon spread to nine other countries. It was to last until January 26, 1982, in the United States and Canada, with other countries ending their boycotts over the next 2 years.

Nestlé was singled out as the sole object of the boycott because of its 50% worldwide market share and the fact that it had attracted more adverse public-ity than other firms that were engaged in the same business practices. The demands of INFACT and the boycotters included: (a) stop altogether the use of milk nurses; (b) stop distributing all free samples; (c) stop promoting infant formula to the health care industry; and (d) stop consumer promotion and advertising of infant formula. The boycott soon had the support of more than

450 local and religious groups across the United States, and proponents claimed it was the largest non-union boycott in U.S. history. Boycott activity was strongest in Boston, Baltimore, and Chicago, where INFACT established an office with five full-time staffers.

Fourth, this boycott was undoubtedly effective, not only directly in causing lost business and profits for the company but also indirectly in crystallizing public opinion against the company and in invoking governmental response. In May 1981, the World Health Organization (WHO) adopted a restrictive advertising code that applied only to the infant food industry. A portion of Article 5 of the code states: "There shall be no advertising or other forms of promotion to the general public of products within the scope of this code." The products covered were infant food formulas and other weaning foods.

Fifth, after luring two of the largest and most expensive public relations firms in the world to improve their corporate image, all to no avail, Nestlé finally decided to clean up its act. The most effective restorative strategy ultimately adopted was the establishment of a 10-member panel of medical experts, clergy, civic leaders, and experts in international public policy to monitor Nestlé's compliance with the WHO code and to investigate complaints against its marketing practices. This Nestlé Infant Formula Audit Commission (NIFAC) gained credibility with the acceptance of the chairmanship by Edmund S. Muskie, former U.S. secretary of state, vice presidential candidate, and Democratic senator from Maine. The commission was established in May 1982.

This so-called Muskie Commission worked with representatives of WHO, the International Nestlé Boycott Committee (INBC), and UNICEF to resolve conflicts in four areas of the WHO code. Points of contention were educational materials, labels, gifts to medical and health professionals, and free or subsidized supplies to hospitals. These were resolved, and Nestlé agreed that, on educational material it distributed, the social and health aspects of formula versus breast-feeding would be addressed. Its infant formula labels would clearly state the dangers of using contaminated water and the superiority of mother's milk. Personal gifts to health officials (which smacked of bribery and seeking preferential treatment) were banned. Finally, free samples of formula distributed to hospitals were to be limited to supplies that go to mothers incapable of breast-feeding their children.

The results in lost business for Nestlé were difficult to pinpoint. Company estimates ranged up to $40 million in lost profits as a direct result of the boycotts. Lost business was probably far greater than this, however, with some coming in the years before the boycotts began as consumers turned to alternative brands from firms with better reputations. Even during the years of boycotts, not all consumers were militant protesters, but they could certainly take their business elsewhere as a silent protest. Admittedly, infant food business accounted for only 3% of total Nestlé sales worldwide, but other Nestlé products were tarnished to an unknown degree by the destroyed public image of this one minor part of the total business. One of the most obvious negative consequences of the boycotts was the loss of meetings and convention business at Nestlé's Stouffer facilities, with some planners choosing to schedule at other locations as a means of avoiding any association with Nestlé's negative image.

In short, the lack of marketing leadership with integrity resulted in loss of lives, worldwide grief-stricken parents, millions of dollars of lost profits in multiple businesses, hostile negative publicity on a global scale, intrusive international regulation of an entire industry, and differential access to bottled infant formula by women in developed and developing countries. (For more details, see Sethi, P. [1994]. *Multinational corporations and the impact of public advocacy on corporate strategy: Nestlé and the infant formula controversy.* Boston: Kluwer.) Also see the videotape, *A case in ethical decision making: Nutritious food and marketing infant formula*, available at the University of Dayton, Philosophy Department.

(4) Business Management/Human Resources/Business Law Minicase: (Case 6D) - Price Waterhouse LLP

Ann Hopkins was a senior manager in the Price Waterhouse LLP Office of Government Services in Washington, D.C. She joined Price Waterhouse in August 1978 as a business manager and was promoted to senior manager in 1981. She specialized in managing larger-scale contracts for government agencies, mostly high-dollar computer systems. She was generally viewed by her management and peers as a highly competent project leader who worked long hours and pushed vigorously to meet deadlines. By 1982, Hopkins had been proposed as a candidate for partnership along with 88 other Price Waterhouse employees. Out of the 88 partnership candidates selected in 1984, she was the only woman candidate. Hopkins had the best new business record of all the candidates. None of the other partnership candidates that year had a comparable record in terms of successfully securing major contracts for partnership. She helped bring in over $40 million of new business during her 6 years at Price Waterhouse. In 1982, Price Waterhouse had 662 partners, 7 of whom were women.

At that time, Price Waterhouse was a nationwide professional accounting partnership, one of the Big Six in the United States. A senior manager became a candidate for partnership when the partners in her office submitted her name for partnership status and went through a relatively unstructured, open-ended evaluation process consisting of either a "long" or "short" form of written comments on each candidate.

After reviewing the comments, the firm's Admissions Committee made recommendations about the partnership candidates to the Price Waterhouse Policy Board. The recommendations consisted of accepting the candidate, denying the promotion, or putting the application on hold. The Policy Board then decided whether to submit the candidate to a vote, reject the candidate, or put the candidacy on hold. There were no limits on the number of persons to whom partnership could be awarded and no guidelines for evaluating positive and negative comments about candidates.

Thirteen of the 32 partners who submitted comments on Hopkins supported her; 3 recommended putting her on hold; 8 said they did not have enough information; and 8 recommended denial. The net result on the vote was that the head partner at Hopkins's office had the job of telling her she had been held over for further consideration. He advised Hopkins that she should "walk more femininely, dress more femininely, wear makeup, have her hair styled, and wear jewelry." In 1985, during the next partnership selection, the partners in the office where Hopkins worked decided not to nominate her for partner. She resigned on notification that she would not be nominated for partner a second time. After exhausting all of her administrative remedies, she filed a sex discrimination suit in federal court.

Hopkins, who litigated the Price Waterhouse denial of her partnership as a violation of Title VII of the Civil Rights Act of 1964 (which prohibits discrimination in employment practices), stated she filed the suit to find out why Price Waterhouse made "such a bad business decision." She did not learn of the partners' comments until discovery during the case. The Supreme Court found for Hopkins. In 1990, on remand, Hopkins was awarded her partnership and $350,000 in damages.

In court, during the discovery period, Hopkins read the Policy Board's following rejection comments:

She may have overcompensated for being a woman . . . she needed to take a course at charm school, . . . many male partners are worse than Ann (language and tough personality), . . . she initially came across as macho . . ˙. she had matured from a tough-talking, somewhat masculine hard-nosed manager into an authoritative, formidable, but much more appealing lady partner candidate.

It appeared as if Price Waterhouse's partners evaluated Ann Hopkins as a woman trying to become a partner, instead of evaluating her simply as a partnership candidate. She was a senior manager at one of the largest accounting firms in the country and she was good at her job. Her success violated many of the partners' gender stereotypes about what a woman is and how a woman should behave. The partners needed to evaluate prospective partnership candidates as business and professional leaders and not as men or women living up or down to gender stereotypes. If there were justifiable business reasons to deny promotions, they should have been proved. In fact, the perceptions of interpersonal incompetence were gender-stereotypical impressions never proved by evidence, and when these impressions were pitted against the exceptional success of her leadership record, the unfairness of the decision became evident (Tannen, 1994a).

The fact that Price Waterhouse's evaluation system gave substantial weight to gender-stereotypical comments rather than had them disregarded in the final tabulation further indicated a discriminatory management process that exposed the partnership to future illegal and unethical conduct.

Today at Price Waterhouse offices in Washington, D.C., 44% of the professional staff are women and 22% are minorities. In accounting firms generally, the number of female principals has grown from 1% in 1983 to 18% today.

In effect, the lack of managerial and legal leadership with integrity resulted in the awarding of a senior partnership that should have been routine with a nondiscriminatory process in place but ended up costing the firm $350,000 in damages, a negative reputation with current and future competent female accounting managers, and sounded a wake-up call to male managers in traditional male occupations. (For more details, see Tavris, C. [1992]. *The mismeasure of women*. New York: Touchstone.)

(5) Technology/Quality Operations/Organizational Behavior Minicase: (Case 6E) - Manville Corporation

Asbestos is a gray-white fibrous mineral that is heat-resistant and possesses great strength. It was mined in Canada and South Africa and processed at plants throughout the world. The largest processors were Johns-Manville (later changed to Manville), Rasbestos Manhattan, Owens-Corning, UNR, AMATEX, and other companies. By the end of the asbestos drama, UNR, AMATEX, and Manville would all have declared Chapter 11 bankruptcy. At the height of its use in the United States, asbestos could be found in items as diverse as hair dryers, potholders, and brake drums.

The first asbestosis death described in medical literature appeared in the *British Medical Journal* in 1924 in an article by Dr. W. E. Cooke, who named the disease asbestosis. Shortly after, state governments began to note workers' compensation claims being filed by asbestos workers. As early as 1928, Johns-Manville sponsored studies by Dr. Leroy U. Gardner, who produced asbestosis in test animals by allowing them to inhale asbestos fibers. These studies, which were not publicly released, were uncovered during litigation in 1971.

The medical inspector of factories for the British Home Office conducted an epidemiological study of asbestos workers in 1928 that showed, among other things, the 81% rate of fibrosis in workers who had been in the industry 20 years or more. On the basis of the study findings, Parliament in 1931 enacted legislation designed to provide protection for asbestos workers. Subsequently, Dr. Anthony Lanza found, in a study he conducted for Metropolitan Life Insurance, that 106 of 126 X-rayed asbestos workers had already developed asbestosis.

During this period of medical discovery in the asbestos industry, so-called silicosis suits began to appear around the country. Damages in these lawsuits, which were brought by workers who alleged harmful exposure to silica dust and resulting lung problems, totaled $300 million by 1934. Alarmed by the increasing numbers of lawsuits, several insurance companies recommended that silicosis and other pulmonary dust diseases be taken out of the courts and covered under workers' compensation. It was also during this period of medical discovery and silicosis suits that Johns-Manville experienced its first asbestos litigation. In 1933, the board of directors of Johns-Manville directed the company's CEO and president to settle asbestosis lawsuits that had been brought against Johns-Manville in New Jersey courts by Samuel Greenstone, an attorney, on behalf of 11 workers. The company made a $30,000 settlement payment in exchange for Greenstone's promise that he would not directly or indirectly participate in the bringing of new actions against the corporation. The settlement terms, documented in the board's minutes, were not revealed until discovery during litigation some 45 years later.

Johns-Manville was then the largest producer of asbestos in the United States. The company also sold asbestos to many other firms for use in other products. Manville had great liability exposure not only through its own sales but also through its sales to other companies and eventually to third-party buyers. Eventually, medical research identified two major diseases that could result from exposure to asbestos dust. The first, the focus of the research, was asbestosis, which is a scarring of the lung tissue. Asbestosis does not appear immediately and may not manifest itself for 10 to 30 years after initial exposure. During this time, the inhaler will appear healthy and normal and will experience no symptoms of the disease. Inhaled asbestos fibers that remain in the lungs, however, cause a tissue reaction that is progressive and, apparently, irreversible. The result is a slow buildup of problems, such as breathing difficulties, that eventually become severe enough to make any physical exertion impossible. The second disease, mesothelioma, is a malignant and extremely painful cancer of the chest lining. This cancer has been associated only with asbestos exposure; it usually is fatal within 1 year after symptoms appear. Like asbestosis, this disease may not appear for 20 years after initial exposure to asbestos. For example, the mother of an asbestos worker, whose only exposure to asbestos came through washing his factory clothes in the 1960s, died of mesothelioma in 1983.

In 1966, attorney Ward Stephenson filed suit against 11 asbestos manufacturers on behalf of his client, Claude Tomplait, an insulator who had developed asbestosis. This was Stephenson's first third-party liability case; it would not be his last. Stephenson also litigated on behalf of Clarence Borel, another insulator who sued several asbestos manufacturers. The trial court found for Borel, but more significantly, its verdict was upheld by the Fifth Circuit Court of Appeals. The appellate decision triggered 25,000 third-party asbestos lawsuits that would be brought against asbestos manufacturers over the next decade. The 1973 *Borel* decision marked the beginning of the end for the asbestos industry. Between 1974 and 1988, asbestos litigation increased tenfold. In 1976, 159 suits had been filed against Johns-Manville; in 1978, 792 suits were filed; and by 1982, suits were being filed at a rate of 6,000 per year. Manville settled asbestos-related suits for an average of $21,000, but by 1982 this settlement amount doubled.

After the asbestos industry tried to get legislative remedies and their attempted congressional bailout failed, asbestos manufacturers faced mounting litigation on their own. Ultimately, it was an accounting rule, FASB-5, that led Manville into Chapter 11. Coopers and Lybrand had taken the position in the previous eight SEC fillings that, under FASB-5, it could not reliably estimate the costs of disposition of the suits and therefore need not make any disclosures about them before certifying the financial statements. Before the ninth SEC filing, however, Litigation Analysis Group (LAG), a litigation consultant for Manville's cases, gave Manville an estimate that the cost of disposition of all future suits would be $1,900,000,000 (1 billion, 900 million dollars!). With this expert opinion in place, Coopers and Lybrand could no longer take its "no estimate possible" position under FASB-5. When Coopers and Lybrand refused to sign off on the financial statements needed for the SEC filing without a disclosure of the litigation liability, Manville dismissed the company and hired Price Waterhouse. But, after reviewing the LAG report, Price Waterhouse reached the same conclusion and refused to certify the financial statements without a disclosure on the litigation. Unable to issue financial statements, Manville filed for Chapter 11 bankruptcy protection on August 26, 1982.

The Committee of Asbestos-Related Litigants was then formed to contest the Manville bankruptcy. The committee filed a motion to dismiss the bankruptcy in November 1982 on the grounds that Manville had filed the Chapter 11 proceedings in bad faith. The committee also had the Senate Judiciary Committee convene a hearing on November 10, 1982, to investigate whether it was proper for a solvent company to file for reorganization under the federal Bankruptcy Code. Despite the significant testimony presented during the hearing, the committee declined to make changes in the Bankruptcy Code.

The big problem in the Manville Chapter 11 proceedings was the disposition of all the actual and pending suits against the company. The issue involved dealing with Manville, its insurers, and the lawyers for the litigants. The bankruptcy proceedings continued through 1989, when Manville and others agreed to the Manville Personal Injury Settlement Trust. Under the agreement, Manville was required to give $2.5 billion in assets (mostly stock) to the trust. Manville was also required, beginning in 1991, to pay annually to the trust $75 million and 20% of its annual net income. So far, 152,000 claims have been filed and 3,000 more are expected. The average settlement had been $42,000. The approval for paying claims came in December 1994, and the resulting payment settlement gave claimants 10 cents on the dollar. Also, $55.7 million of the trust funds were awarded to codefendants who had paid Manville's share of the liability while the trust payments were in litigation.

In 1976, asbestos sales accounted for 31% of Manville's business, or $1.6 billion. Today, 42%, or $2.2 billion, of the company's sales comes from fiberglass insulation. Manville admits to lost customers, however, and a stock price that seems to keep dropping. Some aspects of the asbestos saga remain unresolved. For example, the cleanup of asbestos in Chicago school districts has had an estimated cost of $500 million, and the Illinois Supreme Court has ruled that the school districts can proceed to recover property damages from asbestos manufacturers. The EPA, in turn, has begun issuing complaints against school districts that do not act quickly enough to replace asbestos insulation; those districts that fail to clean up their asbestos problems face a $25,000 fine.

Today, asbestos liability continues for other manufacturers. In mid-1992, after a 2-year jury trial, six other companies were found negligent in installing, manufacturing, or supplying asbestos. The case involved 8,555 plaintiffs, whose damages will be determined in separate proceedings. Punitive damages were awarded in the case as well. Ninety thousand pending claims remain. Twenty former asbestos manufacturers have settled potential future claims for $1 billion. In early 1995, OSHA issued new regulations requiring employer disclosure of the presence of asbestos in the workplace. The impact of exposure remains an issue for regulators, as well as a potential source of liability.

In effect, the lack of leading product safety, employee health, and consumer safety efforts with integrity resulted in the premature loss of lives to asbestos-related illnesses; multiple company bankruptcies; widespread government intervention into occupational safety and health, product, and consumer safety and environmental regulation; and thousands of pending litigation claims. (For more details, see Castleman, B. [1990]. *Asbestos: Medical and legal aspects.* Upper Saddle River, NJ: Prentice Hall.)

(6) Public/Nonprofit/Health Care Administration Minicase: (Case 6F) - The Mercy Hospital System (MHS) and the U.S. Health Care System

The U.S. health care system is experiencing a severe lack of leadership with integrity. People are aware of the need for health care reform because of a range of necessary conflicts about health care quality, cost, and access. But there is no judgment consensus about what to do, the collective resolve to reform has stagnated, and all parties continue to complain about existing services but are not willing to exercise the concerted leadership necessary for meaningful reform (Petrick & Quinn, 1995).

The principal parties in the U.S. health care system are the four major payers (the federal government, employees, state governments, and households) and the four major providers (physicians, hospitals, pharmaceutical and medical supply companies, and types of managed-care organizations).

The first major payer, the federal government, faced with a prospective annual deficit of $400 billion, is poorly positioned to take any initiative that would require substantial new outlays. Matters of resources aside, it would be out of harmony with the U.S. political tradition to expect Congress to act on major health care reform in the face of intense disagreement among the principal pressure groups about the direction that reform should take.

Employers, the second major payer, are deeply divided. Some would welcome the opportunity to end their commitment to provide health insurance benefits to their employees, both active and retired; many others believe that the prospect of unloading this responsibility onto the public sector is doomed to failure. No government plan would match in breadth and depth the benefits that large employers currently provide, which means they would be forced to offer their employees supplemental health benefits.

Furthermore, many employers are disinclined to see their freedom restricted by a possible modification of the Employee Retirement Income Security Acts (ERISA), the federal statute governing employee benefits, which has protected them since 1974 from numerous state taxes and regulations. Moreover, they will avoid any action that might expand the jurisdiction of the federal government over employee benefits. True, employers are disturbed by the large annual increases in the cost of health benefits, but not to the point of taking the leadership initiative to increase federal involvement.

State governments, the third major payer, have been protesting to the administration and Congress since the late 1980s about continuing congressional mandates to extend eligibility and broaden benefits under their Medicaid programs. In 1989, the National Governors Association officially requested that such mandates cease; when Congress turned a deaf ear to their pleas, the states resorted to various financial schemes to enrich federal matching grants for their Medicaid programs. These were of such dubious propriety that the administration and Congress outlawed many of them. Even with additional federal matching money, steeply rising expenditures for Medicaid will inhibit most states from initiating substantial leadership in health care reforms. It is therefore noteworthy that a few—namely, Oregon, Minnesota, and Vermont —are moving ahead with efforts aimed explicitly at providing universal coverage.

Households, the fourth major source of payment, are concerned about deficiencies in insurance coverage and increases in out-of-pocket costs. The number of people with private health insurance has been dropping since 1989, and people with a history of serious medical problems often find that if they lose their coverage, they are unable to replace it at an affordable price. The same is true of people in good health who work in high-risk industries or for a small employer; health insurance, if obtainable at all, comes at a cost that is frequently beyond the reach of employers and employees alike. The failure of Medicare to cover long-term care, either in a nursing home or at home, is a cause of anxiety for many older people, who are disturbed by their growing personal outlays.

In sum, the principal payers—the federal government, employers, state governments, and households—are poorly positioned to assume the leadership in health care reform. The four could provide coverage for the uninsured and make at least limited benefits available for long-term care, but not until U.S. taxpayers change their formidable resistance to higher taxes.

The principal providers—physicians, hospitals, pharmaceutical and medical supply companies, and various types of managed-care organizations—are similarly stalemated. Physicians, the key provider group, generating about 75% of all health care costs, are frustrated by the steady erosion of their clinical autonomy, the avalanche of paper with which they must contend, and the latest assault on their earnings by the Health Care Financing Administration, which under the current resource-based relative-value scale is capping both their fees and the volume of services they provide to Medicare patients. The disruptions caused by malpractice litigation continue, although recent years have seen some reduction on this front. Despite these threats to their professional integrity and career satisfaction, physicians are not in the vanguard of health care reform. Most of them continue to prefer their current fee-for-service arrangements, which yield a mean annual income of about $165,000, to prospective reforms that hold uncertain promise of reducing or eliminating the drawbacks in their current practice environment.

In the late 1970s, hospitals, the second major providers, were able to prevent the Carter administration from introducing new federal regulations aimed at capping their expenditures; since then, they have directed their political efforts at protecting their freedom of decision making regarding new investments and current operations. More recently, governmental payers have reduced their reimbursements for inpatient care, and private-sector payers have applied increasing pressure to obtain price discounts, often in exchange for a guaranteed number of admissions. Although their margins for patient care and their total margins have been declining, most hospitals continue to operate in the black. With an average occupancy rate of slightly more than 60%, many are uncertain about the future, but for now hospital trustees and CEOs generally prefer the status quo to any alternative they see on the horizon.

The pharmaceutical and medical-supply companies, the third major providers, have had few if any reasons to complain in the free-wheeling financing environment of recent decades because of the insatiable appetite of hospitals, physicians, and households for the latest innovations spawned by research and technology. Although a few warning shots have been fired— namely, the requirement by the Health Care Financing Administration that the cost effectiveness of selected new forms of technology be assessed before payment is approved and recent legislation by Congress requiring maximal discounts to the federal government on the purchase of medicines—the large, for-profit manufacturers of health care products have much to gain from the continuation of the status quo. This perception still guides their behavior.

The last of the principal providers are the many for-profit and nonprofit organizations, small and large, that continue to develop new financing and delivery mechanisms, including health maintenance organizations (HMOs), preferred-provider organizations (PPOs), and risk-sharing arrangements between large employers and insurance companies. These entities have grown considerably since the early 1980s, from about 10 million enrollers to close to 40 million, but their future remains uncertain for a variety of reasons: (a) physicians prefer to practice in a fee-for-service system, (b) many of the insured prefer to retain total freedom in their choice of providers, and (c) new risk-sharing systems for the delivery of managed care are difficult to organize. Exacerbating this uncertainty about the future is the limited success these innovations have had in braking costs. A reasonable assumption is that the new entities will continue to expand, but not at a rate that will substantially alter the established patterns of health care financing and delivery in the United States. In short, providers, like payers, do not appear to have any strong drive to assume leadership in the reform of the health care system.

In April 1991, Charles Bowsher, the comptroller general of the United States, testified before the House Ways and Means Committee and offered the following agenda for reform: universal coverage, global budgeting, and administrative simplification. Congress listened and did nothing, taking its lead from interest groups and the public at large. A first challenge is, therefore, to impress the concerned parties and the public that time is running out and that unless a reform effort begins now, the long-term costs will be horrendous.

One type of leadership response by one type of hospital provider is the Mercy Health System (MHS), which developed an integrated community health system in the greater Cincinnati, Ohio, region. The MHS has developed a position paper, similar to a mission statement, to lead its member organizations in developing integrated community health systems. This "system" is defined as an organized group of health care providers who cover the continuum of health care needs. They act in concert to improve the effectiveness and efficiency of services continually. Energy is directed at optimizing the health of enrolled populations and, ultimately, entire communities. An ideal local or regional system will have the following purposes: (a) optimize community health, not maximize medical procedures; (b) maintain incentives for efficiency and effectiveness; (c) eliminate unnecessary duplication, yet promote beneficial competition; (d) maintain continuity among all providers; and (e) hold itself accountable for outcomes and value.

Although many health care organizations have approached integration by using the traditional business model of vertical and horizontal integration, the MHS has defined integration primarily in terms of goal, incentive, and values integration, not structural integration. It has recognized that merger and acquisition is not the only method to meet this definition. The MHS also believes that it is possible for otherwise wholly independent organizations to share common goals, incentives, and values and to achieve a symbiotic relationship. Under these guidelines and definitions, the Mercy Health System-Greater Cincinnati Region (MHS-GCR, or the Region) was developed with four hospitals, including such services as a long-term care facility, a freestanding surgery center, and home care and hospice entities, under a single umbrella.

The system's inner circle of stakeholders, including sponsors and trustees, payers, medical staff, the workforce, and most important, the customers/patients, are placed at the center of concern. Support systems for the customer are the physician and the product line manager of subsystems. The product line manager must ensure that the customer receives coordinated, cost-effective, quality service designed specifically to fit his or her needs. This service is provided through the coordinated interactions of the clinical nurse specialist, case manager, support services, and care providers. The outer circle of stakeholders identifies all the support services required to deliver quality health care in the Region. These services include human resources, information systems, legal services, and other ancillary support services.

In 1995, the Region set four prioritized goals with measurable results to which all regional units were expected to adhere:

1. *Improve quality standards and measurement.* The targeted result for this goal is that quality measures are to be developed and standardized across the network and that not less than a 5% overall improvement in the baseline scores that have been established must be achieved.

2. *Improve clinical and functional integration.* The targeted result for this goal is that at least 15 of 20 identified projects will be complete by the year's end.

3. *Improve physician integration.* Completion of at least 8 out of 10 physician-related projects is the targeted result for this goal.

4. *Improve profitability.* The targeted result is to achieve a combined net operating income of 7% without compromising any of the first three goals.

To achieve the first goal of quality, a task force was formed to develop quality measures to be used throughout the Region. Data-collection and reporting forms were developed for each measure. The patient is identified as the center of all quality activity. Seven quality measures were identified: customer service (e.g., patient satisfaction), waiting time required to access care, revenue enhancement through a Diagnostic Resource Group (DRG) Options program, completion rate of performance appraisals within HRM, reduction of internal cycle times, outcome measures (e.g., unscheduled readmissions), and decrease of length of stay and average charges for six selected DRGs. DRGs selected for regional focus in the last item have characteristics of high volume and high cost. Five of the DRGs were selected by the task force for evaluation, and each acute care facility selected one DRG. Baseline measurements of regional average length of stay and total charges were established. The goal was to reduce both of these by 5% by the end of the year.

A pool of facilitators was trained and educated in team-training and problem-solving methods. These facilitators assist teams working with each quality measure and ensure the development of a consistent approach in the regional quality program. An incentive compensation program was implemented for individuals at the director level and above throughout the Region. Compensation is based on the achievement of the four goals as previously described. The scope of participation was initially limited to a particular level of management, although a proposal has been made to include all employees in such a program in the future.

Mercy Hospital Anderson (MHA), a member of the regional network, has integrated these goals into its quality improvement program. In addition, MHA has implemented other activities to lead the evolution from a functional to a process organization.

The organization's new CEO, an individual who firmly believes that organizations should be quality-driven, took office in April 1994. She has made significant efforts to break down the functional "silos." Although some efforts regarding continuous quality improvement (CQI) and a focus on processes had been previously implemented at MHA, significant barriers were created by the existing strong functional organization. The new CEO stated that her vision was to bring MHA from a functional model to a process model and that her goal was for the organization to be quality-driven and customer-focused.

One of the first actions taken was to change the quality assurance (QA) model that existed in the organization. Under the original structure, clinical and nonclinical activities were completely separated both functionally and through reporting mechanisms. The clinical areas, including clinical departments and medical staff departments, reported to a combined CQI/QA Committee that met monthly. Reports from this committee were subsequently taken to the medical executive committee and finally to the hospital board of directors. The nonclinical areas report to the CQI Advisory Committee, a conduit for information to flow to administration and the hospital board. This committee was formed when the hospital CQI program was developed with the assistance of an outside consultant. The purpose of the committee was to guide the CQI process for the hospital, but it became more of a barrier to the process than a facilitative body. "Permission" had to be obtained from this group before any process improvement activity could take place. This was cumbersome and actually reduced commitment to CQI in the organization.

To improve performance, a multifunctional and multilevel, team-focused approach to improving organizational performance has been developed. The process is based on the mission, vision, and values of MHS-GCR and is shaped by strategic plans and supported by the leadership of the Region. Priorities are established by using preselected criteria, and teams are chartered to guide performance improvement. The team focuses on quality improvement through the development, implementation, and analysis of critical pathways such as chest pain, pneumonia, and total joint replacement. This team receives statistical data from the person coordinating the critical pathways and from the clinical information center. The clinical information center is the source of clinical data that can be obtained through concurrent review and discharge planning. A computer software system named MIDAS is used to collect data and to place it into a meaningful format. Activities of these teams are reported at both the Operations Quality Forum and the Medical Staff Quality Forum.

Both clinical and nonclinical individuals are members of the Operations Quality Forum. Activities from both these forums are reported to the Hospital Board QI Committee.

The change from a QA model to a performance improvement model, plus the development and use of multifunctional teams, focused on addressing specific standards related to the hospital accrediting body (JCAHO), has done more to break down barriers in the organization than any other activity to date.

One other change was made that will affect functional barriers in the future. In the past, MHA had attempted to develop a product line concept in the organization. The conceptual model of the regional organization showed that product line management is the element that helps drive the customer-focused approach. This concept is emphasized at MHA. Essentially, four product lines have been identified: women's health, orthopedics, oncology, and cardiology. A distinction has been made with the concept of "service lines." The emergency department, surgery, and general medical/surgical services have been identified as "service" areas that supply services to the product lines. Because each is important to the profitability of the organization, however, it was thought that emphasis should be placed on them as well.

Many activities of the new CEO at MHA are reflected in the proposed structures. She has made it a point to develop energy and commitment in the organization. Initial discussions with all levels of staff were focused on breaking down the silos that exist in the organization. Entrepreneurial ideas were invited from all levels, and "wisdoms" of the past were subject to scrutiny. Her behavior as a change leader has developed an openness and trust that had not previously been seen in the organization. The efforts made by top management at MHA to explain the need and purpose of the change, to paint what the future will look like, to provide a plan, and to allow individuals to participate have greatly assisted in the transition process.

MHA's nonprofit mission statement focused on continuing the healing ministry of Jesus and bringing better quality to life for all, especially to the poor, vulnerable, and underserved. Enhancement of quality of life is sought for patients and their families, the community, and members of the hospital and medical staff by creating an environment responsive to their physical, spiritual, social, and emotional needs.

MHA has followed a CQI process that was introduced approximately three years ago by a consultant. The staff was trained on how to apply the concepts of this program and the tools of TQM (e.g., brainstorming, sampling, survey, flowcharting, cause-and-effect diagramming). The organization developed many outcome measures; continuous improvement activities have been ongoing. Most of these activities are related to DRGs within the identified product/ service lines. Responsible individual and collective leadership have benefited people and improved processes; leadership has made the difference at Mercy Hospital.

In effect, hospital leadership with integrity provides access to quality health care, paid for and provided by multiple, committed stakeholders, in a cost-effective, efficient manner while protecting the standards of professional care that payers and providers have come to expect. (For more details, see Lindsay, W. & Petrick, J. [1997]. *Total quality and organization development.* Delray Beach, FL: St. Lucie Press.)

(7) International/Environmental/Public Policy Minicase: (Case 6G) - Industrial Ecosystem of Denmark

The idea of "industrial ecosystems" has emerged in recent years to describe a unique form of ecological cooperation that has growing public policy support. The industrial ecosystem idea parallels the natural ecosystem, in which interdependent organisms and their environments exchange resources with each other to survive. For example, in a pond ecosystem, big fish eat little fish, little fish eat insects, insects eat weeds and plankton. The waste products of the fishes serve as resources for the growth of weeds, plankton, and the fish habitats. This arrangement forms a self-sufficient, dynamically balanced ecosystem. As a parallel, the industrial ecosystem consists of a network of organizations that jointly seek to minimize local and/or regional environmental degradation. They use each other's waste and share and minimize the use of natural resources.

A network of companies in Kalundborg, Denmark, demonstrates how an industrial ecosystem operates. It consists of a local power plant, an enzyme plant, a refinery, a chemical plant, and a wallboard plant. These plants use one another's wastes and by-products as raw materials. They coordinate their use of resources and waste management practices, with strong local public policy support.

· The coal-fired Asnaes power plant, for instance, sells its used steam to the Novo Nordisk enzyme plant and the Statoil refinery, instead of condensing it and dumping it into the sea. The power plant also sells its fly ash to a cement company and its surplus heat to the city for heating. Statoil, in turn, supplies

Asnaes with treated wastewater for cooling. It also sells the power plant desulfurized gas to burn, saving 30,000 tons of coal a year. The plant then ships high-sulfur gas emissions to a sulfuric acid plant. Asnaes removes pollutants from its smokestacks and sells the limestone gunk to Gyproc, the wallboard plant; this cuts the imports of mined gypsum. Asnaes warms a fishery that produces 200 tons of trout and turbot each year. Local farms use waste from the fishery and from Novo's enzyme plant as fertilizer.

The impact of this industrial ecosystem on the natural environment is impressive. It conserves water that is pumped from Lake Tisso, 7 miles away. It minimizes the amount of waste sent to landfills. It reduces the pollution that would otherwise be emitted into the atmosphere. It conserves energy resources in the community. It gets companies to cooperate on ecological problems and provides a forum for ongoing improved environmental performance. In addition, it provides participant companies with good image-making publicity.

Viewing organizations as a part of an industrial ecosystem necessitates many fundamental changes in a company's concept of organizational and public policy leadership. It requires a new vision of operational scope, strategies, cost structures, location, and interorganizational management practices. It requires very different criteria for new product development, venture financing, entrepreneurial forms, and infrastructure. It requires rethinking the role of regulations and markets and creating fresh markets for ecologically sound products.

This approach to cooperative regional sustainable development will become increasingly important to regional centers of economic prosperity that successfully participate in the global economy (Ohmae, 1996). As more regional centers (e.g., the Silicon Valley/Bay Area of California, the Osaka/Kansai region of Japan, the Rhone/Alps region of France) compete for human and financial capital to keep their engines of innovation fueled, the quality of the natural environment and the extent of industrial cooperation processes for responsible waste management will add appeal to their gravitational attraction of key resources for the future.

In short, industrial ecosystem leadership with integrity conserves natural resources regionally, reduces the pollution that would otherwise be emitted into the natural environment, promotes sound public policy for the community, provides incentives for interorganizational leadership skill development, and fosters useful cooperation among noncompeting industries/companies. (For more details, see Allenby, B. [1993]. *Industrial ecology.* Upper Saddle River, NJ: Prentice Hall.)

SUMMARY

This chapter covers the multiple dimensions of the function of leading for managers and the four ethical leading subprocesses that build management integrity. In addition, seven management ethics and leading with integrity minicases were presented. By addressing the moral issues entailed in leading ethically and applying the theories and tools from the first part of the book to the structured analysis and principled resolution of leading minicases, sharpened skills in ethical leadership can enhance management integrity.

▧ DISCUSSION/EXPERIENTIAL EXERCISES

Discussion Questions

1. Discuss the nature of managerial leading and culpably negligent leading as they relate to private and public sector managers.
2. Discuss the differences between traditional and total quality leadership and, using the Leading Success Evaluation Matrix (Figure 6.10), provide life/work/school examples from each quadrant.
3. Discuss the people factors (leader and followers) involved in leadership.
4. Discuss the Total Quality Leadership Grid (Figure 6.8) and the phases of team empowerment development.
5. Discuss the relationships among moral development stages, leadership approaches, and likely work performance outcomes.
6. Discuss the parallel alignment of the four key ethics processes and leading subprocesses that build integrity, providing an example of managerial leading for each step.
7. Using the tools and resources from the first part of the book, examine the leading with integrity minicase in your major field or field of concentration.

Experiential Exercises

8. In a group setting, using the tools and resources from the first part of the book, examine two leading with integrity minicases outside your major field or field of concentration.
9. From your own life/work/school experiences, discuss times when leading occurred without integrity, identifying specific adverse impacts that resulted when one or more of the ethical leading steps was omitted or inadequately completed, and how you could have (in the past) or will (in the future) lead with integrity to prevent a recurrence of the problem.

7

Management Ethics:
Controlling With Integrity

The focus of Chapter 7 is on three areas: (a) the dimensions of controlling, (b) ethical controlling processes that build and anchor integrity, and (c) management ethics and controlling with integrity minicases. By addressing the ethical issues involved in the management function of controlling and applying those lessons to the analysis and resolution of controlling minicases, skills in ethical controlling can enhance management ethics and integrity.

▧ DIMENSIONS OF CONTROLLING

Controlling is the intended, coordinated, emergent, and realized pattern of decisions and actions that evaluate current performance in light of expected standards and organizational plans in order to take corrective and/or improvement measures in the future. Just as a football team has an initial game strategy (planning) designed to optimize the use of players and equipment (organizing), with the coach and team captains motivating performance (leading), at halftime the performance is evaluated, necessary corrections are made, and improvement expectations are incorporated for the second half (controlling). In today's work environment, managerial controlling requires performance evaluation, appropriate corrective action, and continuous improvement to

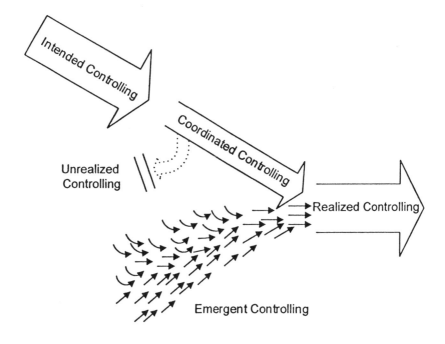

Figure 7.1. Dimensions of Controlling

ensure long-term organizational success. Meritorious controlling is expressly intended, efficiently coordinated, enthusiastically responsive to emergent feedback, and fully realized, as indicated in Figure 7.1.

Managers who generate and articulate compelling visions of future controlling dynamics for an organization that motivate stakeholders are involved in *intended controlling*. Managers who realistically arrange for the proper matching of controlling processes among and between stakeholders are engaged in *coordinated controlling*. Managers who solicit ongoing input and are enthusiastically responsive to critical feedback with regard to controlling processes are involved in *emergent controlling*. The outcomes of the interaction among intended, coordinated, and emergent controlling are realized and unrealized controlling opportunities. *Realized controls* are fully implemented processes that incorporate the evolved patterns of the past, the expectations of the desired future, and the realistic constraints of the present. Managers who analyze the historical precedents of "what worked" and "what didn't work" for

System Performance				
Components	Input	Throughput	Output	Outcome
Types of Control	Preliminary Control	Concurrent Control	Rework Control	Damage Control

Figure 7.2. System Performance and Types of Control

organizations are engaged in realized controlling. *Unrealized controlling* opportunities are intended control projects that never materialize. Among realized organizational control processes, some are successful in that they effectively measure and transform inputs into value-added outputs; other control processes are unsuccessful, realized projects that become barriers to effective organizational and stakeholder performance.

Furthermore, *culpably negligent controlling* includes any and all of the following: (a) absence of explicitly intended control vision, (b) inefficiently coordinated control processes for matching people and system needs, (c) controlling that is rigidly unresponsive to emergent contingencies, (d) inadequately realized control opportunities, (e) unintegrated patterns of control processes and actions, (f) controlling that misdirects core business processes, and (g) control that persists in disrespecting people. The degree of moral culpability for negligent controlling is dependent on the extent to which a manager could have and should have known or anticipated all the factors involved in the control function.

The balance of change and stability to achieve optimal effectiveness in the control function is obtained by addressing system and human (individual and group) performance as they are aligned with organizational planning. The components of system performance and their type of control are indicated in Figure 7.2. Through control of each component of a system's performance, managers can identify and focus on correctional intervention and/or improvement needs.

System input in Figure 7.2 includes all the human and nonhuman resources an organization takes in (e.g., energy, raw natural materials, plant and equipment, technology, people, training, conceptual paradigms, methods and measures of work, transportation systems, information-processing skills). Associated with system input, managers exert *preliminary control* by preventing substandard human and nonhuman resources from entering the organization and proactively improving the quality of all resource inputs used by the organization to produce product/services. By monitoring, enhancing, and certifying the quality of inputs, managers exert control over the performance variation of all subsequent organizational events.

Inadequate preliminary control increases unacceptable variation, which in turn increases the cost of doing business. *Variation* is the change and fluctuation of outcomes over time. The producer and the consumer both benefit from reduced variation at the input stage. The producer benefits by having less need for inspection, less scrap and rework, and higher productivity. The consumer benefits by being ensured that all products/services have similar quality characteristics, thereby encouraging confident bulk and customized purchases. To control variation properly, however, requires that a manager have the statistical skills to identify the common and reduce/eliminate the special causes of variation. *Common causes of variation* represent a natural part of a process resulting in random patterns of performance that fall within acceptable ranges of quality tolerance. Deming believed that 80% of all variation could be accounted for by common causes. The remaining 20% of variation is a result of *special causes of variation* not inherent to the process (e.g., a bad batch of materials purchased from a supplier, a poorly trained operator, excessive tool wear), is easy to detect using statistical methods, and usually is economical to reduce or remove (Evans & Lindsay, 1996; Lindsay & Petrick, 1997).

A *stable system* is a system governed only by common causes of variation. Responsible managers use control to arrive at stable systems, but they can make two fundamental mistakes: (a) treat as a special cause any fault, complaint, mistake, breakdown, accident, or shortage when it actually came from common causes; and (b) attribute to common cause any fault, complaint, mistake, breakdown, accident, or shortage when it actually came from a special cause. In the first case, tampering with a stable system will actually increase undesirable variation in the system. In the second case, managers can miss the opportunity to eliminate unwanted variation by assuming that it is not controllable. Managers who want to control responsibly, therefore, need to measure variation, continually improve the process technologies of an organization, and avoid both overcontrol and undercontrol to keep a stable system improving. Good preliminary control reduces common cause variation to acceptable ranges and eliminates special cause variation to improve the quality of outputs (Evans & Lindsay, 1996; Lindsay & Petrick, 1997).

System throughput in Figure 7.2 includes all the processes, activities, people, and measures used to transform raw input into marketable output (e.g., production processes, warehouse facilities, logistical support services, administrative infrastructure procedures, human resources). Associated with system throughputs is concurrent control. *Concurrent control* is behavior based on real time feedback that identifies unacceptable deviations occurring during the throughput process and takes corrective action automatically (through technology) or personally (through operator intervention). Statistical tools and measures provide managers and employees with the means to spot and react to special cause problems as they occur, as well as to help them understand organizational process capabilities and what they can do to improve operations.

It is particularly important that concurrent control be responsibly exercised. Some persons want managerial roles to "boss others"; they have been "bossed" in the past and want to retaliate on future victims. This approach to concurrent control has a double negative effect. First, by "bossing" people around as if they are special causes of a problem, that actually has a common system cause, a manager further destabilizes the work system. Second, by "bullying" people, a manager does not develop the internal self-control that associates need for eventual self-directed, team leadership. Managers who overcontrol by bossing people to display their power make a mess of the work system and adversely affect morale at the same time (Lindsay, Manning, & Petrick, 1992; Petrick, Lindsay, & Manning, 1991).

System output in Figure 7.2 is the aggregated set of products/services of a system that are deliverable to internal and external customers (e.g., automobiles, computer systems, completed written project reports, consulting services rendered, packaged gifts). Associated with system output is rework control. *Rework control* is action, based on inspection feedback, taken to redo a job. Rework control based on technical testing specialist and/or certification standards is necessary when preliminary and concurrent controls have failed—that is, when defective outputs cannot be sold without first being repaired. Managers who rely solely on rework control are acting irresponsibly because (a) it is more costly to do things twice than it is to do them right the first time, and (b) the range of defects as a result of inadequate design, manufacturing, inspections, instructions, warnings, packaging, and labeling is unlikely to be totally captured if preliminary and concurrent controls are nonexistent. Yet the majority of traditional managerial control is focused on rework resulting from final inspection.

System outcome in Figure 7.2 is the satisfaction effect of outputs on internal and external customers (e.g., the delight that television viewers feel when viewing a popular sitcom, the assurance that a user feels in operating a reliable computer system, the confidence that coworkers feel when they receive output from a competently run work unit). Associated with system outcome is damage control. *Damage control* is action, based on feedback, taken to minimize or eliminate the negative impact of defects or other unacceptable variation impinging on internal or external customers. Damage control may include such actions as apologizing, refunding money, replacing the product, performing the service again, promising to do better in the future, and prolonged reputation management. Managers who ignore or fail to capture negative and positive feedback risk losing both current and future customers, as well as the crucial learning to improve the organizational system in a way that could preclude ongoing damage. Passing on positive feedback from customers to producers also controls the possible damage that results from their loss of morale and feeling unappreciated.

In addition to the types of controlling that managers need to master, there are differences in control emphases between traditional and total quality (TQ) managers. The former tend to emphasize rework and damage control following *a detection paradigm of control*. The latter tend to emphasize preliminary and concurrent control following a prevention paradigm of control. The specific content differences between traditional and total quality (TQ) controlling are indicted in Figure 7.3

The four control steps identified in the left column of Figure 7.3 provide a framework for comparing the assumptions and processes employed in traditional and TQ controlling. The enlarged scope of managerial responsibility entailed in TQ controlling of system variation and improvement is in marked contrast with the more limited traditional approach designed to keep people on track, rather than to promote organizational learning through continuous improvement. The weight accorded traditional controlling relative to TQ controlling depends on whether priority is given to reinforcing past standards or to improving future standards (Lindsay & Petrick, 1997).

TQ controlling entails three continuous improvement process options: incremental improvements, competitive parity improvements, and/or breakthrough improvements (Petrick & Furr, 1995). *Incremental improvement,* known as *kaizen* in Japan, involves small steps taken by individuals and teams in the organization that reduce costs and increase efficiency (e.g., accountants with engineering experience who not only audit financial records to detect deviance but also recommend technical workflow improvements to cut costs). *Competitive parity improvements* involve big steps taken to catch up with the "best-in-class" market leaders. This approach is primarily driven by external competitive "champions" and is better suited to fast-growth economies where

Control Steps	Traditional Controlling	Total Quality Controlling
Set Standards for Control and Improvement	1. Sets standards/objectives that tolerate a range of variation around a target. 2. Tends to develop standards without full consideration of process capabilities that enable people to meet the standards.	1. Sets standards/objectives that progressively require the reduction of variation around target. 2. Tends to develop standards only after full consideration of process capabilities that enable people to meet standards.
Measure Performance	1. Assumes that deviations are discrete events, isolated in time not requiring statistical measurement. 2. Performance measurement usually not widely shared.	1. Assumes that deviations are a part of a pattern of variation over time that can and must be measured statistically. 2. Performance measurement widely shared.
Study Performance Analyses	1. Assumes poor attitudes are the source of substandard system and personal performance. 2. Management by unanalyzed opinions and arbitrary standards.	1. Assumes that poor attitudes are the outcomes of the unstable systems that managers maintain. 2. Management by facts requiring ongoing analysis to develop knowledge about consumers and special causes of variation.
Take Corrective Action	1. Action taken only to fix isolated problems to return performance to past plans. 2. The people are the problems, and deviant individuals are penalized.	1. Action taken to continually reduce variation in performance by acting on the system of causes and raising the level of performance by system design and redesign. 2. The process is the problem, and deviations are managed by shifting process averages.

Figure 7.3. Comparison of Traditional and Total Quality Controlling

keeping pace is critical (e.g., indexing ratio controls to those of market leaders). Finally, *breakthrough improvement* involves quantum leaps taken primarily by visionary leaders in the organization when radical redesign or reengineering is necessary to outdistance all competitors rapidly.

Specific operations management control activities include the following:

Budgetary control that outlines how funds will be obtained and spent in a given period

Ratio analysis control that summarizes the financial position of the organization by calculating ratios based on various financial measures

Materials control that determines the flow of materials from suppliers through an operations system to customers

Cost control that keeps all organizational costs at planned levels

Maintenance control that keeps all equipment and organizational facilities functioning at predetermined work levels either by preventive or repair measures

Inventory control that cuts costs through material-resource planning and that reduces stored inventories to a minimum by arranging for components to be delivered to the production facility just in time (JIT)

Technology control that ensures an adequate amount of state-of-the-art equipment and processes to transform predetermined inputs into competitive, marketable outputs

Informational control that ensures reasonable quantities of high-quality, timely, relevant information contributes to sound decision support and sustained productivity improvements

Audit controls that monitor, measure, and benchmark internal and external progress in organizational finance, accounting, marketing, production, technology, social, ethical, quality, human resource, and health/safety

Certification controls that assess and accredit performance in terms of international, professional, and quality standards (e.g., ISO 9000—the certification series from the International Organization for Standardization).

In addition to system, nonhuman controls, managers need to model and expect appropriate self-control and self-discipline at work. System controls do not relieve anyone of the responsibility for appropriate restraint of self-indulgent urges at work. The human control necessary for personal and group accomplishment requires a moderate degree of self-sacrifice and commitment to the discipline of learning. The opportunity to learn from constructive criticism is a benefit of a well-controlled workplace. The challenge of continually improving performance is the other human side of controlling that routine feedback and measurement provide. The ideal is to avoid human overcontrol (excessive micromanaging) and human undercontrol (excessive macromanaging). By combining TQ knowledge of stable system control and improvement with human sciences/arts knowledge of responsible human conduct, managers can approach balanced system and human control.

To evaluate the efficiency and effectiveness of the dimensions of controlling, Figure 7.4 provides a matrix based on two questions: (1) "Was the in-

Intended Controlling Realized

		Yes	No
Realized Controlling Successful	Yes	Coordinated Controlling Success (*Efficient and Effective*) [A]	Emergent Controlling Success (*Inefficient but Effective*) [C]
	No	Realized Controlling Failure (*Efficient but Not Effective*) [B]	Complete Controlling Failure (*Inefficient and Ineffective*) [D]

Figure 7.4. Controlling Success Evaluation Matrix

tended controlling successfully realized?" and (2) "Did the realized control successfully promote organizational performance?"

In Figure 7.4, the Controlling Success Evaluation Matrix contains four combinations. A yes-yes combination (in Quadrant A) means that the intended, coordinated controlling was successful and fully meritorious; managers set out to do something, they did it efficiently, and the controlling effectively worked. A yes-no designation (in Quadrant B) points toward a realized control failure in which managers efficiently implemented the intended control, which itself is only partially meritorious because that control plan proved to be ineffective. A no-yes designation (in Quadrant C) points toward inefficient implementation of the intended control but effective emergent control; for example, unintended and unanticipated controlling emerges that happens to be effective and is thereby partially meritorious. A no-no designation (in Quadrant D) indicates a complete failure of control because of inefficient implementation of intended controlling and ineffective outcomes.

Now that the dimensions and success standards of controlling have been treated, it is important to address the relationship of ethical controlling process to building management integrity.

▧ ETHICAL CONTROLLING PROCESSES THAT BUILD INTEGRITY

All the dimensions of integrity—judgment, process, and developmental— are important in exercising managerial control with integrity. Whereas the developmental and judgment dimensions anchor and sustain controlling with integrity, the process dimension builds controlling with management integrity. To control in a fully meritorious manner, some form of systematic controlling process must be used. The following four-step sequence of responsible controlling provides a generic model of the controlling subprocesses and their associated developmental tasks:

1. *Controlling Scanning:* enhanced awareness through domestic and global scanning of current external and internal best practices relating to assessment, improvement, and control instruments, tools, and measurements that optimize control benefits

2. *Controlling Formulation and Choice:* control formulation, analysis, and choice of process systems and human performance standards that can most efficiently reduce variation and align resources to accomplish strategic plans and improve organizational performance

3. *Controlling Implementation:* implementing control measures of system and human performance in such a way that interaction (e.g., "playing catchball," rather than organizational "hardball") is emphasized by using operating management tools to improve the organizational readiness to act

4. *Controlling Evaluation and Improvement:* evaluation and improvement of the measured outputs and outcomes of system and human performance by using a variety of performance indicators, audits, international quality standards, feedback, and process improvement tools

Each step in the generic controlling process must be adequately completed to result in a well-controlled company that is both effective and efficient.

The four process integrity steps parallel and permeate the four steps in the generic subprocesses of controlling (controlling scanning, controlling formulation and choice, controlling implementation, and controlling evaluation and improvement). In other words, *controlling with integrity means addressing the elements of the four subprocesses in the context of their parallel control ethics processes to ensure that no step in the controlling function neglects its ethical dimension.* Managers may lack integrity in controlling by neglecting to perform the subtasks entailed in ethics and controlling processes adequately, thereby exposing themselves and their organizations to ethical risk. Controlling with ethical integrity is facilitated by using the appropriate systematic queries from the QL-TOOL in Appendix D for each corresponding step of the generic controlling process. Figure 7.5 depicts the inclusive and sequential alignment of all ethics processes and controlling subprocesses that build management integrity.

Processes	Step 1	Step 2	Step 3	Step 4
Ethics Process	Ethical Awareness	Ethical Judgment	Ethical Intention	Ethical Conduct
Control Subprocesses	Controlling Scanning	Controlling Formulation and Choice	Controlling Implementation	Controlling Evaluation Control, and Improvement

Figure 7.5 Parallel Ethics and Controlling Subprocesses That Build Management Integrity

Ethical Controlling Scanning

With regard to the alignment of ethics processes and controlling subprocesses in Step 1 in Figure 7.5, the scope of ethical controlling scanning includes stakeholder benchmarking in the global and domestic, external and internal organizational environment, specified in detail in queries 1, 2, and 3 from the QL-TOOL (external ecological, technological, economic, legal, sociocultural, and political factors and internal organizational ethics development system factors). Ethical controlling scanning is achieved when the two elements of the ethical awareness process (perception and sensitivity) are adequately addressed by response to queries 1, 2, and 3 of the QL-TOOL. Perception of and sensitivity to external and internal stakeholders results in ethical controlling scanning.

NASA Challenger Disaster Managers
and Unethical Controlling Scanning

On January 28, 1986, the National Aeronautics Space Association (NASA) space shuttle *Challenger* exploded off the coast of Florida, killing all seven astronauts aboard. The primary and contributing causes of the disaster, according to the *Report of the Presidential Commission on the Space Shuttle Challenger Accident* (1986), were, respectively, the technical defect in the O-ring seal reliability in cold weather and a flaw in the managerial decision-making process. The supplier of the O-rings was Morton Thiokol's Wasatch division, which has been described as a rigid, hierarchic unit with an absence of trust between top managers and top engineers, requiring unquestioned loyalty from engineers, such as Roger Boisjoly, who later became the chief whistle blower on the problem of the faulty O-ring seals in cold weather (Boisjoly, Curtis, & Mellican, 1989; Werhane, 1991b). The conflict between the top managerial and political priority of effective action based on balancing risks against benefits, and the top engineering and scientific priority of minimizing risk (better safe than sorry) was also a part of the tension in the NASA public civilian administrative bureaucracy (McConnell, 1987; Newton & Schmidt, 1996).

The inadequacy of ethical control scanning in the *Challenger* disaster case occured at the personal, group, and organizational levels. At the personal level, top individual NASA managers (Smith, Thomas, Aldrich, and Moore) distanced themselves from owning any part of the *Challenger* failure because they claimed not to know about the O-ring objections. Yet they did not acknowledge their top-down responsibility to ask questions regarding the safety of every launch, and their neglect to do so makes them morally culpable (Allinson, 1993). At the group caucus level between NASA and Morton Thiokol's top people (including the lead Thiokol engineers Boisjoly, Thompson, and McDonald), Kilminster, Morton Thiokol's vice president of boosters, initially sided with his engineers on the safety issue but later reversed his decision under peer group pressure from NASA and inability to prioritize engineering concerns over managerial agendas (Harris, Pritchard, & Robins, 1995; Newton & Schmidt, 1996). At the organizational level, in both NASA and Morton Thiokol, a self-imposed, crisis atmosphere that was not conducive to responsible decision making, a lack of standardized criteria for moral decision making, the absence of the exercise of a chain of command in the final decision-making caucuses, and the lack of a specified resolution mechanism (consensus, majority vote) all contributed to inadequate organizational ethical awareness (misperception and insensitivity) of the known risks to the safety of the launch (Allinson, 1993).

The written safety concerns of Boisjoly as an engineer were not perceived (interpreted as valid) by senior Morton Thiokol or NASA managers and thus were not widely shared, thereby depriving both organizations of a broader stakeholder base of ethical perception and sensitivity. Furthermore, once heard, top managers in both organizations did not regard safety issues as more important than the task (launch) completion issue. If both organizations had fostered more bottom-up ethical voice systems with widespread consensus decision-making practices, rather than centralized top-down decision making, the organizations' eyes and ears would have been more attuned and sensitive to the impending moral disaster. At one level, top NASA managers assumed that disasters were inevitable in the inherently risky realm of space exploration, and two perceptual distortions reassured them: (a) The imminent possibility of disaster was denied by the imagined favorable increasing estimate of gambling odds, and (b) the culpable role of a managerial decision process that did not place safety first was denied.

Because the *Challenger* disaster was both foreseen and preventable, the lessons regarding ethical control scanning include (a) the need to institutionalize multiple stakeholder voice systems so that moral challenges to hierarchic authority and ethical consensus about issues can be routinely accepted; (b) developing moral awareness that the "ethical buck" stops everywhere, in the boardroom as well as on the shop floor—that is, collective disasters imply collective responsibility, which top managers cannot evade; and (c) the moral culpability of managers who explain away disasters and allow past faulty control practices to prevail when alternative superior scanning methods are available (Davis, 1989).

Ethical Controlling Formulation and Choice

With regard to the alignment of ethics processes and controlling subprocesses in Step 2 in Figure 7.5, the scope of ethical control formulation and choice includes factors in the global and domestic, external and internal organizational context and judgment, specified in query 4 in the QL-TOOL (supportive external and internal contexts for optimal ethical analysis and resolution in demonstrating judgment integrity). Ethical control formulation and choice are achieved when the two elements of the ethical judgment process (analysis and resolution) are adequately addressed by responses to query 4 of the QL-TOOL. The presence of thorough, multidisciplinary, ethical analysis leads to structured moral dialogue to arrive at balanced, justified resolution of ethically framed issues, and finally, results in ethical control policies formulated responsibly and chosen. The absence of ethical control policy formulation and choice leads to the perception of an organization or industry that is expedient, callous, lacking in judgment integrity, and in short, out of social control, as in the case of the U.S. tobacco industry.

U.S. Tobacco Industry Managers and
Unethical Controlling Formulation and Choice

Although tobacco products have a long global and domestic history of usage, the U.S. tobacco industry formed a united coalition in 1954 with the founding of the Tobacco Institute by the "Big Six" U.S. tobacco companies. These companies, even today, control over 95% of the U.S. cigarette market and include (a) Philip Morris, the largest, with estimated cigarette sales of $194.72 billion in 1993, for 42.2% of the market; (b) R. J. Reynolds (RJR Nabisco), the second largest, with sales of $141 billion and a market share of 30.6%; (c) Brown and Williamson, the third largest, with $50.52 billion in sales and 11% market share; (d) Lorillard, with $32.65 billion, for a 7.1% share; (e) American Tobacco sold $31.12 billion worth of cigarettes, for 6.7% market share; and (f) Liggett trails with $11.17 billion and 2.4% market share. Together under the umbrella of the Tobacco Institute, the tobacco industry leaders contact legislators at all levels and by all means, fund pro-tobacco initiatives from nonindustry sources, rally potential constituencies, and coordinate all activity that may help the industry.

The moral pattern of their coordinated response was set in their 1964 reaction to then Surgeon General Luther Terry's report that identified tobacco products, and cigarette smoking in particular, as threats to the public health. Terry recommended four steps:

1. Immediate educational campaign on the health risks of tobacco product use
2. Ingredient labels on cigarette packs
3. Health hazard warnings stamped on each cigarette pack
4. Restrictions on advertising

The Tobacco Institute's reaction was a denial of wrongdoing and an orchestrated frontal attack (Quinn, 1989).

The ultimate federal government result was that only Terry's third recommendation was legally enacted by Congress. The cigarette warning label, in fact, preempted any legal recourse by the courts for damages incurred after 1964 at the state and local levels. With federal preemption in place, the Tobacco Institute successfully lobbied to achieve two objectives: (a) to take control of tobacco regulation away from the professional experts in the Federal Trade Commission and place it in the congressional political arena where public health would be accorded a lower priority and (b) to ensure that, with federal regulatory preemption, no states or localities could demand any more restrictions of sales, advertising, or labeling within their borders (Quinn, 1989).

The moral pattern of the tobacco industry's response, therefore, was to forestall substantive moral dialogue (and thereby sound moral judgment) by using a range of medical science, public relations, politico-legal, and economic defensive ploys. With regard to the first defensive ploy, medical science forestalling of substitutive moral dialogue, which begins with the honest admission of factual observations, the Tobacco Institute has separately denied the harmful effects of primary and secondary smoke by insisting that the link between smoking and illness has never been conclusively proven (Campbell, 1993; White, 1988). Yet recent medical science research (Editors of the *New England Journal of Medicine*, 1994; McGinnis & Forge, 1993; Schlaadt, 1992) has demonstrated such strong correlations between smoking and illness that the "purported controversy" over scientific evidence is over for most reasonable people, and now the primary question is how much of the proven harm from tobacco products should society permit. The Tobacco Institute, however, has appeared to be engaged in a massive public relations campaign of misinformation to link smoking directly and indirectly with images of health and vitality.

With regard to this second defensive ploy, most cigarette ads feature young persons in the middle of some vigorous activity—volleyball, skiing, surfing, hiking—that is known to be demanding on the heart and lungs. The models in the ads are the very image of cardiovascular and pulmonary health and strength, which runs contrary to the scientific effects of prolonged smoking. The ads clearly attempt to counter the fears that might be raised by warning labels on packs. The ads are designed to neutralize the warnings (Quinn, 1989). Because of the extent of these public relations efforts, some people have termed this tactic of the tobacco industry *disinformation*—an organized campaign of lies so massive, detailed, and self-assured that it overwhelms our ability to disbelieve (Whelan, 1984; White, 1988). Because the objective of this massive campaign is solely to sell a product and increase profits, critics argue that these campaigns constitute fraud—actionable and prosecutable (Whelan, 1984; White, 1988).

With regard to the third defensive ploy, politico-legal emphasis on constitutional rights, the tobacco industry has tried to replace the moral priority of refraining from doing harm to oneself and others with the politico-legal priority of political liberty. The tobacco industry has argued that, in a democratic society, persons have the right to freely make self-regarding, consumption choices without paternalistic protection. The disingenuousness of this political gesture is belied by the following three counterarguments. First, the presumption of self-regarding liberty can and has been challenged because if nicotine is an unsafe addictive drug, as it was classified in 1995 by the Food and Drug Administration (FDA), then the notion that smokers freely choose to smoke is patently unjustified. Furthermore, the purported self-regarding pleas-

pleasure of self-destructive smoking is at the expense of others who experience the grief of loss and/or incur the burden of caring for smokers as their health risks materialize. Second, the unquestioned presumption of business liberty to make and sell tobacco products in a free market economy has also been challenged when tobacco products are known to be unreasonably dangerous. In that event, marketing tobacco products that are known to be unreasonably harmful becomes an unethical practice open to product liability. But for federal preemption, the U.S. tobacco industry would be vulnerable to mass tort product liability lawsuits. Third, the preemption that something is entirely a self-regarding behavior deserving of protection has been refuted by EPA studies that demonstrated that nonsmokers suffered the same diseases as smokers but to a lesser degree (Kennedy & Manderscheid, 1992; Koop, 1986). In effect, an industry marketing policy based on systematic disinformation regarding an unsafe, addictive drug undermines the substantive presumption of liberty, despite the public relations images to the contrary, and undermines the presumption of judgment/industry integrity in moral decision making.

With regard to the fourth defensive ploy, the economic trump card of widespread financial and employment losses from industry overregulation or product banning, the tobacco industry has fomented fears of economic disaster to protect its economic dominance. These economic fears have been countered by larger economic fears regarding the vast negative economic utility (the economic costs of tobacco use outweighs its economic benefits) caused by the tobacco industry in terms of loss of life and health, increased medical and insurance costs, loss of productivity because of death and illness, extensive property damage because of death and illness, extensive property damage because of fires and cleaning costs, and loss of revenue to state governments. Large insurance companies have joined forces with state governments to recoup their financial losses because of increased health and disability benefits obtained by injured smokers and nonsmokers. Furthermore, as tobacco firms have diversified into conglomerates with nontobacco business, the moral double standard applied to tobacco business policies, in contrast with nontobacco policies, has created organizational moral schizophrenia, preventing any genuine sense of organization integrity and efficient uniformity. In addition, exporting unsafe, additive products globally is, in effect, exporting economic and ethical risk to target groups who are vulnerable to exploitation because of lower health and environmental awareness. This cynical policy is as morally reprehensible globally as it is domestically, regardless of international legal permissibility.

In essence, by not according moral priority to integrity in control policy formulation and choice, the tobacco industry has abdicated its responsibility for supporting industrywide integrity in favor of hypocritical, expedient, defensive postures. The total adverse impact of this stance in terms of lost lives, increased health risks, litigation costs, lower stock prices, stigmatized industry reputation, and other related costs cannot yet be fully tallied.

Ethical Control Implementation

With regard to the alignment of the ethics processes and controlling sub-processes in Step 3 in Figure 7.5, the extent of the ethical control implementation can be determined by fully addressing queries 5, 6, and 9 from the QL-TOOL. Ethical control implementation is achieved when the two elements of the ethical intention process (cognitive and volitional readiness to act) are demonstrated by responses to queries 5, 6, and 9 from the QL-TOOL. Obviously, poor implementation of a rationally formulated control design can result in control and moral failure. Less obviously, refusal to consider feedback to modify original control designs in light of operational experience or to replace the intended control design with a more feasible, emergent one is also a control and moral failure. The demands of ethical control implementation in dealing with people, structure, and technology factors can be dramatized in the Ritz-Carlton case.

Ritz-Carlton Hotel Company Managers and Ethical Control Implementation

The Ritz-Carlton Hotel Company, based in Atlanta, operates luxury hotels domestically and globally frequented by industry executives, meeting and corporate travel planners, and affluent travelers, while pursuing the distinction of being the best in each geographic market (Henderson, 1992). In 1992, the Ritz-Carlton became the first hospitality organization to earn the Malcolm Baldrige National Quality Award. The Ritz-Carlton operates from an easy-to-understand definition of service quality that is aggressively communicated and internalized at all levels of the organization. Its motto, We are Ladies and Gentlemen Serving Ladies and Gentlemen, is instilled in all employees. The clear moral message of self-respecting adults providing personalized service and treating guests respectfully is accorded the highest priority.

In addition to controlling implementation through character selection and consistently providing the high level of quality service demanded by customers, the human resource function works closely with the other operational functions. Each hotel has a director of human resources and a training manager, who are assisted by the hotel's quality leader. Each work area has a departmental trainer who is responsible for training and certifying new employees in his or her unit. Ritz-Carlton uses a highly predictive "character-trait recruiting" instrument for determining candidates' fitness for each of 120 job positions.

TQ human resources practitioners enhance selection success by screening for organizational citizenship behavior and service orientation. *Organizational citizenship behavior* (OCB), which is the tendency to be helpful to others, loyal, and considerate of the whole organization, can be ascertained from background checks, reference checks, and behavior-based interviews (Van Dyne et al., 1994). *Service orientation,* which is the psychological predisposition to be helpful to customers, can be predicted by conducting behavior-based interviews using the Service Orientation psychological test, and performing background checks (Hogan et al., 1984).

Other hospitality firms have tried to short-circuit organizational citizenship behavior and service orientation screening by maintaining that desirable employee performance satisfaction can best be accomplished by enforcing appropriate affect display behaviors (feeling rules) to ensure that the interaction between employee and customer appears to be pleasant (Hochschild, 1983). *Feeling rules* are formal and informal norms that require employees to display emotions appropriate to their jobs (e.g., salesclerks are expected to smile frequently, establish eye contact, and thank customers for purchasing). These feeling rules can be extended to internal customers as part of the responsibility of all employees (Rafaeli, 1989). The imposition of feeling rules on anyone, however, even persons with the attitude of a "conscripted employee," is an inappropriate means to the end of TQ service at Ritz-Carlton. There is no substitute for genuine commitment to shared service values and sincere regard for the customer; this spirit of service cannot be coerced, but can only be voluntarily given. The combination of sound character and courteous personality is detected and appreciated by Ritz-Carlton customers. Although it is important to recognize the emotional labor entailed in customer satisfaction, there are alternatives to feeling-rule enforcement to achieve the desired result (e.g., careful selection processes to screen out potential attitude problems, frequent training mini-sessions on commitment to shared values, and/or more frequent breaks from heavy customer contact).

In addition to controlling implementation through character selection, new employees receive two days' orientation in which senior executives demonstrate Ritz-Carlton methods and stress the unique virtues of Ritz-Carlton organizational character. Three weeks later, managers monitor the effectiveness of the instruction and then conduct a follow-up training session. Later, new employees must pass written and skill-demonstration tests to become certified in their work areas.

Every day, in each work area, intellectual, social, emotional, and moral virtues are cultivated in a systematic manner. Each shift supervisor conducts a quality lineup meeting and briefing session. Employees receive instruction for becoming certified as quality managers capable of identifying waste in their work and identifying opportunities to exercise their virtues. Through these and other mechanisms, employees receive more than 100 hours of quality education aimed at fostering anticipatory readiness to act, by exercising the following character-building virtues: social virtues (cooperativeness, cheerfulness, civility, poise), emotional virtues (self-respect, sense of responsibility, caring), moral virtues (self-discipline, dependability, trustworthiness, gratitude) and intellectual virtues (knowledge, resourcefulness, creativity).

The effectiveness of training sessions is regularly evaluated as part of control implementation at four outcome levels: reaction, learning, behavior, and results (Kirkpatrick, 1994). *Reaction* as an outcome measures how those who participate in the training program feel about it. Reactions are measured by postprogram surveys; positive reactions will most likely motivate learning. *Learning* as an outcome is the extent to which participants change attitudes, improve knowledge, and/or increase skill as a result of participating in a training program. These can be measured by pre- and postprogram instruments. *Behavior* as an outcome is the extent to which change in external conduct has occurred because the participant attended a training program. For behavior change to occur, however, four conditions need to be present:

1. The person must have a desire to change
2. The person must know what to do and how to do it
3. The person must work in a supportive work unit climate
4. The person must be rewarded for changing

If the first two conditions are met but the work unit climate is unsupportive and there are no extrinsic or intrinsic rewards for changing, the behavior improvements will not occur. Sometimes learning contracts are implemented at the end of a training program to involve bosses in explicit behavioral change expectations and correlated rewards (Kirkpatrick, 1994). Behavior change instruments and learning contract compliance can measure this output. Finally, *results* as outcomes are the ultimate tangible payoffs for attending training programs (e.g., increased production, decreased costs, reduced turnover). The results of Ritz-Carlton training are indicated below. For example, employees are trusted and empowered to spend up to $2,000 to satisfy a guest swiftly, to be involved in setting plans for their particular work area, and to speak with anyone in the company regarding any problem.

The Ritz-Carlton institutionalizes its character development training by using information technology on a daily basis to gather and use customer satisfaction and quality-related data. Information systems involve every employee and provide critical, responsive data on guest preferences, quantity of error-free products and services, and opportunities for quality improvement. The guest-profiling system records the individual preferences of the hundreds of thousands of guests who have stayed at least three times at any of the hotels. It gives front-desk employees immediate access to such information as whether the guest smokes, whether he or she prefers wine or a rose in the evening, and what kind of pillow he or she prefers.

The implementation results of these training and character-building practices of Ritz-Carlton's quality have been impressive. At the time of winning the Baldrige Award, customer satisfaction was upwards of 95%. Employee turnover was 48%, in an industry where the average is more than 100%. And 100% of key group accounts were retained in 1991. The number of employees needed per guest room during preopening activities of a new hotel was reduced 12%. Within a 3-year period, Ritz-Carlton reduced the number of labor hours per guest room by 8%. Housekeeping costs per occupied room were reduced from $7.90 to $7.30 in less than 1 year. The average amount of time required to clean a room was decreased from 30 to 28.5 minutes, and elevator waiting time was reduced by 33%. Departmental profits per available guest room were nearly five times the industry average.

By using ethical control implementation practices with integrity, Ritz-Carlton and its managers have formed an admirable organizational character that shapes employee readiness to act ethically on a daily basis. Out of showing respect for others, Ritz-Carlton itself has become more respected. It has risen in stature as an organizational role model and can use its enhanced staff readiness to act with integrity as a competitive edge over other service providers domestically and globally.

Ethical Controlling Evaluation and Improvement

With regard to the alignment of the ethics processes and control subprocesses in Step 4 in Figure 7.5, the scope of ethical controlling evaluation and improvement includes stakeholder conduct and reputation in the global and domestic, external and internal organizational environments, specified in detail in queries 7, 8, and 10 from the QL-TOOL (extent to which responsible, ecological, economic, ethical, legal, and philanthropic conduct anchors and builds reputations for integrity). Ethical controlling evaluation and improvement are achieved when the two elements of the ethical conduct process (being responsibly responsive and engaging in sustainable development) are adequately addressed by responses to queries 7, 8, and 10 of the QL-TOOL. Responsible and sustainable conduct results when ethical controlling evaluation and improvement processes are continually developed and used, as in the case of Ben & Jerry's.

Ben & Jerry's Homemade Ice Creams, Inc. Managers
and Ethical Controlling Evaluation and Improvement

Two young American men, Ben Cohen and Jerry Greenfield, established Ben & Jerry's Homemade Ice Creams, Inc. (B&J) in 1978. Their only claim to expertise was a $5 correspondence course on ice cream making in the home kitchen, and a passion for ice cream. Started from their home kitchen, this small business became an international brand and went public in 1984. It has experienced rapid and continuous financial growth and has maintained a solid market share in the super-premium segment of the ice-cream industry.

The controlling vision of B&J has linked prosperity of stakeholders through continued evaluation and improvement of its performance with respect to four missions: product mission, social mission, economic mission, and environmental mission.

First, the product mission is to "make, distribute and sell the finest quality all-natural ice cream and related products in a wide variety of innovative flavors made from Vermont dairy products." The focus on quality, organic ingredients, innovation, and improvement to delight customers and to respond rapidly to customer feedback are not unique to B&J, but are hallmarks of ethical control evaluation, continuous improvement, and quality audits. In addition, B&J responded to increased health consciousness by developing a health line of nonfat yogurt products and by urging moderate consumption of its gourmet line of ice creams.

Second, the social mission is "to operate the company in a way that actively recognizes the central role that business plays in the structure of society by initiating innovative ways to improve the quality of life of a broad community, local, national and international." B&J has creatively designed its core ice creams to be associated with social causes. B&J's Wild Maine Blueberry ice cream uses wild blueberries picked by the Passamaquoddy Native Americans of Maine. They harvest and process blueberries on their reservation. B&J buys $330,000 worth of blueberries from them each year. This gives them a steady source of income and makes them self-reliant. Similarly, B&J buys Brazil nuts and cashew nuts grown and harvested by natives of the Amazonian rain forest. By helping them maintain their traditional lifestyles, the company also helps protect the rain forest. One social cause the company is committed to is supporting family-owned farms, especially in Vermont, so it buys all its cream from a dairy cooperative of such farms. The Fresh Georgia Peach Light ice cream uses peaches from a family farm in Georgia. B&J buys its candy from Community Projects, Inc., a company that donates its profits to rain forest preservation. (B&J created Community Projects, Inc., as a venture to promote social programs.) It buys brownies from Greystone Bakery, which provides training and employment for homeless people. Peace Pops is another product directly linked to a social cause—world peace. The company donates profits from this product to the One Percent for Peace Foundation. The objective of this organization is to divert 1% of the Pentagon budget to social programs and international understanding.

This link between social causes and products has several benefits. It provides concrete support to specific causes. It clarifies and shares the company's core values among employees and stakeholders. It also gives the company a progressive social reputation that, in turn, gives competitive advantage in certain segments of the market (Shrivastava, 1996). As Ben Cohen stated: "As our business supports the community, the community supports us back." B&J goes beyond enlightened egoism into moral altruism, however, through its sustained philanthropic conduct. In 1985, Ben Cohen set up the Ben & Jerry Foundation, which is dedicated to encouraging social change and improvement through the regular donation of 7.5% of B&J's yearly pretax profits. To measure its annual social performance, B&J contracts with an outside expert to conduct a *social audit,* which rates the company in such areas as community involvement, customer service, employee benefits, plant safety, and ecological processes. The social auditor is given access to all employee and corporate documents to conduct the independent audit. The findings of the social audit, positive and negative, are published, unedited, to guarantee complete candor. The inclusion of an uncensored social audit in an annual report is still a rare practice among most world companies, but it enhances the credibility of B&J's reputation.

Third, the economic mission is "to operate the company on a sound financial basis of profitable growth, increasing value for shareholders and creating career opportunities and financial rewards for employees." The Institutional Shareholder Services, Inc., reported, "In all measures of work life, Ben and Jerry's people have a far more favorable view of their jobs, supervision, and company than do employees from American companies in general." B&J's programs have created a highly committed and loyal workforce. Employee wages, benefits, and work conditions are the best in the area. Benefits include the traditional medical leave, stock ownership, and contributory pension plans. The company has also established some innovative new programs: parental leave and adoption assistance, on-site child care, financial counseling for employees, and a military-leave policy that guarantees jobs and pays salary differentials. It tries to maintain the ratio of entry-level wages to highest salaries of 1 to 7 to promote vertical compensation equity and work community morale. B&J is committed to economic growth along with reward equity, measuring the former by financial audits and the later by social audits.

Fourth, the environmental mission is "to motivate and communicate a sense of environmental responsibility throughout Ben & Jerry's community by developing and motivating creative earth-respecting programs." B&J has become a model for small business sustainable development and collaborative partnerships for ecological responsibility. B&J's environmental programs try to compensate for all the environmental effects of company operations. They include management of waste streams, conserving energy and resources, exploring sources of sustainable alternative energy, establishing linkages between products and environmental causes, and setting up community environmental awareness programs (Jennings & Zandbergen, 1995; Shrivastava, 1996). B&J designed a production system that integrates energy conservation, resource management, production, packaging, and waste treatment into a single comprehensive system. The company's energy conservation goal is to reduce energy consumption by 25% over the next 5 years. Periodic corporatewide audits update energy conservation programs. B&J uses compact fluorescent lights, low-wattage light bulbs, and variable-speed drives for condensers. It has installed occupancy sensors that turn off the lights if a room is vacant for 5 minutes; this feature alone saves the company $250,000 per year. B&J is experimenting with high-efficiency refrigeration systems using outdoor air in the winter. It is testing the feasibility of plants that co-generate energy from waste, and of solar-powered delivery trucks and refrigeration systems.

The company's comprehensive *resource conservation* programs involve use reduction, recycling, and reuse of office materials and wastes wherever possible. To maximize the use of raw materials, the company has developed an automated and high-efficiency production system. Company stationery and copier, computer, and laser printer paper are unbleached and 100% recycled. Double-sided copies are made wherever possible. Office pens are refillable. Printer toner cartridges are recycled, and printer ribbons are reinked. Even greeting cards are recycled. Some office paper is reused for packaging and animal bedding. Dishes and flatware in the cafeteria are reused. Reuse of plastic containers for ingredients reduced the amount of cardboard sold for recycling from 1,800 pound/bales per week to 5 pound/bales per week. Production wastes are similarly recycled: 10,000 pounds of plastic egg-yolk pails are recycled each year; the milky liquids (untreatable in the local waste plant) left over from ice-cream manufacture are fed to pigs in the local area, an idea generated by Gail Mayville, head of one of the Green Teams (the company even bought 200 pigs to keep this waste fully used as feed); B&J uses 500 to 700 gallons of ice cream spillage per day to sweeten farmer's manure pits; water and flavoring jugs are recycled. And B&J minimizes generation of solid waste by designing packaging carefully and reusing plastic and cardboard parts. Any extra-clean used fiberboard boxes are sold to a company that reuses them. To remove pollutants from wastewater, the company set up a pilot wastewater treatment system designed by Solar Aquatics. Working on the greenhouse principle, this system uses solar energy and natural vegetation in an artificial marshlands to purify water.

In addition, the company sponsors community projects, campaigns, and events to promote environmental awareness and protection of indigenous peoples. Examples of these include Vermont's Merry Mulching program to recycle Christmas trees and leftover paint cans. B&J made contributions to preserve the cultural tradition of native American and native Brazilian peoples. Together with 17 other companies, B&J also organized a campaign to support congressional legislation calling for auto fuel efficiency standards of 40 miles per gallon by the year 2000. In 1992, B&J signed the Valdez Principles, proposed by the Coalition for Environmentally Responsible Economies (CERES), and agreed to an annual environmental audit (Shrivastava, 1996).

Ethical conduct and managerial reputations are strengthened through ethical controlling, evaluation, and improvement. Managers with a reputation for responsibly responsive and sustainable development controlling are more likely to be regarded as waste eliminators who set higher standards of performance domestically and globally.

⧄ MANAGEMENT ETHICS AND CONTROLLING WITH INTEGRITY MINICASES

To apply managerial ethical decision making and control with integrity, the following minicases are offered for practice analysis. They raise issues in management ethics and controlling with integrity and are categorized into seven allied management application clusters:

1. Accounting/auditing issues
2. Finance/investment issues
3. Marketing/advertising issues
4. Business management/human resources/business law issues
5. Technology/quality operations/organizational behavior issues
6. Public/nonprofit/health care administration issues
7. International/environmental/public policy issues

These clusters are generic categories, and specific cases in any one chapter may not cover all subfields in the cluster, but at least one minicase in Chapters 4 through 7 addresses each subfield in the cluster. Of the 18 subfields contained in the 7 clusters, 28 minicases are provided, ensuring that each subfield is addressed at least once and that overlapping interfield problems are included.

To incorporate the tools and resources of this book to analyze and resolve controlling issues with integrity, the authors recommend that each minicase be approached with three objectives in mind:

1. Systematically apply the QL-TOOL, in an individual or collective setting, to arrive at a principled, feasible resolution.
2. In accomplishing the first objective, consciously engage in ethics dialogue as the guiding method of moral discourse.

3. Select the appropriate components of the OEDS (in Appendix E) and other tools contained in the Appendices that would cultivate, build, and/or sustain dimensions of management integrity in the future.

(1) Accounting/Auditing Minicase: (Case 7A) - The Bank of Credit & Commercial International (BCCI)

The Bank of Credit & Commerce International (BCCI) was a $20 billion banking empire on the surface that operated in 70 countries. Incorporated in Luxembourg and headquartered in London, BCCI owned First American Bankshare in Washington, D.C. (with Clark Clifford, former Secretary of Defense, as chairman), and the National Bank of Georgia.

Clifford had multiple roles at First American, beyond that of chairman. He was also the managing partner of Clifford & Warnke, the law firm that represented First American. Clifford & Warnke also defended BCCI against money-laundering charges in 1988. In addition, Clifford and his law partner, Robert A. Altman, had borrowed $12 million from BCCI to buy shares in First American Bankshare. BCCI found a buyer for Clifford's shares 18 months later, and Clifford realized an $11 million pretax profit.

BCCI had what regulators refer to as a "black network," with 1,500 employees who used spy equipment, arms deals, bribery, espionage, extortion, and drug trafficking to advance its worldwide presence. BCCI was the bank used for the money in the Iran-Contra deals. The CIA also had BCCI accounts. Customers of BCCI included Manuel Noriega, Saddam Hussein, and Ferdinand Marcos.

BCCI was shut down by regulators in 62 countries on July 5, 1991. After the July 5th shutdown of BCCI, mysteries about its operations unfolded. When Manhattan District Attorney Robert Morgenthau announced that BCCI had been indicted on charges of defrauding investors and stealing more than $30 million, he explained that BCCI's structure was nothing more than a global Ponzi scheme in which money was shifted to maintain a facade of fiscal respectability for auditors and regulators while the masterminds kept funds for themselves. BCCI was a meta-nation with its own intelligence service, army, and international bank. It dealt in commodities (oil, drugs, grain, cement, some of the latter of which were laced with bricks of heroin) and was one of the largest arms dealers in the world. Banking was important to this meta-nation's success, but it was far from its only field of operations.

An independent audit undertaken by Price Waterhouse for British authorities, completed and fully released in 1992, concluded that BCCI's board was taken in by a dominant and deceitful management group. Price Waterhouse also concluded that accounts existed for the sole purpose of fraudulently routing funds and laundering money. This is one of the first global bank accounting scandals whose exposure was made possible by the information revolution with its instant transfers of money and real-time, worldwide operations.

Still facing ongoing investigations by various agencies, BCCI pleaded guilty to federal and state charges of racketeering, fraud, and money laundering in December 1991. The fate of the funds of BCCI depositors remains unknown, but U.S. prosecutors continue to pursue the case. A New York grand jury indicted Sheik Khalid bin Mahfouz, a top officer of Saudi Arabia's National Commercial Bank, a BCCI subsidiary, to recover a $170 million fine. Both Clark Clifford and his law partner, Robert Altman, were indicted for conspiracy and concealing material facts in the BCCI downfall.

In effect, the lack of internal controlling of bank managerial accounting practices with integrity invites global regulatory intervention, the loss of millions of dollars, and the destruction of individual careers and industry reputations. (For more details, see Potts, M. [1992]. *Dirty money: BCCI, the inside story of the world's sleaziest bank*. Washington, DC: National Press Books.)

(2) Finance/Investments Minicase: (Case 7B) - Barings Bank

Barings Bank was Britain's oldest merchant bank and, at the time of its crash, was regarded as one of the world's most preeminent financial institutions. Traditionally comparable to other family-controlled financial institutions owned by the Rothschilds or the Hambros, Barings maintained its independence for over 200 years with its founders' direct descendants still at the helm.

Barings had been through many metamorphoses in the course of its long history, surviving by adapting itself to changing circumstances, pushing headlong into new businesses and occasionally taking risks. The most significant change in the history of the bank took place in May 1984 when the Baring Brothers paid just £6 million for a tiny stockbroking company called Henderson Crosthwaite (Far East), later to become Barings Securities. It was to prove an inspired purchase, transforming the bank's fortunes during the 1980s, but in it lay a future that was to seal the fate of the House of Barings.

In the 5 years after Baring Securities set up its Asian headquarters in Tokyo, Japan underwent a period of extraordinary economic growth. Between February 1985 and February 1988, the value of the yen more than doubled against the dollar; people expected the economy to slip into recession, but suddenly Japan's domestic demand boomed, and far from slumping, the economy expanded at its fastest rate for 6 years, with corporate profits growing lustily. Japan's strong economic growth, tight labor markets, increasing domestic demand, and expanding domestic liquidity sent the Japanese stock market shooting skyward.

Nick Leeson joined the London back office's settlements department of Barings Securities in 1989. Barings Securities was at the height of its research-driven probe into Southeast Asia, and the foundation laid by the firm's network of research offices paved the way for its sales and trading activities in the emerging markets. Most of the firm's expansion had been in the front office, which encompassed research teams, sales staff, and traders, whereas the back office, which consisted of the people and processes for settling trades and accounts, had fallen behind. In fact, although the back office settlement staff performed 80% of the workload associated with completing any single trade once it was made, they were generally regarded as second-class citizens. But for Nick Leeson, it was a start, and after two prior jobs, he was ambitiously working toward a front office trader position.

As Leeson became more proficient in back office operations, handled operational problems in Asia (Japan and Indonesia), and formed a political alliance with Ian Martin, the Chief Operating Officer of Barings Securities, he was promoted to head the new Singapore operation of Barings. There was some initial confusion about reporting and control lines for Leeson: whether there should be local control by James Box in Singapore, regional control by Fernando Gueler in Tokyo, or global control by Ian Martin in London.

By 1992, an increasing amount of Barings Securities' business in futures and options was moving offshore from Japan to Singapore for several reasons: (a) increased financial restrictions by the Japanese Ministry of Finance; (b) U.S. clients' preference for open-outcry markets, such as the one at the Singapore International Monetary Exchange (SIMEX); and (c) the substantially less expensive commissions required by SIMEX. When Leeson arrived in Singapore, the clarity of reporting and control lines became further blurred because of the operational and geographic separation of the Barings Securities office, headed by Box on the 24th floor, and the Barings Futures office, headed by Leeson on the 14th floor.

In addition to the ambiguity of managerial control within Barings, the norms of conduct for traders on the open-outcry trading floor emphasized individualism, competition, greed, cultivating a macho image of financial success, concealing losses, and fear of public humiliation as a loser. Furthermore, in many Baring's derivatives trading offices, over 75% were composed of aggressive young males whose hypercompetitive bravado, complete absorption in the market, and illusion of invulnerability predisposed them as traders to arrogant risk-taking conduct. As an expatriate financial manager, Leeson also experienced isolation and, with the sudden increase in wealth and the trappings of socioeconomic status, a certain elitist superiority.

Given these individual and contextual factors, Leeson took advantage of the loose operational controls and trading flow norms to engage in high-risk derivative deals that brought down the 200-year-old Barings in three short months from December 1994 to February 1995. Leeson bought futures on the SIMEX, the value of which would increase if the Nikkei 225 index increased. Because Leeson had a limited formal education of financial management and had only recently experienced the booming Japanese futures market, he adopted the uncritical trader assumption that a declining market would always rebound in a timely manner, so "doubling down" (e.g., doubling long investment in contracts in a declining market) was automatic. This is precisely what Leeson did. After massive futures purchases in January 1995, the Nikkei 225 index went into a persistent downward trend in February, and Leeson doubled his long position in a concealed margin account numbered 88888 (a number chosen for its lucky auspices in Chinese numerology). Finally, on February 23, the Nikkei 225 crashed below the 18,000 level and Leeson/Barings Securities lost £65 million in one day. Leeson left Barings Futures on that day, and on February 27, the Nikkei market opened 880 points down, thereby causing Barings to go bust. Leeson flew out of Singapore and was apprehended in Germany within a week.

Nick Leeson's unauthorized trading activities were the catalyst for the collapse of Barings. He stands accused of fabricating and shredding documents relating to his trading activities; juggling accounts, money, and positions; lying to auditors and management; falsifying trading reports to the Singapore exchange authorities; and dodging meetings with senior Barings executives seeking clarification of his activities. In addition, Barings was brought down by the inadequacy of managerial control processes within and outside the bank.

At least seven lines of procedure control should have prevented Leeson's unauthorized and imprudent trading activities but did not. They included internal management; external and internal auditors; regulatory bodies in Singapore, Tokyo, and Osaka; and the Bank of England. Among the internal management control failures were (a) failure to segregate Leeson's duties:

throughout, he was permitted to remain in charge of both the front and back offices in Singapore despite warnings of the dangers inherent in this position in an internal audit; (b) failure of senior executives and settlements staff to ensure that £742 million—over twice the bank's reported capital—sent out to Leeson's derivatives speculation, actually matched client accounts or the bank's own positions as declared by Leeson; (c) failure of both top management and the designated members of the derivatives group to fully understand and introduce effective trading limits on the business that Leeson was supposed to be undertaking, despite vast reported profits and funding requirements; and (d) failure to conduct a serious investigation of Leeson's activities despite market rumors throughout January and February 1995, and expressions of concern at high levels from reputable sources, including the Bank for International Settlements. On May 21, Barings senior managers from London, Tokyo, and Singapore, with functional responsibility for the Singapore derivatives business, all resigned.

The absence of regular monitoring communication between the exchanges of Japan and SIMEX and between the exchanges and Barings contributed to a lack of extraorganizational regulatory control of derivatives' abuses. Finally, although the Board of Banking Supervision of the Bank of England stated that no fundamental change in the national framework of financial regulation seemed warranted, the BCCI and Barings scandals indicate a rupture in the integrity of the British financial system. A strong case can now be made for the Bank of England to retain only its monetary role, handing over regulatory supervision to an independent body as does the German Bundesbank.

In effect, the lack of financial control with integrity resulted in the downfall of the oldest merchant bank in England, hundreds of millions in losses for investors, hundreds of lost jobs, ruined management careers, and loss of international investor confidence in global derivatives and global traders. (For more details, see Rawnsley, J. [1995]. *Total risk: Nick Leeson and the fall of Barings Bank*. New York: Harper Business.)

(3) Marketing/Advertising Minicase: (Case 7C) -
Dow Corning and Implants

Dow Corning was incorporated in Michigan in 1943 by Corning Glass Works and Dow Chemical Company. It is owned equally by these two major corporations. Dow Corning is principally engaged in the development, production, and sale of silicone and related products. Corporate offices and principal R&D facilities are in Midland, Michigan.

Although far smaller than its parents, Dow Corning was still of considerable size. Sales in 1990 were $1.7 billion, with a net income of $171 million. As of December 31, 1990, the company had approximately 8,000 employees. Although the company was a leading manufacturer of implants, this business represented less than 1% of the company's product line and had accumulated 5 years of financial losses. Robert Rylee, Dow Corning's health care general manager, said that the company had been staying in the implant business because the medical profession and millions of women had been counting on Dow.

At about the same time, John Swanson, Dow Corning's director of employee and management communications, did not share Rylee's sanguine assessment. He believed that his company had failed to prove that silicone breast implants were safe before selling them to surgeons for implantation in hundreds of thousands of women. He believed that the company had failed to follow up promptly on studies that showed that silicone might cause severe health problems. He concluded that the company had failed to fully apprise women of the known risks of its breast implants so that they could make genuinely informed decisions. In his view, the company had underestimated and downplayed the complication rates for breast implants and had subsequently tried to deny any wrongdoing. Swanson believed that some managers had tried to keep the facts about problems with the product not only from the public but also from the senior management of the company.

These were all violations of the corporate code of ethics that Swanson had spent most of his career at Dow Corning promoting. Dow Corning, thought Swanson, was failing to live up to its own rhetoric, its own professed standards of right and wrong. It was failing to exhibit process and developmental integrity. It even crossed Swanson's mind that growing media scrutiny of the implant crisis would undermine the career he envisioned for himself when his days at Dow Corning were over—as an advocate of strong corporate ethics programs. Who would take him seriously once the company he worked for was widely attacked for its failure to properly test a product destined to be put into the human body?

For months, he had been brooding over the decision to recuse himself from the breast implant decision (have nothing to do with it) although he had only a few years until retirement. It meant that the manager who had once helped promote the devices and even helped draft a defense of them for *Ms.*

magazine would refuse to discuss implants, create memos about them, or help the company defend itself against future criticism. He might lose his job, or worse, become a pariah in the community to which he had devoted the better part of his life. Midland, after all, was the silicone capital of the world and fully supported its hometown Fortune 500 company. But Swanson could no longer live with the secret that even as he worked as an executive at Dow Corning, his wife had been diagnosed as having silicone-related diseases. The fact that he had assured her at the onset that the implants were safe, on what he considered impeccable authority, added a grim edge to their ordeal.

Swanson had watched his wife's mystifying physical health decline for years, never considering that her implants could be the cause. At first, she had suffered dreadful migraine headaches, lower back problems, and numbness in both arms and hands. She would become so tired at the end of the day that she would climb into bed before dark. Then her breasts had become rock hard, and she felt a constant burning in her chest. In time, nearly unbearable pain began to sear through her left arm and hand, down into her ring and index fingers. It spread to her hips and neck. From time to time, periodic rashes would break out over her upper body, rendering her chest as red and shiny as a severe sunburn. Her illnesses, each growing into the next like an endless series of waves lapping a beach, extracted a devastating cost, eroding her energy and her life. At one point, her weight dwindled to 89 pounds. The once perky and attractive woman John Swanson had married was a mere shadow of herself. She finally endured the painful removal of the implants and would be disfigured for the rest of her life.

On September 18, 1991, Swanson, the guardian of Dow Corning's highly trusted organizational ethics program, went into recusal about the breast implant issue. Swanson never acted as a whistle blower and quietly retired from Dow Corning to live in Bloomington, Indiana, with his wife.

Within three months of his recusal, a California woman with Dow Corning implants, who suffered severe joint aches, muscle pain, fatigue, and weight loss, won a $7.3 million judgment against the company that would be upheld on appeal. In early January 1992, the FDA called for a 45-day moratorium on all sales of silicone breast implants. Damaging news reports—largely based on documents once sealed in numerous court cases—would charge that the company's safety studies had been inadequate and that serious questions raised by its own research and by doctors' complaints had not been answered. Finally, on April 16, 1992, the FDA determined that adequate data to demonstrate the safety and effectiveness of silicone breast implants did not exist and would ban their use. Thousands of women, including Swanson's wife, filed lawsuits against Dow Corning, leading the company to file for federal bankruptcy protection on May 15, 1995.

The controversy and crisis are likely to plague the company for many years. Questions are now being raised about the company's other silicone medical products, from jaw replacements to penile implants. Many observers believe that a $4.23 billion accord to settle most of the claims brought by implant victims against Dow Corning and other makers of silicone breast implants will collapse. Even though it is the largest product-liability settlement in history, a federal judge has found that Dow Corning is significantly underfunded to handle the 410,000 claims that have been filed by women with implants. Moreover, thousands of other women are still pursuing their own lawsuits against Dow Corning—a circumstance that forced the company to take a pretax write-off of $241 million in January 1995.

In effect, the lack of marketing control with integrity resulted in the loss of lives, disfigured women, a corporate bankruptcy, millions of dollars already paid out in lawsuits with continued legal exposure to future litigation, the loss of a hard-won corporate reputation for institutionalizing ethics, the ironic personal and family tragedy of the Swansons that gained international notoriety, and the loss of credibility of the marketing/advertising efforts for other silicone medical products.

This case demonstrates the need for comprehensive anchoring, building, and maintaining organization integrity on an ongoing basis. Organization integrity requires managing people and processes morally, internalizing the values embedded in a company's code of ethics so that stakeholder complaints are listened to, so that unknown risks are not displaced on others who lack informed consent, so that ethical judgments are made in tune with corporate values, so that the collective readiness to act ethically (the strength of corporate character that eschews betrayal of principles) is summoned by morally courageous leaders, and so that the actual conduct that demonstrates ethical performance occurs repeatedly. In the absence of demonstrated process, developmental, and judgment integrity, no amount of public relations, Harvard-based glamorization of showcase ethics programs, or legal maneuvering can compensate for the absence of the real thing—management and organization integrity in everyday decision making. (For more details, see Byrne, J. [1996]. *Informed consent: Inside the Dow Corning breast implant controversy.* New York: McGraw-Hill.)

(4) Business Management/Human Resources/Business Law Minicase: (Case 7D) - The Xieng Case and Accent Discrimination

The massive shifts in global population between 1975 and 2000 present major managerial challenges for the United States, Europe, and Japan (Petrick & Quinn, 1993). The infusion of immigrant resources, with their distinctive accents, into the mainstream of host country economic systems promises to heighten aggregate productivity while it simultaneously strains the communication tolerance levels of host nation peoples.

The issue of accent discrimination is one concrete instance of human resource discrimination based on national origin that will become increasingly important as global immigration patterns change. This type of prevalent discrimination is embedded in cultures and is often overlooked, until recently in the U.S. legal system. Accent discrimination by U.S. managers abroad was acceptable practice before the New Civil Rights Act of 1991, which extended the discrimination policies of Title VII of the Civil Rights Act of 1964 to all employees in U.S. corporations abroad. As a result of the legislation, U.S. corporations are formulating accent discrimination policies to ensure legal compliance.

Support for accent equality, however, is evident in the increasing international, not merely U.S., consensus for nondiscriminatory employment policies in the U.N. Declaration of Human Rights and the International Labor Office Tripartite Declaration (Bellace, 1991).

In U.S. law, Title VII states that discrimination against a person based on accent amounts to national origin discrimination. In particular, national origin discrimination includes discriminating against an individual because he or she shares the linguistic characteristics of a national origin group. The only time an employer may claim that an employee's accent is a legitimate reason for not hiring or promoting an employee is if that accent interferes materially with job performance.

A major issue in applying Title VII of the U.S. Civil Rights Act to accent discrimination cases is making the distinction between accents that potentially or actually inhibit job performance and those that are just different from socially accepted norms. Only the former are legally relevant to decisions in U.S. courts. The latter provide the moral challenges for U.S. and other global managers to recognize and overcome arbitrary biases that impede workplace productivity.

In dealing with accents, one must remember that not only must the sender of the spoken word be taken into consideration, but also the receiver. Communication is carried out between two or more people with a certain amount of noise involved in the communication channel. An accent may contribute to the noise in that channel, but prejudice on the part of the receiver can also interfere with transmission. The act of listening involves a tacit choice of message interpretations frequently based on socialized acceptance of positive or negative stereotypes. On the global scale, stereotypical communication in the form of accent discrimination plays out in regional preferences accorded individuals from the Northern Hemisphere over those from the Southern Hemisphere and those from Western Europe over those from Eastern Europe. Changing immigration patterns will invariably increase instances of accent discrimination based on national origin. For example, during the 1970s and 1980s, nine countries—Mexico, the Philippines, South Korea, Hong Kong, China, the Dominican Republic, Haiti, India, and Jamaica—provided 51% of the legal immigrants to the United States. Fewer immigrants are coming from Eastern and Western Europe than came in the 1800s and early 1900s. Today, 46% of new immigrants come from Asia and 37% come from Latin America, with Mexico representing the lead in immigration population to the United States. These numbers are in drastic contrast with those from the turn of the century, when nearly 100% of immigrants came from Europe to the United States.

The risk of differential accent discrimination exists in the United States and is reflected in the fact that the EEOC has not seen any cases of discrimination on the basis of accent involving Western European immigrants. This fact leads one to believe that there are major differences in the way people with different accents have been treated in the United States. It seems as though low-status accents are more likely to be interpreted as difficult to understand and indicative of incompetence, whereas high-status accents are more likely to be interpreted as easily understood and suggestive of competence (Petrick & Quinn, 1993).

Along with the different types of accents come the different classifications in which people can be placed. In the United States, someone with a British accent is stereotypically looked upon as being well educated and upper class. In contrast, someone with a Hispanic or Asian accent is looked upon warily as a possible illegal immigrant and/or as a member of a lower class.

Such was the human resource concern raised in *Xieng v. People's National Bank of Washington* in 1991, which paved the way for a new U.S. accent discrimination policy. The case involves Phanna Xieng, a Cambodian immigrant who came to the United States in 1972. He was very well educated, completing undergraduate and graduate studies in Cambodia, France, and the United States. He had held many positions that required a strong command of the English language since beginning work in the United States in 1976. In 1979, he began working for the People's National Bank of Washington as a vault and payroll teller. His career progressed, and in 1981 he was selected to participate in a management training program. Throughout the program, Xieng received positive performance appraisals, and although it was noted that his English communication skills were an area for future improvement, it was never suggested that his Cambodian accent interfered with his job performance. Several of his supervisors even recommended him for promotion.

Xieng filled in virtually full-time as a grade 11 credit authorizer but continued to be paid at the lower level of grade 9 coordinator. Despite his positive evaluations, Xieng was denied promotion for years, and he finally brought suit against the bank.

In addition to suffering emotional distress, Xieng had been successfully doing the job to which he felt he should have been promoted, and therefore it was rather obvious that he was being discriminated against by not getting the promotion. In this case, it was clear that his accent did not "interfere materially with his job performance" because he had already been completing the tasks of the job. Xieng eventually won the case, and the seeds of U.S. accent discrimination policy were laid in the U.S. courts.

In discriminating against a person on the basis of accent, U.S. managers are disregarding not only broader legal responsibilities but also moral and public policy responsibilities that endorse principles of utility, justice, liberty, and dignity. With regard to utility, immigrant people with "understandable" accents add to the GNP, pay taxes, and reduce unemployment costs. In Germany alone, it has been estimated that immigrant groups have significantly contributed to reunification efforts by adding 1.3% to gross domestic product (GDP) and $14 million in taxes and by reducing unemployment by 0.2%.

With regard to justice, contributory justice standards are violated because the most deserving are penalized by accent discrimination. In addition, unfair distribution of benefits and burdens forces those people with unacceptable accents to bear the burden of being unemployed more so than those people without accents.

With regard to liberty, discriminating against individuals with unacceptable accents also takes away their individual right to make a choice about the manner in which they are employed. If persons with an accent make a choice to pursue a career in a certain field and if they are discriminated against, they have been denied their freedom as U.S. citizens to make this kind of choice. In a capitalistic society, persons may choose how they want to make a living, but by discriminating against people because of accent, economic freedom is severely impaired.

Finally, in discriminating against people because of unacceptable accents, managers are denying them the fundamental respect for human dignity that is due everyone. Everyone should have the right to a certain amount of self-respect and self-esteem, and by denying persons employment because of their accents, individuals who are perfectly capable of doing the job may be denied the self-respect to which they are entitled. This point is illustrated in the *Xieng* case: Xieng was obviously capable of doing the job into which he should have been promoted, and with that he was entitled to a certain amount of dignity and self-respect in knowing that he could perform the job at the next level, but he was denied this opportunity because of his accent.

To address these serious legal and moral lapses, an internationally responsive U.S. accent discrimination policy is emerging. Its contours can be described in terms of the four processes necessary for routine implementation. First, when recruiting a person for U.S. employment, evaluating that person's ability to communicate effectively in English and also evaluating the level of communication required by the position should be mandatory. Different levels of unaccented fluency are materially relevant to job performance in various positions. Second, every job applicant, regardless of national origin, should be required to take an oral and written English test to assess the language proficiency of the person. If a person is able to satisfactorily pass one of the two sections of this test, and assuming that the person has all the other abilities needed to fulfill the requirements of the job, the person will be hired with the understanding that he or she must complete certified English language courses and within 1 year be able to attain the required score on the portion of the English test where deficiency was spotted. Because the level of communication required of each job varies, passing grades on the English test should also vary. Third, during the probationary year, the company should make reasonable accommodations; arrangements should be made to relieve the person of any duties that he or she cannot effectively complete because of the inability to communicate in English at an optimal level. Fourth, each position in a U.S. company should be evaluated on the basis of English language and host country language communication requirements. A rating will be assigned to each position by using a numerical scale of 1 to 10, with a rating of 1 meaning that communication in English or host country language is of very little importance in completing the tasks required of the job, and 10 meaning that effectively being able to communicate in English is of the utmost importance in being able to perform job duties.

In short, the lack of controlling accent discrimination with integrity results in the loss of competition-enhancing, company contributions from global human resource talent because of arbitrary decisions, unfair distribution of workplace benefits and burdens, the loss of employment options by materially competent people, and the loss of human dignity by socially induced humiliation. Although talented people may have an accent, they do not think in accents. (For more details, see Simons, G., Vazquez, C., & Harris, P. [1993]. *Transcultural leadership: Empowering the diverse workplace.* Houston: Gulf.)

(5) Technology/Quality Operations/Organizational Behavior Minicase: (Case 7E) - The A. H. Robins Company

The A. H. Robins Company, headquartered in Richmond, Virginia, was a relatively small company ($135 million in sales at the time), but it had subsidiaries in more than 12 foreign countries. It was best known for such products as Robitussin cough syrup, ChapStick lip balm, and Sergeant's Flea and Tick collars. It was no fly-by-night company; for more than a century, it had been a solid family business, exercising social responsibility in the community.

When a grandson, Edwin Claiborne Robins, took over management in 1933 with dreams of expanding, he stopped selling medicines directly to the public and turned instead to selling prescription drugs to physicians and pharmacists. The first such product was a stomach remedy, Donnatel, which is still a major product. After World War II, the company became a major manufacturer of mass-marketed prescription and nonprescription drugs. In 1963, with net sales of $47 million and profits near $5 million, the firm went public. In the process, E. Claiborne Robins, Sr., turned his family into one of the wealthiest in Virginia. In 1978, E. Claiborne Robins, Jr., became president and CEO.

Since 1965, the company had been interested in the birth-control market and particularly in intrauterine devices (IUDs), although it had never made or sold a medical device or gynecological product before and had no obstetrician or gynecologist on its staff. It had considered buying the rights for the Lippes Loop, but then the Dalkon Shield opportunity surfaced.

The potential for IUDs as a group seemed attractive, but perhaps the biggest plus for IUDs was that they did not require filing a New-Drug Application (NDA) with the FDA. Because the agency only had jurisdiction over drugs and not over medical devices (which was how IUDs were classified), a manufacturer did not have to file an NDA demonstrating that it had established relative safety with reliable and sufficient clinical and animal testing. Thus, lengthy research safety testing of the Dalkon Shield could be avoided. (On May 28, 1976, the Medical Device Amendments were enacted to bring medical devices under the supervision of the FDA, but these amendments came 5 years after the Dalkon Shield was first brought to market.)

Robins quickly made plans to bring the Shield to market, and its assembly was assigned to the ChapStick division. The company saw an urgent need to get into the market before potential competitors could rush in. In January 1971, only 6 months after Robins acquired the rights, the Dalkon Shield was ready for national distribution. The profitability potential was intriguing; the production cost was only about 25 cents, whereas the Shield was priced at $4.35. Although some quality control problems arose, they were deemed not to be particularly serious.

An aggressive marketing strategy was put in place. Several hundred salespeople were trained to contact physicians. The advertising itself was directed at both medical professionals—physicians as well as agencies and clinics that provided IUDs—and women directly, to persuade them to accept the Shield if their physicians should so recommend, and even to request and insist on the device if their physicians were skeptical. Consequently, in addition to medical journals, *Family Circle, Mademoiselle,* and similar magazines carried Dalkon Shield advertising.

Robins wanted to position the Shield as a superior product. In 1970, it was promoted as a modern, superior IUD, with the lowest pregnancy rate (1.1%), lowest expulsion rate (2.3%), and highest continuation rate (94%). Other promotional literature stated that it was the only IUD anatomically engineered for optimal uterine placement, fit, tolerance, and retention.

In the ads in major medical journals, Dr. Davis (the original researcher and coinventor) was shown as an impressive research physician, with citations from the articles he had published. Not disclosed was his financial interest in the product and the fact that he was hardly the objective and unbiased researcher deemed essential to sound medical research.

Between 1971 and 1975, Robins sold more than 4 million Dalkon Shield IUDs in 80 countries. In so doing, it ignored ever-increasing concerns of physicians and others about the Shield's effectiveness and safety. In the United States alone, more than 2 million women were fitted with the inadequately tested contraceptive device by doctors who believed the optimistic claims of the company. As a result, thousands of women suffered serious damage caused by the Shield—pelvic infection, sterility, miscarriage, and even death.

In December 1974, Alexander Schmidt, then commissioner of the FDA, announced that Robins could continue to market the Shield as long as accurate records were kept of all wearers.

Where the FDA failed, the judicial system took over. By March 1975, 186 suits had been filed against Robins. Also in March, the first judicial award was made: $10,000 compensatory and $75,000 punitive damages against Robins. In May, a $475,000 judgment was awarded to the estate of a woman who had died while using the Shield. In August 1975, Robins formally announced that it would not remarket the Shield, but it insisted that women who had had it inserted previously were in no danger.

Not until September 1980, 6 years after problems with the Shield had begun to surface, did Robins finally send a letter to 200,000 doctors, urging them to remove the device from all women who were still using it. The company stated that a "new" study showed that other problems, such as an infection called pelvic actinomycosis, were more likely the longer the device was worn. This move followed a $6.8 million judgment in Colorado in June 1980, in which $600,000 was awarded in compensatory damages and $6.2 million in punitive damages. The punitive award was of serious concern to the company because Robins's liability insurance covered only compensatory damages.

By 1980, 4,300 suits were pending against Robins. Some attorneys were spending their entire time suing Robins; this became so popular a cause that a newsletter was published covering IUD litigation, and 4-day yearly seminars were held so that more experienced lawyers could instruct on how best to sue Robins.

The company's 1981 annual report noted that 2,300 cases were still pending and that 4,200 had been settled. Up to now, the company and its insurer (Aetna) had paid out $98 million for Dalkon Shield litigation. Lawsuits continued to multiply, and they became increasingly expensive for the company to deal with. For example, the average settlement in 1976 was $8,000; in 1984, the average was in the $400,000 range.

In 1984, E. Claiborne Robins, Jr., company president and CEO, Carl Lunsford, Director of Research, and William Forrest, Jr., company general counsel, were all chastised by Judge Lord in federal district court because health and safety impacts of the Dalkon Shield reproductive technology were callously ignored to pursue profits.

In 1984, hounded by ever-mounting legal costs and judgments and running out of liability insurance coverage from Aetna, Robins took an extraordinary charge of $615 million as a reserve for claims. This resulted in a paper loss of $461.6 million in 1984. In August 1985, Robins filed Chapter 11 bankruptcy. Under Chapter 11 bankruptcy, all litigation against a company is stayed while the company and its creditors attempt to devise a plan to pay the bankrupt company's debts. E. Claiborne Robins, Jr., said the action was necessary to protect the company's economic survival against those who would destroy it for the benefit of the few. Attorneys for the victims found this action to be fraudulent and in bad faith, an attempt by Robins to escape responsibility for the thousands of injuries the Shield had caused.

The legal strategy to file bankruptcy switched the interactional context, language, and blame from one of legal tortfeasance and victims to one of economic debtors and creditors. In the former arena, Robins was held legally responsible for its tortuous conduct in terms of compensatory damages and punitive awards. In the latter arena, Robins was accorded a "fresh start" as a debtor to pay off creditors and avoid future insolvency. The goal of the bankruptcy interactions was not retributive justice (blame and penalty proportionate to harm done), but distributive justice (speedy settlement to pay as many creditor litigants as soon as possible). The switched venues jeopardized the foundations of managerial and organizational moral responsibility for killing and maiming women and provided a convenient tactic to recoil into a legal den of corporate immunity—absolved of full moral and legal responsibility for tortuous misconduct.

A lively bidding war developed for the troubled Robins Company in bankruptcy court. On January 20, 1988, the bid by American Home Products (AHP) was accepted. John Stafford, chairman and CEO of AHP, was interested in Robins because of the tax advantages and the acquisition of two popular consumer brands: Robitussin and Dimetapp. AHP could deduct its funding of Dalkon Shield liabilities from federal taxes.

In effect, the lack of quality technology and organizational behavior control with integrity resulted in lost lives and lacerated uteruses in thousands of women, public fraud and coverups of suspect technological research data necessary for informed consent, forced intervention of government, jail sentences for family and corporate executives with large attached fines, the destruction of an entire company and its reputable tradition, the reprehensible exporting of Dalkon Shields to developing countries, and the contraction of the IUD/contraception industry in the United States. (For more details, see Mintz, M. [1995]. *At any cost: Corporate greed, women, and the Dalkon Shield.* New York: Pantheon.)

(6) Public/Nonprofit/Health Care Administration Minicase:
(Case 7F) - The Housing and Urban Development (HUD) Scandal

The U.S. Secretary of Housing and Urban Development (HUD) for two terms during the 1980s was Samuel Pierce. Ultimately, his shameful dereliction of the public manager's duty to control resources led to his resignation and indictment. A congressional panel concluded, after 14 months of investigation, that widespread fraud and political abuse, influence peddling, blatant favoritism, monumental waste, and gross absence of managerial control were rampant at HUD (Welfeld, 1992).

The tone of cabinet-level administrative control of HUD resources was set by Pierce's managerial attitude of getting-ahead-by-going-along-with Republican and crony interests. It was reported that having lived with racial prejudice left Pierce with a firm political conviction that, for a black man to get ahead, he had to play by upper-class, white man's rules. This is what Pierce did by displaying a majestic disinterest in hands-on managerial control (which by disposition and political ideology mirrored the Reagan era); he failed to keep informed about key HUD program/progress details and was woefully lax in exercising control over HUD subordinates.

Although several HUD programs and personnel were harshly criticized in the Lantos congressional hearings, the inept handling of the Coinsurance Program was typical of HUD mismanagement. In May 1983, HUD began the Section 223f Coinsurance Program. Legislation authorizing coinsurance was enacted in 1974 and became Section 244 of the National Housing Act. Congress, in the same legislation, also enacted a new paragraph (f) under Section 223 (Miscellaneous Housing Provisions), which authorized the HUD Secretary to provide mortgage insurance for the purchase and/or refinancing of existing buildings. HUD's role in multifamily housing was to ensure the maintenance of the existing unsubsidized stock of residential real estate. Not having a staff to run even a small multifamily insurance program, HUD put its limited resources into coinsurance. It was a convenient fit: real businesspersons who did not rely on the crumbs of subsidy and faster processing, fewer federal employees, and less red tape.

HUD appeared to be protected on paper. The coinsurer would be responsible for the first 5% of the loss. The Federal Housing Authority (FHA) would pay for 85% of the balance of the loss, and the private lender would be responsible for the remainder. With this risk, the private lender was granted a great deal of power; the lender was to perform all loan underwriting functions, monitor property management agents, handle any foreclosures, and determine disposition of all real estate projects. After the acquired property was sold, the lender could apply to HUD for payment of HUD's share of the loss. The loss was the difference between the sales price and the unpaid mortgage plus costs of foreclosure, accrued interest, and maintenance of the property.

For their efforts, HUD permitted the private lenders to collect from the borrowers up-front fees that could be included in the loan. These included an application fee of 0.3%, a financing fee of 2%, and a placement fee of 1.5%. The lender also received 0.35% from the HUD initial mortgage insurance premium. Thus, at the initiation of the loan, the fees totalled 4.15%. In addition, the private lender received a 0.10% premium from the annual renewal of mortgage insurance premium plus an annual loan servicing fee of 0.25%. If securities were issued, backed by the coinsured loans and guaranteed by the Government National Mortgage Association (GNMA), the lender received another 0.07%. The fees alone made this a profitable venture with minimal downside risk as a government-backed financial instrument.

By mid-1988, 5 years after the Coinsurance Program was inaugurated, participating lenders had coinsured 846 loans. The amount of the mortgages totaled $4.8 billion.

By late 1988, however, led by the highest-flying firm in the business, DRG, under the direction of its CEO, Donnie DeFranceaux (Donnie De), the program became an unregulated disaster: 106 loans, having an outstanding principal and accrued interest amount of over $700 million, went into default. The largest coinsurer in the program, DRG, which had 272 coinsured mortgages, contributed 79 defaults and a $500 million in losses. The program was in a free fall descent: 65 of DRG defaults had occurred in late 1988. By March 1990, the dollar volume of defaults had reached $1.6 billion and HUD was furiously trying to shut the program down to limit its coinsurance liabilities.

Donnie De hired the former Republican HUD Secretary Carla Hills, and Lynda Murphy, a close friend of Debbie Dean, Pierce's powerful executive assistant (some even claimed she was the de facto boss of HUD) to protect DRG from immediate investigation. In fact, although DRG was chastised in a letter for failure to get HUD approval of its loan processors, inadequate review of borrower financial statements, inflated income projections, underestimated expenses, and overvalued properties, it was officially absolved of major default liability and did not even have to submit loans to HUD before it insured future mortgages.

Eventually, because DRG was an issuer of GNMA mortgage-backed securities, it was required to pass on the sales proceeds from the coinsured projects to the holders of those securities. Because DRG could not do so because of cashflow problems, GNMA took control of the entire portfolio of coinsured loans. After careful auditing, it was disclosed that two thirds of the 214 co-insured DRG loans were in default by 1989, totalling over $709 million, an amount that needed to be absorbed at taxpayers' expense.

A number of public managerial control lapses were present in this fiasco. First, the lenders in the multifamily coinsurance business were thinly capitalized (as low as $1 of capital for every $40 of loans). They were in the business for the fees, rather than for the interest payments, and 98% of the loans were pooled and sold to GNMA. Because the "profitability" of the lender increased with the size of the loan, overmortgaging was rampant and uncontrolled.

Second, it was a borrower's dream come true. Lenders were competing for consumers, and the one with the most liberal appraisers and optimistic underwriters (many former HUD employees) made the loans. Borrowers, by mortgaging out of existing buildings, could make money without concern about occupancy of the buildings. The coinsurers were essentially in the same position as savings and loan institutions. GNMA's guarantee of the securities that were backed by coinsured loans was the equivalent of federal deposit insurance. GNMA agreed to guarantee full payment (and FHA agreed to indemnify it against any loss from the coinsurer's failure to pay its share). This gave coinsurers a huge source of funds, with most risk displaced onto the taxpayers.

Third, purchasers of government coinsured mortgages were willing to buy the government securities regardless of the quality of the loans, in the same manner as insured depositors in savings and loans could disregard the quality of a particular bank's portfolio. It was the "full faith and credit of the United

States" on which the reliance was being placed, and it was the government, and ultimately each taxpayer, that was left holding the bag.

In effect, the lack of public managerial control with integrity resulted in the loss of hundreds of millions of taxpayer dollars, severe erosion of public confidence in government fiduciary control of housing, ruined careers, and the betrayal of public trust in its democratically elected and appointed leaders. (For more details, see Welfeld, I. [1992]. *The HUD scandal: Howling headlines and silent fiasco.* New York: Transaction.)

(7) International/Environmental/Public Policy Minicase:
    (Case 7G) - Komineft and the CIS Oil Spill

On December 8, 1991, reflecting the collapse of socialism and the increased sovereignty of the republics, the Union of Soviet Socialist Republics (USSR) became the Commonwealth of Independent States (CIS). The CIS is approximately 34,000 miles long and borders 13 countries: North Korea, China, Mongolia, Afghanistan, Iran, Turkey, Romania, Hungary, Slovakia, the Czech Republic, Poland, Finland, and Norway. The Bering Strait separates the CIS from the United States. Water resources of the CIS are both scarce and abundant; with approximately 3 million rivers and 4 million inland bodies of water, the CIS holds the largest fresh, surface water resources of any country. Unfortunately, more than 80% of the water flows through sparsely populated areas and into the Arctic and Pacific Oceans.

The CIS has abundant supplies of nearly every major type of natural resource. It has become the world leader in the production of oil, iron ore, manganese, and asbestos. The CIS has the world's largest proven reserves of natural gas, and in 1984 it surpassed the United States in the production of this increasingly important fuel. It has enormous coal reserves and is the world's second-largest producer. The CIS has developed its huge and widely dispersed resource base with the motivation to become self-sufficient. It remains a source of pride that the CIS, alone among the industrialized countries of the world, can satisfy almost all the requirements of its economy for decades by using its own natural resources. Large amounts of oil products are used in the CIS for electric power, agriculture, transportation, and export. The abundance of fossil fuels not only supplies the domestic needs of the CIS but also allows for surplus supplies to be exported to consumers in Eastern and Western Europe. Most of the convertible currency of the CIS is earned from these exports, and the currency finances the purchase of critical import commodities.

The increased distance from oil wells to consumers has grown to be a major concern for the oil industry. Pipelines link the oil fields with the refineries, and the refineries are linked to main user areas or export outlets (e.g., ports). Over 90% of oil is transported by pipeline. The oil pipeline system doubled in length between 1970 and 1983, reaching close to 127,000 miles. Before 1960, the system was composed of 25,000 miles of pipeline. As oil production leveled off in the 1980s, so did pipeline construction. By 1986, the pipeline system measured almost 136,000 miles. In 1986, almost 653 million tons of crude oil and refined petroleum products were transported through the network of pipelines.

The CIS has more than 100,000 miles of gas and oil pipelines, many of them poorly maintained and in a deteriorating condition. Each year, up to 20% of the total oil production of the CIS is lost either to theft or to leakage. The number of accidents involving oil pipelines that resulted in oil discharges increased from 1990 to 1991. About 2,000 accidental discharges of pollutants were reported in 1992, causing damage estimated to cost 3 billion rubles. According to the national environmental report for 1992, annual social and economic damage from industrial accidents in the CIS cost between 15 and 19 million rubles. In 1991, there were 280 reported cases of environmental pollution by oil products. According to officials, 15% of the country's territory, containing 20% of the total population, qualified as environmental disaster zones.

The Komi Autonomous Republic (Komi), Maine's Soviet sister state and five times its size, is a 90-minute flight northeast of Moscow, crossing the Arctic Circle at the north. It boasts Europe's largest paper mill and is named after the indigenous Komi people, who are now a minority on their own soil. Komi is located in the tundra zone, where less than 1% of the CIS population lives. The long, harsh winters and the lack of sunshine allow only mosses, lichens, dwarf willows, and shrubs to grow. Although the great Siberian rivers flow slowly through this zone to the Arctic Ocean, drainage of the numerous lakes, ponds, and swamps is hampered by partial and intermittent thawing. Frost weathering is the most important physical process in this area. Fishing and port industries of the Kola Peninsula, the paper industries, and the huge oil and gas fields of northwestern Siberia are the largest employers in the tundra zone. The prolonged periods of cold weather have a profound effect on almost every aspect of life in the CIS, and energy demands multiply with the extended periods of darkness and cold.

Komi appeared in international news in 1994, when the CIS revealed a major oil spill in the Komi Republic. This major oil spill, about 40% of the size of the *Exxon Valdez* spill, poured from a ruptured 26-inch diameter pipeline. The 31-mile pipeline, made of mild steel with no protective coating, was built in 1975 to move oil from a Komi field to a terminal at Usinsk, a city 30 miles south. The pipeline had been poorly maintained and in need of major repairs or replacement since at least 1988, when the first leaks appeared. The owners of the pipeline are the Russian Oil Company, Komineft, and two financial partners, Gulf Canada Resources and British Gas. More than 17,000 barrels per day flow through the pipeline from the Komi fields south to the refineries in Moscow. Komineft is reportedly one of the most consistent offenders of oil leaks in the CIS. The oil magazine, *Nefte Compass*, alleges that the Komineft pipelines have averaged about 10 leaks every month during the past 6 years.

The neglect of the oil pipelines by Komineft's management has had a devastating effect on Komi's environment. The inhabitants of Komi, human and nonhuman alike, are suffering from the effects of the oil spill. The land from which humans and nonhumans gain their nourishment and the rivers and streams from which they drink and fish have all been contaminated by the oil spill.

Rather than stop the flow of oil and income, however, the Russian oil company Komineft has continued to pump oil after the leaks in the pipeline were discovered. The government never told the company to shut down production when the leaks began, nor were shipments stopped. The CIS Government Emergency Situations Commission (GESC) estimated the Komi spill to be the biggest oil pipeline spill in Russia's history.

The first environmental law in the history of the former Soviet Union, "On Environmental Protection," was signed by Boris Yeltsin in December 1991. The CIS government has declared a commitment to restoring the country's environment. The issue has gained ministry rank with the newly established Ministry for the Environment and the Rational Use of Natural Resources. Unfortunately, the new ministry must still depend on the Ministry of Hydrology and Meteorology. Because of this, it must compromise with powerful energy and resource ministries on many pollution issues. In 1993, Environment Minister Viktor Danilov-Danilyan announced a new government cleanup initiative aimed at a range of environmental problems. The budget established for this initiative, however, was extremely low. The large federal deficit in the CIS has led to an even more severe conflict between environmental goals and economic growth. According to some estimates, the environmental damage in the early 1990s was between 15% and 17% of the GDP. Only 1.3% of the GDP was allocated to environmental protection.

Since 1991, laws have been upgraded, and new concepts such as licensing, charging for resource usage, and fines for pollution have been introduced. Some of the additional money generated from these initiatives is used for environmental cleanup efforts. Marxist doctrine, however, previously accorded oil no inherent value except for the labor used to transform it. Therefore, oil had been virtually free for domestic users. Other significant changes have included the shift to decentralized environmental management, environmental impact assessments of industrial projects, and the introduction of litigation procedures for environmental damage. Although much action has taken place to reform environmental law, the country is still governed by the old Constitution, adopted by the former Russian Soviet Federative Socialist Republic. Many amendments have been made, but many contradictions exist, and it is still inadequate to address the current needs of the CIS.

In the absence of strong, just background institutions in the CIS, it is politically difficult to support Komi and control the unsustainable development policies of Komineft. It is evident that Komineft did not engage in preliminary control by assessing the anticipated human and nonhuman risks associated with the potential environmental hazards of its oil pipeline operations. Responsible risk assessment involves four steps:

1. Hazard identification, which includes information about comparisons of molecular structures, short-term studies, animal bioassay data, and epidemiological studies.
2. Dose-response assessment, which determines the response of humans to various levels of exposure, typically encompassing assessments of animal studies.
3. Exposure assessment, which includes the determination of which populations would be exposed to the substance(s) and the dosages that would lead to acute or chronic conditions.
4. Risk characterization is the final step involving the severity judgments of qualified assessors.

Although Komineft did not conduct these responsible risk-assessment activities, it is imperative that it now engage itself in risk-management efforts with strong local, state, and federal government support.

The Russian government has fined Komineft 62 billion rubles (U.S. $20.2 million). The amount of the fine was calculated on the basis of an accidental spill of 14,000 tons of oil, which is Komineft's estimate. Komineft agreed to pay the fine in October 1994. Although this fine is appropriate by CIS standards, it is only a token for the environmental devastation caused by Komineft's lack of managerial control. The massive oil spill in Komi because of the managerial incompetence at Komineft and the lack of just background institutions in the CIS are casting Russia into the role of the national global example of how not to live.

In effect, the lack of organizational and governmental environmental control with integrity resulted in regional ecocide on such a scale of contamination as to serve as an ecological threat to the entire planet; loss of lives, health, safety, and property value for an entire region and the Barents Sea; token fines that demonstrate the weak infrastructural support for sustainable development; and the absence of effective preliminary, concurrent, rework, and damage controls at all levels. (For more details, see Feshback, M., & Friendly, A., Jr. [1992]. *Ecocide in the USSR: Health and nature under siege*. New York: Basic Books.)

SUMMARY

In summary, this chapter covers the multiple dimensions of the function of controlling for managers and the four ethical controlling subprocesses that build management integrity. In addition, seven management ethics and controlling with integrity minicases were presented. By addressing the moral issues embedded in controlling ethically and applying the theories and tools from the first part of the book to the structured analysis and principled resolution of control minicases, sharpened skills in ethical controlling can enhance management integrity.

▧ DISCUSSION/EXPERIENTIAL EXERCISES

Discussion Questions

1. Discuss the nature of managerial controlling and culpably negligent controlling as they relate to private and public sector managers.
2. Discuss the differences between traditional and TQ controlling and, using the Controlling Success Evaluation Matrix (Figure 7.4), provide life/work/school examples from each quadrant.
3. Discuss the parallel alignment of the four key ethics processes and controlling subprocesses that build integrity, providing an example of managerial controlling for each step.
4. Using the tools and resources from the first part of the book, examine the controlling with integrity minicase in your major field or field of concentration.

Experiential Exercises

5. In a group setting, using the tools and resources from the first part of the book, examine two controlling with integrity minicases outside your major field or field of concentration.
6. From your own life/work/school experiences, discuss times when controlling occurred without integrity, identifying specific adverse impacts that resulted when one or more of the ethical controlling steps was omitted or inadequately completed, and how you could have (in the past) or will (in the future) control with integrity to prevent a recurrence of the problem.

Management Style Assessment (MSA)

PURPOSE: The purpose of this self-assessment instrument is to determine your current preferred management style.

DIRECTIONS: Listed below are some statements that describe managerial practices. Indicate how often you engage in, or would engage in, the following conduct. Anchor your point of reference to one work or nonwork setting throughout the exercise and use the scale below to respond to each statement. Place a number from 1 to 7 in the space beside each question.

Almost never   1   2   3   4   5   6   7   Almost always

A: ASSESSMENT INSTRUMENT
   (As a manager, how often would you . . .)

_____   1. Come up with inventive ideas.

_____   2. Exert upward influence in the organization.

_____   3. Ignore the need to achieve unit goals.

_____   4. Continually clarify the unit's purpose.

_____   5. Search for innovations and potential improvements.

_____   6. Make the unit's role very clear.

_____ 7. Maintain tight logistical control.

_____ 8. Keep track of what goes on inside the unit.

_____ 9. Develop consensual resolution of openly expressed differences.

_____ 10. Listen to the personal problems of subordinates.

_____ 11. Maintain a highly coordinated, well-organized unit.

_____ 12. Hold open discussion of conflicting opinions in groups.

_____ 13. Push the unit to meet objectives.

_____ 14. Surface key differences among group members and then work participatively to resolve them.

_____ 15. Monitor compliance with the rules.

_____ 16. Treat each individual in a sensitive, caring way.

_____ 17. Experiment with new concepts and procedures.

_____ 18. Show empathy and concern in dealing with subordinates.

_____ 19. Seek to improve the work group's technical capacity.

_____ 20. Get access to people at higher levels.

_____ 21. Encourage participative decision making in the group.

_____ 22. Compare records, reports, and so on to detect discrepancies.

_____ 23. Solve scheduling problems in the unit.

_____ 24. Get the unit to meet expected goals.

_____ 25. Do problem solving in creative, clear ways.

_____ 26. Anticipate workflow problems to avoid crisis.

_____ 27. Check for errors and mistakes.

_____ 28. Persuasively sell new ideas to higher-ups.

_____ 29. See that the unit delivers on stated goals.

_____ 30. Facilitate consensus building in the work unit.

_____ 31. Clarify the unit's priorities and direction.

_____ 32. Show concern for the needs of subordinates.

_____ 33. Maintain a "results" orientation in the unit.

_____ 34. Influence decisions made at higher levels.

_____ 35. Regularly clarify the objectives of the unit.

_____ 36. Bring a sense of order and coordination into the unit.

B: INSTRUMENT SCORING PROCEDURES

Step 1: Compute Managerial Role Competency Scores: (a) Place the evaluation numbers (1-7) that you inserted in front of each statement in their corresponding statement numbers below—for example, if you rated Question 1 a 5, then go to the Innovator subsection below, where #1 is listed, and place a 5 in the blank space next to #1; (b) Total the scores for each role competency and divide the total by the designated figure (4 or 5) to arrive at the average role competency score.

The Facilitator	The Mentor
#9_____	#10_____
#12_____	#16_____
#14_____	#18_____
#21_____	#32_____
#30_____	
Total_____ / 5 = _____	Total_____ / 4 = _____

The Innovator	The Broker
#1_____	#2_____
#5_____	#20_____
#17_____	#28_____
#25_____	#34_____
Total_____ / 4 = _____	Total_____ / 4 = _____

The Producer	The Director
#3_____ (Reverse)	#4_____
#13_____	#6_____
#19_____	#24_____
#29_____	#31_____
#33_____	#35_____
Total_____ / 5 = _____	Total_____ / 5 = _____

The Coordinator	The Monitor
#7_____	#8_____
#11_____	#15_____
#23_____	#22_____
#26_____	#27_____
#36_____	
Total_____ / 5 = _____	Total_____ / 4 = _____

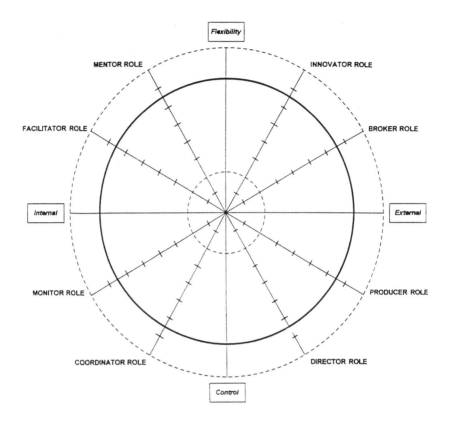

Figure A.1. Management Style Profile

Step 2: Plot Management Style Profile: (a) Using the average role competency score, plot (place a dot on) the corresponding managerial role spoke in Figure A.1; (b) Continue the previous step for all eight roles, using the bull's-eye point within the three circles as point zero, connect all eight dots to produce a graphic profile of your management style, and shade in the area.

C: INTERPRETATION OF RESULTS

Step 1: The shaded area of your management style profile depicts the current range of your self-perceived role competence. The quadrant that contains the longest connecting lines, and thereby the largest shaded area, indicates your primary managerial strength, on which you can rely and capitalize.

Step 2: The quadrant that contains the shortest connecting lines, and therefore the smallest shaded area, indicates your primary managerial weakness, which may need priority attention to achieve well-rounded managerial competence.

Step 3: Areas outside the shaded profile but within the outer limit of the second circle provide opportunities for managerial competency development in all four quadrants, so that the balanced profile of the master manager can be approximated. Shaded quadrant areas within the first and third circle outer limits indicate managerial role under- and overdevelopment, respectively.

SOURCE: DiPadova, L. (1990). *Instructor's manual to becoming a master manager.* New York: John Wiley. Modified by the authors with permission.

Caux Round Table Principles for Business

Caux Round Table principles are rooted in two basic ethical ideals: *kyosei* and human dignity. The Japanese concept of *kyosei* means living and working together for the common good—enabling cooperation and mutual prosperity to coexist with healthy and fair competition. *Human dignity* refers to the sacredness or value of each person as an end, not simply as a means to the fulfillment of other's purposes or even majority prescription.

The General Principles in Section 2 seek to clarify the spirit of *kyosei* and *human dignity;* the specific Stakeholder Principles in Section 3 are concerned with their practical application.

Section 1. Preamble

The mobility of employment, capital, products, and technology is making business increasingly global in its transactions and its effects.

Laws and market forces are necessary but insufficient guides for conduct.

Responsibility for the policies and actions of business and respect for the dignity and interests of its stakeholders are fundamental.

Shared values, including a commitment to shared prosperity, are as important for a global community as for communities of smaller scale.

For these reasons and because business can be a powerful agent of positive social change, we offer the following principles as a foundation for dialogue and action by by business leaders in search of business responsibility. In so doing, we affirm the necessity for moral values in business decision making. Without them, stable business relationships and a sustainable world community are impossible.

Section 2. General Principles

Principle 1. The Responsibilities of Businesses:
Beyond Shareholders Toward Stakeholders

The value of a business to society is the wealth and employment it creates and the marketable products and services it provides to consumers at a reasonable price commensurate with quality. To create such value, a business must maintain its own economic health and viability, but survival is not a sufficient goal.

Businesses have a role to play in improving the lives of all their customers, employees, and shareholders by sharing with them the wealth they have created. Suppliers and competitors as well should expect businesses to honor their obligations in a spirit of honesty and fairness. As responsible citizens of the local, national, regional, and global communities in which they operate, businesses share a part in shaping the future of those communities.

Principle 2. The Economic and Social Impact of Businesses:
Toward Innovation, Justice, and World Community

Businesses established in foreign countries to develop, produce, or sell should also contribute to the social advancement of those countries by creating productive employment and by helping to raise the purchasing power of their citizens. Businesses should also contribute to human rights, education, welfare, and vitalization of the countries in which they operate.

Businesses should contribute to economic and social development not only in the countries in which they operate but also in the world community at large, through effective and prudent use of resources, free and fair competition, and emphasis on innovation in technology, production methods, marketing, and communications.

Principle 3. Business Behavior: Beyond the Letter of
the Law Toward a Spirit of Trust

While accepting the legitimacy of trade secrets, businesses should recognize that sincerity, candor, truthfulness, the keeping of promises, and transparency contribute not only to their own credibility and stability but also to the smoothness and efficiency of business transactions, particularly on the international level.

Principle 4. Respect for Rules

To avoid trade frictions and to promote freer trade, equal conditions for competition, and fair and equitable treatment for all participants, businesses should respect international and domestic rules. In addition, they should recognize that some behavior, though legal, may still have adverse consequences.

Principle 5. Support for Multilateral Trade

Businesses should support the multilateral trade systems of the GATT World Trade Organization and similar international agreements. They should cooperate in efforts to promote the progressive and judicious liberalization of trade, and to relax those domestic measures that unreasonably hinder global commerce, while giving due respect to national policy objectives.

Principle 6. Respect for the Environment

Businesses should protect and, where possible, improve the environment, promote sustainable development, and prevent the wasteful use of natural resources.

Principle 7. Avoidance of Illicit Operations

Businesses should not participate in or condone bribery, money laundering, or other corrupt practices: indeed, they should seek cooperation with others to eliminate these practices. They should not trade in arms or other materials used for terrorist activities, drug traffic, or other organized crime.

Section 3. Stakeholder Principles

Customers

We believe in treating all customers with dignity, irrespective of whether they purchase our products and services directly from us or otherwise acquire them in the market. We therefore have a responsibility to:

- provide our customers with the highest-quality products and services consistent with their requirements
- treat our customers fairly in all aspects of our business transactions, including a high level of service and remedies for their dissatisfaction
- make every effort to ensure that the health and safety of our customers, as well as the quality of their environment, will be sustained or enhanced by our products and services

- ensure respect for human dignity in products offered, marketing, and advertising
- respect the integrity of the culture of our customers

Employees

We believe in the dignity of every employee and in taking employee interest seriously. We therefore have a responsibility to:

- provide jobs and compensation that improve workers' living conditions
- provide working conditions that respect each employee's health and dignity
- be honest in communications with employees and open in sharing information, limited only by legal and competitive restraints
- listen to and, where possible, act on employee suggestions, ideas, requests, and complaints
- engage in good-faith negotiations when conflict arises
- avoid discriminatory practices and guarantee equal treatment and opportunity in areas such as gender, age, race, and religion
- promote in the business itself the employment of differently abled people in places of work where they can be genuinely useful
- protect employees from avoidable injury and illness in the workplace
- encourage and assist employees in developing relevant and transferable skills and knowledge
- be sensitive to serious unemployment problems frequently associated with business decisions, and work with governments, employee groups, other agencies, and each other in addressing these dislocations

Owners/Investors

We believe in honoring the trust that our investors place in us. We therefore have a responsibility to:

- apply professional and diligent management to secure a fair and competitive return on our owners' investment
- disclose relevant information to owners/investors subject only to legal requirements and competitive constraints
- conserve, protect, and increase the owners'/investors' assets
- respect owners'/investors' requests, suggestions, complaints, and formal resolutions

Suppliers

Our relationship with suppliers must be based on mutual respect. We therefore have a responsibility to:

- seek fairness and truthfulness in all our activities, including pricing, licensing, and rights to sell
- ensure that our business activities are free from coercion and unnecessary litigation
- foster long-term stability in the supplier relationship in return for value, quality, competitiveness, and reliability
- share information with suppliers and integrate them into our planning processes
- pay suppliers on time and in accordance with agreed terms of trade
- seek, encourage, and prefer suppliers and subcontractors whose employment practices respect human dignity

Competitors

We believe that fair economic competition is one of the basic requirements for increasing the wealth of nations and, ultimately, for making possible the just distribution of goods and services. We therefore have a responsibility to:

- foster open markets for trade and investment
- promote competitive behavior that is socially and environmentally beneficial and that demonstrates mutual respect among competitors
- refrain from either seeking or participating in questionable payments or favors to secure competitive advantages
- respect both tangible and intellectual property rights
- refuse to acquire commercial information by dishonest or unethical means, such as industrial espionage

Communities

We believe that, as global corporate citizens, we can contribute to such forces of reform and human rights as are at work in the communities in which we operate. We therefore have a responsibility in those communities to:

- respect human rights and democratic institutions and promote them wherever practicable

- recognize government's legitimate obligation to society at large and support public policies and practices that promote human development through harmonious relations between business and other segments of society
- collaborate with those forces in the community dedicated to raising standards of health, education, workplace safety, and economic well-being
- promote and stimulate sustainable development and play a leading role in preserving and enhancing the physical environment and conserving the earth's resources
- support peace, security, diversity, and social integration
- respect the integrity of local cultures
- be a good corporate citizen through charitable donations, educational and cultural contributions, and employee participation in community and civic affairs.

A Business Charter for
Sustainable Development

INTRODUCTORY PREAMBLE: To become ecologically sustainable, managers and organizations must begin with some acceptable principles for sustainable action. In April 1991, 700 industrialists met at the Second World Industry Conference on Environmental Management. They adopted a set of 16 principles as guidelines for creating sustainable corporations. Since then, top managements of several hundred companies, government organizations, and industry associations have endorsed these principles.

1. *Corporate Priority:* To recognize environmental management as among the highest corporate priorities and as a key determinant to sustainable development; to establish policies, programs, and practices for conducting operations in an environmentally sustainable manner.

2. *Integrated Management:* To integrate these policies, programs, and practices fully into each business as an essential element of management in all its functions.

3. *Process of Improvement:* To continue to improve corporate policies, programs, and environmental performance, taking into account technological developments, scientific understanding, consumer needs, and community expectations, with legal regulations as a starting point; and to apply the same environmental criteria internationally.

4. *Employee Education:* To educate, train, and motivate employees to conduct their activities in an environmentally responsible manner.

5. *Prior Assessment:* To assess environmental impacts before starting a new activity or project and before decommissioning a facility or leaving a site.

6. *Products and Services:* To develop and provide products or services that have no undue environmental impacts and are safe in their intended use, that are efficient in their consumption of energy and natural resources, and that can be recycled, reused, or disposed of safely.

7. *Customer Advice:* To advise, and where relevant, educate customers, distributors, and the public in the safe use, transportation, storage, and disposal of products provided; and to apply similar considerations to the provision of services.

8. *Facilities and Operations:* To develop, design, and operate facilities and conduct activities, taking into consideration the efficient use of energy and materials, the sustainable use of renewable resources, the minimization of adverse environmental impact and waste generation, and the safe and responsible disposal of residual waste.

9. *Research:* To conduct or support research on environmental impacts of raw materials, products, processes, emissions, and wastes associated with the enterprise and on the means of minimizing such adverse impacts.

10. *Precautionary Approach:* To modify the manufacture, marketing, or use of products or services or the conduct of activities, consistent with scientific and technical understanding, to prevent serious and irreversible environmental degradation.

11. *Contractors and Suppliers:* To promote the adoption of these principles by contractors acting on behalf of the enterprise, encouraging and, where appropriate, requiring improvements in their practices to make them consistent with those of the enterprise; and to encourage wider adoption of these principles by suppliers.

12. *Emergency Preparedness:* To develop and maintain, where significant hazards exist, emergency preparedness plans in conjunction with the emergency services, relevant authorities, and the local community, recognizing potential boundary impacts.

13. *Transfer of Technology:* To contribute to the transfer of environmentally sound technology and management methods throughout the industrial and public sectors.

14. *Contributing to the Common Effort:* To contribute to the development of public policy and to business, government, and intergovernmental programs and educational initiatives that will enhance environmental awareness and protection.

15. *Openness to Concerns:* To foster openness and dialogue with employees and the public, anticipating and responding to their concerns about the potential hazards and impacts of operations, products, wastes, or services, including those of transboundary or global significance.

16. *Compliance and Reporting:* To measure environmental performance; to conduct regular environmental audits and assessments of compliance with company requirements, legal requirements, and these principles; and periodically to provide appropriate information to the board of directors, shareholders, employees, the authorities, and the public.

Qualitative Ethical Decision-Making Tool (QL-TOOL)

PURPOSE: The purpose of the QL-TOOL is to provide a comprehensive, sequentially structured, qualitative framework to responsibly analyze and resolve moral issues and promote management integrity.

INSTRUCTIONS: The QL-TOOL consists of 10 key clusters of ethical decision-making questions and incorporates the dimensions of integrity and the ethics dialogue process from initial to enacted moral proposals. Compare written responses to each of the questions and/or use them as a discussion framework for ethics dialogue. Each of the bracketed concepts refers to steps in the ethics dialogue process.

Numeric weights on a scale of 1 to 10 can be applied to each of the 10 key clusters of questions. For example, after each question, two columns can be created, one representing the current situation and one the desired situation. The current situation column is to be weighted with numbers on a scale of 1 to 10, 10 usually meaning the respondent regards this element as *currently* the most relevant, fully implemented, and/or most important contribution to building personal and organizational ethical integrity; that is, the respondent should ask him- or herself with regard to each factor, "How much *does* this element, in fact, exist to contribute to personal and organizational integrity?" The desired future column is weighted in a similar 1 to 10 manner, 10 usually meaning the respondent regards this element as one that *should be* the most relevant, fully implemented, and/or most important contribution; that is, the respondent should ask him- or herself with regard to each factor, "How much *should* this element contribute to personal and organizational integrity?" The quantitative differences between scores in the second and third columns among respondents indicate the nature and extent of ethical agreement and disagreement that exists on an issue; severe differences can then be prioritized to efficiently address large disparities first.

THE QL-TOOL

1. Current Ethical Awareness (Process Integrity): [INITIAL PROPOSAL AND OB-SERVATIONS]

   a. What is the ethical issue and how does it relate to a management function?

   b. How important is the ethical issue?

   (Who is doing what to whom ethically or unethically, and so what?)

2. Impact and Intensity of Ethical Issue (Process Integrity) (Developmental Integrity): [OBSERVATIONS]

   a. Who are the affected stakeholders? What is the scope of the moral domain?

   b. How intensely does this moral issue affect each of the stakeholders?

3. Supportive Environmental Context (Developmental Integrity): [OBSERVATIONS, VALUE PRIORITIZATION, ASSUMPTIONS, AND OPPOSING VIEWS DIALOGUE]

   a. What is the extent of ethical opportunity support from background extraorganizational factors for an optimal ethical resolution of the issue?

   b. What is the extent of ethical opportunity support from background intraorganizational factors for an optimal ethical resolution of the issue?

   c. To what extent is the organizational ethical work culture characterized by both supportive democratic participation and principled decision making with respect to this issue?

   d. To what extent is the work unit ethical work culture characterized by both supportive democratic participation and principled decision making with respect to this issue?

   e. To what extent is the personal moral development of each agent characterized by respect for majority opinion and principled decision making on this issue?

4. Current Ethical Judgment (Process Integrity) (Judgment Integrity): [OBSERVATIONS, VALUE PRIORITIZATION, ASSUMPTIONS, AND OPPOSING VIEWS DIALOGUE]

a. How adequate is the ethical analysis of this issue?

b. How adequately did the agent(s) use ethical dialogue to analyze the ethical issue?

c. How soundly are each of the ethics theories (teleological ethics—the weighted values of *utility and happiness;* deontological ethics—the weighted values of *freedom and dignity;* virtue ethics—the weighted values of *justice and caring;* and system development ethics—the weighted values of *improvement and creativity)* argued to adequately justify the ethical action with respect to this issue?

d. To what extent do each of the cognate resource theories (management, law, and communications) support the analysis and resolution of this issue?

e. How adequate and balanced is the ethical resolution of this issue?

f. How extensively were the alternative viable resolution options of this issue considered?

g. How capable is the resolution of this issue of withstanding careful scrutiny from qualified inquirers?

h. To what extent does the resolution of this issue demonstrate judgment integrity?

5. Ethical Intention (Process Integrity) (Developmental Integrity): [OBSERVA-TIONS, VALUE PRIORITIZATION, ASSUMPTIONS, AND OPPOSING VIEWS DIALOGUE]

a. How strong is the cognitive readiness to act ethically on this issue by the moral agent(s)?

b. How extensively are the intellectual virtues of the moral agent(s) cultivated at work on this issue?

c. How strong is the volitional readiness of the moral agent(s) to act ethically at work as they relate to this issue?

d. How extensively are the emotional virtues of the moral agent(s) cultivated at work on this issue?

e. How extensively are the social virtues of the agent(s)' characters cultivated at work on this issue?

f. How extensively are the moral virtues of the agent(s)' characters cultivated at work on this issue?

g. How strong-willed and resolute are the moral agent(s) to act ethically at work on this issue?

6. *Sustained Character Development (Developmental Integrity): [OBSERVATIONS, VALUE PRIORITIZATION, ASSUMPTIONS, AND OPPOSING VIEWS DIA-LOGUE]*

a. How extensively have managers cultivated intellectual virtues in people as ingrained parts of organizational and work unit character with respect to this issue?

b. How extensively have managers cultivated emotional virtues in people as ingrained parts of organizational character and work unit with respect to this issue?

c. How extensively have managers cultivated moral virtues in people as ingrained parts of organizational and work unit character with respect to this issue?

d. How extensively have managers cultivated social virtues in people as ingrained parts of organizational and work unit character with respect to this issue?

e. How resolute is the collective character of the organization and work unit to act ethically with regard to this issue?

7. Ethical Conduct (Process Integrity): [OBSERVATIONS, VALUE PRIORITIZATION, ASSUMPTIONS, AND OPPOSING VIEWS DIALOGUE]

a. To what extent do moral agent(s) engage in and visibly endorse responsibly responsive conduct on the domestic realm with regard to this issue?

b. To what extent do moral agent(s) engage in and visibly endorse responsibly responsive conduct in the global realm with regard to this issue?

c. To what extent do moral agent(s) engage in and visibly endorse sustainable development practices in the domestic realm with regard to this issue?

d. To what extent do moral agent(s) engage in and visibly endorse sustainable development practices in the global realm with regard to this issue?

8. Sustained Reputation Development (Developmental Integrity): [OBSERVATIONS, VALUE PRIORITIZATION, ASSUMPTIONS, AND OPPOSING VIEWS DIALOGUE]

a. How extensively have managers cultivated responsibly responsive conduct norms as credible and visible parts of the organizational and work unit domestic reputation?

b. How extensively have managers cultivated responsibly responsive conduct norms as credible and visible parts of the organizational and work unit global reputation?

c. How extensively have managers cultivated sustainable development practices as credible and visible parts of the organizational and work unit domestic reputation?

d. How extentively have managers cultivated sustainable development practices as credible and visible parts of the organizational and work unit global reputation?

9. Ethical Decision Implementation (Judgment Integrity) (Process Integrity): [OBSERVATIONS AND OPPOSING VIEWS DIALOGUE]

a. How well is the ethical resolution of this issue implemented or capable of being implemented?

b. How feasible is the ethical resolution of this issue, given the current nonhuman, contextual constraints?

c. How feasible is the ethical resolution of this issue, given the current human, contextual constraints?

d. How adequate is the measurement system for detecting moral progress of this issue?

e. How ample are the resources committed to implementing the ethical decision on this issue?

f. To what extent is there a widespread sense of "ownership" of and commitment to implementing the ethical decision on this issue?

10. Ethical Decision Evaluation, Control, and Improvement (Judgment Integrity) (Process Integrity) (Developmental Integrity): [ENACTED PROPOSAL AND OBSERVATIONS]

a. How well will the ethical resolution of this issue be monitored?

b. How well will the ethical resolution of this issue be evaluated?

c. How well will the ethical resolution of this issue be controlled?

d. How regularly will the ethical decision-making outcomes be audited?

e. How well will corrective feedback about ethical decision making on this issue be acted on?

f. How well will lessons learned from mistakes be shared for future improvement?

g. How well will individuals or groups who enacted successful resolutions be recognized?

h. How well will moral progress be measured and benchmarked?

i. How well will individuals be protected from moral overcontrol and undercontrol by statistically determining and maintaining acceptable variations in moral conduct?

Organization Ethics Development System (OEDS) Components and Their Collective Work Culture Environments

(OEDS) Components	Collective Connivance	Collective Compliance	Collective Commitment
1. Moral Leadership and Ethical Influence Patterns	Either nonexistent or self-interested use of power	Transactional exchanges in a bureaucratic, hierarchic, and/or legal context	Transformational relationships that raise leaders and followers to higher levels of motivation and morality
2. Ethical Work Culture and Ethics Needs Assessment	Assessments either nonexistent or done out of reaction to crises with no disclosure of results	Assessments either nonexistent or completed as part of a compliance program to meet externally imposed standards of disclosure	Assessments regularly conducted with results publicly benchmarked and used to direct ongoing improvement efforts

(OEDS) Components	Collective Connivance	Collective Compliance	Collective Commitment
3. Ethics in Organizational Strategy and Structure	Either nonexistent or short-term strategy to maximize competitive economic advantage with highly centralized command and control authority	Intermediate term strategy to ensure internal alignment and regulatory compliance with centralized, bureaucratic, hierarchic authority	Long-term strategy to promote sustainable development of resources with nonhierarchical, decentralized, participative authority
4. Ethics Steering Committee	Either nonexistent or ethics policy formulation, guidance, coordination, and updating completed with exclusive input from powerful insiders	Ethics policy formulation, guidance, coordination, and updating completed with selective input from external sources through the process of influencing public policy and eventual compliance with external legislative/regulatory enactments (e.g., Federal Sentencing Guidelines)	Ethics policy formulation, guidance, coordination, and updating with inclusive external and internal input regarding the process of influencing public policy and eventual institutionalization of self-regulatory systems that exceed external requirements
5. Formal Statement of Prioritized Values and Written Codes of Conduct	Nonexistent, informal, or unprioritized value statement and/or exacting written codes of conduct used to terrorize "bad apples"	Formal statement of prioritized values and written code of conduct to ensure public relations' "window-dressing" and/or to deter government intervention by complying with latest laws and regulations affecting the organization	Formal statement of prioritized values and written code of conduct to ensure internal character development and external reputation development for internalized self-regulation

(OEDS) Components	Collective Connivance	Collective Compliance	Collective Commitment
6. Ethics Policy and Procedure Manuals	Nonexistent or narrow in scope/content and unincorporated into organizational practice; no ethics handbook	Policies and procedures designed and implemented to conform with externally imposed standards and to prevent criminal/illegal behavior; no ethics handbook, but compliance manual	Policies and procedures designed for self-governance according to chosen value priorities and standards that enable committed, responsible conduct and organizational integrity; ethics handbook and compliance manual
7. Ethics in the Human Resource Selection, Socialization, and Performance Subsystems	Nonexistent or selective, reactive response to deter or punish unethical conduct after the fact	Preventive integrity testing and regulatory orientation to detect actual or probable unethical conduct to avoid risk exposure and to censure misconduct	Preventive integrity and organization citizenship behavior testing, and regulatory orientation to identify people who assume individual and systemic responsibility for ongoing improvement

(OEDS) Components	Collective Connivance	Collective Compliance	Collective Commitment
8. Ethics in Human Resource Appraisal, Reward/ Recognition/ Incentive, and Development Subsystems	Nonexistent or selective, reactive responses that ignore or delay punishment of unethical conduct and/or ignore or delay commendation of exemplary conduct; no career, work system, or organization development efforts undertaken; no useful feedback provided to give direction, enable empowerment, or foster intrinsic motivation at work	Human resource policies that evaluate, reward, and develop individuals to commend conventional conformity and legal compliance as being ethically adequate or superior moral behavior; career, work system, and organization development efforts occasionally undertaken; some useful feedback provided to give direction, enable empowerment, or foster intrinsic motivation at work	Human resource policies that factor in moral integrity and ethical conduct in individual and team appraisal, reward/recognition/ incentive, and development subsystems to ensure organizational justice above and beyond the law, and to establish a tradition of commendation for moral excellence and fair, swift censuring of individual and collective wrongdoing; career, work system, and organizational development efforts routinely undertaken; comprehensive, useful feedback provided to give direction, enable empowerment, or foster intrinsic motivation at work

(OEDS) Components	Collective Connivance	Collective Compliance	Collective Commitment
9. Ethics in Formal and Informal Communication Processes and Work Attitudes	Nonexistent or unaligned, downward, formal, and informal communication processes that ignore or trivialize moral discourse and promote negative, cynical work attitudes; no ethics dialogue or discussion	Aligned, formal, and informal communication processes that are credible and multimedia; downward communications that legitimate moral conformity that is backed by legal/regulatory standards and that promotes compliant work attitudes and conventional accountability; ethics discussion or debate, but no ethics dialogue	Aligned, formal, and informal communication processes that are prioritize construc- tive challenging of authority; multidirectional communications that institutionalize ethics discourse and encourage commitment to sustaining individual and organizational integrity, rather than mere compliance; ethics dialogue and ethics discussion.
10. Ethics Training and Education Programs	Nonexistent or narrow focus on career success through techniques that glorify gamesmanship and reinforce securing "bottom-line" advantage at any cost; occasional moral "pep" talk	Formal training and education to prevent criminal misconduct by focusing on compliance with externally imposed standards; concern for letter and spirit of the law; ethics compliance training	Formal and informal training and education to enable moral autonomy and responsible conduct that focuses on legally inclusive but ethics-driven decision making that exceeds external compliance standards and promotes cooperative self-governance according to rationally justified commitments; ethics compliance training and moral decision-making education

(OEDS) Components	Collective Connivance	Collective Compliance	Collective Commitment
11. Ethics in Decision-Making Processes	Nonexistent or normless ethical disenfranchisement and alienation that perpetuates and rewards an atmosphere of self-interested confrontation and negativism	Formal adherence to group decision-making norms, role expectations, obedience to unilateral hierarchic authority, and compliance with externally imposed standards of decision making	Formal and informal inclusion of legal and ethical principle-driven factors to enable personal accountability, moral empowerment, and group responsibility for preventing "group-think" and for promoting participative self-governing, cooperative relationships

(OEDS) Components	Collective Connivance	Collective Compliance	Collective Commitment
12. Ethics Officer and/or Delegated Organizational Ethics Operational Role Responsibility	Nonexistent or discretionary operational responsibilities diffused among line supervisors or security departments to detect, deter, and control costs of ethical violations; no external ethics consultants hired or moral benchmarking done	Formal centralized or decentralized authority delegated to operationally coordinate ethics policies; investigate, analyze, and resolve ethical disputes; and enforce ethical standards that sanction unethical behavior by adhering to due process, due diligence, and compliance requirements (e.g., Federal Sentencing Guidelines); external ethics consultants occasionally hired for compliance programs and moral benchmarking occasionally performed	Formal centralized or decentralized authority delegated to operationally coordinate ethics policies and to promote systemwide internalization of responsibility for organizational integrity through the investigation, analysis, and resolution of ethical disputes and enforcement of ethical standards that censure unethical conduct and encourage commendable conduct by adhering to due process and compliance standards, as well as by supporting conduct and commitment to raising standards of organizational trust; external ethics consultants regularly hired and moral benchmarking routinely performed

(OEDS) Components	Collective Connivance	Collective Compliance	Collective Commitment
13. Ethics Reporting and Conflict Resolution Processes	Nonexistent or retaliation against whistle-blowers condoned because of stigmatized disloyalty; minimal open-door policy with ad hoc, case-by-case discretionary resolution	Reporting of questionable ethical practices to Ethics Officer; formal grievance procedures that protect confidentiality and due process through in-company or conventional outside grievance resolution forums in compliance with mandated, whistle-blower protection laws to minimize lawsuits and prevent unionization	Contacting Ethics Officer to report questionable ethical practices and to solicit ethical advice prior to decision making; formal grievance and continuous informal feedback expected to provide guidance, support, and consultation for ongoing ethical conflict resolution, which protects and rewards whistle-blowers for constructive loyalty
14. Enforcement Processes of Ethical Standards	Nonexistent, arbitrary, capricious, or delayed direct or indirect managerial punishments for unethical conduct, action taken to display power and engender fear	Management of swift and fair enforcement of group norms and legal compliance standards with direct or indirect punishment of unethical conduct to pressure people to conform and do what they are told	Management and peer enforcement of fair and swift justice that directly or indirectly punishes unethical conduct and provides internal and external rewards for exemplary ethical conduct

(OEDS) Components	Collective Connivance	Collective Compliance	Collective Commitment
15. Ethics Audit and Evaluation Subsystems	Nonexistent or detection and dismissal processes to control unethical behavior and adversarially react to government standards, with no attempt to document ethics system effectiveness	Perform and oversee periodic ethical compliance audits; engage in public policy initiatives to minimize government regulatory intervention but eventually accommodate law-abiding expectations; use of Federal Sentencing Guidelines as key factors in ethics audits	Perform and oversee regular, ongoing ethics audit and evaluation processes to continuously assess and develop individual ethical performance and organization integrity systems; engage in proactive public policy and quality benchmarking to ensure private and public accountability for organizational ethical and social responsibility performance
16. Ethics System and Work Process Control and Improvement	Nonexistent or reactive crisis management of ethical disasters based on avoidance of legal liabilities and financial costs; no attempt to monitor and improve ethics system; work processes are unknown and/or only partially understood and documented	Formal ethics system controls and corrective actions taken to accommodate legal mandates and to prevent ethical disasters; emphasis on embracing legal norms; documented work processes usually meet customer expectations effectively and/or efficiently without waste; process measurements of variance taken, but system unstable	Formal and informal ethics system controls and corrective actions taken to ensure legal compliance and ongoing improvement of ethical standards to proactively promote individual and organization integrity development; documented work processes are error-free (highly effective and streamlined) and/or world-class (superior and continuously improving) within acceptable variance ranges in a statistically stable work system

Leadership Empowerment
Readiness Assessment (LERA)

PURPOSE: The purpose of this assessment instrument is to determine individual and/or group total quality leadership empowerment readiness. It can be used as a personal or group self-assessment instrument or by a manager considering another individual for promotion or group members for a project, or can be distributed for anonymous collective feedback about a prospective individual or group empowerment activity or promotion decision.

DIRECTIONS: For each of the assessment dimensions listed below, circle the number that most closely represents your perception of the individual or group under consideration, using the rating scale below. Comments are optional. Then use the LERA scoring sheet to determine task, psychosocial, and moral maturity levels. Finally, interpret the results.

High			Moderate				Low
8	7	6	5	4	3	2	1

A. ASSESSMENT DIMENSIONS   *Comments*

1. Job/project knowledge

Has job/   Does not have job/
project knowledge   knowledge

| 8 | 7 | 6 | 5 | 4 | 3 | 2 | 1 | _____ |

2. Achievement motivation

Has high desire   Has little desire
to achieve   to achieve

| 8 | 7 | 6 | 5 | 4 | 3 | 2 | 1 | _____ |

3. Honesty

Always honest   Never honest

| 8 | 7 | 6 | 5 | 4 | 3 | 2 | 1 | _____ |

4. Total quality problem-solving ability

Solves problems   Unable to solve
by using total   problems by using
quality tools   total quality tools

| 8 | 7 | 6 | 5 | 4 | 3 | 2 | 1 | _____ |

5. Communication style

Communicates   Does not communicate
effectively at work   effectively at work

| 8 | 7 | 6 | 5 | 4 | 3 | 2 | 1 | _____ |

6. Trustworthy

Always trustworthy   Never trustworthy

| 8 | 7 | 6 | 5 | 4 | 3 | 2 | 1 | _____ |

7. Past job/project experience

Has relevant experience   No relevant experience

| 8 | 7 | 6 | 5 | 4 | 3 | 2 | 1 | _____ |

8. Sense of humor

Always exhibits   Never exhibits
an appropriate   an appropriate
sense of humor   sense of humor

| 8 | 7 | 6 | 5 | 4 | 3 | 2 | 1 | _____ |

9. Justice/fairness

Always fair and just   Never fair and just

8   7   6   5   4   3   2   1   _____

10. Relevant computer literacy

Always uses   Never uses
computer   computer
effectively at work   effectively at work

8   7   6   5   4   3   2   1   _____

11. Work attitude

Has "can do—   Has "can't do—
enjoy making it   thank goodness
happen" attitude   it's Friday" attitude

8   7   6   5   4   3   2   1   _____

12. Respectfully caring

Always respectfully caring   Never respectfully caring

8   7   6   5   4   3   2   1   _____

13. Organization knowledge

Knows the   Does not know
organization   the organization
as a whole system   as a whole system

8   7   6   5   4   3   2   1   _____

14. Interdependent cooperation

Works   Does not work
cooperatively   cooperatively
with others   with others

8   7   6   5   4   3   2   1   _____

15. Good judgment

Always exhibits   Never exhibits
good judgment   good judgment

8   7   6   5   4   3   2   1   _____

16. Takes responsibility for an envisioned future

Envisions a   Does not envision
future and takes   a future or take
responsibility for it   responsibility for it

8   7   6   5   4   3   2   1   _____

17. Uses and shares power effectively

Uses and shares power effectively				Uses and shares power ineffectively				
8	7	6	5	4	3	2	1	_____

18. Courage

Always exhibits courage				Never exhibits courage				
8	7	6	5	4	3	2	1	_____

B. LERA SCORING SHEET

1. *Task maturity:* Add the numbers circled for Questions 1, 4, 7, 10, 13, and 16, and divide the total by 6.

2. *Psychosocial maturity:* Add the numbers circled for Questions 2, 5, 8, 11, 14, and 17, and divide the total by 6.

3. *Moral maturity:* Add the numbers circled for Questions 3, 6, 9, 12, 15, and 18, and divide the total by 6.

C: INTERPRETATION OF RESULTS

Average scores for any of the factors:

1—4.0 = Individual or group is not ready for total quality leadership empowerment at this time.

4.1—7.0 = Individual or group is ready for regular participation in total quality leadership teamwork.

7.1—8.0 = Individual or group is ready for self-directed, high-performance, total quality leadership teamwork.

STEP 1: *Identify Leadership Empowerment Training Needs:* Use your lowest average factor score as a place to begin preparing yourself and/or your group for responsible leadership empowerment. Individuals or groups who are prematurely empowered (e.g., promoted without being ready to assume their commensurate responsibilities) eventually become problems for themselves, others, and the total quality system ("The Peter Principle" of institutionalized incompetence). Training and development are warranted.

STEP 2: *Identify Leadership Empowerment Promotion/Delegation Candidates:* Individuals or groups who are ready for high-performance, leadership empowerment deserve your support and are the most likely to make best use of limited resources to achieve success with integrity. Consider them for promotion/delegation opportunities.

References

Ackerman, R., & Bauer, R. (1976). *Corporate social responsiveness: The modern dilemma.* Reston, VA: Reston.

Adams, J. S. (1963). Toward an understanding of inequity. *Journal of Abnormal and Social Psychology, 67*(5), 422-436.

Adams, S. (1996). *The Dilbert principle.* New York: Harper Business.

AFL-CIO Committee on the Evolution of Work. (1994). *The new American workplace: A labor perspective.* Washington, DC: AFL-CIO Publishing.

Agarwal, H., & Narain, S. (1991). *Global warming in an unequal world: A case of environmental colonialism.* New Delhi, India: Center for Science and Environment.

Alderfer, C. P. (1972). *Existence, relatedness, and growth: Human needs in organizational settings.* New York: Free Press.

Alexander, S., & Ruderman, M. (1987). The role of procedural and distributive justice in organizational behavior. *Social Justice Research, 1,* 177-198.

Allinson, R. E. (1993). *Global disasters.* Upper Saddle River, NJ: Prentice Hall.

Andersson, L., & Bateman, T. (1994). *Cynicism in the workplace: Some causes and effects* (Working Paper). Chapel Hill: University of North Carolina, Kenan-Flagler Business School.

Andrews, G. (1991). *Citizenship.* London: Lawrence & Wishalt.

Ansoff, H. L. (1988). *The new corporate strategy.* New York: John Wiley

Aquinas, T. (1959). Summa theologica I-II treatise on law. In C. Morris (Ed.), *The great legal philosophers* (pp. 74-93). Philadelphia: University of Pennsylvania Press. (Original work published 1250)

Aristotle. (1985). Nicomachean ethics. In T. Irwin (Ed.), *The works of Aristotle.* Indianapolis: Hackett. (Original work published 350 B.C.)

Armstrong, M. B. (1993). *Ethics and professionalism.* Cincinnati: South-Western.

Armstrong, S., & Botzler, R. (Eds.). (1993). *Environmental ethics: Divergence and convergence.* New York: McGraw-Hill.

Arpoes, J., & Braithwaite, J. (1992). *Responsive regulation.* New York: Oxford University Press.

August, R. (1993). *International business law.* Upper Saddle River, NJ: Prentice Hall.

August, R. (1995). *Public international law.* Upper Saddle River, NJ: Prentice Hall.

Austin, J. (1954). *The province of jurisprudence determined.* London: Clarendon. (Original work published 1885)

Austin, L. (1962). *How to do things with words.* Cambridge, MA: Harvard University Press.

Axelrod, R. (1984). *The evolution of cooperation.* New York: Basic Books.

Axelrod, R., & Dion, D. (1988). The further evolution of cooperation. *Science, 242,* 1385-1390.

Ayres, I., & Braithwaite, J. (1992). *Responsive regulation.* New York: Oxford University Press.

Bailey, F. G. (1988). *Humbuggery and manipulation: The art of leadership.* Ithaca: Cornell University Press.

Baily, M., Burtless, G., & Litan, R. (1993). *Growth with equity: Economic policy making for the next century.* Washington, DC: Brookings Institution.

Ball, G. A., Trevino, L. K., & Sims, H. P., Jr. (1994). Just and unjust punishment: Influences on subordinate performance and citizenship. *Academy of Management Journal, 37*(2), 299-322.

Bandura, A. (1976). Self-reinforcement: Theoretical and methodological considerations. *Behaviorism, 4*(3), 135-155.

Bandura, A. (1982). Self-efficacy mechanism in human behavior. *American Psychologist, 37*(7), 122-147.

Bandura, A., & Walters, R. H. (1963). *Social learning and personality development.* New York: Holt, Rinehart & Winston.

Bartlett, K. T. (1993). *Gender and law: Theory, doctrine, commentary.* Boston: Little, Brown.

Bass, B. M. (1985). *Leadership and performance beyond expectation.* New York: Free Press.

Bass, B. M. (1990a). *Bass and Stogdill's handbook on leadership* (3rd ed.). New York: Free Press.

Bass, B. M. (1990b). From transactional to transformational leadership: Learning to share the vision. *Organizational Dynamics, 4*(2), 19-32.

Baxter, B. (1974). *People and penguins: The case for optimal pollution.* New York: Columbia University Press.

Bayles, M. D. (1989). *Professional ethics* (2nd ed.). Belmont, CA: Wadsworth.

Bazerman, M., Messick, D., Tenbrunsel, A., & Wade-Benzoni, K. (Eds.). (1997). *Psychological perspectives on human behavior in relation to the national environment.* San Francisco: Jossey-Bass.

Bazerman, M. H. (1994). *Judgment in managerial decision making.* New York: John Wiley.

Beck-Dudley, C., & Conry, E. (1995). Legal reasoning and practical reasonableness. *American Business Law Journal, 33*(1), 91-130.

Bellace, J. (1991). The international dimension of Title VII. *Cornell International Law Journal, 24,* 1-24.

Bennett, W. J. (1993). *The book of virtues.* New York: Simon & Schuster.

Bentham, J. (1948). *An introduction to the principles of morals and legislation.* Oxford: Clarendon. (Original work published 1789)

Berman, H. J., & Greiner, W. R. (1980). *The nature and functions of law* (4th ed.). Mineola, NY: Foundation Press.

Bhide, A., & Stevenson, H. H. (1990). Why be honest if honesty doesn't pay? *Harvard Business Review, 9*(10), 121-129.

Binstein, M., & Bowden, C. (1993). *Trust me: Charles Keating and the missing billions.* New York: Random House.

Bird, F. B., & Waters, T. A. (1989). The moral muteness of managers. *California Management Review, 16*(4), 73-88.

Blackburn, J. D., Klayman, E. I., & Malin, M. H. (1994). *The legal environment of business* (5th ed.). Burr Ridge, IL: Irwin.

Blasi, A. (1980). Bridging moral cognition and moral action: A critical review of the literature. *Psychological Bulletin, 88,* 1-45.

Blinder, A. S. (1990). *Paying for productivity: A look at the evidence.* Washington, DC: Brookings Institution.

Boatright, J. (1993). *The shareholder-management relation and the stakeholder paradox.* Paper presented at the annual meeting of the Society for Business Ethics, Washington, DC.

Boatright, J. R. (1997). *Ethics and the conduct of business* (2nd ed.). Upper Saddle River, NJ: Prentice Hall.

Boisjoly, R., Curtis, M., & Mellican, D. (1989). Roger Boisjoly and the *Challenger* disaster: The ethical dimensions. *Journal of Business Ethics, 8*(4), 217-230.

Bolton, R., & Bolton, D. G. (1984). *Social styles/management styles: Developing productive work relationships.* New York: AMACOM.

Bork, R. H. (1990). *The tempting of America: The political seduction of the law.* New York: Touchstone.

Bounds, G. M. (1996). *Cases in quality.* Chicago: Irwin.

Bounds, G. M., Dobbins, G. H., & Fowler, O. S. (1995). *Management: A total quality perspective.* Cincinnati: South-Western.

Bounds, G. M., Yorks, L., Adams, M., & Ranney, G. (1994). *Beyond total quality management.* New York: McGraw-Hill.

Bowie, N. (1982). *Business ethics.* Upper Saddle River, NJ: Prentice Hall.

Bowie, N. E. (1991). Challenging the egoistic paradigm. *Business Ethics Quarterly, 1*(1), 1-23.

Boyhan, W. S. (1992). Approaches to eliminating chlorofluorocarbon use in manufacturing. *Proceedings of the National Academy of Sciences of the U.S., 89,* 812-814.

Brest, P. (1981). The fundamental rights controversy: The essential contradictions of normative constitutional scholarship. *Yale Law Journal, 90,* 1091-1092.

Breyer, S. (1982). *Regulation and its reform.* Cambridge, MA: Harvard University Press.

Brookfield, H. (1992). Environmental colonialism, tropical reforestation, and concerns other than global warming. *Global Environmental Change, 2*(2), 93-96.

Brooks, S., & Vance, R. (1995). *Organizational cynicism: Development of a concept.* Paper presented at the annual meeting of the Academy of Management, Vancouver, British Columbia.

Brown, M. T. (1990). *Working ethics.* San Francisco: Jossey-Bass.

Brunsson, N. (1989). *The organization of hypocrisy: Talk, decisions, and actions in organizations.* New York: John Wiley.

Buchholz, E., Evans, W., & Wagley, R. (1994). *Managerial responses to public policy issues* (3rd ed.). Upper Saddle River, NJ: Prentice Hall.

Buchholz, R. A. (1994). *Business environment and public policy.* Upper Saddle River, NJ: Prentice Hall.

Buchholz, R. A., Marcus, A., & Post, J. (1992). *Managing environmental issues: A case book.* Upper Saddle River, NJ: Prentice Hall.

Buchholz, R. A. (1991). *Principles of environmental management.* Englewood Cliffs, NJ: Prentice-Hall.

Bunker, B. B., & Rubin, J. Z. (Eds.). (1995). *Conflict, cooperation, and justice.* San Francisco: Jossey-Bass.

Burns, J. M. (1979). *Leadership.* New York: Harper & Row.

Burris, D. (1993). *Technotrends.* New York: Harper Business.

Callahan, D., & Bok, S. (Eds.). (1980). *The teaching of ethics in higher education.* Hastings-on-the-Hudson, NY: Hastings Center.

Cameron, K. (1980). Crucial questions in assessing organizational effectiveness. *Organizational Dynamics, 9,* 140-167.

Cameron, K., & Freeman, S. (1991). Cultural consequences, strengths, and type: Relationships to effectiveness. *Research in Organizational Development, 5,* 23-58.

Camp, R. C. (1995). *Business process benchmarking: Finding and implementing best practices.* Milwaukee, WI: ASQC Quality Press.

Campbell, T. (1993). *The politics of despair: Power and resistance in the tobacco wars.* Lexington: University Press of Kentucky.

Carillo, P., & Kopelman, R. (1991). Organizational structure and productivity: Effects of subunit size, vertical complexity, and administrative intensity on operating efficiency. *Group and Organizational Studies, 16,* 44-59.

Carroll, A. B. (1991). The pyramid of corporate social responsibility: Toward the moral management of organizational stakeholders. *Business Horizons, 34*(4), 39-48.

Carroll, A. B. (1996). *Business and society* (3rd ed.). Cincinnati, OH: South-Western.

Cavanagh, G. F. (1984). *American business values.* Upper Saddle River, NJ: Prentice Hall.

Cederblom, J., & Dougherty, C. T. (1990). *Ethics at work.* Belmont, CA: Wadsworth.

Certo, S. C. (1994). *Modern management* (6th ed.). Needham Heights, MA: Allyn & Bacon.

Chandler, A. D., Jr. (1977). *The visible hand: The managerial revolution in American business.* Cambridge, MA: Harvard University Press.

Chandler, A. D., Jr. (1980). *Scale and scope.* Cambridge, MA: Belknap.

Ciulla, J. B. (1995). Leadership ethics: Mapping the territory. *Business Ethics Quarterly, 5*(1), 5-28.

Clarkson, M. B. E. (1991). Defining, evaluating, and managing corporate social performance: A stakeholder management model. In J. E. Preston (Ed.), *Research in corporate social performance and society* (pp. 89-101). Greenwich, CT: JAI.

Cohen, D. V. (1993). Creating and maintaining ethical work climates. *Business Ethics Quarterly, 3*(4), 343-358.

Cohen, J., Pant, L., & Sharp, D. (1993). A validation and extension of a multidimensional ethics scale. *Journal of Business Ethics, 12,* 13-26.

Cohen, S., & Bran, R. (1993). *Total quality management in government.* San Francisco: Jossey-Bass.

Cohen, S., & Eimicke, W. (1995). *The new effective public manager.* San Francisco: Jossey-Bass.

Colby, A., & Damon, W. (1994). *Some do care: Contemporary lives of moral commitment.* New York: Free Press.

Colby, A., & Kohlberg, L. (1987). *The measurement of moral judgment: Theoretical foundations and research validation.* Cambridge, MA: Cambridge University Press.

Collins, D. (1989). Organizational harm, legal condemnation, and stakeholder retaliation: A typology, research agenda, and application. *Journal of Business Ethics, 2,* 1-13.

Common Cause. (1989). *Conflict of interest legislation in the states.* Washington, DC: Author.

Conference Board. (1991). *Employee buy-in to total quality.* New York: Author.

Congressional Ethics Committee Staff. (1992). *Congressional ethics history, facts, and controversy.* Washington, DC: Congressional Quarterly.

Congressional Research Service. (1994). *Congressional Research Service, legislative ethics in democratic countries: Comparative analysis of financial standards.* Washington, DC: U.S. Congress.

Conry, E. J., & Nelson, D. R. (1989). Business law and moral growth. *American Business Law Journal, 27*(1), 1-39.

Cooper, D. E. (1996). *World philosophies.* Cambridge, MA: Blackwell.

Cooper, T. (1986). *The responsible administrator: An approach to ethics for the administrative role.* New York: Associated Faculty Press.

Council of Better Business Bureaus, Inc. (1983). *Self-regulatory guidelines for children's advertising* (3rd ed.). Washington, DC: Author.

Covey, S. R. (1989). *The seven habits of highly effective people: Restoring the character ethic.* New York: Simon & Schuster.

Covey, S. R. (1994). *First things first.* New York: Simon & Schuster.

Crawford, J. M. B., & Quinn, J. F. (1991). *The Christian foundations of criminal responsibility.* New York: Mellon.

Crosette, B. (1995, August 20). A global gauge of greased palms. *New York Times,* p. 3.

Cullen, J., Victor, B., & Stephens, C. (1989). An ethical weather report: Assessing the organization's ethical climate. *Organizational Dynamics, 18,* 82-101.

Dansereau, F., Graen, G., & Haga, W. (1975). A vertical dyad linkage approach to leadership in formal organizations. *Organizational Behavior and Human Performance, 13,* 46-78.

Daufman, P. W. (1994). *Cross-cultural leadership research: Issues and assumptions.* Paper presentation at the annual symposium of the Social Issues in Management Division, Nashville, TN.

D'Aveni, R. A. (1994). *Hypercompetition: Managing the dynamics of strategic maneuvering.* New York: Free Press.

Davidson, R. H., & Oleszek, W. J. (1994). *Congress and its members* (4th ed.). Washington, DC: CQ Press.

Davis, M. (1989). Explaining wrongdoing. *Journal of Social Philosophy, 20,* 74-90.

Dean, J. (1976). *Blind ambition.* New York: Simon & Schuster.

Dean, J., & Brandes, P. (1995). *Organizational cynicism.* Manuscript submitted for publication.

DeGeorge, R. T. (1997). *Business ethics* (5th ed.). Upper Saddle River, NJ: Prentice Hall.

DeGeorge, R. T. (1993). *Competing with integrity in international business.* New York: Oxford University Press.

Deming, W. E. (1982). *Quality, productivity, and competitive position.* Cambridge: MIT.

Deming, W. E. (1988). *Out of the crisis.* New York: Cambridge University Press.

Denison, D., Hoojiberg, R., & Quinn, R. (1995). Paradox and performance: Toward a theory of behavioral complexity in managerial leadership. *Organization Science, 6*(5), 524-540.

Deresky, H. (1997). *International management: Managing across borders.* Reading, MA: Addison-Wesley.

Dienesh, R., & Liden, R. (1986). Leader-member exchange model of leadership: A critique and further development. *Academy of Management Review, 11,* 618-634.

Dinavo, J. (1995). *Privatization in developing countries: Its impact on economic development and democracy.* New York: Praeger.

DiPadova, L. (1990). *Instructor's manual to becoming a master manager.* New York: John Wiley.

Dobel, J. P. (1990). Integrity in public service. *Public Administration Review, 50,* 354-366.

Doig, J., & Hargrove, E. (Eds.). (1990). *Leadership and innovation; Entrepreneurs in government.* Baltimore: Johns Hopkins University Press.

Donahue, W., & Kolt, R. (1992). *Managing interpersonal conflict.* Newbury Park, CA: Sage.

Donaldson, T. (1989). *The ethics of international business.* New York: Oxford University Press.

Donaldson, T. (1994). When integration fails. *Business Ethics Quarterly, 4*(2), 157-169.

Donaldson, T., & Dunfee, T. W. (1994). Toward a unified conception of business ethics: Integrative social contracts theory. *Academy of Management Review, 9*(2), 252-284.

Donaldson, T., & Preston, L. (1995). The stakeholder theory of the corporation: Concepts, evidence, and implications. *Academy of Management Review, 20,* 15-91.

Dove, M. R. (1994). North-South differences, global warming, and the global system. *Chemosphere, 29*(5), 1063-1077.

Downie, U. S. (1971). *Roles and values: An introduction to social ethics.* New York: Methuen.

Downs, A. (1995). *Corporate executions.* New York: AMACOM.

Drake, B., & Baasten, M. (1990). *Facilitating moral dialogue and debate: A new leadership dimension.* Paper presented at the annual meeting of the Western Academy of Management, Shizuoka, Japan.

Driscoll, D. M., Hoffman, M. W., & Petry, E. S. (1995). *The ethical edge: Tales of organizations that have faced moral crises.* New York: Master Media.

DuBrin, A. T. (1995). *Leadership: Research findings, practice, and skills.* Boston: Houghton Mifflin.

Dukerich, J. M., Nichols, M., Elm, D., & Vollrath, D. A. (1990). Moral reasoning in groups: Leaders make a difference. *Human Relations, 43*(5), 473-493.

Dworkin, R. (1978). *Taking rights seriously* (2nd ed.). Cambridge, MA: Harvard University Press.

Dworkin, R. (1985). *A matter of principle.* Cambridge, MA: Belknap.

Dworkin, R. (1986). *Law's empire.* Cambridge, MA: Harvard University Press.

Eagly, A., & Johnson, B. (1990). Gender and leadership style: A meta-analysis. *Psychological Bulletin, 108*(2), 251-273.

Earley, P. C. (1993). East meets West meets Mideast: Further explorations of collectivistic and individualistic work groups. *Academy of Management Journal, 36,* 319-348.

Editors of the *New England Journal of Medicine.* (1994). The human costs of tobacco use. *New England Journal of Medicine, 330,* 907.

Ehrlich, E. (1936). *Fundamental principles of the sociology of law.* Cambridge, MA: Harvard University Press. (Original work published 1913)

Elkins, P. (1992). *Green economics.* Garden City, NY: Doubleday.

Elm, D. R., & Weber, J. (1994). Measuring moral judgment: The moral judgment interview or the defining issues test. *Journal of Business Ethics, 13*(2), 341-355.

Ely, J. H. (1980). *Democracy and distrust: A theory of judicial review.* New York: Harper & Row.

Emmet, D. (1966). *Rules, roles, and relations.* Boston: Beacon.

Enderle, G. (1987). Some perspectives of managerial ethical leadership. *Journal of Business Ethics, 6*(8), 657-663.

Epstein, R. A. (1985). *Takings: Private property and the power of eminent domain.* Cambridge, MA: Harvard University Press.

Ettorre, B. (1994). The contingency workforce moves mainstream. *Management Review, 83*(2), 12.

Etzioni, A. (1988). *The moral dimension.* New York: Free Press.

Evans, J., & Lindsay, W. (1996). *The management and control of quality* (3rd ed.). St. Paul, MN: West.

Evans, M. G. (1986). *Path-goal theory of leadership: A meta-analysis.* Unpublished manuscript, University of Toronto.

Ewing, D. W. (1977). *Freedom inside the organization.* New York: McGraw-Hill.

Fairholm, G. W. (1991). *Values leadership: Toward a new philosophy of leadership.* New York: Praeger.

Farh, J., Podsakoff, P., & Organ, D. (1990). Accounting for organizational citizenship behavior: Leader fairness and task scope versus satisfaction. *Journal of Management, 16*(4), 705-721.

Feinberg, J. (1970). *Essays on the theory of responsibility.* Princeton, NJ: Princeton University Press.

Feinberg, J. (1995). *Philosophy of law.* Belmont, CA: Wadsworth.

Feldman, D., Dolipinghaus, H., & Turnley, W. (1994). Managing temporary workers: A permanent HRM challenge. *Organizational Dynamics, 23*(2), 49-58.

Fernandez, J. (1991). *Managing a diverse workplace.* New York: Free Press.

Ferrell, O. C., & Fraedrich, J. (1997). *Business ethics* (3rd ed.). Boston: Houghton Mifflin.

Ferrell, O. C., Gresham, L. G., & Fraedrich, J. J. (1989). A synthesis of ethical decision models for marketing. *Journal of Macromarketing, 9,* 5-16.

Fiedler, F., & Chemers, M. (1982). *Improving leadership effectiveness: The leader match concept* (2nd ed.). New York: John Wiley.

Finnis, J. (1980). *Natural law and natural rights.* New York: Oxford University Press.

Finnis, J. (1986). The natural law tradition. *Journal of Legal Education, 36,* 492-510.

Fiorelli, P. E. (1992). Fine reductions through effective ethics programs. *Albany Law Review, 56*(2), 403-440.

Fiorelli, P. E., and Rooney, C. (1996). *The federal sentencing guidelines: Guidelines for internal auditors.* Orlando, FL: Institute of Internal Auditors—Research Foundation.

Fisher, W. (1987). *Human conversation as narration: Toward a philosophy of reason, value, and action.* Columbia: University of South Carolina Press.

FitzGerald, C. (Ed.). (1996). Editorial comments. *Total Quality Environmental Management, 5*(4), 107-113.

Flores, A. (1988). *Professional ideals.* Belmont, CA: Wadsworth.

Folger, R., & Konovsky, M. A. (1989). Effects of procedural and distributive justice on reactions to pay raise decisions. *Academy of Management Journal, 32,* 115-130.

Fombrun, C. J. (1996). *Reputation: Realizing value from the corporate image.* Boston, MA: Harvard Business School Press.

Fox, M. (1994). *The reinvention of work: A new vision of livelihood for our time.* New York: HarperCollins.

Frank, R. (1988). *Passions within reason: The strategic role of the emotions.* New York: Norton.

Frederick, W. C. (1986). Toward CSR's: Why ethical analysis is indispensable and unavoidable in corporate affairs. *California Management Review, 28*(2), 126-141.

Frederick, W. C. (1995). *Values, nature, and culture in the American corporation.* New York: Oxford University Press.

Freeman, K. (1993). *Feminist jurisprudence.* New York: Free Press.

Freeman, R. E. (1984). *Strategic management: A stakeholder approach.* Boston: Pitman.

Freeman, R. E. (1994). The politics of stakeholder theory: Some cultural directions. *Business Ethics Quarterly, 4,* 409-422.

Freeman, R. E., & Gilbert, D., Jr. (1988). *Corporate strategy and the search for ethics.* Upper Saddle River, NJ: Prentice Hall.

French, W. A., & Granrose, J. (1995). *Practical business ethics.* Upper Saddle River, NJ: Prentice Hall.

Fukuyama, F. (1995). *Trust: The social virtues and the creation of prosperity.* New York: Free Press.

Fuller, L. L. (1964). *The morality of the law.* New York: Macmillan.

Gahl, L. L. (1984). Moral courage: The essence of leadership. *Presidential Studies Quarterly, 14*(1), 43-52.

Galbraith, T. R., & Kazanjian, R. K. (1986). *Strategy implementation: Structure, systems, and process.* St. Paul, MN: West.

Galston, W. (1991). *Liberal purposes: Goods, virtues, and duties in the liberal state.* Cambridge, UK: Cambridge University Press.

Gattiger, U. (1990). *Technology management in organizations.* Newbury Park, CA: Sage.

Gauthier, D. (1986). *Morals by agreement.* Oxford, UK: Oxford University Press.

General Accounting Office (GAO). (1987). *Ethics enforcement: Process by which conflict of interest allegations are investigated and resolved* (GAO/GGD-87-83BR). Washington, DC: Author.

Giacalone, R., & Greenberg, J. (Eds.). (1997). *Antisocial behavior in organizations.* Thousand Oaks, CA: Sage.

Giacalone, R., & Rosenfeld, P. (Eds.). (1991). *Applied impression management.* Newbury Park, CA: Sage.

Gilligan, C. (1982). *In a different voice: Psychological theory and women's development.* Cambridge, MA: Harvard University Press.

Gilligan, C., Ward, J. V., & Taylor, J. M. (Eds.). (1989). *Mapping the moral domain.* Cambridge, MA: Harvard University Press.

Gini, A. (1996). Moral leadership and business ethics. In B. Adams & S. Webster (Eds.), *Kellogg Leadership Studies Project: Ethics and leadership working papers* (pp.1-22). College Park, MD: Center for Political Leadership and Participation.

Gioia, D. (1992). Pinto fines and personal ethics: A script analysis of missed opportunities. *Journal of Business Ethics, 11*(5), 379-389.

Gittines, R. (1993). *Technotrends.* New York: Harper Business.

Gladwin, T. N., Kennelly, J. J., & Krause, T. S. (1995). Shifting paradigms for sustainable development: Implications for management theory and research. *Academy of Management Review, 20*(4), 874-907.

Gladwin, T. N., & Krause, T. S. (1997). *Business, nature, and society: Toward sustainable enterprise.* Burr Ridge, IL: Irwin.

Glance, N. S., & Huberman, B. A. (1994). The dynamics of social dilemmas. *Scientific American, 270*(3), 76-81.

Glass, L. (1992). *He says, she says: Closing the communication gap between the sexes.* New York: Perigee.

Glendon, M. A. (1991). *Rights talk: The impoverishment of political discourse.* New York: Free Press.

Glendon, M. A. (1994). *A nation under lawyers.* New York: Farrar, Strauss & Giroux.

Goldberg v. Kelly, 397 U.S. 254 (1970).

Goldfarb, J. (1991). *The cynical society.* Chicago: University of Chicago Press.

Goldsmith, T. H. (1991). *The biological roots of human nature: Forging links between evolution and behavior.* New York: Oxford University Press.

Goodpaster, K. (1991). Business ethics and stakeholder analyses. *Business Ethics Quarterly, 1*(1), 53-73.

Gortner, H. F. (1991). *Ethics for public managers.* New York: Praeger.

Graen, G., & Scandura, T. (1987). Toward a psychology of dyadic organizing. *Research in Organizational Behavior, 9,* 175-208.

Graen, G., & Uhl-Bren, M. (1991). The transformation of work group professionals into self-managing and partially self-designing contributors: Toward a theory of leadership making. *Journal of Management Systems, 3*(3), 33-48.

Graham, J. W. (1991). Servant-leadership in organizations: Inspirational and moral. *Leadership Quarterly, 2*(2), 105-119.

Graham, J. W. (1995). Leadership, moral development, and citizen behavior. *Business Ethics Quarterly, 5*(1), 43-54.

Green, D. M. (1994). *The ethical manager.* New York: Macmillan.

Greenberg, J. (1990). Looking fair v. being fair: Managing impressions of organizational justice. In B. M. Staw & L. L. Cummings (Eds.), *Research in organizational behavior* (pp. 111-157). Greenwich, CT: JAI.

Greenberg, J. (1996). *The quest for justice on the job: Essays and experiments.* Thousand Oaks, CA: Sage.

Greene, R. T. (1993). *Global quality: A synthesis of the world's best management methods.* Milwaukee: ASQC Quality Press.

Greenleaf, R. K. (1977). *Servant leadership.* New York: Paulist Press.

Grey, T. C. (1975). Do we have an unwritten constitution? *Stanford Law Review, 27,* 703.

Grey, T. C. (1978). Origins of the unwritten constitution: Fundamental law in American thought. *Stanford Law Review, 30,* 843-859.

Grey, T. C. (1984). The constitution as scripture. *Stanford Law Review, 37,* 40-61.

Guastello, S., Rieke, M., Guastello, D., & Billings, S. (1992). A study of cynicism, personality, and work values. *Journal of Psychology, 126,* 37-48.

Hambrick, D. C., & Cannella, H. A. (1989). Strategy implementation as substance and style. *Academy of Management Executive, 28,* 18-27.

Hand, L. (1958). *The bill of rights.* Cambridge, MA: Harvard University Press.

Hansen, R. S. (1992). A comment on "A multidimensional scale for measuring business ethics": A purification and refinement. *Journal of Business Ethics, 11*(7), 523-534.

Harkness, S., Edwards, C. P., & Super, C. M. (1981). Social roles and moral reasoning: A case study in a rural African community. *Developmental Psychology, 17,* 595-603.

Harrington, H. J. (1995). *Total improvement management.* New York: McGraw-Hill.

Harrington, M. (1991). *Business process improvement.* New York: McGraw-Hill.

Harris, C. E., Pritchard, M. S., & Robins, M. J. (1995). *Engineering ethics.* Belmont, CA: Wadsworth.

Hart, H. L. A. (1961). *The concept of law.* New York: Oxford University Press.

Hart, S., & Quinn, R. (1993). Roles executives play: CEOs, behavioral complexity, and firm performance. *Human Relations, 46*(3), 115-142.

Hartley, R. F. (1994). *Management mistakes and successes* (4th ed.). New York: John Wiley.

Heater, D. (1990). *Citizenship: The civic ideal in world history, politics, and education.* White Plains, NY: Longman.

Hecht, M. L., Collier, M. J., & Ribeau, S. A. (1993). *African American communication: Ethnic identity and cultural interpretation.* Newbury Park, CA: Sage.

Heifitz, V. A. (1994). *Leadership without easy answers.* Cambridge, MA: Harvard University Press.

Helgesen, S. (1990). *The female advantage: Women's ways of leadership.* New York: Doubleday Currency.

Henderson, C. (1992). Putting on the Ritz. *TQM Magazine, 2*(5), 292-296.

Heneman, H., & Heneman, R. (1994). *Staffing organizations.* Burr Ridge, IL: Irwin.

Hersey, P. (1984). *The situational leader.* New York: Warner.

Hersey, P., & Blanchard, P. (1977). *Management of organizational behavior.* Upper Saddle River, NJ: Prentice Hall.

Heymann, P. B. (1987). *The politics of public management.* New Haven, CT: Yale University Press.

Hill, T. (1991). Weakness of will and character. In G. W. Mortimore (Ed.), *Autonomy and self-respect* (pp. 120-125). Cambridge, UK: Cambridge University Press.

Himmelfarb, G. (1994). *The de-moralization of society.* New York: Random House.

Hinter, J. E. (1986). Cognitive ability, cognitive attitudes, job knowledge, and job performance. *Journal of Vocational Behavior, 29*(3), 340-362.

Hirschman, E., & Holbrook, M. (1992). *Postmodern consumer research: The study of consumption as text.* Newbury Park, CA: Sage.

Hochschild, A. R. (1983). *The managed heart.* Berkeley: University of California Press.

Hocker, J. L., & Wilmot, W. W. (1995). *Interpersonal conflict* (4th ed.). Madison, WI: Brown & Benchmark.

Hoffman, M. L. (1975). Developmental synthesis of affect and cognition and its implications for altruistic motivation. *Developmental Psychology, 11*, 607-622.

Hoffman, M. L. (1976). Empathy, role taking, guilt, and the development of altruistic motives. In T. Lickona (Ed.), *Moral development and behavior* (pp. 47-59). New York: Holt, Rinehart & Winston.

Hoffman, W. M. (1995). A blueprint for corporate ethical development. In W. M. Hoffman & R. E. Frederick (Eds.), *Business ethics* (pp. 87-98). New York: McGraw-Hill.

Hofstede, G. (1980). *Culture's consequences: International differences in work-related values.* Beverly Hills, CA: Sage.

Hofstede, G. (1991). *Cultures and organizations: Software of the mind.* New York: McGraw-Hill.

Hofstede, G. (1993). Cultural constraints in management theories. *Academy of Management Executive, 7*(1), 81-93.

Hofstede, G., & Bond, M. (1988). The Confucian connection: From cultural roots to economic growth. *Organizational Dynamics, 16*(4), 4-21.

Hogan, J., Hogan, R., & Busch, C. M. (1984). How to measure service orientation. *Journal of Applied Psychology, 8*(1), 167-173.

Hogan, R., Curphy, G. J., & Hogan, J. (1994). What we know about leadership effectiveness and personality. *American Psychologist, 49,* 493-504.

Hollander, E. P., & Offermann, L. R. (1990). Power and leadership in organizations. *American Psychologist, 15,* 179-189.

Hollist, W. L., & Tullis, F. L. (1987). Pursuing international food security: Strategies and obstacles in Africa, Asia, and North America. In *International economy yearbook.* Vienna: Balden.

Holmberg, J. (Ed.). (1992). *Making development sustainable.* Washington, DC: Island.

Holmes, R. L. (1993). *Basic moral philosophy.* Belmont, CA: Wadsworth.

Hoojiberg, R., & Quinn, R. (1992). Behavioral complexity and the development of effective managers. In R. Phillips & J. Hunt (Eds.), *Strategic leadership: A multiorganizational-level perspective* (pp. 44-61). Westport, CT: Quorum.

Hosmer, L. T. (1994a). *Moral leadership in business.* Burr Ridge, IL: Irwin.

Hosmer, L. T. (1994b). Why be moral? A different rationale for managers. *Business Ethics Quarterly, 4*(2), 191-204.

Hosmer, L. T. (1995). Trust: The connecting link between organizational theory and psychological ethics. *Academy of Management Review, 20*(2), 379-403.

Hosmer, L. T. (1996). *The ethics of management* (3rd ed.). Burr Ridge, IL: Irwin.

Houck, J., & Williams, O. (Eds.). (1996). *Is the good corporation dead? Social responsibility in a global economy.* Lanham, MD: Rowman & Littlefield.

House, R. J. (1971). A path-goal theory of leader effectiveness. *Administrative Science Quarterly, 16,* 321-339.

Houston, B., & Vavak, C. (1991). Cynical hostility: Developmental factors, psychosocial correlates, and health behaviors. *Health Psychology, 10,* 9-17.

Howard, P. (1995). *The death of common sense: How law is suffocating America.* New York: Random House.

Howell, J. M., & Avalco, B. I. (1992). The ethics of charismatic leadership: Submission or liberation? *Academy of Management Executive, 6,* 43-54.

Ibarra, H., & Andrews, S. (1993). Power, social influence, and sense making: Effects of network centrality and proximity on employee perceptions. *Administrative Science Quarterly, 38,* 277-303.

Israedel, T. E., & Crutzen, P. J. (1995). *Atmosphere, climate, and change.* New York: Scientific American Library.

Ivy, D. K., & Backhind, P. (1994). *Exploring gender speak: Personal effectiveness in gender communications.* New York: McGraw-Hill.

Jackall, R. (1988). *Moral mazes.* New York: Oxford University Press.

Janis, I. L. (1983). *Groupthink* (2nd ed.). Boston: Houghton Mifflin.

Jeannot, T. M. (1989). Moral leadership and practical wisdom. *International Journal of Social Economics, 16*(16), 14-38.

Jennings, M. M. (1996). *Case studies in business ethics* (2nd ed.). St. Paul, MN: West.

Jennings, P. D., & Zandbergen, P. A. (1995). Ecologically sustainable organizations: An institutional approach. *Academy of Management Review, 20*(4), 1015-1052.

Johannsen, R. L. (1990). *Ethics in human communication.* Prospect Heights, IL: Waveland.

Johnson, R. S. (1993). *TQM: Leadership for the quality transformation.* Milwaukee: ASQC Quality Press.

Joiner, B. L. (1994). *Fourth-generation management.* New York: McGraw-Hill.

Jones, T. M. (1991). Ethical decision making by individuals in organizations: An issue contingent model. *Academy of Management Review, 16*(2), 366-395.

Jones, T. M. (1995). Instrumental stakeholder theory: A synthesis of ethics and economics. *Academy of Management Review, 20*(2), 404-437.

Josephson, M. (1992). *Making ethical decisions.* Marina Del Rey, CA: Josephson Institute of Ethics.

Kahn, W., & Kram, K. (1994). Authority at work: Internal models and their organizational consequences. *Academy of Management Review, 19,* 17-50.

Kahneman, D., Knetsch, J. L., & Thaler, R. (1986). Fairness as a constraint on profit seeking: Entitlements in the market. *American Economic Review, 76,* 728-741.

Kanfer, R., & Ackerman, P. L. (1989). Motivation and cooperative abilities: An integrative/aptitude treatment interaction approach to skill acquisition. *Journal of Applied Psychology, 74*(3), 657-690.

Kant, I. (1938). *Fundamental principles of the metaphysics of morals.* New York: Appleton-Century. (Original work published 1785)

Kanter, R. M. (1977). *Men and women of the corporation.* New York: Basic Books.

Kanungo, R., & Mendonca, M. (1996). *Ethical dimensions of leadership.* Thousand Oaks, CA: Sage.

Katzenbach, J., & the RCL Team (1995). *Real change leaders: How you can create growth and high performance at your company.* New York: Times Business.

Katzenbach, J., & Smith, D. (1993). *The wisdom of teams.* New York: Harper Business.

Kaufman, R. (1988). Preparing useful performance indicators. *Training and Development Journal, 10*(4), 80-85.

Kearns, D. (1990). Leadership through quality. *Academy of Management Executive, 4*(2), 88-91.

Kearns, D., & Nadler, D. (1992). *Prophets in the dark: How Xerox reinvented itself and beat back the Japanese.* New York: HarperCollins.

Kellerman, B. (1986). *Leadership and multidisciplinary perspectives.* Pittsburgh: University of Pittsburgh Press.

Kelley, R. E. (1988). In praise of followers. *Harvard Business Review, 66*(6), 142-148.

Kelman, H. C., & Hamilton, V. L. (1989). *Crimes of obedience.* New Haven, CT: Yale University Press.

Kelsen, H. (1957). *What is justice?* Berkeley: University of California Press.

Kennedy, C., & Manderscheid, R. W. (1992). SSDI and SSI disability beneficiaries with mental disorders. In K. W. Manderscheid & M. A. Sorrenschein (Eds.), *Mental health, United States* (pp. 417-429). Washington, DC: Government Printing Office.

Kilmann, R. H. (1984). *Beyond the quick fix: Managing five tracks to organizational success.* San Francisco: Jossey-Bass.

Kim, W., & Mauborgne, R. (1993). Procedural justice, attitudes, and subsidiary top management compliance with multinationals' corporate strategic decisions. *Academy of Management Journal, 36,* 502-526.

Kimball, L. A. (1992). *Forging international agreements: Strengthening intergovernmental institutions for environmental development.* Washington, DC: World Resource Institute.

King, D. (1987). *The new right: Politics, markets, and citizenship.* London: Macmillan.

Kingwell, M. (1994). *A civil tongue: Justice, dialogue, and the politics of pluralism.* University Park: Pennsylvania State University Press.

Kirkpatrick, D. L. (1994). *Evaluating training programs.* San Francisco: Berrett-Koehler.

Knowdell, R. L., Branstead, E., & Moravec, M. (1994). *From downsizing to recovery.* Palo Alto, CA: Consulting Psychologist Press.

Koehn, D. (1995). *The ground of professional ethics.* Boston: Routledge & Kegan Paul.

Kohlberg, L. (1973). *Collected papers on moral development and moral education.* Cambridge, MA: Harvard University Press.

Kohlberg, L. (1984). *The psychology of moral development: The nature and validity of moral stages.* New York: Harper & Row.

Kohn, A. (1993). *Punished by rewards.* Boston: Houghton Mifflin.

Koop, C. E. (1986). *The health consequences of involuntary smoking.* Rockville, MD: U.S. Department of Health and Human Services.

Korten, D. (1996). *When corporations rule the world.* San Francisco: Berrett-Koehler.

Kothari, R. (1990). Environmental technology and ethics. In J. R. Engel (Ed.), *Ethics of environment and development.* Tucson: University of Arizona Press.

Kouzes, J. M., & Posner, B. Z. (1990). *The leadership challenge.* San Francisco: Jossey-Bass.

Kouzes, J. M., & Posner, B. Z. (1991). *Credibility: How leaders gain and lose it and why people demand it.* San Francisco: Jossey-Bass.

KPMG Peat Marwick Forensic and Investigative Services. (1994). *The 1994 fraud survey.* Washington, DC: Author.

Kramer, R. M., & Tyler, T. R. (Eds.). (1995). *Trust in organizations.* Newbury Park, CA: Sage.

Kruschwitz, R. B., & Roberts, R. C. (1987). *The virtues.* Belmont, CA: Wadsworth.

Kubasek, N. K., Brennan, B. A., & Browne, M. N. (1996). *The legal environment of business.* Upper Saddle River, NJ: Prentice Hall.

Kupfer, J., & Klett, L. (1993). Client empowerment and counselor integrity. *Professional Ethics, 2*(1), 35-49.

Kupperman, J. (1968). Confucius and the problem of naturalness. *Philosophy East and West, 18*(2), 42-51.

Kupperman, J. (1989). Character and ethical theory. *Midwest Studies in Philosophy, 13,* 98-111.

Kurschner, D. (1996). The 100 best corporate citizens. *Business Ethics, 10*(3), 24-35.

Lakoff, R. T. (1990). *Talking power: The politics of language in our lives.* New York: Basic Books.

Lane, R. E. (1988). Procedural goods in a democracy: How one is treated versus what one gets. *Social Justice Research, 2,* 177-192.

Larrabee, M. J. (Ed.). (1993). *An ethic of care; Feminist and interdisciplinary perspectives.* Boston: Routledge & Kegan Paul.

Larson, M. S. (1977). *The rise of professionalism.* Berkeley: University of California Press.

Lawrence, P. R., & Lorsch, J. W. (1967). *Organization and environment.* Cambridge, MA: Harvard University Press.

Lax, D., & Sebenius, J. (1986). *The manager as negotiator: Bargaining for cooperation and competitive gain.* New York: Free Press.

Leaptrott, N. (1996). *Rules of the game: Global business protocol.* Cincinnati, OH: Thomson Executive.

Lee, J. A. (1988). Changes in managerial values. *Business Horizons, 5*(4), 29-37.

Leonard-Barton, D. (1995). *Wellsprings of knowledge.* Cambridge, MA: Harvard Business School Press.

Lewis, C. W. (1991). *The ethics challenge in public service.* San Francisco: Jossey-Bass.

Liedtka, J. M. (1996). Feminist morality and competitive reality: A role for an ethic of care? *Business Ethics Quarterly, 6*(2), 179-200.

Lind, E. A., Kanfer, R., & Earley, A. C. (1990). Voice, control, and procedural justice: Instrumental and uninstrumental concerns in fairness judgments. *Journal of Personality and Social Psychology, 59*(5), 952-959.

Lind, E. A., & Tyler, T. R. (1988). *The social psychology of procedural justice.* New York: Plenum.

Lindsay, W. M., Manning, G. E., & Petrick, J. A. (1992). Work morale in the 1990s. *SAM Advanced Management Journal, 57*(3), 43-48.

Lindsay, W. M., & Petrick, J. A. (1997). *Total quality and organization development.* Delray Beach, FL: St. Lucie.

Littleton, C. A. (1987). Reconstructing sexual equality. *California Law Review, 75,* 1279.

Llewellyn, K. (1950). *The bramble bush.* Dobbs Ferry, NY: Oceana.

Locke, J. (1690). *Two treatises on government.* London: Cambridge University Press.

Loden, M. (1985). *Feminine leadership, or how to succeed in business without being one of the boys.* New York: Times Books.

Lord, R. (1985). An information-processing approach to social perception, leadership, and behavioral measurement in organizations. In B. M. Staw & L. L. Cummings (Eds.), *Research in organizational behavior* (pp. 27-39). Greenwich, CT: JAI.

Lozano, J. M. (1996). Ethics and management: A controversial issue. *Journal of Business Ethics, 15,* 223-236.

Ludwig, D. C., & Longenecker, C. O. (1993). The Bathsheba syndrome: The ethical failure of successful leaders. *Journal of Business Ethics, 12,* 265-273.

Macedo, S. (1990). *Liberal virtues: Citizenship, virtue, and community.* New York: Oxford University Press.

MacIntyre, A. (1984). *After virtue* (2nd ed.). Notre Dame, IN: University of Notre Dame.

MacIntyre, A. (1988). *Whose justice? Which rationality?* Notre Dame, IN: University of Notre Dame.

Maniero, L. (1992). *Office romance: Love, sex, and power in the workplace.* New York: McGraw-Hill.

Manley, W. (1991). *Executive handbook of model business conduct codes.* Upper Saddle River, NJ: Prentice Hall.

Manz, C., & Sims, H. (1989). *Superleadership: Leading others to lead themselves.* Upper Saddle River, NJ: Prentice Hall.

Marshall, T. H. (1965). *Class, citizenship, and social development.* New York: Anchor.

Martin, J. (1985). *Common courtesy.* New York: Atheneum.

Martin, J. (1995). *The great transition.* New York: AMACOM.

Martin, M. W. (1986). *Self-deception and morality.* Lawrence: University Press of Kansas.

Martin, M. W. (1995). *Everyday morality*. Belmont, CA: Wadsworth.

Maslow, A. (1970). *Motivation and personality* (2nd ed.). New York: Harper & Row.

Mason, R. O., Mason, F. M., & Culnan, M. J. (1995). *Ethics of information management*. Newbury Park, CA: Sage.

Mayer, D. (1994). *Hypernorms and integrative social contracts theory*. Paper presented at the annual meeting of the Society for Business Ethics, Dallas, TX.

Mayhew, D. R. (1991). *Divided we govern*. New Haven, CT: Yale University Press.

Mayo, E. (1933). *The human problems of an industrial civilization*. New York: Macmillan.

McAdams, T. A., Freeman, J., & Pincus, L. B. (1995). *Law, business, and society* (4th ed.). Burr Ridge, IL: Irwin.

McAllister, D. J. (1995). Affect- and cognition-based trust as foundations for interpersonal cooperation in organizations. *Academy of Management Journal, 38*(1), 24-59.

McCall, M. (1994). Identifying leadership potential in future international executives: Developing a concept. *Consulting Psychology Journal, 46*, 49-63.

McClelland, D. C. (1963). *The achieving society*. Princeton, NJ: Van Nostrand.

McConnell, M. (1987). *Challenger, a major malfunction: A true story of politics, greed, and the wrong stuff*. Garden City, NY: Doubleday.

McFall, L. (1987). Integrity. *Ethics, 98*(4), 5-20.

McGinnis, J., & Forge, W. (1993). Actual causes of death. *Journal of the American Medical Association, 270*, 2207-2212.

McLaughlin, B. P., & Rorty, A. (Eds.). (1988). *Perceptions of self-deception*. Berkeley: University of California Press.

Mead, R. (1994). *International management: Cross-cultural dimensions*. Oxford, UK: Blackwell.

Meister, J. (1994). *Corporate quality universities: Lessons in building a world-class workforce*. Burr Ridge, IL: Irwin.

Mele, A. R. (1987). *Irrationality: An essay on evasion, self-deception, and self-control*. New York: Oxford University Press.

Mendl, J. R. (1989). Managing to be fair: An exploration of values, motives, and leadership. *Administrative Science Quarterly, 39*(2), 252-276.

Mensen, T. (1990). Ethics and state budgeting. *Public Budgeting and Finance, 10*, 95-108.

Merchant, C. (1992). *Radical ecology: The search for a livable world*. New York: Routledge, Chapman & Hall.

Merrill, D. W., & Reid, R. H. (1981). *Personal styles and effective performance*. Radnor, PA: Chilton.

Messick, D. M., & Bazerman, M. H. (1994). *Ethics for the 21st century: A decision-making perspective.* Unpublished manuscript, International Consortium for Executive Development Research, New York.

Metzger, M. , Mallor. J., Barnes, A., Bowers, T., Phillips, M., & Langvardt, A. (1995). *Business law and the regulatory environment.* Burr Ridge, IL: Irwin.

Micheli, L. (1979). *Kellogg Company: Sugar, children, and TV advertising.* Boston: Harvard Business School.

Michelman, R. (1979). Welfare rights in a constitutional democracy. *Washington University Law Quarterly, 10*(659).

Midgley, M. (1984). *Wickedness: A philosophical essay.* Boston: Routledge & Kegan Paul.

Miles, H. H. (1987). *Managing the corporate social environment: A grounded theory.* Upper Saddle River, NJ: Prentice Hall.

Miller, V., & Quinn, J. F. (1993). How green is the transnational corporation? *Business Strategy and the Environment, 2*(1), 13-25.

Milo, R. D. (1984). *Immorality.* Princeton, NJ: Princeton University Press.

Minton, T. W. (1988). *Justice, satisfaction, and loyalty: Employee withdrawal and voice in the din of inequity.* Unpublished doctoral dissertation, Duke University, Durham, NC.

Mintzberg, H. (1994). *The rise and fall of strategic planning.* New York: Free Press.

Mitnick, B. M. (1980). *The political economy of regulation: Creating, designing, and removing regulatory forms.* New York: Columbia University Press.

Mitnick, B. M. (1993). *Organizing research in corporate social performance: The CSA system as core paradigm.* Paper presented at the annual meeting of the International Association for Business and Society, San Diego, CA.

Moberg, D. J. (1994). *The moral conundrum of sub-unit partiality in organizations.* Paper presented at the annual meeting of the Society of Business Ethics, Dallas, TX.

Moore, M. H. (1995). *Creating public value: Strategic management in government.* Cambridge, MA: Harvard University Press.

Moore, M. H., & Sparrow, M. K. (1990). *Ethics in government: The moral challenges of public leadership.* Upper Saddle River, NJ: Prentice Hall.

Morrison, A. (1992). *The new leaders: Guidelines on leadership diversity in America.* San Francisco: Jossey-Bass.

Mortimer, G. W. (1971). *Weakness of will.* New York: St. Martin's.

Mosher, F. (1982). *Democracy and the public service.* New York: Oxford University Press.

Murray, C. (1984). *Losing ground: American social policy, 1950-1980.* New York: Basic Books.

Murray, H. A. (1938). *Explorations in personality.* New York: Oxford University Press.

Murphy, K. R. (1993). *Honesty in the workplace.* Pacific Grove, CA: Brooks/Cole.

Murphy, P., & Enderle, G. (1995). Managerial ethical leadership. *Business Ethics Quarterly, 5*(1), 117-128.

Naess, A. (1987). *Ecology, community, and lifestyle.* Cambridge, UK: Cambridge University Press.

Nash, L. L. (1990). *Good intentions aside.* Boston: Harvard Business School Press.

Nash, R. (1989). *The rights of nature.* Madison: University of Wisconsin Press.

Navran, F. J. (1991). *Desktop guide to total ethics management.* Atlanta, GA: Navran Associates.

Navran, F. J. (1995a). *Feeding the hog: A practical guide to ethical leadership.* Atlanta, GA: Navran Associates.

Navran, F. J. (1995b). *Trust and truth: The first two victims of downsizing.* Alberta, Canada: Athabasca University Press.

Neave, H. R. (1990). *The Deming dimension.* Knoxville, TN: SPC Press.

Newton, L. H., & Schmidt, D. P. (1996). *Wake-up calls: Classic cases in business ethics.* Belmont, CA: Wadsworth.

Noddings, N. (1984). *Caring: A feminine approach to ethics and moral education.* Berkeley: University of California Press.

Noer, D. M. (1993). *Healing the wounds: Overcoming the trauma of lay-offs and revitalizing downsized organizations.* San Francisco: Jossey-Bass.

Noonan, J. (1980). *Persons and masks of the law.* Berkeley: University of California Press.

Norton, D. L. (1976). *Personal destinies: A philosophy of ethical individualism.* Princeton, NJ: Princeton University Press.

Nozick, R. (1974). *Anarchy, state, and utopia.* New York: Basic Books.

Nussbaum, M. C. (1986). *The fragility of goodness.* Cambridge, UK: Cambridge University Press.

Ohmae, K. (1996). *The evolving global economy.* Boston: Harvard Business School Press.

Olasky, M. (1992). *The tragedy of American compassion.* Washington, DC: Regnery Gateway.

O'Leary-Kelly, A., Griffin, R., & Glew, D. (1996). Organization-motivated aggression: A research framework. *Academy of Management Review, 21*(1), 225-253.

Olian, J., & Rynes, S. (1991). Making total quality work: Aligning organizational processes, performance, measures, and stakeholders. *Human Resource Management, 30*(3), 310-325.

Olmstead, B., & Smith, S. (1994). *Creating a flexible workplace: How to select and manage alternative work options.* New York: AMACOM.

Olson, M. (1965). *The logic of collective action.* Cambridge, MA: Harvard University Press.

Ones, D. S., Visyvesvaran, C., & Schmidt, F. (1993). Comprehensive meta-analysis of integrity test validities: Findings and implications for personnel selection and theories of job performance. *Journal of Applied Psychology, 78*(2), 270-292.

Organization for Economic Cooperation and Development (OECD) Government Outlay Group. (1996). *European Commission report on government outlays.* Paris, France: OECD Publications.

Osborne, J., & Gaebler, S. (1992). *Reinventing government.* Reading, MA: Addison-Wesley.

O'Toole, J. (1995). *Leading change: Overcoming the ideology of comfort and the tyranny of custom.* San Francisco: Jossey-Bass.

Paine, L. S. (1991). Ethics as character development: Reflections on the objective of ethics education. In E. Freeman (Ed.), *Business ethics: State of the art* (pp. 61-79). New York: Oxford University Press.

Paine, L. S. (1994a). Law, ethics, and managerial judgment. *Journal of Legal Studies Education, 12*(2), 153-169.

Paine, L. S. (1994b). Managing for organizational integrity. *Harvard Business Review, 2,* 106-117.

Paine, L. S. (1996). Moral thinking in management: An essential capability. *Business Ethics Quarterly, 6*(4), 461-476.

Paine, L. S. (1997). *Cases in leadership, ethics, and organizational integrity.* Burr Ridge, IL: Irwin.

Parks, M. J. M. (1992). *The role of incomplete contracts and their governance in delinquency, in-role, and extra-role behaviors.* Paper presented at the annual meeting of the Society for Industrial and Organizational Psychology, Montreal, Canada.

Payne, S. L. (1994). Epistemological and ethical development in human resource professionals. *Business and Professional Ethics Journal, 13,* 35-50.

Payne, S. L., & Giacalone, R. A. (1990). Social psychological approaches to the perception of ethical dilemmas. *Human Relations, 43*(3), 649-665.

Pearce, J. A., & Robinson, R. B., Jr. (1994). *Strategic management* (5th ed.). Burr Ridge, IL: Irwin.

Peck, M. S. (1993). *A world waiting to be born: Civility rediscovered.* New York: Bantam.

Peery, N. S., Jr. (1995). *Business, government, and society.* Upper Saddle River, NJ: Prentice Hall.

Pegis, A. C. (Ed.). (1945). *Basic writings of Saint Thomas Aquinas.* New York: Random House.

Pepper, G. L. (1995). *Communicating in organizations: A cultural approach.* New York: McGraw-Hill.

Petrick, J., Lindsay, W., & Manning, G. (1991). Mapping work group morale. *Journal for Quality and Participation, 14*(2), 100-107.

Petrick, J., & Manning, G. (1990). Developing an ethical climate for excellence. *Journal for Quality and Participation, 14*(2), 84-90.

Petrick J., & Pullins, E. (1992). Organizational ethics development and the expanding role of the human resource professional. *Healthcare Supervisor, 11*(2), 52-61.

Petrick, J., & Russell-Robles, L. (1992). Challenges in the education of the contemporary U.S. international manager. *The International Executive, 34*(3), 251-261.

Petrick, J., Scherer, R., & Claunch, W. (Eds.). (1991). *Institutionalizing organizational ethics programs: Contemporary perspectives*. Dayton, OH: Wright State University Press.

Petrick, J., Scherer, R., Wilson, J., & Westfall, F. (1994). Benchmarking and improving core competencies: Lessons from a Baldrige award winner. *Journal for Quality and Participation, 17*(4), 82-86.

Petrick, J., Von der Embse, T., & Wagley, R. (1991). Structured ethical decision making and the prospect of managerial success. *SAM Advanced Management Journal, 56*(1), 72-78.

Petrick J., & Wagley, R. (1992). Enhancing responsible strategic management in organizations. *Journal of Management Development, 11*(4), 57-72.

Petrick, J. A., & Furr, D. S. (1995). *Total quality in managing human resources*. Delray Beach, FL: St. Lucie.

Petrick, J. A., & Manning, G. E. (1993). Paradigm shifts in quality management and ethics development. *Business Forum, 18*(4), 15-18.

Petrick, J. A., & Quinn, J. F. (1993). Emerging strategic human resource challenges in managing accent discrimination and ethnic diversity. *Journal of Applied Human Resource Management Research, 4*(2), 79-93.

Petrick, J. A., & Quinn, J. F. (1994a). Agenda 21: Productivity and responsible land use planning and management. *Proceedings of the Interdisciplinary Conference on Ethical Issues Embedded in the U.N. Program for Environment and Development,* United Nations, New York, 112-122.

Petrick, J. A., & Quinn, J. F. (1994b). Indonesian deforestation: A policy framework for sustainable development. *Journal of Asian Business, 10*(2), 39-54.

Petrick, J. A., & Quinn, J. F. (1995). Organizational ethics in a health care setting. In H. Hoivik & A. Fallesdal (Eds.), *Ethics and consultancy: European perspectives*. Hingham, MA: Kluwer.

Pierce, R. J. (1991). *Leadership, perspective, and restructuring for total quality*. Milwaukee, WI: ASQC Quality Press.

Pierson, C. (1991). *Beyond the welfare state: The new political economy of welfare*. University Park: Pennsylvania State University Press.

Pincoffs, E. L. (1985). Two cheers for Meno's The definition of the virtues. In E. E. Shelp (Ed.), *Virtue and medicine* (pp. 95-111). Dordrecht, The Netherlands: D. Reidel.

Pincoffs, E. L. (1986). *Quandaries and virtues.* Lawrence: University Press of Kansas.

Plato (1968). The republic. In A. Bloom (Ed.). *The works of Plato.* New York: Basic Books. (Original work published 367 B.C.)

Podsakoff, P. M., MacKenzie, S. B., Moorman, R. H., & Fetter, R. (1990). Transformational leader behaviors and their effects on followers' trust in leader, satisfaction, and organizational citizenship behaviors. *Leadership Quarterly, 1*(2), 107-142.

Porter, M. (1980). *Competitive strategy.* New York: Free Press.

Porter, M. (1985). *Competitive advantage: Creating and sustaining superior performance.* New York: Free Press.

Porter, M. (1990). *The competitive advantage of nations.* New York: Free Press.

Posner, B., & Schmidt, W. (1984). Values and the American manager: An update. *California Management Review, 26*(3), 202-216.

Posner, B., & Schmidt, W. (1992). Values and the American manager: An update updated. *California Management Review, 34*(3), 80-94.

Posner, R. A. (1986). *Economic analysis of law* (3rd ed.). Cambridge, MA: Harvard University Press.

Poundstone, W. (1992). *Prisoner's Dilemma.* New York: Anchor.

Powell, G. (1993). *Men and women in the workplace.* Newbury Park, CA: Sage.

Powers, C. W., & Vogel, D. (1980). *Ethics in the education of business managers.* Hastings-on-Hudson, NY: Hastings Center.

Premeaux, S. R., & Mondy, W. R. (1993). Linking management behavior to ethical philosophy. *Journal of Business Ethics, 12,* 349-357

Quinn, J. B., & Mintzberg, H. (1996). *The strategy process* (2nd ed.). Upper Saddle River, NJ: Prentice Hall.

Quinn, J. F. (1989). Moral theory and defective tobacco advertising and warnings: The business ethics of *Cippollone v. Liggett* group. *Journal of Business Ethics, 8,* 831-840.

Quinn, J. F. (1995). Development in the underdeveloped world: A new challenge for business ethics. In S. Stewart & G. Dunleavy (Eds.), *Whose business values?* (pp. 77-91). Hong Kong: Hong Kong University Press.

Quinn, J. F., & Petrick, J. A. (1994). U.S. international competitiveness and the challenge of expanding the jurisdiction of human dignity. In W. M. Hoffman, J. B. Kamm, R. E. Frederick, & E. Petry, Jr. (Eds.), *Emerging global business ethics* (pp. 107-118). Westport, CT: Quorum.

Quinn, R. E. (1988). *Beyond rational management: Mastering the paradoxes and competing demands of high performance.* San Francisco: Jossey-Bass.

Quinn, R. E., Faerman, S. R., Thompson, M. P., & McGrath, M. R. (1996). *Becoming a master manager* (2nd ed.). New York: John Wiley.

Quinn, R. E., Hildebrandt, H. W., Rogers, P. S., & Thompson, M. P. (1991). A competing values framework for analyzing presentational communication in management contexts. *Journal of Business Communication, 23*(3), 213-232.

Quinn, R. E., Sendelbach, N., & Spreitzer, G. (1991). Education and empowerment: A transformational model of managerial skills development. In J. Bigelow (Ed.), *Managerial skills: Explorations in practical knowledge* (pp. 47-60). Newbury Park, CA: Sage.

Quinn, R. E., Spreitzer, G., & Hart, S. (1992). Integrating the extremes: Crucial skills for managerial effectiveness. In S. Srivastva & Associates (Eds.), *Executive and organizational continuity: Managing the paradoxes of stability and change* (pp. 92-109). San Francisco: Jossey-Bass.

Rafaeli, A. (1989). When clerk meets customer: A test of variables related to emotional expressions on the job. *Journal of Applied Psychology, 74*(3), 385-393.

Rahim, M. A. (1986). *Managing conflict in organizations.* New York: Praeger.

Rawls, J. (1971). *A theory of justice.* Cambridge, MA: Harvard University Press.

Reich, R. (1964). The new property. *Yale Law Journal, 73*(133).

Reich, R. (1991). *The work of nations.* New York: Knopf.

Reidenbach, E., & Robin, D. (1990). Toward the development of a multidimensional scale for improving evaluations of business ethics. *Journal of Business Ethics, 9,* 639-653.

Reinhardt, F. L., & Vietor, R. (1996). *Business management and the natural environment.* Cincinnati: South-Western.

Report of the Presidential Commission on the Space Shuttle Challenger Accident. (1986). Washington, DC: Government Printing Office.

Rest, J. R. (1979). *Development in judging moral issues.* Minneapolis: University of Minnesota Press.

Rest, J. R. (1984). The major components of morality. In W. M. Kurtines & J. L. Gerwitz (Eds.), *Morality, moral behavior, and moral development* (pp. 58-71). New York: John Wiley.

Rest, J. R. (1986). *Moral development: Advances in research and theory.* New York: Praeger.

Rest, J. R., & Narvaez, D. (Eds.). (1994). *Moral development in the professions: Psychology and applied ethics.* Hillsdale, NJ: Lawrence Erlbaum.

Richards, E. (1994). *Law for global business.* Burr Ridge, IL: Irwin.

Rion, M. (1990). *The responsible manager: Practical strategies for ethical decision making.* New York: HarperCollins.

Robbins, S. P. (1990). *Organizational theory: Structure, design, and applications.* Upper Saddle River, NJ: Prentice Hall.

Robin, D., Gordon, G., Jordan, C., & Reidenbach, E. (1996). The empirical performance of cognitive moral development in predicting behavioral intent. *Business Ethics Quarterly, 6*(4), 493-515.

Robin, D. P., & Reidenbach, E. (1991). A conceptual model of corporate moral development. *Journal of Business Ethics, 10*(4), 273-284.

Robinson, S., Kraatz, M., & Rousseau, D. (1994). Changing obligations and the psychological contract: A longitudinal study. *Academy of Management Journal, 37*(5), 137-152.

Rorty, R. (1989). *Contingency, irony, and solidarity.* Cambridge, UK: Cambridge University Press.

Rose, J. (1995). *Growth and change in (social security) recipient population: Call for reexamining the program.* Washington DC: General Accounting Office.

Rost, J. (1991). *Leadership for the 21st century.* New York: Praeger.

Rost, J. (1993). Leadership development in the new millenium. *Journal of Leadership Studies, 1*(1), 109-110.

Rousseau, D. (1995). *Psychological contracts in organizations.* Newbury Park, CA: Sage.

Rousseau, D. (1996). Changing the deal while keeping the people. *Academy of Management Executive, 10*(1), 50-61.

Rousseau, J. J. (1959-1969). *Œuvres complètes* (Vols. 1-4). Paris: Librarie Gallimard. (Original work published 1762)

Sachs, J., & Huizinga, H. (1987). U.S. commercial banks and the developing country debt issues. Washington DC: Brookings Institution.

Samovar, L. A., & Porter, R. E. (1994). *Intercultural communication: A reader.* Belmont, CA: Wadsworth.

Sandel, M. J. (1996). *Democracy's discontent.* Cambridge, MA: Harvard University Press.

Sargent, C., & Bass, S. (1992). The future shape of forests. In J. Holmberg (Ed.), *Making development sustainable* (p. 207). Washington, DC: Island Press.

Sayre, R. (1996). *Inside ISO 14000: The competitive advantage of environmental management.* Delray Beach, FL: St. Lucie.

Schein, E. H. (1972). *Professional education.* New York: McGraw-Hill.

Schein, E. H. (1985). *Organizational culture and leadership.* San Francisco: Jossey-Bass.

Scherkenbach, W. W. (1991). *Deming's road to continual improvement.* Knoxville, TN: SPC.

Schlaadt, R. G. (1992). *Tobacco and health.* Guilford, CT: Dushkin.

Schmidheiny, S. (1992). *Changing course.* Cambridge: MIT Press.

Schmidt, W., & Posner, B. (1982). *Managerial values and expectations: The silent power in personal and organizational life.* New York: AMACOM.

Schminke, M. (Ed.). (1997). *Managerial ethics: Morally managing people and processes.* Hillsdale, NJ: Lawrence Erlbaum.

Schnitzer, M. (1983). *Contemporary government and business regulation.* Boston: Houghton Mifflin.

Scholtes, P. R. (1988). *The team handbook.* Madison, WI: Joiner Associates.

Schon, D. (1983). *The reflective practitioner.* New York: Basic Books.

Schutz, W. (1994). *The human element.* San Francisco: Jossey-Bass.

Schwartz, H. (1990). *Narcissistic process and corporate decay.* New York: New York University Press.

Searle, T. (1969). *Speech acts.* Cambridge, UK: Cambridge University Press.

Sejersted, F. (1996). Managers as consultants and manipulators: Reflections on the suspension of ethics. *Business Ethics Quarterly, 6*(1), 75-83.

Selznick, P. (1957). *Leadership in administration.* New York: Harper & Row.

Sendelbach, N. (1993). The competing values framework for management training and development: A tool for understanding complex issues and tasks. *Human Resource Management, 32*(1), 75-99.

Senge, P. M. (1990). *The fifth discipline: The art and practice of the learning organization.* Garden City, NY: Doubleday.

Senge, P. M. (1993). The leader's new work: Building learning organizations. *Sloan Management Review, 32*(1), 7-23.

Sethi, S. P. (1975). Dimensions of corporate social performance: An analytic framework. *California Management Review, 3,* 58-64.

Shames, L. (1989). *The hunger for more.* New York: Vintage.

Shaw, W. H., & Barry, V. (1995). *Moral issues in business.* Belmont, CA: Wadsworth.

Sheaffer, R. C. (1988). *Resentment against achievement.* Buffalo, NY: Prometheus.

Sheppard, B. H., Lewicki, R. J., & Minton, J. W. (1992). *Organizational justice: The search for fairness in the workplace.* Lexington, MA: Lexington Books.

Shiba, S., Graham, A., & Walden, D. (1993). *A new American TQM: Four practical revelations in management.* Cambridge, MA: Productivity.

Shiner, R. (1992). *Norm and nature: The movements of legal thought.* Oxford, UK: Clarendon.

Shklar, J. (1984). *Ordinary vices.* Cambridge, MA: Harvard University Press.

Shklar, J. (1991). *American citizenship: The quest for inclusion.* Cambridge, MA: Harvard University Press.

Shockley-Zalabak, P. (1994). *Understanding organizational communication: Cases, commentaries, and conversations.* White Plains, NY: Longman.

Shrader-Frechette, K. S. (1991). *Risk and rationality.* Berkeley: University of California Press.

Shrivastava, P. (1995a). Ecocentric management for a risk society. *Academy of Management Review, 20*(1), 118-137.

Shrivastava, P. (1995b). The role of corporations in achieving ecological sustainability. *Academy of Management Review, 20*(4), 936-960.

Shrivastava, P. (1996). *Greening business: Profiting the corporation and the environment.* Cincinnati: Thomson Executive Press.

Shue, H. (1980). *Basic rights: Subsistence, affluence, and U.S. foreign policy.* Princeton, NJ: Princeton University Press.

Sigler, J. A., & Murphy, J. E. (1988). *Interactive corporate compliance: An alternative to regulatory compulsion.* New York: Quorum.

Simon, Y. R. (1965). *The tradition of natural law: A philosopher's reflections.* New York: Fordham University Press.

Singh, J. B., & Lakhan, V. C. (1989). Business ethics and the international trade in hazardous wastes. *Journal of Business Ethics, 8*(8), 83-92.

Skelly, J. (1995). The Caux Round Table principles for business: The rise of international ethics. *Business Ethics, 10*(4), 17-18.

Skinner, B. F. (1971). *Beyond freedom and dignity.* New York: Baltimore.

Slote, M. (1992). *From morality to virtue.* New York: Oxford University Press.

Smith, H. J. (1994). *Managing privacy: Information technology and corporate America.* Chapel Hill: University of North Carolina Press.

Snyder, C., Higgins, R., & Stucky, R. (1983). *Excuses.* New York: John Wiley.

Solberg, J. J. (1995). Has *Harris v. Forklift* brightened the behavioral line in sexual harassment cases in the Seventh Circuit? *Proceedings of the Tristate Business Law Association,* Bloomington, IN, 83-97.

Solomon, R. C. (1977). *The passions.* New York: Anchor.

Solomon, R. C. (1990a). *Love: Emotion, myth, and metaphor.* Buffalo, NY: Prometheus.

Solomon, R. C. (1990b). *A passion for justice.* Reading, MA: Addison-Wesley.

Solomon, R. C. (1992). *Ethics and excellence: Cooperation and integrity in business.* New York: Oxford University Press.

Solomon, R. C., & Higgins, K. M. (1996). *A short history of philosophy.* New York: Oxford University Press.

Spreitzer, G., McCall, M., & Mahoney, J. (1995). *The early identification of international leadership potential: Dimensions, measurement, and validation.* Paper presented at the annual meeting of the Academy of Management, Vancouver, British Columbia.

Spitzer, T. (1995). *People and their jobs: What's real and what's rhetoric.* Princeton, NJ: Kepner-Tregoe.

Srivastva, S., & Associates (1988). *Executive integrity.* San Francisco: Jossey-Bass.

Stahl, M., & Bounds, G. (1990). *Competing globally through customer value.* Cambridge, MA: Blackwell.

Stahl, M. J. (1995). *Management: Total quality in a global environment.* Cambridge, MA: Blackwell.

Starik, M., & Rands, G. P. (1995). Weaving an integrated web: Multi-level and multi-system perspectives on ecologically sustainable organizations. *Academy of Management Review, 20*(4), 908-935.

Stead, W. E., & Stead, J. G. (1996). *Management for a small planet* (2nd ed.). Thousand Oaks, CA: Sage.

Steers, R., Porter, L., & Begley, G. (1996). *Motivation and leadership at work* (6th ed.). New York: McGraw-Hill.

Steiner, G. A., & Steiner, J. F. (1991). *Business, government, and society* (6th ed.). New York: McGraw-Hill.

Stewart, S., & Donleavy, G. (1995). *Whose business values? Some Asian and cross-cultural perspectives.* Hong Kong: Hong Kong University Press.

Stewart, T. (1994). Your company's most valuable asset: Intellectual capital. *Fortune, 130*(7), 68-74.

Stone, D. L., & Eddy, E. R. (1996). A model of individual and organizational factors affecting quality-related outcomes. *Journal of Quality Management, 1*(1), 21-48.

Sullivan, W. M. (1995). *Work and integrity: The crisis and promise of professionalism in America.* New York: Harper Business.

Tannen, D. (1993). *Framing in discourse.* New York: Oxford University Press.

Tannen, D. (1994a). *Gender and discourse.* New York: Oxford University Press.

Tannen, D. (1994b). *Talking from 9 to 5.* New York: William Morrow.

Tannen, D. (1994c). *Words at work.* New York: William Morrow.

Tavris, C. (1982). *Anger.* New York: Touchstone.

Taylor, F. W. (1911). *The principles of scientific management.* New York: Harper & Brothers.

Taylor, G. (1987). *Pride, shame, and guilt.* Oxford, UK: Clarendon.

Terry, L. D. (1990). Leadership in the administrative state: The concept of administrative conservatorship. *Administration and Society, 21*(4), 395-412.

Terry, R. W. (1993). *Authentic leadership: Courage in action.* San Francisco: Jossey-Bass

Thompson, D. F. (1987). *Political ethics and public office.* Cambridge, MA: Harvard University Press.

Thompson, D. F. (1995). *Ethics in Congress: From individual to institutional corruption.* Washington, DC: Brookings Institution.

Tichy, N. M., & Devanna, M. A. (1986). *The transformational leader.* New York: John Wiley.

Tobias, M. (1994). *World War III.* Santa Fe, NM: Bear.

Toffler, B. L. (1991). *Managers talk ethics.* New York: John Wiley.

Tomasko, R. M. (1990). *Downsizing.* New York: MACOM.

Torbert, W. (1991). *The power of balance.* New York: Oxford University Press.

Touche Ross Management Consultants. (1990). *Reducing consumption of ozone depleting substitutes in India: Phase 1. The cost of complying with the Montreal Protocol.* London: Author.

Toulman, S. (1984). *An introduction to reasoning* (2nd ed.). New York: Macmillan.

Transparency International. (1996). *International Corruption Perception Index.* Gottingen, Germany: Gottingen University.

Trevino, L. K., & Nelson, K. (1995). *Managing business ethics.* New York: John Wiley.

Trevino, L. K., & Youngblood, S. A. (1990). Bad apples in bad barrels: A causal analysis of ethical decision-making behavior. *Journal of Applied Psychology, 75*(4), 308-338.

Tronto, J. (1993). *Moral boundaries: A political argument for an ethic of care.* New York: Routledge.

Tyler, T., & Dawes, R. M. (1993). Fairness in groups: Comparing the self-interest and social identity perspectives. In B. A. Mellens & T. Baron (Eds.), *Psychological perspectives on justice* (pp. 87-108). New York: Cambridge University Press.

Tyler, T. R. (1994). Psychological models of the justice motive: Antecedents of distributive and procedural justice. *Journal of Personality and Social Psychology, 67*, 850-863.

Vaill, P. (1991). *Managing as a performing art.* San Francisco: Jossey-Bass.

Vanasco, R., & Quinn, J. F. (1995). *Internal control reporting: A global perspective.* Paper presented at the annual symposium of the International Conference on Contemporary Accounting Issues, Taipei, Taiwan University.

Van Dyne, L., Graham, J. W., & Dienesch, R. M. (1994). Organizational citizenship behavior: Construct redefinition, measurement, and validation. *Academy of Management Journal, 37*(4), 765-802.

Velasquez, M. (1996). Why ethics matters: A defense of ethics in business organizations. *Business Ethics Quarterly, 6*(2), 201-222.

Velasquez, M. G. (1994). *Business ethics.* Upper Saddle River, NJ: Prentice Hall.

Victor, B., & Stephens, C. (1994). Business ethics: A synthesis of normative philosophy and empirical science. *Business Ethics Quarterly, 4*(2), 145-155.

Viscott, D. (1996). *Emotional resilience.* New York: Harmony.

Vogel, D. (1992). The globalization of business ethics: Why America remains distinctive. *California Management Review, 35*(1), 30-49.

Vogel, U., & Moran, M. (1991). *The frontiers of citizenship.* New York: St. Martin's.

Vorherr, P., Petrick, J., Quinn, J., & Brady, T. (1995). The impact of gender and major in ethical perceptions of business students: Management implications for the accounting profession. *Journal of Academy of Business Administration, 1*(1), 46-66.

Vroom, V. H. (1964). *Work and motivation.* New York: John Wiley.

Wagner, J. A., & Hollenbeck, J. R. (1995). *Management of organizational behavior* (2nd ed.). Upper Saddle River, NJ: Prentice Hall.

Waldman, D. A. (1993). A theoretical consideration of leadership and total quality management. *Leadership Quarterly, 4*(2), 65-79.

Wallace, J. D. (1978). *Virtues and vices.* Ithaca, NY: Cornell University Press.

Walton, C. C. (1988). *The moral manager.* New York: Harper Business.

Walton, D. (1986). *Courage: A philosophical investigation.* Berkeley: University of California Press.

Walton, M. (1989). *Deming management at work.* Rutherford, NJ: G. P. Putnam.

Walzer, M. (1983). *Spheres of justice.* New York: Basic Books.

Walzer, M. (1992). The civil society argument. In C. Mouffe (Ed.), *Dimensions of radical democracy: Pluralism, citizenship, and community* (pp. 37-50). London: Routledge.

Wamsley, G. L., Bacher, R. N., Goodsell, C. T., Knonenberg, P. S., Rohr, J. A., Stivers, O. F., & Wolf, J. F. (1990). *Refounding public administration.* Newbury Park, CA: Sage.

Wanous, J., Reichers, A., & Austin, T. (1994). Organizational cynicism: An initial study. *Academy of Management Best Papers Proceedings, 269-273.*

Wanous, J. P., & Zwang, A. (1977). A cross-sectional treatment of need hierarchy theory. *Organizational Behavior and Human Performance, 18*(3), 78-97.

Waterman, R. H., Jr. (1994). *What America does right: Learning from companies that put people first.* New York: Norton.

Waters, J. A. (1988). Integrity management: Learning and implementing ethical principles in the workplace. In S. Srivastva & Associates (Eds.), *Executive integrity* (pp. 172-196). San Francisco: Jossey-Bass.

Weaver, G. R., & Trevino, L. K. (1994). Normative and empirical business ethics. *Business Ethics Quarterly, 4*(2), 129-143.

Weber, M. (1921). *Theory of social and economic organization.* London: Oxford University Press.

Weidenbaum, M. R., & Warren, T. D (1995). *Costs of regulation and benefits of reform.* St. Louis: Center for the Study of American Business.

Weiss, J. W. (1994). *Business ethics.* Belmont, CA: Wadsworth.

Welfeld, I. (1992). *The HUD scandal: Howling headlines and silent fiasco.* New Brunswick, NJ: Transaction.

Wellman, C. (1975). *Morals and ethics.* Glenview, IL: Scott, Foresman.

Werhane, P. H. (1991a). *Adam Smith and his legacy for modern capitalism.* New York: Oxford University Press.

Werhane, P. H. (1991b). Engineers and management: The challenge of the *Challenger* incident. *Journal of Business Ethics, 10,* 605-616.

Wever, G. H. (1996). *Strategic environmental management: Using TQEM and ISO 14000 for competitive advantage.* New York: John Wiley.

Wheelen, T. L., & Hunger, D. T. (1992). *Strategic management and business policy.* Reading, MA: Addison-Wesley.

Whelan, E. (1984). *A smoking gun: How the tobacco industry gets away with murder.* Philadelphia: George F. Stekey.

White, L. C. (1988). *Merchants of death: The American tobacco industry.* New York: William Morrow.

Wilkins, A. L. (1989). *Developing corporate character: How to successfully change an organization without destroying it.* San Francisco: Jossey-Bass.

Willig, J. T. (1994). *Environmental TQM.* New York: McGraw-Hill.

Wilson, J. Q. (1989). *Bureaucracy.* New York: Basic Books.

Wilson, J. Q. (1993). *The moral sense.* New York: Free Press.

Wilson, R. (Ed.). (1996). *Character above all.* New York: Simon & Schuster.

Winograd, T., & Flores, F. (1986). *Understanding computers and cognition: A new foundation of design.* Norwood, NJ: Ablex.

Wood, D. T. (1994). *Business and society* (2nd ed.). New York: HarperCollins.

Yarbrough, E., & Wilmot, W. (1994). *Mediation at work.* Boulder, CO: Yarbrough.

Yukl, G. C. (1994). *Leadership in organizations* (3rd ed.). Upper Saddle River, NJ: Prentice Hall.

Zahariadis, N. (1995). *Markets, states, and public policy: Privatization in Britain and France.* Ann Arbor: University of Michigan Press.

Zaleznik, A. (1990). The leadership gap. *Academy of Management Executive, 4*(1), 7-22.

Zemke, R. (1986). Employee theft: How to cut your losses. *Training, 14*(5), 17-78.

Zey-Ferrell, M., & Ferrell, O. C. (1982). Role set configuration and opportunity as predictors of unethical behavior in organizations. *Human Relations, 35*(3), 587-604.

Index

About the Authors

Joseph A. Petrick is Associate Professor of Management at Wright State University in Dayton, Ohio. He earned his Ph.D. in comparative philosophy and cultural anthropology from Pennsylvania State University, University Park, as a Woodrow Wilson Fellow. He completed his MBA in quality management and marketing at the University of Cincinnati, with advanced international graduate work at the University of Bonn in Germany and the University of Tokyo in Japan. He is certified as a Senior Professional in Human Resources (SPHR) and a Registered Organization Development Professional (RODP). He has taught graduate and undergraduate courses in the disciplines of management and philosophy as a tenured professor in both fields. He was elected Vice President of the Entrepreneurship Division of the United States Association of Small Business and Entrepreneurship, is President-Elect of the Midwestern Human Resources/Industrial Relations Society, and is an active member of the following professional associations: Society for Business Ethics, Academy of Legal Studies in Business, Academy of Management, American Philosophical Association, American Society for Quality Control, and Society for Human Resource Management.

Dr. Petrick coauthored *Total Quality in Managing Human Resources* (1995) and *Total Quality and Organization Development* (1997), coedited *Institutionalizing Organizational Ethics Programs* (1991), and has published in a wide range of professional anthologies and journals, including *Emerging Global Business Ethics* (Center for Business Ethics), *Ethics and Consultancy: European*

Perspectives, Managerial Ethics: Morally Managing People and Processes, Journal of Managerial Psychology, Journal of General Management, SAM Advanced Management Journal, Journal of Management Development, International Executive, Personnel Journal, Industrial Management, Journal of Health and Human Resource Management, Journal for Quality and Participation, and *Journal of Asian Business.* He has firsthand management experience in the private, public, and nonprofit sectors and is the principal and founder of Organizational Ethics Associates (OEA) and the CEO of Performance Leadership Associates (PLA), both in Cincinnati. The former firm designs and delivers ethics consulting, training, and development services domestically and globally; the latter firm focuses on quality leadership enhancement services for managerial, group, and organizational performance in the North American market.

John F. Quinn is Associate Professor of Philosophy at the University of Dayton, in Dayton, Ohio, where he has been since completion of his graduate studies at the University of Washington, Seattle. His interest in applied philosophy (philosophy of law, environmental ethics, aesthetics, business ethics, and jurisprudence for the law school) was supplemented by study at the University of Dayton, School of Law, where he completed his legal studies in 1982 and the bar in 1983. He has practiced law in such areas as employment discrimination, environment and health, and safety. He has become adjunct in business law and management, where his work has become focused on the relationships among ethics, law, and management. He has taught CPA review classes, business law both domestic and international, multinational corporations, human resource management, government and business, corporate responsibility, women and management, and business and the natural environment.

In 1991, Dr. Quinn published *The Christian Foundations of Criminal Responsibility* (with J. M. B. Crawford) and became a Senior Partner at Organizational Ethics Associates in Cincinnati, where he has made use of his early certification in engineering, as well as certifications in human resource management (PHR) and organization development (RODP). His academic and consulting activities have taken him to the four corners of the globe, where he has worked with organizations and presented papers on an array of management ethics topics. He has published in a wide range of professional journals and anthologies, such as *Journal of Business Ethics, Business and Professional Ethics Journal, Business Strategy and the Environment, Journal of Asian Business, Dialogue and Universalism, Journal of Social Philosophy, Ethics and Consultancy: European Perspectives, Emerging Global Business Ethics* (Center for Business

Ethics), *Journal of Applied Human Resource Management, Whose Business Values* (Center for Values in Business—Hong Kong), and *Review of Business.* He belongs to numerous professional associations, including the American Trial Lawyers Association, Academy of Legal Studies in Business, Society for Business Ethics, International Association of Business, Economics and Ethics, American Philosophical Association, and Association of Practical and Applied Philosophy.